Homeland Security Preparedness and Information Systems:

Strategies for Managing Public Policy

Christopher G. Reddick
University of Texas at San Antonio, USA

A volume in the Advances in Digital Crime, Forensics, and Cyber Terrorism (ADCFCT) Book Series

Director of Editorial Content: Kristin Klinger
Senior Managing Editor: Jamie Snavely
Assistant Managing Editor: Michael Brehm
Publishing Assistant: Sean Woznicki
Typesetter: Michael Brehm, Michael Killian
Cover Design: Lisa Tosheff

Published in the United States of America by
Information Science Reference (an imprint of IGI Global)
701 E. Chocolate Avenue
Hershey PA 17033
Tel: 717-533-8845
Fax: 717-533-8661
E-mail: cust@igi-global.com
Web site: http://www.igi-global.com

Library of Congress Cataloging-in-Publication Data

Reddick, Christopher G.
Homeland security preparedness and information systems : strategies for managing public policy / by Christopher G. Reddick.
p. cm.
Includes bibliographical references and index.
Summary: "This book examines the impact of Homeland Security Information Systems (HSIS) on government, discussing technologies used in a national effort to prevent and respond to terrorist attacks and emergencies such as natural disasters"--Provided by publisher.
ISBN 978-1-60566-834-5 (hardcover) -- ISBN 978-1-60566-835-2 (ebook) 1. Emergency management--United States. 2. Terrorism--United States--Prevention. 3. Preparedness--Government policy--United States. 4. Information technology--Government policy--United States. I. Title.
HV551.3.R3934 2009
363.34068'4--dc22
2009007010

This book is published in the IGI Global book series Advances in Digital Crime, Forensics, and Cyber Terrorism (ADCF-CT) Book Series (ISSN: 2327-0381; eISSN: 2327-0373)

British Cataloguing in Publication Data
A Cataloguing in Publication record for this book is available from the British Library.

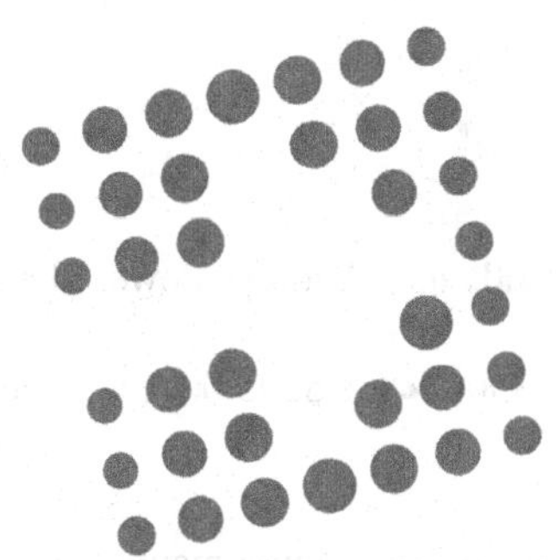

Advances in Digital Crime, Forensics, and Cyber Terrorism (ADCFCT) Book Series

ISSN: 2327-0381
EISSN: 2327-0373

Mission

The digital revolution has allowed for greater global connectivity and has improved the way we share and present information. With this new ease of communication and access also come many new challenges and threats as cyber crime and digital perpetrators are constantly developing new ways to attack systems and gain access to private information.

The **Advances in Digital Crime, Forensics, and Cyber Terrorism (ADCFCT) Book Series** seeks to publish the latest research in diverse fields pertaining to crime, warfare, terrorism and forensics in the digital sphere. By advancing research available in these fields, the **ADCFCT** aims to present researchers, academicians, and students with the most current available knowledge and assist security and law enforcement professionals with a better understanding of the current tools, applications, and methodologies being implemented and discussed in the field.

Coverage

- Computer Virology
- Cryptography
- Cyber Warfare
- Database Forensics
- Digital Crime
- Encryption
- Identity Theft
- Malware
- Telecommunications Fraud
- Watermarking

IGI Global is currently accepting manuscripts for publication within this series. To submit a proposal for a volume in this series, please contact our Acquisition Editors at Acquisitions@igi-global.com or visit: http://www.igi-global.com/publish/.

The Advances in Digital Crime, Forensics, and Cyber Terrorism (ADCFCT) Book Series (ISSN 2327-0381) is published by IGI Global, 701 E. Chocolate Avenue, Hershey, PA 17033-1240, USA, www.igi-global.com. This series is composed of titles available for purchase individually; each title is edited to be contextually exclusive from any other title within the series. For pricing and ordering information please visit http://www.igi-global.com/book-series/advances-digital-crime-forensics-cyber/73676. Postmaster: Send all address changes to above address.

Titles in this Series

For a list of additional titles in this series, please visit: www.igi-global.com

The Psychology of Cyber Crime Concepts and Principles
Gráinne Kirwan (Dun Laoghaire Institute of Art, Design and Technology, Ireland) and Andrew Power (Dun Laoghaire Institute of Art, Design and Technology, Ireland)
Information Science Reference • copyright 2012 • 372pp • H/C (ISBN: 9781613503508) • US $195.00 (our price)

Cyber Crime and the Victimization of Women Laws, Rights and Regulations
Debarati Halder (Centre for Cyber Victim Counselling (CCVC), India) and K. Jaishankar (Manonmaniam Sundaranar University, India)
Information Science Reference • copyright 2012 • 264pp • H/C (ISBN: 9781609608309) • US $195.00 (our price)

Digital Forensics for the Health Sciences Applications in Practice and Research
Andriani Daskalaki (Max Planck Institute for Molecular Genetics, Germany)
Medical Information Science Reference • copyright 2011 • 418pp • H/C (ISBN: 9781609604837) • US $245.00 (our price)

Cyber Security, Cyber Crime and Cyber Forensics Applications and Perspectives
Raghu Santanam (Arizona State University, USA) M. Sethumadhavan (Amrita University, India) and Mohit Virendra (Brocade Communications Systems, USA)
Information Science Reference • copyright 2011 • 296pp • H/C (ISBN: 9781609601232) • US $180.00 (our price)

Handbook of Research on Computational Forensics, Digital Crime, and Investigation Methods and Solutions
Chang-Tsun Li (University of Warwick, UK)
Information Science Reference • copyright 2010 • 620pp • H/C (ISBN: 9781605668369) • US $295.00 (our price)

Homeland Security Preparedness and Information Systems Strategies for Managing Public Policy
Christopher G. Reddick (University of Texas at San Antonio, USA)
Information Science Reference • copyright 2010 • 274pp • H/C (ISBN: 9781605668345) • US $180.00 (our price)

Table of Contents

Section 1: Background Information

Section 1 of this book is a collection of three chapters that provides background information on homeland security preparedness, citizen-centric e-government, and collaboration and e-government. The message of this section is that one cannot understand the impact of homeland security information systems (HSIS) on governments without understanding these three key pillars that drive the implementation of HSIS.

Section 2:
Homeland Security Information Systems in Government

The second section of this book examines the implementation of HSIS in the federal government, state emergency management, and local governments. The chapters in Section 2 provide evidence on the impact of HSIS on the different levels of government in the United States.

Section 3:
Emerging Issues

The final section of this book examines some emerging issues in the realm of HSIS. These important issues discussed in Section 3, faced by governments, are citizens' use of terrorism information for preparedness, information security, and an assessment of information on emergency management websites. The conclusion summarizes the main findings of the book and provides recommendations for future research on this important subject matter.

Section 4: Selected Readings from the Author

Foreword

Reading Christopher G. Reddick's *Homeland Security Preparedness and Information Systems: Strategies for Managing Public Policy* was a reminder of how far the information technology (IT) revolution has come in 25 years. My first computer in graduate school was the boxy, heavy Kayrpo II, which served as a typewriter upgrade and dumb terminal to connect (via a very slow phone modem) to Florida State University's mainframe. We have come a long way in that quarter century, and the computer has become a central part of most Americans' lives. And as Professor Reddick details, it has become a mainstay of one of the most important policy "spaces" of the 21st Century—Homeland Security.

The centrality of the IT to bolster Homeland Security is a central theme of this work. But as Dr. Reddick notes, implementation of enhancements in the Homeland Security Information Systems (HSIS) realm does not come easily. IT facilitates the sharing of information across multiple agencies and levels of governments, but this capacity conflicts with deep-seated cultural preferences for privacy and transparency. Increasing citizen involvement is a cornerstone of effective HSIS, but America still suffers from a digital divide that puts older, less-educated citizens at a disadvantage in their ability to provide or gather information on natural or manmade disasters. Meanwhile, a younger generation of Americans will view the Internet as their primary source of information, but it remains to be seen if many cities and states have the financial and human resources needed to build information systems that can "bridge" to these cyber-savvy Americans.

Dr. Reddick also reminds us of one of the critical bugaboos of implementation in American public administration: the mixed blessing of the Federal system. Multiple layers of government have served to blunt hyper-centralized top-down administrative policies. But this structure also presents challenges to effective information sharing and may exacerbate the differences between "have" and "have not" IT entities at the sub-national levels. The 21st Century and IT offer breathtaking opportunities for bringing a frequently disillusioned citizenry back into fold of governance. This indeed is a "force multiplier" in terms of enhancing IT's potential for improving Homeland Security. That said, without appropriate infrastructure and computer literacy, IT may provide nothing more than a glorified Yellow Pages for contacting public officials.

One of the central themes of this book is that organizational culture matters. Senior IT officials cannot expect their employees to learn about cyber security through osmosis. Building organizational roots that grow awareness of threats to security requires intensive training and commitment. All governments operate in an IT environment that is highly regulated in many dimensions. Yet as Dr. Reddick notes, most breakdowns in cyber-security are not the result of onerous regulations but rather, the inability of organizations to adequately train personnel in appropriate procedures.

Dr. Reddick bolsters his findings with surveys of "real world" officials in senior ranks. This buttresses the validity of his findings while underscoring the often broad chasm between the potential and reality of what IT can deliver in helping to improve prevention and mitigation of natural and manmade disasters. Thusly, Reddick's work is both informative and thought-provoking.

Professor Howard Frank
Florida International University,
Miami, Florida, USA

Howard A. Frank *is Professor of Public Administration at Florida International University in Miami, Florida, USA where he joined the faculty in 1988. Dr. Frank's major research interests are in the areas of local government budgeting and productivity. Professor Frank has held a number of administrative positions during his tenure at FIU and currently serves as Managing Editor of the* Journal of Public Budgeting, Accounting, and Financial Management*. Professor Frank earned his PhD at the Florida State University and worked in several local and federal agencies prior to his academic career.*

Preface

This book examines the impact of Homeland Security Information Systems (HSIS) on government. HSIS can be defined as technologies used in a national effort to prevent and respond to terrorist attacks and emergencies such as natural disasters. This book has included both the study of terrorist attacks and emergency management in its definition, since both are critical for protecting the homeland. This definition is different from the typical response by police, firefighter's, and other first responders to emergencies since it involves a multi-jurisdictional and national effort. Therefore, the severity of the emergency requires a more coordinated effort across different levels of government than what one government can handle alone.

Some notable incidents of homeland security were the terrorist attacks of September 11, 2001 on the World Trade Center and the Pentagon and Hurricane Katrina that devastated large parts of the Gulf Coast in 2005. In these notable national disasters, the response to both of them were criticized because the different levels of government lacked adequate preparation and collaboration when responding to these incidents (Wise and Nader, 2002; Wise, 2006). This book provides knowledge of the impact and use of HSIS on all levels of government in the United States. The argument is made that in order to more successfully implement HSIS, one must understand its current impact on governments. This book through a collection of surveys of public officials, in all levels of government in the United States, provides an assessment of the degree of adoption of HSIS and its effectiveness on government.

This book makes a unique contribution through its examination of electronic government (or e-government) and homeland security preparedness research. This book melds both research themes to examine this important issue. What is especially noteworthy in this research is survey evidence presented in each of the chapters to provide baseline knowledge of what key officials in government think about HSIS and its impact on their government. The majority of the surveys were conducted by the author, with some other survey evidence provided by notable organizations such as the International City/County Management Association (ICMA) and Pew Internet and American Life Project.

Existing research on e-government focuses generally on its adoption in public sector organizations (Moon, 2002; West, 2004; Norris and Moon, 2005; Torres, Pina, and Acerete 2005; Melitski and Holzer, 2007). This book examines the development of e-government by focusing specifically on HSIS adoption at all levels of government in the United States. The purpose of this book is to outline the extent to which HSIS has impacted government. What this book does not do, is provide an elaborative discussion of all technologies available in homeland security, as other works cover that important dimension (Pine, 2006; Cutter, Emrich, and Adams, et al. 2007). The following section presents a chapter-by-chapter overview and plan for the book.

OVERVIEW OF THE BOOK

Section 1 of this book is a collection of three chapters that provides background information on homeland security preparedness, e-government and citizens, and collaboration and e-government. The message of this section is that one cannot understand the impact of HSIS on governments without understanding these three pillars that drive the implementation of HSIS.

Chapter 1 provides the reader with a knowledge base about some of the issues associated with homeland security preparedness. The focus on this chapter is the experiences of local governments in the realm of homeland security preparedness, since they are normally first on the scene if a natural disaster or terrorist incident occurs. This chapter indentifies the important organizational, management, and collaborative elements that impact homeland security preparedness. There is a case study of information systems used in the response to Hurricane Katarina. After reading this chapter, the reader should be able to understand the salient issues in homeland security preparedness that governments face.

Chapter 2 provides research on how e-government is thought to create more citizen-centric government. Since HSIS is part of the e-government effort, it is important to know about the relationship between e-government and citizens, since citizens are thought to be one of the main determinates in the advancement and success of e-government. Many definitions of e-government include expanding outreach to citizens with their government because of power of the internet.

Chapter 3 provides an examination of collaboration and its impact on e-government. The purpose of this chapter is to discuss one of the most often cited and pressing issues in the realm of homeland security of collaboration and demonstrates how this is related to the e-government literature. It is essentially to know about the issues associated with collaboration, since it is the most common challenge that government face when preparing and responding to homeland security. This chapter examines some best practices of collaboration and shows how state governments measure up against some noted principles of collaboration.

The second section of this book has three chapters that examine the implementation of HSIS in the federal, state, and local governments. The chapters in this section provide evidence on the impact of HSIS on the different levels of government in the United States.

Chapter 4 provides details on the federal government, the largest purchaser of information technology in the world, and its use of HSIS. This chapter focuses on the impact of HSIS on federal departments and agencies through a survey of CIOs. This chapter covers the important pieces of federal legislation in HSIS and outlines the scope of its impact on Chief Information Officers (CIO) and their departments/agencies. The result of this chapter indicate that HSIS has significantly changed the roles and responsibilities of federal CIOs.

Chapter 5 examines the impact of IT on emergency management function through the key areas of emergency management, which are mitigation, preparedness, response, and recovery. The focus here is on state governments' and their use of emergency management and IT. There is an examination of the impact of IT on emergency management planning efforts of state governments. The effectiveness of IT on various technologies used by emergency management departments is also assessed. Some of the barriers to the adoption of IT in emergency management are also discussed in this chapter.

Chapter 6 examines the impact of HSIS on local government, relative to other homeland security priorities. Some of the topics covered in this chapter are the assessment of the quantity and quality of information sharing from federal and state governments with local governments. There is a discussion of the financing of homeland security for local governments and where HSIS fits into local budget priorities. There is mention of the need for training in the area of local government HSIS.

The final section of this book examines some emerging issues in the realm of HSIS. These important issues faced by governments are citizens' use of terrorism information for preparedness, information security, and assessment of information on emergency management websites.

Chapter 7 examines the impact of citizens' use of the Internet and information on homeland security. The focus of this chapter is to assess why individuals go online for information, providing an assessment of the barriers to Internet access. There is a survey presented that shows citizens preferred methods of contacting government for information and how homeland security fits into their preferences for online information.

Chapter 8 examines the important issue of information security, with a focus on a survey from Texas state agencies. Information security is a top challenge and priority according to public and private sector CIOs. The results of this chapter give the reader information on the information security environment and the challenges that governments face in this post 9/11 world. Some of the issues discussed are the management and organizational culture and its impact on information security. There also is a discussion of the information security threats faced by government and strategies that they use to mitigate these threats.

Chapter 9 examines through a content analysis of state government emergency management websites some of the information that can be found on these websites to aid communities in preparation for an emergency. This chapter is used to provide a baseline of knowledge of the features that emergency management departments have placed on their websites, and to determine how effective this information is for their citizens and the communities that they serve.

Chapter 10 is the conclusion and provides a discussion of the main findings of the book. There also are some recommendations for future research on the implementation of HSIS in government.

HSIS is an important area of inquiry since information technology can have a tremendous influence on the preparation and response of government to a terrorist attack or natural disaster. This book will show that HSIS has pervaded many elements of preparedness and response in homeland security across all levels of government in the United States. It provides a baseline of knowledge through the use of surveys of public officials that are directly involved in homeland security preparedness efforts.

REFERENCES

Cutter, S.L., Emrich, C.T., Adams, B.J., Huyck, C.K., & Eguchi, R.T. (2007). New Information Technologies in Emergency Management. In W.L. Waugh, & K.Tierney (eds.)., *Emergency Management: Principles and Practices for Local Government*, (pp. 279-297). Washington, DC: International City/County Management Association.

Melitski, J., & Holzer, M. (2007). Assessing Digital Government at the Local Level Worldwide: An Analysis of Municipal Web Sites throughout the World. In D. F. Norris (Ed.), *Current Issues and Trends in E-government Research*. Hershey, PA: Cybertech Publishing.

Moon, M.J. (2002). The Evolution of E-Government among Municipalities: Rhetoric or Reality? *Public Administration Review, 62*(4), 424-433.

Norris, D.F., & Moon, M.J. (2005). Advancing E-Government at the Grassroots: Tortoise or Hare? *Public Administration Review, 65*(1), 64-75.

Pine, J.C. (2006). *Wiley Pathways Technology in Emergency Management.* Hoboken, NJ: John Wiley & Sons.

Torres, L., Pina, V., & Acerete, B. (2005). E-government Developments on Delivering Public Services among EU Cities. *Government Information Quarterly, 22*(2), 217-238.

West, D.M. (2004). E-government and the Transformation of Service Delivery and Citizen Attitudes. *Public Administration Review, 64*(1), 15-27.

Wise, C.R. (2006). Organizing for Homeland Security after Katrina: Is Adaptive Management What's Missing? *Public Administration Review, 66*(3), 302-318.

Wise, C.R., & Nader, R. (2002). Organizing the Federal System for Homeland Security: Problems, Issues, and Dilemmas. *Public Administration Review, 62* (Special Issue), 44-57.

Acknowledgment

I am very grateful for the helpful comments of the peer reviewers for the book. I would also like to thank the staff, especially Julia Mosemann, at IGI Global for their support. On a personal note, I would like to thank my family, especially Cathy, for their support and encouragement through the production of this book.

Christopher G. Reddick
University of Texas at San Antonio, USA

Section 1
Background Information

Section 1 of this book is a collection of three chapters that provides background information on homeland security preparedness, citizen-centric e-government, and collaboration and e-government. The message of this section is that one cannot understand the impact of homeland security information systems (HSIS) on governments without understanding these three key pillars that drive the implementation of HSIS.

Chapter 1
Homeland Security Preparedness

Our first priority must always be the security of our nation...America is no longer protected by vast oceans. We are protected from attack only by vigorous action abroad, and increased vigilance at home. (President George W. Bush, State of the Union Address, January 29, 2002)

INRODUCTION

September 11, 2001 or 9/11 has put extra pressures on public officials and their agencies in the United States to prepare for new terrorist threats (Rosenthal, 2003). After 9/11 the idea of homeland security became a part of American thinking and behavior (Beresford, 2004). In this relatively new environment that governments must contend with, it is important to be aware of some issues associated with homeland security preparedness. The traditional distinction among the major sectors of the government has blurred, since the war on terrorism is no longer just the purview of military agencies (Wise and Nader, 2002). In this new environment both civilian and military agencies share the responsibility in protecting the homeland.

This chapter attempts to address homeland security preparedness by focusing on city governments examining organizational, collaboration, and management elements of homeland security. The main purpose of this chapter is to set the context of homeland security preparedness. It is vital to know some of the issues that governments face in homeland security in order to understand how Homeland Security Information Systems (HSIS) might be used to address these issues.

In order to accomplish this task this chapter first provides background information and an overview of some of the existing homeland security literature in public administration. There is a discussion of the research methods of this article and the results of a homeland security preparedness survey are presented. A conclusion demonstrates the significance of the key findings found in this chapter.

DOI: 10.4018/978-1-60566-834-5.ch001

Essentially, this chapter shows that there is not much funding for homeland security in local governments. There is improved cooperation with other levels of government. There is a high managerial capacity in government to deal with homeland security preparedness. Finally, there is a low terror threat perceived by these local governments.

BACKGROUND

Homeland security is defined by the federal government as a concerted national effort to prevent terrorist attacks within its territory, reduce vulnerability to terrorism, and minimize the damage and recover from attacks that occur (Whitehouse, 2002). Perhaps the most important piece of federal legislation is the Homeland Security Act of 2002 (Appendix A). The Homeland Security Act defines the role of homeland security and established a 22 agency Department of Homeland Security (DHS) to oversee this important function. An overarching and perhaps more applicable definition of homeland security to this chapter is all actions taken at every level state, local, private and citizen can use to deter, defend against, and mitigate attacks within the U.S. or to respond to other major domestic emergencies (Beresford, 2004). Homeland security brings in specific challenges and requirements to each level of government (Wise and Nader, 2002). Homeland security requires a reconfiguration to significant portions of public service.

Although resources for homeland security are mainly national, the responsibility to define the situation, initiate a government response, evaluate population needs, and plan a relief effort still lies with state and local governments (Wise and Nader, 2002). Therefore, because of their critical role local government are examined in this chapter through a survey of city managers in cities serving 100,000 residents or greater in the United States.

The U.S. Census Bureau defines cities as "urban places," which typically have populations of 2,500 residents or greater. The Census Bureau also defines metropolitan areas, which is a more accurate depiction of what is studied in this chapter, having cities with populations generally exceeding 50,000. In terms of administrative structure most cities in the U.S. have a council-manager form of government, where a city manager (or chief administrative officer) reports directly to the city council and has full authority to administer the city, develop and propose a budget, and hire and fire all personnel (DeSantis and Renner, 2002).

The relationship between homeland security and cities and the federal government has evolved much like the traditional emergency management system. The initial responsibility for planning, preparing, and response falls upon local governments – such as police, fire department, emergency medical personnel, and public health agencies. For its part, the federal government has primarily provided leadership, training, and funding assistance to local governments. The federal government's role in responding to major disasters has historically been defined by the *Safford Act (P.L. 93-288)* which makes most federal assistance contingent upon finding that the disaster is so severe as to be beyond the capacity of state and local governments to respond effectively (GAO, 2002). The federal government essentially has four policy tools - grants, regulations, tax incentives, and information sharing mechanisms to motivate or mandate other levels of government to address homeland security concerns. In order to understand homeland security preparedness, it is important to show the relationship between institutions and e-government research.

ORGANIZATIONAL BEHAVIOR AND INFORMATION TECHNOLOGY

Fountain advocates for an institutional understanding of e-government reform in the United States (Fountain, 2001; 2007). This institutional approach integrates politics, organizational structure, and policy into studies on e-government. There are both formal institutions and informal networks that support e-government adoption. There are several other important studies that incorporate institutional analysis in the study of e-government (Gasco, 2003; Danziger, 2004; Heeks and Bailur, 2007). HSIS can be seen as one core element in an overall government reform effort within government.

Specifically, relating homeland security and institutional analysis Waugh (2003) points out that in the United States, there are several governmental agencies that deal with terrorism. The most important agencies are the Department of Homeland Security, the Department of Justice, the Department of Defense and state and local government law enforcement (Waugh, 2003). In addition, there is Health and Human Services which would deal with bioterrorism and Federal Emergency Management Agency (FEMA), which would work with the coordinating effort for disaster response. There are of course other nongovernmental entities such as the network of nonprofit agencies such as the Red Cross and private firms that provide assistance during and after terrorist incidents and disasters. In addition, President Bush established the Citizen Corps (http://www.citizencorps.gov) to be coordinated by FEMA to organize and mobilize citizen volunteers in the event of a major disaster. Waugh (2003) argues that there is hundreds, if not thousands of, organizations that compose the national emergency management network in the United States. As a result, in order to understand HSIS one must grasp the vast network involved in this area and the major issues of preparedness. In fact, each of these members of the network would have different technology needs to incorporate into their preparedness efforts. This book argues that one of the keys to unlocking government reform is through HSIS.

One potential use for IT is to create a virtual restructuring of the organization through information systems that identify and link the needs of the organization to answer critical questions (Kettl, 2003). To create a system that is more flexible and responsive to changing needs of homeland security is where classical organizational theory falls behind. However, Kettl believes that information systems might change this because of its ability to coordination, communicate, and share homeland security information.

Comfort (2007) presents one model of communicating information in the time of a disaster. In this model new information is “fanned out” to and “fanned in” to interested parties. The emergency operations center transmits this data to emergency personnel chiefs who interpret the data with reference to the emergency. These emergency chiefs adjust their operations in light of the new information. In this theoretical model, information technology can be used to facilitate both the fanning in and out of information in a disaster. Combining all of the different stakeholders and their information there is data collection, analysis, and organizational action on the basis of the interpretation of the data. This may be one theoretical interpretation of what could potentially happen, but of course there are numerous notable incidents of this not taking place such as September 11, 2001 and Hurricane Katrina noted towards the end of the book.

ADMINISTRATIVE AND ORGANIZATIONAL ASPECTS OF HOMELAND SECURITY

In emergencies, such as terrorist threats, Carroll (2001) believes that the government response is shaped by operational, administrative, and sociological components. The actual service provided by the government is said to be the operational aspect, administrative is how government entity is run, and sociological is both internal and external impacts on emergency management. Wise and Nader (2002) describe the organizational aspects of homeland security in terms of areas of intergovernmental relationships, operational, financial, legal and regulatory, and political. Essentially, the literature demonstrates the importance of the surrounding organizational environment, both internal and external, and its impact on homeland security preparedness.

Homeland security mandates from higher levels of government put tremendous pressure on the finances of local governments and dictate intensified administrative oversight (Caruson and MacManus, 2005). In a national survey of American cities, there was evidence that resource capacity, budgetary constraints, and administrative capacity are tied to homeland security preparedness (Gerber et al., 2005). To exemplify this, in a survey of city officials, 58% of respondents believed it was unlikely that residents would support additional local taxes to fund homeland security (Baldassare and Hoene, 2002). Also, according to a survey of Florida county and city government officials, the greatest impact of homeland security legislation on local governments has been financial and administrative (Caruson and MacManus, 2005). Therefore, the administrative environment that city managers face in homeland security is very constrained, with very limited resources and a public generally unwilling to accept tax increases to fund these activities.

One of the most important administrative aspects of homeland security is the sharing of information between the federal, state, and local governments. The Government Accountability Office (GAO) conducted a national survey of all levels of government of homeland security information sharing (GAO, 2003a). The results show that the federal, state, and city governments do not perceive the current sharing process of information as "effective" or "very effective" because they believed (1) that they are not routinely receiving the information they need to protect the homeland; (2) that when information is received, it is not very useful, timely, accurate, or relevant; and (3) that the federal government still perceives the fight against terrorism to be generally a federal responsibility.

Local officials and first responders in the state of Florida also do not give the federal homeland security advisory system (or the color coded system developed by the U.S. Department of Homeland Security to provide information on terrorist threat levels) very high marks. More officials tend to depend on information sources other than the federal government for threat data (MacManus and Caruson, 2006). Therefore, information should drive the response from local government to disasters and preparedness efforts. Local government officials tend to depend heavily on state and local outlets for threat information, suggesting that federal sources are not providing the level of specificity desired by officials (MacManus and Caruson, 2006). The following section of the chapter provides information on the level of collaboration between and among department and agencies in homeland security. The literature argues that effective collaboration is vital for homeland security preparedness.

HOMELAND SECURITY COLLABORATION

One of the most important lessons learned from the events of 9/11 is the importance of coordination among the governmental agencies and organizations that are responsible for disaster management (Caruson and MacManus, 2006). Homeland security preparedness requires numerous federal, state, local, and private entities to be prepared to operate in close coordination to meet the threat and to mitigate its consequences (Wise and Nader, 2002).

Waugh (1988) explains that this tendency for a lack of collaboration among different levels of governments in emergency preparedness is attributed to three factors. This author demonstrates the complex relationship between the different levels of government in U.S. emergency management system. First, vertical fragmentation is due to the division of powers between federal and state governments, and the limited powers given to local governments. Second, horizontal fragmentation is due to the jurisdictional issues of all the agencies involved. Finally, there is the unwillingness of the federal government to assume the lead role in disaster preparedness.

This fragmentation is also evident in homeland security grant funding. The GAO (2003b) has reported that mission fragmentation and program overlap are widespread in the federal government and that the cross cutting program efforts are not well coordinated in homeland security grants. Therefore, scholars have argued that the federal system inhibits the responsiveness of governments to possible terrorist threats, which is exemplified through the existing grant funding system.

In a homeland security survey, evidence shows some increased level of collaborations after 9/11. In this survey of city officials there were high ratings for collaborative efforts of governments, agencies, and other organizations in their region (Baldassare and Hoene, 2002). There were even higher marks given for coordination between departments and agencies within their own city governments. In a survey of county and city officials in Florida, roughly two thirds of survey respondents reported an improvement in intergovernmental cooperation since 9/11 (Caruson and MacManus, 2006). The change in the homeland security collaboration may be partially explained by the adaptive management model.

ADAPTIVE MANAGEMENT AND HOMELAND SECURITY

The term "adaptive management" first appeared in the natural resources management literature in the mid-1970s (Hollings, 1978). This theory has been subsequently used to explain homeland security preparedness and planning after 9/11 (Wise, 2006). Adaptive management calls for the integration of science and management and for researchers and managers to work collaboratively with each other and with the public (Graham and Kruger, 2002). Adaptive management attempts to incorporate the views and knowledge of all interested parties. It begins with bringing together interested stakeholders to discuss management problems and to develop models to express participants' collective understanding of how the system operates (Johnson, 1999).

In adaptive management there is citizen and organizational learning whereby professionals learn about the conditions affected by alternative courses of action (Graham and Kruger, 2002). Adaptive management begins with the central tenet that management involves a continual learning process (McLain and Lee, 1996). Indeed, public opinion research has found that the more people talk about terrorism, the greater the chance that reason rather than fear will dictate reactions (West and Orr, 2005). This implies that if governments have increased dialogues with citizens on homeland security, this may relieve some of their anxiety about homeland security concerns.

Wise (2006) makes the case that given the turbulent environment of homeland security, the most suitable approach seems to be the adaptive management model. Adaptive management requires managers to change their approach as new information arrives (Alexander, 2002; Wise, 2006). This mode of management differs from traditional forms of management by emphasizing the importance of feedback in shaping policy, followed by further systematic experimentation and evaluation of policy as new information arises (Wise, 2006). The following section provides information on a survey that examines homeland security preparedness in United States local governments.

RESEARCH METHODS

The chapter uses data collected from a mail survey in 2006 of city managers that serve populations greater than 100,000 residents. City managers were chosen for this survey because they hold the highest administrative position in the city and have the responsibility for overseeing homeland security. A comprehensive mailing list of cities was obtained from the National League of Cities. Out of 191 cities that were sent a survey 126 responded, giving a response rate of 66%. The response rate for this survey is higher than the typical response rate of around 40% for International City/County Management Association (ICMA) surveys of Chief Administrative Officers (CAO). This high participation rate can most likely be attributed to the timeliness of homeland security at all levels of government since 9/11.

The survey methods involved sending a cover letter along with the survey to city managers. In order to get more candid responses, the survey respondents were ensured anonymity with only summary responses reported in the analysis. This is especially important given some of the sensitive information asked on the survey. A reminder letter and another copy of the survey were sent one month after the initial mailing to city mangers' who did not respond to the first mailing. The following section outlines the characteristics of cities that responded to the survey to determine how representative the sample is of the overall population.

DESCRIPTIVE CHARACTERISTICS OF CITY MANAGERS AND THEIR GOVERNMENTS

Table 1 examines how representative this sample is compared to all cities in the United States serving a population of 100,000 residents or greater. In size of city government, this study uses a broad measure of full-time equivalent (FTE) employment. The findings indicate that the typical city that responded to the survey employees between 1,000 and 2,499 FTE employees. Therefore, the cities that participated in the survey are rather large and should be representative of larger-sized cities in the United States. There were 17 very large cities that responded to the survey, having 5,000 or more FTE employees.

This survey also asked questions on the fiscal capacity, economic development climate, and political climate of each city in order to gain a better perspective of the environment in which these cities operate (Table 1). The fiscal capacity of a typical city was favorable according to 35% of respondents (adding up favorable and very favorable responses). About three quarters of city managers believed that the economic development climate of their city was favorable. Only 7% of cities believed that their economic

Table 1. City managers and their governments

Full-time equivalent (FTE) employees	Frequency	Percent
99 or less	1	0.8
100 to 499	8	6.3
500 to 999	24	19
1,000 to 2,499	56	44.4
2,500 to 4,999	20	15.9
5,000 or more	17	13.5
Fiscal capacity		
Very Favorable	7	5.6
Favorable	37	29.4
Neither Favorable/Unfavorable	40	31.7
Unfavorable	31	24.6
Very Unfavorable	11	8.7
Economic development climate		
Very Favorable	23	18.3
Favorable	71	56.3
Neither Favorable/Unfavorable	23	18.3
Unfavorable	9	7.1
Very Unfavorable	0	0
Political climate		
Very Favorable	30	23.8
Favorable	71	56.3
Neither Favorable/Unfavorable	21	16.7
Unfavorable	4	3.2
Very Unfavorable	0	0
Gender		
Male	112	88.9
Female	14	11.1
Age range		
25-34	5	4
35-44	24	19
45-54	55	43.7
55-64	39	31
65 or over	3	2.4
Graduate degree		
Yes	82	65.1
No	44	34.9

development climate was unfavorable. Table 1 also shows the views of city managers on the political climate of their city. Around 80% of city managers believed that the political climate of their city was favorable. Overall, in terms of the environment in which city managers find themselves there is a limited amount of fiscal capacity, but the economic development and political climate are favorable.

The demographic characteristics of the sample showed that 89% of city managers were males. There was 44% of the sample being composed of city managers in the age range of 45 to 54. Finally, the majority of city managers held a graduate degree (65%). The following section provides the opinions of city managers on possible terrorist threats to local governments. The information that follows helps to set the context for understanding HSIS discussed more thoroughly in later chapters.

POSSIBLE TERRORIST THREATS

Table 2 provides information on the level of concern that city managers have of different types of terrorist threats in 2007 for their municipality. The results in this table indicate that the greatest concerns are an individual/suicide bomb, car or truck bomb, biohazard/biological, chemical, cyber-terrorism, and dirty bomb. There seems to be less consensus among city managers about radiological, nuclear, and airplane used as a bomb. Overall, the findings in Table 2 indicate that most city managers are concerned about many possible terrorist threats in their municipality. The following section provides information on the equipment that has been purchased to respond to a terrorist attack.

TYPES OF HOMELAND SECURITY EQUIPMENT PURCHASED

There are various types of equipment that can be used to complete a city government's homeland security goals. Table 3 lists the most common equipment that city managers have purchased. HAZMAT (or Hazardous Material) suits and apparatuses were the most frequently purchased by 89% of cities (This is a garment worn as protection from hazardous materials or substances. It may be used by firefighters and

Table 2. Perceived terrorist threats

How concerned are you about the following terrorist threats over the next year in your locality?	Very Concerned %	Concerned %	Neither Concerned/ Unconcerned %	Unconcerned %	Very Unconcerned %
Individual/suicide bomb	19.8	32.5	31.0	13.5	3.2
Car or truck bomb	18.3	51.6	20.6	8.7	0.8
Biohazard/biological	15.1	57.1	17.5	8.7	1.6
Chemical	15.1	55.6	19.0	8.7	1.6
Cyber-terrorism	15.1	47.6	27.0	8.7	1.6
Combination (dirty bomb)	13.5	43.7	27.8	11.1	4.0
Radiological	9.5	36.5	33.3	13.5	7.1
Nuclear	7.9	27.8	38.1	19.0	7.1
Airplane used as a bomb	7.1	31.7	38.1	16.7	6.3

Table 3. Types homeland security equipment purchased

	Frequency	Percent
HAZMAT suits, apparatuses	112	88.9
Communications	107	84.9
Information technology	79	62.7
Surveillance devices	72	57.1
Access control devices	69	54.8
Identification technology	52	41.3
Other	19	15.1

other emergency personnel to respond to toxic spills). Communications equipment was purchased by 85% of cities to meet their homeland security goals. The third most commonly purchased equipment for homeland security was information technology. There were 15% of cities who responded to the "other" category which included medications, a central command unit, and specialized vehicles. Overall, the results in Table 3 are not surprising given the need for more effective communication technologies to respond to terrorist threats. The question that city managers must be cognizant of, where is the money coming from to fund their homeland security goals?

HOMELAND SECURITY FUNDING

Table 4 provides information on homeland security funding in city governments. This question specifically asked for information on how homeland security was paid for, the proportion not covered by federal and/or state government grants. The most common method of paying for homeland security was through the general fund or existing budget of a city with 71% of cities using this method. All of the other funds were used less frequently with only 22%, for example, used asset seizure funds. The smallest number of cities actually raised property taxes to fund homeland security (1.6%). Only 4% of cities used a special sales tax to pay for homeland security. Overall the results in Table 4 indicate that

Table 4. How has your city government paid for its portion of homeland security costs (i.e., that portion not covered by federal and/or state grants)?

	Frequency	Percent
General fund/existing budget	89	70.6
Asset seizure funds	28	22.2
Reallocate/cut spending	23	18.3
Issue bonds	6	4.8
Dedicate a special sales tax	5	4.0
Raise utility rates	4	3.2
Raise property taxes	2	1.6
Other	1	0.5

most of the cities are paying for their homeland security initiatives (not covered by grants) through the general fund. Not surprisingly, given taxpayer resistance there is much less use of increasing taxes or users fees to fund homeland security.

The average amount of grant funding in 2005 that a city government received from federal and/or state sources was $250,000 to $499,000 (not shown). A small proportion of cities, around 6% did not receive any grant funding. The survey results revealed that 23% of cities received more than one million in federal and/or state homeland security grants. Essentially, homeland security preparedness has become another issue on the agenda for U.S. cities, but very little funding has been allocated towards it compared to other priorities.

COLLABORATION AND HOMELAND SECURITY

Table 5 provides information on what organizations/agencies city governments tend to collaborate with on homeland security issues. Not surprisingly, the most common is their state government, with 94% of cities collaborating with this level of government. The second highest was 91% of cities that collaborated with other local governments. A regional organization was the third most common collaborating entity with 83% of cities working with them. Some of the responses for the 9% of cities that indicated "other" were collaborating with the Red Cross, the Department of Energy, and the Center for Disease Control.

HOMELAND SECURITY INFORMATION ASSESSMENT

Homeland security information that cities receive is critical for effective preparedness and response. In terms of the current information received by federal and/or state agencies on terrorist threats, 48% of city managers believed that this was effective (Table 6). The survey results showed that 24% of cities believed that federal and/or state information received was ineffective. The color coded homeland security advisory system was not viewed by city managers in their planning efforts as extremely effec-

Table 5. Organizations/Agencies that city governments collaborate with on homeland security

	Frequency	Percent
Your state government	118	93.7
Other local governments	114	90.5
A regional organization, such as regional planning agency	105	83.3
FBI/Department of Justice	98	77.8
DHS/FEMA	93	73.8
HHS (Health and Human Services)	67	53.2
Non-governmental organizations	65	51.6
Local military installations	59	46.8
DOD (Department of Defense)	34	27.0
Other state governments	21	16.7
Other	11	8.7

Table 6. Homeland security information assessment

For your city government, how effective is the...	Very Effective %	Effective %	Neither Effective/ Ineffective %	Ineffective %	Very Ineffective %
Current information received by federal and/or state agencies on terrorist threats.	4.8	42.9	28.6	19.8	4.0
Homeland Security Advisory System (the color-coded system developed by the U.S. Department of Homeland Security) in your planning efforts.	1.6	23.8	42.9	23.0	8.7

Table 7. Rating homeland security coordination and collaboration across governments

How would you rate the extent of homeland security coordination and collaboration...	Very High %	High %	Neither High/ Low %	Low %	Very Low %
Among departments and agencies in your city government.	45.2	42.1	7.9	4.0	0.8
Across levels of government, agencies, and other organizations in your region.	26.2	43.7	23.0	6.3	0.8
Across levels of government, agencies, and other organizations statewide.	14.3	43.7	29.4	11.9	0.8

tive, with only one quarter of them believing this was the case. Indeed, 32% actually believed that the advisor system was ineffective.

RATING HOMELAND SECURITY COLLABORATION

Table 7 reports on the extent of homeland security coordination and collaboration across governments. City managers generally believed that there was a high level of collaboration among departments and agencies in their city government (87%). In addition, collaboration was high across levels of government, agencies, and other organizations in their region (70%). A majority of cities believed that collaboration on homeland security was high across levels of government, agencies, and other organizations statewide (58%). Overall, the results in Table 7 indicated that collaboration was rated the highest in their city, followed by their region, then statewide.

HOMELAND SECURITY COLLABORATION AND ADAPTIVE MANAGEMENT

Table 8 provides an assessment of the level of homeland security collaboration in city government and across other governments in their community. This provides some evidence of the prevalence of the adaptive management model in city government homeland security preparedness. There was a high level of agreement that homeland security efforts have established a common strategy, addressed the need to leverage resources, established compatible policies and procedures, agreed on roles and responsibilities for planning, developed mechanisms to monitor, evaluate, and report on collaborative efforts. However,

Table 8. Assessment of homeland security collaboration

Homeland security collaboration in our city government, and across other governments, in our locality has. . .	Strongly Agree %	Agree %	Neutral %	Disagree %	Strongly Disagree %
Established a common strategy.	22.2	54.0	15.1	8.7	0.0
Addressed the need to leverage resources.	18.3	61.9	14.3	5.6	0.0
Established compatible policies and procedures.	15.1	51.6	25.4	7.9	0.0
Agreed on roles and responsibilities for planning.	14.3	61.9	18.3	5.6	0.0
Developed mechanisms to monitor, evaluate, and report on collaborative efforts.	7.9	50.0	31.0	11.1	0.0
Reinforced accountability for collaborative efforts through performance systems.	5.6	27.0	45.2	19.8	2.4

there was not as much agreement that homeland security used performance measures, with only 33% of cities agreeing to this. Overall, homeland security collaboration was high for city governments, supporting one of the main principles of the adaptive management model. With respect to cities actually measuring whether they achieved results, there was not as much agreement among city officials.

MANAGEMENT CONCERNS AND HOMELAND SECURITY

Table 9 provides survey evidence on the management concerns of homeland security. The greatest management concern, not surprisingly, was lack of money, according to 79% of cities surveyed. The second greatest concern was personnel limitations, with 64% of cities believing this was an issue. The third greatest concern was technology/interoperability, with half of city managers citing this as a problem. External cooperation being a management concern was found in 26% of cities. In addition, the lack of clear plan/roles was a problem in 21% of cities. One of the responses for the 2.4% who responded "other" was sustaining funding levels for homeland security. These homeland security management concerns are consistent with general management issues that cities face in the United States.

Table 9. Management concerns and homeland security

	Frequency	Percent
Lack of money	100	79.4
Personnel limitations	81	64.3
Technology/interoperability	63	50.0
Lack of health care capacity	58	46.0
Lack of external cooperation	33	26.2
Lack of clear plan/roles	27	21.4
Lack of internal cooperation	7	5.6
Other	3	2.4

Table 10. Organizational aspects of homeland security

Homeland security planning in our city government...	Strongly Agree %	Agree %	Neutral %	Disagree %	Strongly Disagree %
Has a high level of cooperation between city departments and the city manager's office.	57.9	34.9	5.6	1.6	0.0
Has open lines of communication.	42.1	48.4	7.9	1.6	0.0
Is regularly monitored and evaluated.	31.0	55.6	10.3	2.4	0.8
Tends to focus on the long-term issues.	18.3	48.4	21.4	11.9	0.0
Includes input from citizens and businesses.	11.9	46.8	25.4	15.1	0.8
Has tended to emphasize preparedness over response.	8.7	40.5	31.7	17.5	1.6

ORGANIZATIONAL ASPECTS OF HOMELAND SECURITY

Table 10 showed that there was a very high level of cooperation between city departments and the city managers' offices in homeland security planning; with 93% of cities believing this was the case. There was a similarly high level of agreement that there were open lines of communication on homeland security planning (91%). There was less agreement that homeland security planning tended to emphasize preparedness over response (49%). Overall, the results in Table 10 demonstrated that communication, focusing on long-term issues, and monitoring and evaluating homeland security was very strong in city governments. There was less agreement of an emphasis being placed on preparedness over response in homeland security planning, which would be especially critical for city governments since the terrorist attacks of 9/11.

CITY GOVERNMENT HOMELAND SECURITY ASSESSMENT

Table 11 provides information on the overall evaluation by city managers of their city government's homeland security preparedness. City managers believed that their governments had a high managerial capacity to coordinate and control homeland security, with 81% of them agreeing to this statement. Similarly, 73% of city managers believed that they have a high level of current homeland security preparedness. The most interesting finding in Table 11was that 35% of city managers believed that they have a low probability of being a future terrorist target. Overall, city managers are of the opinion that their cities are well prepared for a terrorist attack, but are not confident that one will materialize in the near

Table 11. City government homeland security assessment

How would you assess your city's...	Very High %	High %	Neither High/Low %	Low %	Very Low %
Managerial capacity to coordinate and control homeland security.	18.3	62.7	15.1	4.0	0.0
Current homeland security preparedness.	10.3	62.7	20.6	5.6	0.8
Probability of being a future terrorist target.	4.8	23.8	36.5	22.2	12.7

future. The following section provides a case study of the use of information systems in the response to Hurricane Katrina; this provides an illustration of homeland security preparedness in action.

HURRICANE KATRINA, INFORMATION SYSTEMS AND PREPAREDNESS

A report by the Select Bipartisan Committee to Investigate the Preparation for and Response to Hurricane Katrina (2006) entitled "A Failure of Initiative" provides some unique insights into how information systems failed in American's worst natural disaster. One of the key findings of the Select Committee was the following:

The federal government is the largest purchaser of information technology in the world, by far. One would think we could share information by now. But Katrina again proved we cannot. We reflect on the 9/11 Commission's finding that "the most important failure was one of imagination." The Select Committee believes Katrina was primarily a failure of initiative. But there is, of course, a nexus between the two. Both imagination and initiative – in other words, leadership – require good information. And a coordinated process for sharing it. And a willingness to use information – however imperfect or incomplete – to fuel action. With Katrina, the reasons reliable information did not reach more people more quickly are many, and these reasons provide the foundation for our findings (Select Committee, 2006, p. 1).

The Select Committee came to the conclusion that the preparation and response to Hurricane Katrina was a failure of initiative. With Hurricane Katrina reliable information did not reach individuals quickly and this was one of the foundations of the Select Committee's findings. Emergency responders were overwhelmed and unable to perform their duties effectively, despite ample warnings through forecasting of this natural disaster potentially happening to the Gulf Coast. Similarly to the findings of the 9/11 commission, the Select Committee came to the conclusion that there is a risk adverse culture in the federal government, when it should be more agile and responsive to the needs of its citizens.

Specifically, with regards to information systems the Select Committee (2006) found that there was "massive interoperability had the biggest effect on communications, limiting command and control, situational awareness, and federal, state, and local officers' ability to address unsubstantiated media reports." (Select Committee, 2006, p. 3). The Select Committee's report mentions that massive interoperability was the biggest communication problem in the response to Hurricane Katrina. For example, FEMA could have prepositioned mobile communications in New Orleans, but did not because it believed that it must be first asked to do so by local authorities. Other examples of the Select Committee's findings on examples of IT communication problems are listed below (p. 164):

- More than three million customer telephone lines were knocked down in Louisiana, Mississippi, and Alabama. As of September 28, 2005, over 260,000 customer lines remained out of service, including 238,000 in Louisiana and 22,000 in Mississippi.
- The entire communications infrastructure on the Mississippi Gulf coast was destroyed.
- Significant damage was inflicted both on the wire line switching centers that route calls and on the lines used to connect buildings and customers to the network.
- Thirty-eight 911 call centers went down. Thirty days after landfall, two call centers in Louisiana remained out of service.

- Two telephone company switches in New Orleans responsible for routing 911 calls for the surrounding parishes were knocked out by flooding, resulting in one of the most significant losses of capacity in and around New Orleans.
- Local wireless networks also sustained considerable damage, with up to 2,000 cell sites out of service. A month after landfall, approximately 820 cell sites remained out of service, the majority within New Orleans and other areas of Louisiana.
- Over 20 million telephone calls did not go through the day after the hurricane.
- 37 of 41 broadcast radio stations in New Orleans and surrounding areas were knocked off the air (2 AM and 2 FM stations continued to broadcast).

During Hurricane Katarina there were hundreds of New Orleans first responders trying to communicate only on two way radios on a backup system (Select Committee, 2006). These first responders would essentially have to wait for an opening in communications traffic to transmit and receive critical information. Hurricane Katrina demonstrates one of the most commonly found problems in emergency management preparedness of difficulties in communications.

As mentioned, Hurricane Katrina was a communication crisis according to Select Bipartisan Committee to Investigate the Preparation for and Response to Hurricane Katrina (Select Committee, 2006). There was massive interoperability of communication technology that has been well documented (Garnett and Kouzmin, 2007). Research shows that communication plays a crucial role in the time of crisis. Most of the time failure in crisis can be contributed to problems in communication failures, and Hurricane Katrina has become a noted example.

Information systems should aid inter-organizational cooperation and in response and recovery. Essentially, during a crisis communication technologies are showcased (Garnett and Kouzmin, 2007). Disasters are able to demonstrate the value of certain information technologies to the response and recovery efforts of first responders. Showcasing can gain acceptance of emergency management personnel before it becomes more mainstream. There also is the added benefit of being able to test out the actual effectiveness of technology in the time of crisis. For example, Hurricane Katrina showed that much of the communications technology that was used was made useless because of water, wind, and mismanagement (Garnett and Kouzmin, 2007).

Comfort (2006) argues that a self-organizing, resilient city is built on the ability of it to coordinate its groups in the city. Since urban areas are exposed to various risks, they can function more effectively with the help of IT. This author uses the example of the failure of communication systems after Hurricane Katrina exasperated the coordination among first responders to this natural disaster. Comfort essentially argues that IT is one component of creating cities that are more resilient to risks that are created because of major disasters.

CONCLUSION

This chapter provided an overview of the organizational, administrative, collaboration, and management issues of homeland security preparedness. The primary aim was to provide a broad overview of some of the issues that governments face in the realm of homeland security preparedness. In order to more effectively understand HSIS, this chapter was written to provide baseline knowledge of some of the important issues that governments face with regards to homeland security. This chapter finally provided a case study of the response to Hurricane Katrina as an example of HSIS in action in government.

Some of the most interesting survey results indicate that city managers are concerned about terrorist threats such as a car or truck bomb, biohazard/biological, and chemical attack. However, there was less concern about radiological, nuclear, and airplane used as a bomb as possible terrorist attacks. There was no general consensus among city managers of the most likely terrorist attack their cities could face.

The two most common types of homeland security equipment purchased by city governments were HAZMAT suits (and apparatuses) and communications equipment. As existing research shows, most of the cities used their general fund (the portion not covered by grants) to pay for homeland security. According to city managers, the possibility of raising taxes to fund homeland security was very unlikely. The average amount of grant funding that a city government received was very small at only $250,000 to $499,000.

Another issue was the level of cooperation and collaboration between city government and among other levels of governments in homeland security. In terms of collaboration, the most common governments that cities worked with in order of frequency were their state governments, other local governments, and regional planning authorities. What is interesting is that federal agencies are not near the top of this list. This was echoed in the views of city managers on the information that they received from the federal government, with 32% of respondents believed that the color-coded homeland security advisory system was ineffective. This is a surprising finding since the federal government is in charge of coordinating the national homeland security effort.

According to city managers, there is a very high level of collaboration between and among agencies and different levels of government in homeland security preparedness. This is somewhat surprising and may be explained by the new type of environment that these city governments are facing post 9/11. A similar result was found in a survey of Florida local government officials of increased collaboration in homeland security in a time of crisis (Caruson and MacManus, 2006).

In the application of the adaptive management model to homeland security, the results in this study showed that some of the key elements of collaboration identified in the adaptive management literature were supported in the survey evidence. The only exception was performance systems not being as commonly used to gain accountability in city government homeland security. The most pronounced homeland security management concerns, not surprisingly, were the lack of money and personnel limitations that cities faced. Near the bottom of the list was lack of cooperation, which further supports a high level of cooperation and collaboration in homeland security for city governments.

Finally, there is an interesting split between city managers believing that they are well prepared for an attack and the relatively low probability of being a future terrorist target. On a brighter note, city managers believe that the managerial capacity is there in their governments to coordinate and control homeland security. This finding is especially important given the key role that city managers' play in homeland security preparedness. The following chapter provides an examination of the e-government literature and evidence of HSIS creating more citizen centric government.

REFERENCES

Alexander, D. (2002). *Principles of Emergency Planning and Management*. New York: Oxford University Press.

Baldassare, M., & Hoene, C. (2002). *Coping with Homeland Security: Perceptions of City Officials in California and the United States*. San Francisco, CA: Public Policy Institute of California.

Beresford, A. D. (2004). Homeland Security as an American Ideology: Implications for U.S. Policy and Action. *Journal of Homeland Security and Emergency Management, 1*(3). Retrieved May 27, 2006, from http://www.bepress.com/jhsem/vol1/iss3/301

Carroll, J. (2001). Emergency Management on a Grand Scale: A Bureaucrat's Analysis. In A. Farazmand, (Ed.) *Handbook of Crisis and Emergency Management*. New York: Marcel Dekker, Inc.

Caruson, K., & MacManus, S. A. (2005). Homeland Security Preparedness: Federal and State Mandates and Local Government. *Spectrum . The Journal of State Government, 78*(2), 25–28.

Caruson, K., & MacManus, S. A. (2006). Mandates and Management Challenges in the Trenches: An Intergovernmental Perspective on Homeland Security. *Public Administration Review, 66*(4), 522–536. doi:10.1111/j.1540-6210.2006.00613.x

Comfort, L. K. (2006). Cities at Risk: Hurricane Katrina and the Drowning of New Orleans. *Urban Affairs Review, 41*(4), 501–516. doi:10.1177/1078087405284881

Comfort, L. K. (2007). Crisis Management in Hindsight: Cognition, Communication, Coordination, and Control. *Public Administration Review, 67*(s1), 189–197.

Danziger, J. (2004). Innovation in innovation? The technology enactment framework. *Social Science Computer Review, 22*(1), 100–110. doi:10.1177/0894439303259892

DeSantis, V. S., & Renner, T. (2002). City Government Structures: An Attempt at Clarification. *State and Local Government Review, 34*(2), 95–104.

Fountain, J. E. (2001). *Building the Virtual State: Information Technology and Institutional Change*. Washington, DC: The Brookings Institution Press.

Fountain, J. E. (2007). *Bureaucratic Reform and E-Government in the United States: An Institutional Perspective*. Retrieved January 26, 2009, from http://www.umass.edu/digitalcenter/research/working_papers/07_006FountainBureauReform.pdf.

Garnett, J. L., & Kouzmin, A. (2007). Communicating throughout Katrina: Competing and Complementary Conceptual Lenses on Crisis Communication. *Public Administration Review, 67*(s1), 171–188. doi:10.1111/j.1540-6210.2006.00705_3.x

Gasco, M. (2003). New technologies and institutional change in public administration. *Social Science Computer Review, 21*(1), 6–14. doi:10.1177/0894439302238967

Gerber, B. J., Cohen, D. B., Cannon, B., Patterson, D., & Stewart, K. (2005). On the Front Line: American Cities and the Challenge of Homeland Security Preparedness. *Urban Affairs Review, 41*(2), 182–210. doi:10.1177/1078087405279900

Graham, A. C., & Kruger, L. E. (2002). *Research in Adaptive Management: Working Relations and the Research Process* (PNW-RP-538). Portland, OR: U.S. Department of Agriculture.

Heeks, R., & Bailur, S. (2007). Analyzing e-government research: Perspective, philosophies, theories, methods, and practice. *Government Information Quarterly, 24*(2), 243–265. doi:10.1016/j.giq.2006.06.005

Hollings, C. S. (1978). *Adaptive Environmental Assessment and Management.* Editor. John Wiley: New York, NY.

Johnson, B. L. (1999). The Role of Adaptive Management as an Operational Approach for Resource Management Agencies. *Ecology and Society, 3*(2). Retrieved May 27, 2006, from http://www.consecol.org/vol3/iss2/art8

Kettl, D. F. (2003). Contingent Coordination: Practical and Theoretical Puzzles for Homeland Security. *American Review of Public Administration, 33*(3), 253–277. doi:10.1177/0275074003254472

MacManus, S. A., & Caruson, K. (2006). Code Red: Florida City and County Officials Rate Threat Information Sources and the Homeland Security Advisory System. *State and Local Government Review, 38*(1), 12–22.

McLain, R. J., & Lee, R. G. (1996). Adaptive Management: Promises and Pitfalls. *Environmental Management, 20*(4), 437–448. doi:10.1007/BF01474647

Rosenthal, U. (2003). September 11: Public Administration and the Study of Crisis and Crisis Management. *Administration & Society, 35*(2), 129–143. doi:10.1177/0095399703035002001

Select Committee. (2006). *A Failure of Initiative: Final Report of the Select Bipartisan Committee to Investigate the Preparation for and Response to Hurricane Katrina.* Retrieved January 26, 2009, from http://www.gpoaccess.gov/serialset/creports/katrina.html

United States Government Accountability Office. (GAO) (2002). *Homeland Security: Intergovernmental Coordination and Partnership will be Critical to Success.* (GAO-02-901T). Washington, D.C: U.S. Government Printing Office.

United States Government Accountability Office. (GAO) (2003a). *Homeland Security: Efforts to Improve Information Sharing Need to be Strengthened.* (GAO-03-760). Washington, DC: U.S. Government Printing Office.

United States Government Accountability Office. (GAO) (2003b). *Homeland Security: Reforming Federal Grants to Better Meet Outstanding Needs.* (GAO-03-1146T). Washington, DC: U.S. Government Printing Office.

Waugh, W. L. (1988). Current Policy and Implementation Issues in Disaster Preparedness. In L.K. Comfort, (Ed.) *Managing Disaster: Strategies and Policy Perspectives*. Durham, NC: Duke University Press.

Waugh, W. L. (2003). Terrorism, Homeland Security and the National Emergency Management Network. *Public Organization Review, 3*(4), 373–385. doi:10.1023/B:PORJ.0000004815.29497.e5

West, D. M., & Orr, M. (2005). Managing Citizen Fears: Public Attitudes toward Urban Terrorism. *Urban Affairs Review, 41*(1), 93–105. doi:10.1177/1078087405278642

Whitehouse (2002). *The National Strategy for Homeland Security*. Washington, DC: Office of Homeland Security. Retrieved January 5, 2007, from http://www.whitehouse.gov/homeland/book/nat_strat_hls.pdf.

Wise, C. R. (2006). Organizing for Homeland Security after Katrina: Is Adaptive Management What's Missing? *Public Administration Review*, *66*(3), 302–318. doi:10.1111/j.1540-6210.2006.00587.x

Wise, C. R., & Nader, R. (2002). Organizing the Federal System for Homeland Security: Problems, Issues, and Dilemmas. *Public Administration Review*, *62*(Special Issue), 44–57. doi:10.1111/1540-6210.62.s1.8

APPENDIX A: CONGRESSIONAL RESEARCH SERVICE SUMMARY OF THE HOMELAND SECURITY ACT OF 2002

H.R.5005 Title: To establish the Department of Homeland Security, and for other purposes. **Sponsor:** Rep Armey, Richard K. [TX-26] (by request) (introduced 6/24/2002) Cosponsors (118) **Related Bills:** H.RES.502, H.R.4635, H.R.4660, H.R.5506, H.R.5710, S.1534, S.2452, S.2546, S.2554, S.2794 **Latest Major Action:** Became Public Law No: 107-296 **House Reports:** 107-609 Part 1 **Note:** On 11/19/2002, S.Amdt. 4901 substituted text essentially the same as H.R. 5710 in H.R. 5005. The House agreed to the Senate amendment on 11/22/2002. Other earlier bills included H.R. 4660, S. 1534, S. 2452, and S. 2794.

SUMMARY AS OF: 11/19/2002--Passed Senate amended.

Homeland Security Act of 2002 –

Title I: Department of Homeland Security -

(Sec. 101) Establishes a Department of Homeland Security (DHS) as an executive department of the United States, headed by a Secretary of Homeland Security (Secretary) appointed by the President, by and with the advice and consent of the Senate, to: (1) prevent terrorist attacks within the United States; (2) reduce the vulnerability of the United States to terrorism; (3) minimize the damage, and assist in the recovery, from terrorist attacks that occur within the United States; (4) carry out all functions of entities transferred to DHS; (5) ensure that the functions of the agencies and subdivisions within DHS that are not related directly to securing the homeland are not diminished or neglected except by a specific Act of Congress; (6) ensure that the overall economic security of the United States is not diminished by efforts, activities, and programs aimed at securing the homeland; and (7) monitor connections between illegal drug trafficking and terrorism, coordinate efforts to sever such connections, and otherwise contribute to efforts to interdict illegal drug trafficking. Vests primary responsibility for investigating and prosecuting acts of terrorism in Federal, State, and local law enforcement agencies with proper jurisdiction except as specifically provided by law with respect to entities transferred to DHS under this Act.

(Sec. 102) Directs the Secretary to appoint a Special Assistant to carry out specified homeland security liaison activities between DHS and the private sector.

(Sec. 103) Creates the following: (1) a Deputy Secretary of Homeland Security; (2) an Under Secretary for Information Analysis and Infrastructure Protection; (3) an Under Secretary for Science and Technology; (4) an Under Secretary for Border and Transportation Security; (5) an Under Secretary for Emergency Preparedness and Response; (6) a Director of the Bureau of Citizenship and Immigration Services; (7) an Under Secretary for Management; (8) not more than 12 Assistant Secretaries; and (9) a General Counsel. Establishes an Inspector General (to be appointed under the Inspector General Act of 1978). Requires the following individuals to assist the Secretary in the performance of the Secretary's functions: (1) the Commandant of the Coast Guard; (2) the Director of the Secret Service; (3) a Chief Information Officer; (4) a Chief Human Capital Officer; (5) a Chief Financial Officer; and (6) an Officer for Civil Rights and Civil Liberties.

Title II: Information Analysis and Infrastructure Protection –

Subtitle A: Directorate for Information Analysis and Infrastructure Protection; Access to Information – (Sec. 201) Establishes in the Department: (1) a Directorate for Information Analysis and Infrastructure Protection, headed by an Under Secretary for Information Analysis and Infrastructure Protection; (2) an Assistant Secretary for Information Analysis; and (3) an Assistant Secretary for Infrastructure Protection.

Requires the Under Secretary to: (1) access, receive, and analyze law enforcement and intelligence information from Federal, State, and local agencies and the private sector to identify the nature, scope, and identity of terrorist threats to the United States, as well as potential U.S. vulnerabilities; (2) carry out comprehensive assessments of vulnerabilities of key U.S. resources and critical infrastructures; (3) integrate relevant information, analyses, and vulnerability assessments to identify protection priorities; (4) ensure timely and efficient Department access to necessary information for discharging responsibilities; (5) develop a comprehensive national plan for securing key U.S. resources and critical infrastructures; (6) recommend necessary measures to protect such resources and infrastructure in coordination with other entities; (7) administer the Homeland Security Advisory System; (8) review, analyze, and make recommendations for improvements in policies and procedures governing the sharing of law enforcement, intelligence, and intelligence-related information and other information related to homeland security within the Federal Government and between the Federal Government and State and local government agencies and authorities; (9) disseminate Department homeland security information to other appropriate Federal, State, and local agencies; (10) consult with the Director of Central Intelligence (DCI) and other appropriate Federal intelligence, law enforcement, or other elements to establish collection priorities and strategies for information relating the terrorism threats; (11) consult with State and local governments and private entities to ensure appropriate exchanges of information relating to such threats; (12) ensure the protection from unauthorized disclosure of homeland security and intelligence information; (13) request additional information from appropriate entities relating to threats of terrorism in the United States; (14) establish and utilize a secure communications and information technology infrastructure for receiving and analyzing data; (15) ensure the compatibility and privacy protection of shared information databases and analytical tools; (16) coordinate training and other support to facilitate the identification and sharing of information; (17) coordinate activities with elements of the intelligence community, Federal, State, and local law enforcement agencies, and the private sector; and (18) provide intelligence and information analysis and support to other elements of the Department. Provides for: (1) staffing, including the use of private sector analysts; and (2) cooperative agreements for the detail of appropriate personnel.

Transfers to the Secretary the functions, personnel, assets, and liabilities of the following entities: (1) the National Infrastructure Protection Center of the Federal Bureau of Investigation (other than the Computer Investigations and Operations Section); (2) the National Communications System of the Department of Defense; (3) the Critical Infrastructure Assurance Offices of the Department of Commerce; (4) the National Infrastructure Simulation and Analysis Center of the Department of Energy and its energy security and assurance program; and (5) the Federal Computer Incident Response Center of the General Services Administration.

Amends the National Security Act of 1947 to include as elements of the intelligence community the Department elements concerned with analyses of foreign intelligence information.

(Sec. 202) Gives the Secretary access to all reports, assessments, analyses, and unevaluated intelligence relating to threats of terrorism against the United States, and to all information concerning infrastructure or other vulnerabilities to terrorism, whether or not such information has been analyzed. Requires all Federal agencies to promptly provide to the Secretary: (1) all reports, assessments, and analytical information relating to such threats and to other areas of responsibility assigned to the Secretary; (2) all information concerning the vulnerability of U.S. infrastructure or other U.S. vulnerabilities to terrorism, whether or not it has been analyzed; (3) all other information relating to significant and credible threats of terrorism, whether or not it has been analyzed; and (4) such other information or material as the President may direct. Requires the Secretary to be provided with certain terrorism-related information from law enforcement agencies that is currently required to be provided to the DCI.

Subtitle B: Critical Infrastructure Information - Critical Infrastructure Information Act of 2002 - (Sec. 213) Allows a critical infrastructure protection program to be so designated by either the President or the Secretary.

(Sec. 214) Exempts from the Freedom of Information Act and other Federal and State disclosure requirements any critical infrastructure information that is voluntarily submitted to a covered Federal agency for use in the security of critical infrastructure and protected systems, analysis, warning, interdependency study, recovery, reconstitution, or other informational purpose when accompanied by an express statement that such information is being submitted voluntarily in expectation of such nondisclosure protection. Requires the Secretary to establish specified procedures for the receipt, care, and storage by Federal agencies of critical infrastructure information voluntarily submitted. Provides criminal penalties for the unauthorized disclosure of such information.

Authorizes the Federal Government to issue advisories, alerts, and warnings to relevant companies, targeted sectors, other governmental entities, or the general public regarding potential threats to critical infrastructure.

Subtitle C: Information Security - (Sec. 221) Requires the Secretary to establish procedures on the use of shared information that: (1) limit its re-dissemination to ensure it is not used for an unauthorized purpose; (2) ensure its security and confidentiality; (3) protect the constitutional and statutory rights of individuals who are subjects of such information; and (4) provide data integrity through the timely removal and destruction of obsolete or erroneous names and information.

(Sec. 222) Directs the Secretary to appoint a senior Department official to assume primary responsibility for information privacy policy.

(Sec. 223) Directs the Under Secretary to provide: (1) to State and local government entities and, upon request, to private entities that own or operate critical information systems, analysis and warnings related to threats to and vulnerabilities of such systems, as well as crisis management support in response to threats to or attacks upon such systems; and (2) technical assistance, upon request, to private sector and other government entities with respect to emergency recovery plans to respond to major failures of such systems.

(Sec. 224) Authorizes the Under Secretary to establish a national technology guard (known as NET Guard) to assist local communities to respond to and recover from attacks on information systems and communications networks.

(Sec. 225) Cyber Security Enhancement Act of 2002 - Directs the U.S. Sentencing Commission to review and amend Federal sentencing guidelines and otherwise address crimes involving fraud in connection with computers and access to protected information, protected computers, or restricted data in interstate or foreign commerce or involving a computer used by or for the Federal Government. Requires a Commission report to Congress on actions taken and recommendations regarding statutory penalties for violations. Exempts from criminal penalties any disclosure made by an electronic communication service to a Federal, State, or local governmental entity if made in the good faith belief that an emergency involving danger of death or serious physical injury to any person requires disclosure without delay. Requires any government entity receiving such a disclosure to report it to the Attorney General.

Amends the Federal criminal code to: (1) prohibit the dissemination by electronic means of any such protected information; (2) increase criminal penalties for violations which cause death or serious bodily injury; (3) authorize the use by appropriate officials of emergency pen register and trap and trace devices in the case of either an immediate threat to a national security interest or an ongoing attack on a protected computer that constitutes a crime punishable by a prison term of greater than one year; (4) repeal provisions which provide a shorter term of imprisonment for certain offenses involving protection from the unauthorized interception and disclosure of wire, oral, or electronic communications; and (5) increase penalties for repeat offenses in connection with unlawful access to stored communications.

Subtitle D: Office of Science and Technology - (Sec. 231) Establishes within the Department of Justice (DOJ) an Office of Science and Technology whose mission is to: (1) serve as the national focal point for work on law enforcement technology (investigative and forensic technologies, corrections technologies, and technologies that support the judicial process); and (2) carry out programs that improve the safety and effectiveness of such technology and improve technology access by Federal, State, and local law enforcement agencies. Sets forth Office duties, including: (1) establishing and maintaining technology advisory groups and performance standards; (2) carrying out research, development, testing, evaluation, and cost-benefit analyses for improving the safety, effectiveness, and efficiency of technologies used by Federal, State, and local law enforcement agencies; and (3) operating the regional National Law Enforcement and Corrections Technology Centers (established under this Subtitle) and establishing additional centers. Requires the Office Director to report annually on Office activities.

(Sec. 234) Authorizes the Attorney General to transfer to the Office any other DOJ program or activity determined to be consistent with its mission. Requires a report from the Attorney General to the congressional judiciary committees on the implementation of this Subtitle.

(Sec. 235) Requires the Office Director to operate and support National Law Enforcement and Corrections Technology Centers and, to the extent necessary, establish new centers through a merit-based, competitive process. Requires such Centers to: (1) support research and development of law enforcement technology; (2) support the transfer and implementation of such technology; (3) assist in the development and dissemination of guidelines and technological standards; and (4) provide technology assistance, information, and support for law enforcement, corrections, and criminal justice purposes. Requires the Director to: (1) convene an annual meeting of such Centers; and (2) report to Congress assessing the effectiveness of the Centers and identifying the number of Centers necessary to meet the technology needs of Federal, State, and local law enforcement in the United States.

(Sec. 237) Amends the Omnibus Crime Control and Safe Streets Act of 1968 to require the National Institute of Justice to: (1) research and develop tools and technologies relating to prevention, detection, investigation, and prosecution of crime; and (2) support research, development, testing, training, and evaluation of tools and technology for Federal, State, and local law enforcement agencies.

Title III: Science and Technology in Support of Homeland Security –

(Sec. 301) Establishes in DHS a Directorate of Science and Technology, headed by an Under Secretary for Science and Technology, to be responsible for: (1) advising the Secretary regarding research and development (R&D) efforts and priorities in support of DHS missions; (2) developing a national policy and strategic plan for, identifying priorities, goals, objectives and policies for, and coordinating the Federal Government's civilian efforts to identify and develop countermeasures to chemical, biological, radiological, nuclear, and other emerging terrorist threats; (3) supporting the Under Secretary for Information Analysis and Infrastructure Protection by assessing and testing homeland security vulnerabilities and possible threats; (4) conducting basic and applied R&D activities relevant to DHS elements, provided that such responsibility does not extend to human health-related R&D activities; (5) establishing priorities for directing, funding, and conducting national R&D and procurement of technology systems for preventing the importation of chemical, biological, radiological, nuclear, and related weapons and material and for detecting, preventing, protecting against, and responding to terrorist attacks; (6) establishing a system for transferring homeland security developments or technologies to Federal, State, and local government and private sector entities; (7) entering into agreements with the Department of Energy (DOE) regarding the use of the national laboratories or sites and support of the science and technology base at those facilities; (8) collaborating with the Secretary of Agriculture and the Attorney General in the regulation of certain biological agents and toxins as provided in the Agricultural Bioterrorism Protection Act of 2002; (9) collaborating with the Secretary of Health and Human Services and the Attorney General in determining new biological agents and toxins that shall be listed as select agents in the Code of Federal Regulations; (10) supporting U.S. leadership in science and technology; (11) establishing and administering the primary R&D activities of DHS; (12) coordinating and integrating all DHS R&D activities; (13) coordinating with other appropriate executive agencies in developing and carrying out the science and technology agenda of DHS to reduce duplication and identify unmet needs; and (14) developing and overseeing the administration of guidelines for merit review of R&D projects throughout DHS and for the dissemination of DHS research.

(Sec. 303) Transfers to the Secretary: (1) specified DOE functions, including functions related to chemical and biological national security programs, nuclear smuggling programs and activities within the proliferation detection program, the nuclear assessment program, designated life sciences activities of the biological and environmental research program related to microbial pathogens, the Environmental Measurements Laboratory, and the advanced scientific computing research program at Lawrence Livermore National Laboratory; and (2) the National Bio-Weapons Defense Analysis Center of DOD.

(Sec. 304) Requires the HHS Secretary, with respect to civilian human health-related R&D activities relating to HHS countermeasures for chemical, biological, radiological, and nuclear and other emerging terrorist threats, to: (1) set priorities, goals, objectives, and policies and develop a coordinated strategy for such activities in collaboration with the Secretary to ensure consistency with the national policy and strategic plan; and (2) collaborate with the Secretary in developing specific benchmarks and outcome measurements for evaluating progress toward achieving such priorities and goals.

Amends the Public Health Service Act to: (1) authorize the HHS Secretary to declare that an actual or potential bioterrorist incident or other public health emergency makes advisable the administration of a covered countermeasure against smallpox to a category or categories of individuals; (2) require the HHS Secretary to specify the substances to be considered countermeasures and the beginning and ending dates of the period of the declaration; and (3) deem a covered person to be an employee of the Public Health Service with respect to liability arising out of administration of such a countermeasure.

Extends liability to the United States (with an exception) with respect to claims arising out of an administration of a covered countermeasure to an individual only if: (1) the countermeasure was administered by a qualified person for the purpose of preventing or treating smallpox during the effective period; (2) the individual was within a covered category; or (3) the qualified person administering the countermeasure had reasonable grounds to believe that such individual was within such category. Provides for a rebuttable presumption of an administration within the scope of a declaration in the case where an individual who is not vaccinated contracts vaccinia Makes the remedy against the United States provided under such Act exclusive of any other civil action or proceeding against a covered person for any claim or suit arising out of the administration of a covered countermeasure.

(Sec. 305) Authorizes the Secretary, acting through the Under Secretary, to establish or contract with one or more federally funded R&D centers to provide independent analysis of homeland security issues or to carry out other responsibilities under this Act.

(Sec. 306) Directs the President to notify the appropriate congressional committees of any proposed transfer of DOE life sciences activities.

(Sec. 307) Establishes the Homeland Security Advanced Research Projects Agency to be headed by a Director who shall be appointed by the Secretary and who shall report to the Under Secretary. Requires the Director to administer the Acceleration Fund for Research and Development of Homeland Security Technologies (established by this Act) to award competitive, merit-reviewed grants, cooperative agreements, or contracts to public or private entities to: (1) support basic and applied homeland security research to promote revolutionary changes in technologies that would promote homeland security; (2) advance the development, testing and evaluation, and deployment of critical homeland security technologies; and (3) accelerate the prototyping and deployment of technologies that would address homeland security vulnerabilities. Allows the Director to solicit proposals to address specific vulnerabilities. Requires the Director to periodically hold homeland security technology demonstrations to improve contact among technology developers, vendors, and acquisition personnel.

Authorizes appropriations to the Fund. Earmarks ten percent of such funds for each fiscal year through FY 2005 for the Under Secretary, through joint agreement with the Commandant of the Coast Guard, to carry out R&D of improved ports, waterways, and coastal security surveillance and perimeter protection capabilities to minimize the possibility that Coast Guard cutters, aircraft, helicopters, and personnel will be diverted from non-homeland security missions to the ports, waterways, and coastal security mission.

(Sec. 308) Requires the Secretary, acting through the Under Secretary, to: (1) operate extramural R&D programs to ensure that colleges, universities, private research institutes, and companies (and consortia thereof) from as many areas of the United States as practicable participate; and (2) establish a university-based center or centers for homeland security which shall establish a coordinated, university-based system to enhance the Nation's homeland security. Authorizes the Secretary, through the Under Secretary, to: (1) draw upon the expertise of any Government laboratory; and (2) establish a headquarters laboratory for DHS and additional laboratory units.

(Sec. 309) Allows the Secretary, in carrying out DHS missions, to utilize DOE national laboratories and sites through: (1) a joint sponsorship arrangement; (2) a direct contact between DHS and the applicable DOE laboratory or site; (3) any "work for others" basis made available by that laboratory or site; or (4) any other method provided by law. Allows DHS to be a joint sponsor: (1) with DOE of one or more DOE national laboratories; and (2) of a DOE site in the performance of work as if such site were a federally funded R&D center and the work were performed under a multiple agency sponsorship arrangement with DHS Directs the Secretary and the Secretary of DOE to ensure that direct contracts between DHS and the operator of a DOE national laboratory or site for programs or activities transferred from DOE to DHS are separate from the direct contracts of DOE with such operator.

Establishes within the Directorate of Science and Technology an Office for National Laboratories which shall be responsible for the coordination and utilization of DOE national laboratories and sites in a manner to create a networked laboratory system to support DHS missions.

(Sec. 310) Directs the Secretary of Agriculture to transfer to the Secretary the Plum Island Animal Disease Center of the Department of Agriculture and provides for continued Department of Agriculture access to such Center.

(Sec. 311) Establishes within DHS a Homeland Security Science and Technology Advisory Committee to make recommendations with respect to the activities of the Under Secretary.

(Sec. 312) Directs the Secretary to establish the Homeland Security Institute, a federally funded R&D center. Includes among authorized duties for the Institute: (1) determination of the vulnerabilities of the Nation's critical infrastructures; (2) assessment of the costs and benefits of alternative approaches to enhancing security; and (3) evaluation of the effectiveness of measures deployed to enhance the security of institutions, facilities, and infrastructure that may be terrorist targets.

(Sec. 313) Requires the Secretary to establish and promote a program to encourage technological innovation in facilitating the mission of DHS, to include establishment of: (1) a centralized Federal clearinghouse to further the dissemination of information on technologies; and (2) a technical assistance team to assist in screening submitted proposals.

Title IV: Directorate of Border and Transportation Security –

Subtitle A: Under Secretary for Border and Transportation Security – (Sec. 401) Establishes in DHS a Directorate of Border and Transportation Security to be headed by an Under Secretary for Border and Transportation Security. Makes the Secretary, acting through the Under Secretary for Border and Transportation Security, responsible for: (1) preventing the entry of terrorists and the instruments of terrorism into the United States; (2) securing the borders, territorial waters, ports, terminals, waterways, and air, land, and sea transportation systems of the United States; (3) carrying out the immigration enforcement functions vested by statute in, or performed by, the Commissioner of Immigration and Naturalization immediately before their transfer to the Under Secretary; (4) establishing and administering rules governing the granting of visas or other forms of permission to enter the United States to individuals who are not citizens or aliens lawfully admitted for permanent residence in the United States; (5) establishing national immigration enforcement policies and priorities; (6) administering the customs laws of the United States (with certain exceptions); (7) conducting the inspection and related administrative functions of the Department of Agriculture transferred to the Secretary; and (8) ensuring the speedy, orderly, and efficient flow of lawful traffic and commerce in carrying out the foregoing responsibilities.

(Sec. 403) Transfers to the Secretary the functions, personnel, assets, and liabilities of: (1) the U.S. Customs Service; (2) the Transportation Security Administration; (3) the Federal Protective Service of the General Services Administration (GSA); (4) the Federal Law Enforcement Training Center of the Department of the Treasury; and (5) the Office for Domestic Preparedness of the Office of Justice Programs of the Department of Justice (DOJ).

Subtitle B: United States Customs Service - (Sec. 411) Establishes in DHS the U.S. Customs Service (transferred from the Department of the Treasury, but with certain customs revenue functions remaining with the Secretary of the Treasury). Authorizes the Secretary of the Treasury to appoint up to 20 new personnel to work with DHS personnel in performing customs revenue functions.

(Sec. 414) Requires the President to include a separate budget request for the U.S. Customs Service in the annual budget transmitted to Congress.

(Sec. 416) Directs the Comptroller General to report to Congress on all trade functions performed by the executive branch, specifying each agency that performs each such function.

(Sec. 417) Directs the Secretary to ensure that adequate staffing is provided to assure that levels of current customs revenue services will continue to be provided. Requires the Secretary to notify specified congressional committees prior to taking any action which would: (1) result in any significant reduction in customs revenue services (including hours of operation provided at any office within DHS or any port of entry); (2) eliminate or relocate any office of DHS which provides customs revenue services; or (3) eliminate any port of entry.

(Sec. 419) Amends the Consolidated Omnibus Budget Reconciliation Act of 1985 to create in the Treasury a separate Customs Commercial and Homeland Security Automation Account to contain merchandise processing (customs user) fees. Authorizes appropriations for FY 2003 through 2005 for establishment of the Automated Commercial Environment computer system for the processing of merchandise that is entered or released and for other purposes related to the functions of DHS.

Subtitle C: Miscellaneous Provisions - (Sec. 421) Transfers to the Secretary the functions of the Secretary of Agriculture relating to agricultural import and entry inspection activities under specified animal and plant protection laws.

Requires the Secretary of Agriculture and the Secretary to enter into an agreement to effectuate such transfer and to transfer periodically funds collected pursuant to fee authorities under the Food, Agriculture, Conservation, and Trade Act of 1990 to the Secretary for activities carried out by the Secretary for which such fees were collected.

Directs the Secretary of Agriculture to transfer to the Secretary not more than 3,200 full-time equivalent positions of the Department of Agriculture.

(Sec. 423) Directs the Secretary to establish a liaison office within DHS for the purpose of consulting with the Administrator of the Federal Aviation Administration before taking any action that might affect aviation safety, air carrier operations, aircraft airworthiness, or the use of airspace.

(Sec. 424) Requires the Transportation Security Administration to be maintained as a distinct entity within DHS under the Under Secretary for Border Transportation and Security for two years after enactment of this Act.

(Sec. 425) Amends Federal aviation law to require the Under Secretary of Transportation for Security to take certain action, if, in his discretion or at the request of an airport, he determines that the Transportation Security Administration is not able to deploy explosive detection systems at all airports required to have them by December 31, 2002. Requires the Under Secretary, in such circumstances, to: (1) submit to specified congressional committees a detailed plan for the deployment of explosive detection systems at such airport by December 31, 2003; and (2) take all necessary action to ensure that alternative means of screening all checked baggage is implemented.

(Sec. 426) Replaces the Secretary of Transportation with the Secretary of Homeland Security as chair of the Transportation Security Oversight Board. Requires the Secretary of Transportation to consult with the Secretary before approving airport development project grants relating to security equipment or the installation of bulk explosive detection systems.

(Sec. 427) Directs the Secretary, in coordination with the Secretary of Agriculture, the Secretary of Health and Human Services, and the head of each other department or agency determined to be appropriate by the Secretary, to ensure that appropriate information concerning inspections of articles that are imported or entered into the United States, and are inspected or regulated by one or more affected agencies, is timely and efficiently exchanged between the affected agencies. Requires the Secretary to report to Congress on the progress made in implementing this section.

(Sec. 428) Grants the Secretary exclusive authority to issue regulations with respect to, administer, and enforce the Immigration and Nationality Act (INA) and all other immigration and nationality laws relating to the functions of U.S. diplomatic and consular officers in connection with the granting or refusal of visas, and authority to refuse visas in accordance with law and to develop programs of homeland security training for consular officers, which authorities shall be exercised through the Secretary of State. Denies the Secretary authority, however, to alter or reverse the decision of a consular officer to refuse a visa to an alien.

Grants the Secretary authority also to confer or impose upon any U.S. officer or employee, with the consent of the head of the executive agency under whose jurisdiction such officer or employee is serving, any of these specified functions.

Authorizes the Secretary of State to direct a consular officer to refuse a visa to an alien if the Secretary of State deems such refusal necessary or advisable in the foreign policy or security interests of the United States.

Authorizes the Secretary to assign employees of DHS to any diplomatic and consular posts abroad to review individual visa applications and provide expert advice and training to consular officers regarding specific security threats relating to such applications and to conduct investigations with respect to matters under the Secretary's jurisdiction.

Directs the Secretary to study and report to Congress on the role of foreign nationals in the granting or refusal of visas and other documents authorizing entry of aliens into the United States.

Requires the Director of the Office of Science and Technology Policy to report to Congress on how the provisions of this section will affect procedures for the issuance of student visas.

Terminates after enactment of this Act all third party screening visa issuance programs in Saudi Arabia. Requires on-site personnel of DHS to review all visa applications prior to adjudication.

(Sec. 429) Requires visa denial information to be entered into the electronic data system as provided for in the Enhanced Border Security and Visa Entry Reform Act of 2002. Prohibits an alien denied a visa from being issued a subsequent visa unless the reviewing consular officer makes specified findings concerning waiver of ineligibility.

(Sec. 430) Establishes within the Directorate of Border and Transportation Security the Office for Domestic Preparedness to: (1) coordinate Federal preparedness for acts of terrorism, working with all State, local, tribal, county, parish, and private sector emergency response providers; (2) coordinate or consolidate systems of communications relating to homeland security at all levels of government; (3) direct and supervise Federal terrorism preparedness grant programs for all emergency response providers; and (4) perform specified other related duties.

Subtitle D: Immigration Enforcement Functions - (Sec. 441) Transfers from the Commissioner of Immigration and Naturalization to the Under Secretary for Border and Transportation Security all functions performed under the following programs, and all personnel, assets, and liabilities pertaining to such programs, immediately before such transfer occurs: (1) the Border Patrol program; (2) the detention and removal program; (3) the intelligence program; (4) the investigations program; and (5) the inspections program.

(Sec. 442) Establishes in the Department of Homeland Security (DHS) the Bureau of Border Security, headed by the Assistant Secretary of the Bureau of Border Security who shall: (1) report directly to the Under Secretary; (2) establish and oversee the policies for performing functions transferred to the Under Secretary and delegated to the Assistant Secretary by the Under Secretary; and (3) advise the Under Secretary with respect to any policy or operation of the Bureau that may affect the Bureau of Citizenship and Immigration Services.

Directs the Assistant Secretary to: (1) administer the program to collect information relating to nonimmigrant foreign students and other exchange program participants; and (2) implement a managerial rotation program.

Establishes the position of Chief of Policy and Strategy for the Bureau of Border Security, who shall: (1) make immigration enforcement policy recommendations; and (2) coordinate immigration policy issues with the Chief of Policy and Strategy for the Bureau of Citizenship and Immigration Services.

(Sec. 443) Makes the Under Secretary responsible for: (1) investigating noncriminal allegations of Bureau employee misconduct, corruption, and fraud that are not subject to investigation by the Inspector General for DHS; (2) inspecting and assessing Bureau operations; and (3) analyzing Bureau management.

(Sec. 444) Authorizes the Under Secretary to impose disciplinary action pursuant to policies and procedures applicable to FBI employees.

(Sec. 445) Requires the Secretary of Homeland Security to report on how the Bureau will enforce relevant INA provisions.

(Sec. 446) Expresses the sense of Congress that completing the 14-mile border fence project near San Diego, California, mandated by the Illegal Immigration Reform and Immigrant Responsibility Act of 1996 should be a priority for the Secretary.

Subtitle E: Citizenship and Immigration Services - (Sec. 451) Establishes in DHS a Bureau of Citizenship and Immigration Services, headed by the Director of the Bureau of Citizenship and Immigration Services, who shall: (1) establish the policies for performing and administering transferred functions; (2) establish national immigration services policies and priorities; and (3) implement a managerial rotation program.

Authorizes the Director to implement pilot initiatives to eliminate the backlog of immigration benefit applications.

Transfers all Immigration and Naturalization Service (INS) adjudications and related personnel and funding to the Director.

Establishes for the Bureau positions of: (1) Chief of Policy and Strategy; (2) legal adviser; (3) budget officer; and (4) Chief of the Office of Citizenship to promote citizenship instruction and training for aliens interested in becoming naturalized U.S. citizens.

(Sec. 452) Establishes within the DHS a Citizenship and Immigration Services Ombudsman, with local offices, to: (1) assist individuals and employers resolve problems with the Bureau; (2) identify problem areas; and (3) propose administrative and legislative changes.

(Sec. 453) Makes the Director responsible for (1) investigating noncriminal allegations of Bureau employee misconduct, corruption, and fraud that are not subject to investigation by the Inspector General of DHS; (2) inspecting and assessing Bureau operations; and (3) analyzing Bureau management.

(Sec. 454) Authorizes the Director to impose disciplinary action pursuant to policies and procedures applicable to FBI employees.

(Sec. 456) Sets forth transfer of authority and transfer and allocation of appropriations and personnel provisions.

(Sec. 457) Amends the INA to repeal the provision permitting fees for adjudication and naturalization services to be set at a level that will ensure recovery of the costs of similar services provided without charge to asylum applicants.

(Sec. 458) Amends the Immigration Services and Infrastructure Improvements Act of 2000 to change the deadline for the Attorney General to eliminate the backlog in the processing of immigration benefit applications to one year after enactment of this Act.

(Sec. 459) Directs the Secretary to report on how the Bureau of Citizenship and Immigration Services will efficiently complete transferred INS adjudications.

(Sec. 460) Directs the Attorney General to report on changes in law needed to ensure an appropriate response to emergent or unforeseen immigration needs.

(Sec. 461) Directs the Secretary to: (1) establish an Internet-based system that will permit online information access to a person, employer, immigrant, or nonimmigrant about the processing status of any filings for any benefit under the INA; (2) conduct a feasibility study for online filing and improved processing; and (3) establish a Technology Advisory Committee.

(Sec. 462) Transfers to the Director of the Office of Refugee Resettlement of the Department of Health and Human Services (HHS) INS functions with respect to the care of unaccompanied alien children (as defined by this Act).

Sets forth the responsibilities of the Office for such children, including: (1) coordinating and implementing the care and placement of unaccompanied alien children who are in Federal custody, including appointment of independent legal counsel to represent the interests of each child; (2) identifying and overseeing individuals, entities, and facilities to house such children; (3) family reunification; (4) compiling, updating, and publishing at least annually a State-by-State list of professionals or other entities qualified to provide guardian and attorney representation services; (5) maintaining related biographical and statistical information; and (6) conducting investigations and inspections of residential facilities.

Directs the Office to: (1) consult with juvenile justice professionals to ensure such children's safety; and (2) not release such children upon their own recognizance.

Subtitle F: General Immigration Provisions - (Sec. 471) Abolishes INS upon completion of all transfers from it as provided for by this Act.

(Sec. 472) Authorizes the Attorney General and the Secretary to make voluntary separation incentive payments, after completion of a strategic restructuring plan, to employees of: (1) INS; (2) the Bureau of Border Security of DHS; and (3) the Bureau of Citizenship and Immigration Services of DHS.

(Sec. 473) Directs the Attorney General and the Secretary to conduct a demonstration project to determine whether policy or procedure revisions for employee discipline would result in improved personnel management.

(Sec. 474) Expresses the sense of Congress that: (1) the missions of the Bureau of Border Security and the Bureau of Citizenship and Immigration Services are equally important and should be adequately funded; and (2) the functions transferred should not operate at levels below those in effect prior to the enactment of this Act.

(Sec. 475) Establishes within the Office of Deputy Secretary a Director of Shared Services who shall be responsible for: (1) information resources management; and (2) records, forms, and file management.

(Sec. 476) Provides for budgetary and funding separation with respect to the Bureau of Citizenship and Immigration Services and the Bureau of Border Security.

(Sec. 477) Sets forth reporting and implementation plan provisions.

(Sec. 478) Directs the Secretary to annually report regarding: (1) the aggregate number of all immigration applications and petitions received, and processed; (2) regional statistics on the aggregate number of denied applications and petitions; (3) application and petition backlogs and a backlog elimination plan; (4) application and petition processing periods; (5) number, types, and disposition of grievances and plans to improve immigration services; and (6) appropriate use of immigration-related fees.

Expresses the sense of Congress that: (1) the quality and efficiency of immigration services should be improved after the transfers made by Act; and (2) the Secretary should undertake efforts to guarantee that such concerns are addressed after such effective date.

Title V: Emergency Preparedness and Response –

(Sec. 501) Establishes in DHS a Directorate of Emergency Preparedness and Response, headed by an Under Secretary.

(Sec. 502) Requires the responsibilities of the Secretary, acting through the Under Secretary, to include: (1) helping to ensure the effectiveness of emergency response providers to terrorist attacks, major disasters, and other emergencies; (2) with respect to the Nuclear Incident Response Team, establishing and certifying compliance with standards, conducting joint and other exercises and training, and providing funds to the Department of Energy and the Environmental Protection Agency for homeland security planning, training, and equipment; (3) providing the Federal Government's response to terrorist attacks and major disasters; (4) aiding recovery from terrorist attacks and major disasters; (5) building a comprehensive national incident management system with Federal, State, and local governments to respond to such attacks and disasters; (6) consolidating existing Federal Government emergency response plans into a single, coordinated national response plan; and (7) developing comprehensive programs for developing interoperative communications technology and helping to ensure that emergency response providers acquire such technology.

(Sec. 503) Transfers to the Secretary the functions, personnel, assets, and liabilities of: (1) the Federal Emergency Management Agency (FEMA); (2) the Integrated Hazard Information System of the National Oceanic and Atmospheric Administration, which shall be renamed FIRESAT; (3) the National Domestic Preparedness Office of the FBI; (4) the Domestic Emergency Support Teams of DOJ; (5) the Office of Emergency Preparedness, the National Disaster Medical System, and the Metropolitan Medical Response System of HHS; and (6) the Strategic National Stockpile of HHS.

(Sec. 504) Requires the Nuclear Incident Response Team, at the direction of the Secretary (in connection with an actual or threatened terrorist attack, major disaster, or other emergency in the United States), to operate as an organizational unit of DHS under the Secretary's authority and control.

(Sec. 505) Provides that, with respect to all public health-related activities to improve State, local, and hospital preparedness and response to chemical, biological, radiological, and nuclear and other emerging terrorist threats carried out by HHS (including the Public Health Service), the Secretary of HHS shall set priorities and preparedness goals and further develop a coordinated strategy for such activities in collaboration with the Secretary.

(Sec. 506) Defines the Nuclear Incident Response Team to include: (1) those entities of the Department of Energy that perform nuclear or radiological emergency support functions, radiation exposure functions at the medical assistance facility known as the Radiation Emergency Assistance Center/Training Site (REAC/TS), radiological assistance functions, and related functions; and (2) Environmental Protection Agency entities that perform such support functions and related functions.

(Sec. 507) Includes in the homeland security role of FEMA: (1) all functions and authorities prescribed by the Robert T. Stafford Disaster Relief and Emergency Assistance Act; and (2) a comprehensive, risk-based emergency management program of mitigation, of planning for building the emergency management profession, of response, of recovery, and of increased efficiencies. Maintains FEMA as the lead agency for the Federal Response Plan established under Executive Orders 12148 and 12656. Requires the FEMA Director to revise the Plan to reflect the establishment of and incorporate DHS.

(Sec. 508) Directs the Secretary, to the maximum extent practicable, to use national private sector networks and infrastructure for emergency response to major disasters.

(Sec. 509) Expresses the sense of Congress that the Secretary should: (1) use off-the-shelf commercially developed technologies to allow DHS to collect, manage, share, analyze, and disseminate information securely over multiple channels of communication; and (2) rely on commercial sources to supply goods and services needed by DHS.

Title VI: Treatment of Charitable Trusts for Members of the Armed Forces of the United States and Other Governmental Organizations –

(Sec. 601) Sets forth requirements a charitable corporation, fund, foundation, or trust must meet to designate itself as a Johnny Micheal Spann Patriot Trust (a charitable trust for the spouses, dependents, and relatives of military and Federal personnel who lose their lives in the battle against terrorism that is named after the first American to die in such service following the September 11th terrorist attacks). Requires at least 85 percent of each Trust corpus to be distributed to such survivors and prohibits more than 15 percent from being used for administrative purposes. Prohibits: (1) any Trust activities from violating any prohibition against attempting to influence legislation; and (2) any such Trust from participating in any political campaign on behalf of a candidate for public office. Requires: (1) audits of each Trust that annually receives contributions of more than $1 million; and (2) Trust distributions to be made at least once a year. Provides for the notification of Trust beneficiaries.

Title VII: Management –

(Sec. 701) Makes the Secretary, acting through the Under Secretary for Management, responsible for the management and administration of DHS. Details certain responsibilities of the Under Secretary with respect to immigration statistics. Transfers to the Under Secretary functions previously performed by the Statistics Branch of the Office of Policy and Planning of the Immigration and Naturalization Service (INS) with respect to: (1) the Border Patrol program; (2) the detention and removal program; (3) the intelligence program; (4) the investigations program; (5) the inspections program; and (6) INS adjudications.

(Sec. 702) Requires a chief financial officer, a chief information officer, and a chief human capital officer to report to the Secretary. Requires the chief human capital officer to ensure that all DHS employees are informed of their rights and remedies under merit system protection and principle provisions.

(Sec. 705) Requires the Secretary to appoint an Officer for Civil Rights and Civil Liberties who shall: (1) review and assess information alleging abuses of civil rights, civil liberties, and racial and ethnic profiling by employees and officials of DHS; and (2) make public information on the responsibilities and functions of, and how to contact, the Office.

(Sec. 706) Requires the Secretary to develop and submit to Congress a plan for consolidating and co-locating: (1) any regional offices or field offices of agencies that are transferred to DHS under this Act, if their officers are located in the same municipality; and (2) portions of regional and field offices of other Federal agencies, to the extent such offices perform functions that are transferred to the Secretary under this Act.

Title VIII: Coordination With Non-Federal Entities; Inspector General; United States Secret Service; Coast Guard; General Provisions –

Subtitle A: Coordination with Non-Federal Entities - (Sec. 801) Establishes within the Office of the Secretary the Office for State and Local Government Coordination to oversee and coordinate Department homeland security programs for and relationships with State and local governments.

Subtitle B: Inspector General - (Sec. 811) Places the DHS Inspector General under the authority, direction, and control of the Secretary with respect to audits or investigations, or the issuance of subpoenas, that require access to sensitive information concerning intelligence, counterintelligence, or counterterrorism matters; criminal investigations or proceedings; undercover operations; the identify of confidential sources; and certain matters of disclosure.

Amends the Inspector General Act of 1978 to: (1) give such Inspector General oversight responsibility for internal investigations performed by the Office of Internal Affairs of the United States Customs Service and the Office of Inspections of the United States Secret Service; and (2) authorize each Inspector General, any Assistant Inspector General for Investigations, and any special agent supervised by such an Assistant Inspector General to carry a firearm, make arrests without warrants, and seek and execute warrants. Allows the latter only upon certain determinations by the Attorney General (exempts the Inspector General offices of various executive agencies from such requirement). Provides for the rescinding of such law enforcement powers. Requires the Inspector General offices exempted from the determinations requirement to collectively enter into a memorandum of understanding to establish an external review process for ensuring that adequate internal safeguards and management procedures continue to exist to ensure the proper utilization of such law enforcement powers within their departments.

Subtitle C: United States Secret Service - (Sec. 821) Transfers to the Secretary the functions of the United States Secret Service, which shall be maintained as a distinct entity within DHS.

Subtitle D: Acquisitions - (Sec. 831) Authorizes the Secretary to carry out a five-year pilot program under which the Secretary may exercise specified authorities in carrying out: (1) basic, applied, and advanced research and development projects for response to existing or emerging terrorist threats; and (2) defense prototype projects. Requires a report from the Comptroller General to specified congressional committees on the use of such authorities.

(Sec. 832) Permits the Secretary to procure temporary or intermittent: (1) services of experts or consultants; and (2) personal services without regard to certain pay limitations when necessary due to an urgent homeland security need.

(Sec. 833) Authorizes the Secretary to use specified micro purchase, simplified acquisition, and commercial item acquisition procedures with respect to any procurement made during the period beginning on the effective date of this Act and ending on September 30, 2007, if the Secretary determines that the mission of DHS would be seriously impaired without the use of such authorities. Requires a report from the Comptroller General.

(Sec. 834) Requires the Federal Acquisition Regulation to be revised to include regulations with regard to unsolicited proposals.

(Sec. 835) Prohibits the Secretary from entering into a contract with a foreign incorporated entity which is treated as an inverted domestic corporation. Sets forth requirements for such treatment. Authorizes the Secretary to waive such prohibition in the interest of homeland security, to prevent the loss of any jobs in the United States, or to prevent the Government from incurring any additional costs.

Subtitle E: Human Resources Management - (Sec. 841) Expresses the sense of Congress calling for the participation of DHS employees in the creation of the DHS human resources management system.

Amends Federal civil service law to authorize the Secretary, in regulations prescribed jointly with the Director of the Office of Personnel Management (OPM), to establish and adjust a human resources management system for organizational units of DHS. Requires the system to ensure that employees may organize, bargain collectively, and participate through labor organizations of their own choosing in decisions which affect them, subject to an exclusion from coverage or limitation on negotiability established by law. Imposes certain requirements upon the Secretary and the OPM Director to ensure the participation of employee representatives in the planning, development, and implementation of any human resources management system or system adjustments.

Declares the sense of Congress that DHS employees are entitled to fair treatment in any appeals that they bring in decisions relating to their employment.

Terminates all authority to issue regulations under this section five years after enactment of this Act.

(Sec. 842) Prohibits any agency or agency subdivision transferred to DHS from being excluded from coverage under labor-management relations requirements as a result of any order issued after June 18, 2002, unless: (1) the mission and responsibilities of the agency or subdivision materially change; and (2) a majority of the employees within the agency or subdivision have as their primary duty intelligence, counterintelligence, or investigative work directly related to terrorism investigation. Declares that collective bargaining units shall continue to be recognized unless such conditions develop. Prohibits exclusion of positions or employees for a bargaining unit unless the primary job duty materially changes or consists of intelligence, counterintelligence, or investigative work directly related to terrorism investigation. Waives these prohibitions and recognitions in circumstances where the President determines that their application would have a substantial adverse impact on the Department's ability to protect homeland security.

Subtitle F: Federal Emergency Procurement Flexibility - (Sec. 852) Provides that the simplified acquisition threshold to be applied for any executive agency procurement of property or services that is to be used to facilitate the defense against or recovery from terrorism or nuclear, biological, chemical, or radiological attack and that is carried out in support of a humanitarian or peacekeeping operation or a contingency operation shall be: (1) $200,000 for a contract to be awarded and performed, or a purchase to be made, inside the United States; or (2) $300,000 for a contract to be awarded and performed, or a purchase to be made, outside the United States.

(Sec. 854) Authorizes the head of each agency to designate certain employees to make such procurements below a micro-purchase threshold of $7,500 (currently $2,500) under the Office of Federal Procurement Policy Act.

(Sec. 855) Permits executive agencies to apply to any such procurement specified provisions of law relating to the procurement of commercial items, without regard to whether the property and services are commercial items. Makes the $5 million limitation on the use of simplified acquisition procedures inapplicable to purchases of property or services to which such provisions apply.

(Sec. 856) Requires executive agencies to use specified streamlined acquisition authorities and procedures for such procurements. Waives certain small business threshold requirements with respect to such procurements.

(Sec. 857) Requires the Comptroller General to review and report to specified congressional committees on the extent to which procurements of property and services have been made in accordance with requirements of this Subtitle.

(Sec. 858) Requires each executive agency to conduct market research to identify the capabilities of small businesses and new entrants into Federal contracting that are available to meet agency requirements in furtherance of defense against or recovery from terrorism or nuclear, biological, chemical, or radiological attack.

Subtitle G: Support Anti-terrorism by Fostering Effective Technologies Act of 2002 - Support Anti-terrorism by Fostering Effective Technologies Act of 2002 or SAFETY Act - (Sec. 862) Authorizes the Secretary to designate anti-terrorism technologies that qualify for protection under a risk management system in accordance with criteria that shall include: (1) prior Government use or demonstrated substantial utility and effectiveness; (2) availability for immediate deployment in public and private settings; (3) substantial likelihood that such technology will not be deployed unless protections under such system are extended; and (4) the magnitude of risk exposure to the public if such technology is not deployed. Makes the Secretary responsible for administration of such protections.

(Sec. 863) Provides a Federal cause of action for sellers suffering a loss from qualified anti-terrorism technologies so deployed. Prohibits punitive damages from being awarded against a seller.

(Sec. 864) Requires sellers of qualified anti-terrorism technologies to obtain liability insurance in amounts certified as satisfactory by the Secretary.

Subtitle H: Miscellaneous Provisions - (Sec. 871)Authorizes the Secretary to establish, appoint members of, and use the services of advisory committees as necessary.

(Sec. 872) Grants the Secretary limited authority to reorganize DHS by allocating or reallocating functions within it and by establishing, consolidating, altering, or discontinuing organizational units.

(Sec. 873) Requires the Secretary to comply with Federal requirements concerning the deposit of proceeds from property sold or transferred by the Secretary. Requires the President to submit to Congress a detailed Department budget request for FY 2004 and thereafter.

(Sec. 874) Requires each such budget request to be accompanied by a Future Years Homeland Security Program structured in the same manner as the annual Future Years Defense Program.

(Sec. 876) Provides that nothing in this Act shall confer upon the Secretary any authority to engage in war fighting, the military defense of the United States, or other military activities or limit the existing authority of the Department of Defense or the armed forces to do so.

(Sec. 878) Directs the Secretary to appoint a senior DHS official to assume primary responsibility for coordinating policy and operations within DHS and between DHS and other Federal departments and agencies with respect to interdicting the entry of illegal drugs into the United States and tracking and severing connections between illegal drug trafficking and terrorism.

(Sec. 879) Establishes within the Office of the Secretary an Office of International Affairs, headed by a Director, to: (1) promote information and education exchange on homeland security best practices and technologies with friendly nations; (2) identify areas for homeland security information and training exchange where the United States has a demonstrated weakness and another friendly nation has a demonstrated expertise; (3) plan and undertake international conferences, exchange programs, and training activities; and (4) manage international activities within DHS in coordination with other Federal officials with responsibility for counter-terrorism matters.

(Sec. 880) Prohibits any Government activity to implement the proposed component program of the Citizen Corps known as Operation TIPS (Terrorism Information and Prevention System).

(Sec. 881) Directs the Secretary to review the pay and benefit plans of each agency whose functions are transferred to DHS under this Act and to submit a plan for ensuring the elimination of disparities in pay and benefits throughout DHS, especially among law enforcement personnel, that are inconsistent with merit system principles.

(Sec. 882) Establishes within the Office of the Secretary the Office of National Capital Region Coordination, headed by a Director, to oversee and coordinate Federal homeland security programs for and relationships with State, local, and regional authorities within the National Capital Region. Requires an annual report from the Office to Congress on: (1) resources needed to fully implement homeland security efforts in the Region; (2) progress made by the Region in implementing such efforts; and (3) recommendations for additional needed resources to fully implement such efforts.

(Sec. 883) Requires DHS to comply with specified laws protecting equal employment opportunity and providing whistle blower protections.

(Sec. 885) Authorizes the Secretary to establish a permanent Joint Interagency Homeland Security Task Force, composed of representatives from military and civilian agencies, for the purpose of anticipating terrorist threats and taking actions to prevent harm to the United States.

(Sec. 886) Reaffirms the continued importance of Federal criminal code proscriptions on the use of the armed forces as posse comitatus and expresses the sense of Congress that nothing in this Act shall be construed to alter the applicability of such proscriptions to any use of the armed forces to execute the laws.

(Sec. 887) Requires the annual Federal response plan developed by DHS to be consistent with public health emergency provisions of the Public Health Service Act . Requires full disclosure of public health emergencies, or potential emergencies, among HHS, DHS, the Department of Justice, and the Federal Bureau of Investigation.

(Sec. 888) Transfers to DHS the authorities, functions, personnel, and assets of the Coast Guard, which shall be maintained as a distinct entity within DHS. Prohibits the Secretary from substantially or significantly reducing current Coast Guard missions or capabilities, with a waiver of such prohibition upon a declaration and certification to Congress that a clear, compelling and immediate need exists. Requires the DHS Inspector General to annually review and report to Congress on performance by the Coast Guard of its mission requirements. Requires the Commandant of the Coast Guard, upon its transfer, to report directly to the Secretary. Prohibits any of the above conditions and restrictions from applying to the Coast Guard when it is operating as a service in the Navy. Directs the Secretary to report to specified congressional committees on the feasibility of accelerating the rate of procurement in the Coast Guard's Integrated Deepwater System from 20 to ten years.

(Sec. 889) Requires the inclusion in the President's annual budget documents of a detailed homeland security funding analysis for the previous, current, and next fiscal years.

(Sec. 890) Amends the Air Transportation Safety and System Stabilization Act, with respect to the September 11th Victim Compensation Fund of 2001, to limit"agents" of an air carrier engaged in the business of providing air transportation security to persons that have contracted directly with the Federal

Aviation Administration on or after February 17, 2002, to provide such security and that had not been or are not debarred within six months of that date.

Subtitle I: Information Sharing - Homeland Security Information Sharing Act - (Sec. 891) Expresses the sense of Congress that Federal, State, and local entities should share homeland security information to the maximum extent practicable, with special emphasis on hard-to-reach urban and rural communities.

(Sec. 892) Directs the President to prescribe and implement procedures for Federal agency: (1) sharing of appropriate homeland security information, including with DHS and appropriate State and local personnel; and (2) handling of classified information and sensitive but unclassified information. Authorizes appropriations.

(Sec. 893) Requires an implementation report from the President to the congressional intelligence and judiciary committees.

(Sec. 895) Amends the Federal Rules of Criminal Procedure to treat as contempt of court any knowing violation of guidelines jointly issued by the Attorney General and DCI with respect to disclosure of grand jury matters otherwise prohibited. Allows disclosure to appropriate Federal, State, local, or foreign government officials of grand jury matters involving a threat of grave hostile acts of a foreign power, domestic or international sabotage or terrorism, or clandestine intelligence gathering activities by an intelligence service or network of a foreign power (threat), within the United States or elsewhere. Permits disclosure to appropriate foreign government officials of grand jury matters that may disclose a violation of the law of such government. Requires State, local, and foreign officials to use disclosed information only in conformity with guidelines jointly issued by the Attorney General and the DCI.

(Sec. 896) Amends the Federal criminal code to authorize Federal investigative and law enforcement officers conducting communications interception activities, who have obtained knowledge of the contents of any intercepted communication or derivative evidence, to disclose such contents or evidence to: (1) a foreign investigative or law enforcement officer if the disclosure is appropriate to the performance of the official duties of the officer making or receiving the disclosure; and (2) any appropriate Federal, State, local, or foreign government official if the contents or evidence reveals such a threat, for the purpose of preventing or responding to such threat. Provides guidelines for the use and disclosure of the information.

(Sec. 897) Amends the Uniting and Strengthening America by Providing Appropriate Tools Required to Intercept and Obstruct Terrorism Act (USA PATRIOT ACT) of 2001 to make lawful the disclosure to appropriate Federal, State, local, or foreign government officials of information obtained as part of a criminal investigation that reveals such a threat.

(Sec. 898) Amends the Foreign Intelligence Surveillance Act of 1978 to allow Federal officers who conduct electronic surveillance and physical searches in order to acquire foreign intelligence information to consult with State and local law enforcement personnel to coordinate efforts to investigate or protect against such a threat.

Title IX: National Homeland Security Council –

(Sec. 901) Establishes within the Executive Office of the President the Homeland Security Council to advise the President on homeland security matters.

(Sec. 903) Includes as members of the Council: (1) the President; (2) the Vice President; (3) the Secretary; (4) the Attorney General; and (5) the Secretary of Defense.

(Sec. 904) Requires the Council to: (1) assess the objectives, commitments, and risks of the United States in the interest of homeland security and make recommendations to the President; and (2) oversee and review Federal homeland security policies and make policy recommendations to the President.

(Sec. 906) Authorizes the President to convene joint meetings of the Homeland Security Council and the National Security Council.

Title X: Information Security –

Federal Information Security Management Act of 2002 - (Sec. 1001) Revises Government information security requirements. Requires the head of each agency operating or exercising control of a national security system to ensure that the agency: (1) provides information security protections commensurate with the risk and magnitude of the harm resulting from the unauthorized access, use, disclosure, disruption, modification, or destruction of the information; and (2) implements information security policies and practices as required by standards and guidelines for national security systems. Authorizes appropriations for FY 2003 through 2007.

(Sec. 1002) Transfers from the Secretary of Commerce to the Director of the Office of Management and Budget (OMB) the authority to promulgate information security standards pertaining to Federal information systems.

(Sec. 1003) Amends the National Institute of Standards and Technology Act to revise and expand the mandate of the National Institute of Standards and Technology to develop standards, guidelines, and associated methods and techniques for information systems. Renames the Computer System Security and Privacy Advisory Board as the Information Security and Privacy Board and requires it to advise the Director of OMB (instead of the Secretary of Commerce) on information security and privacy issues pertaining to Federal Government information systems.

Title XI: Department of Justice Divisions –

Subtitle A: Executive Office for Immigration Review - (Sec. 1101) Declares that there is in the Department of Justice (DOJ) the Executive Office for Immigration Review (EOIR), which shall be subject to the direction and regulation of the Attorney General under the INA.

(Sec. 1102) Amends the INA to grant the Attorney General such authorities and functions relating to the immigration and naturalization of aliens as were exercised by EOIR, or by the Attorney General with respect to EOIR, on the day before the effective date of the Immigration Reform, Accountability and Security Enhancement Act of 2002.

Subtitle B: Transfer of the Bureau of Alcohol, Tobacco and Firearms to the Department of Justice - (Sec. 1111) Establishes within DOJ, under the Attorney General's authority, the Bureau of Alcohol, Tobacco, Firearms, and Explosives (the Bureau). Transfers to DOJ the authorities, functions, personnel, and assets of the Bureau of Alcohol, Tobacco and Firearms (BATF), which shall be maintained as a distinct entity within DOJ, including the related functions of the Secretary of the Treasury.

Provides that the Bureau shall be headed by a Director and shall be responsible for: (1) investigating criminal and regulatory violations of the Federal firearms, explosives, arson, alcohol, and tobacco smuggling laws; (2) such transferred functions; and (3) any other function related to the investigation of violent crime or domestic terrorism that is delegated to the Bureau by the Attorney General.

Retains within the Department of the Treasury certain authorities, functions, personnel, and assets of BATF relating to the administration and enforcement of the Internal Revenue Code.

Establishes within the Department of the Treasury the Tax and Trade Bureau, which shall retain and administer the authorities, functions, personnel, and assets of BATF that are not transferred to DOJ.

(Sec. 1113) Amends the Federal criminal code to authorize special agents of the Bureau, as well as any other investigator or officer charged by the Attorney General with enforcing criminal, seizure, or forfeiture laws, to carry firearms, serve warrants and subpoenas, and make arrests without warrant for offenses committed in their presence or for felonies on reasonable grounds. Authorizes any special agent to make seizures of property subject to forfeiture to the United States. Sets forth provisions regarding seizure, disposition, and claims pertaining to property.

(Sec. 1114) Establishes within the Bureau an Explosives Training and Research Facility at Fort AP Hill in Fredericksburg, Virginia, to train Federal, State, and local law enforcement officers to: (1) investigate bombings and explosions; (2) properly handle, utilize, and dispose of explosive materials and devices; (3) train canines on explosive detection; and (4) conduct research on explosives. Authorizes appropriations.

(Sec. 1115) Transfers the Personnel Management Demonstration Project to the Attorney General for continued use by the Bureau and to the Secretary of the Treasury for continued use by the Tax and Trade Bureau.

Subtitle C: Explosives - Safe Explosives Act - (Sec. 1122) Rewrites Federal criminal code provisions regarding the purchase of explosives to create a new "limited permit" category. Prohibits a holder of a limited permit: (1) from transporting, shipping, causing to be transported, or receiving in interstate or foreign commerce explosive materials; (2) from receiving explosive materials from a licensee or permittee whose premises are located outside the holder's State of residence; or (3) on more than six separate occasions during the period of the permit, from receiving explosive materials from one or more licensees or permittees whose premises are located within the holder's State of residence.

Requires license, user permit, and limited permit applicants to include the names of and identifying information (including fingerprints and a photograph of each responsible person) regarding all employees who will be authorized by the applicant to possess explosive materials. Caps the fee for limited permits at $50 for each permit. Makes each limited permit valid for not longer than one year.

Modifies criteria for approving licenses and permits. Requires the Secretary of the Treasury to issue to the applicant the appropriate license or permit if, among other conditions: (1) the applicant is not a person who is otherwise prohibited from possessing explosive materials (excluded person); (2) the Secretary verifies by inspection or other appropriate means that the applicant has a place of storage for explosive materials that meets the Secretary's standards of public safety and security against theft (inapplicable to an applicant for renewal of a limited permit if the Secretary has verified such matters by inspection within the preceding three years); (3) none of the applicant's employees who will be authorized to possess explosive materials is an excluded person; and (4) in the case of a limited permit, the applicant has certified that the applicant will not receive explosive materials on more than six separate occasions during the 12-month period for which the limited permit is valid. Authorizes the Secretary to inspect the storage places of an applicant for or holder of a limited permit only as provided under the code. Requires the Secretary of the Treasury to approve or deny an application for licenses and permits within 90 days.

Requires the Secretary: (1) upon receiving from an employer the name and other identifying information with respect to a person or an employee who will be authorized to possess explosive materials, to determine whether such person or employee is an excluded person; (2) upon determining that such person or employee is not an excluded person, to notify the employer and to issue to the person or employee a letter of clearance confirming the determination; and (3) upon determining that such person or employee is an excluded person, to notify the employer and issue to such person or employee a document that confirms the determination, explains the grounds, provides information on how the disability may be relieved, and explains how the determination may be appealed.

(Sec. 1123) Includes among aliens who may lawfully receive or possess explosive materials any alien who is in lawful non-immigrant status, is a refugee admitted under the INA, or is in asylum status under the INA and who is: (1) a foreign law enforcement officer of a friendly government; (2) a person having the power to direct the management and policies of a corporation; (3) a member of a North Atlantic Treaty Organization or other friendly foreign military force; or (4) lawfully present in the United States in cooperation with the DCI and the shipment, transportation, receipt, or possession of the explosive materials is in furtherance of such cooperation.

(Sec. 1124) Requires: (1) licensed manufacturers, licensed importers, and those who manufacture or import explosive materials or ammonium nitrate to furnish samples and relevant information when required by the Secretary; and (2) the Secretary to authorize reimbursement of the fair market value of samples furnished, as well as reasonable shipment costs.

(Sec. 1125) Sets penalties for the destruction of property of institutions receiving Federal financial assistance.

(Sec. 1127) Requires a holder of a license or permit to report any theft of explosive materials to the Secretary not later than 24 hours after discovery. Sets penalties for failure to report.

(Sec. 1128) Authorizes appropriations.

Title XII: Airline War Risk Insurance Legislation –

(Sec. 1201) Amends Federal aviation law to extend the period during which the Secretary of Transportation may certify an air carrier as a victim of terrorism (and thus subject to the $100 million limit on aggregate third-party claims) for acts of terrorism from September 22, 2001, through December 31, 2003.

(Sec. 1202) Directs the Secretary of Transportation to extend through August 31, 2003, and authorizes the Secretary to extend through December 31, 2003, the termination date of any insurance policy that the Department of Transportation (DOT) issues to an American aircraft or foreign-flag aircraft against loss or damage arising out of any risk from operation, and that is in effect on enactment of this Act, on no less favorable terms to such air carrier than existed on June 19, 2002. Directs the Secretary, however, to amend such policy to add coverage for losses or injuries to aircraft hulls, passengers, and crew at the limits carried by air carriers for such losses and injuries as of such enactment, and at an additional premium comparable to the premium charged for third-party casualty under the policy.

Limits the total premium paid by an air carrier for such a policy to twice the premium it was paying for its third party policy as of June 19, 2002. Declares that coverage in such a policy shall begin with the first dollar of any covered loss incurred.

(Sec. 1204) Directs the Secretary of Transportation to report to specified congressional committees concerning: (1) the availability and cost of commercial war risk insurance for air carriers and other aviation entities for passengers and third parties; (2) the economic effect upon such carriers and entities of available commercial war risk insurance; and (3) the manner in which DOT could provide an alternative means of providing aviation war risk reinsurance covering passengers, crew, and third parties through use of a risk-retention group or by other means.

Title XIII: Federal Workforce Improvement –

Subtitle A: Chief Human Capital Officers - Chief Human Capital Officers Act of 2002 - (Sec. 1302) Requires the heads of Federal departments and agencies currently required to a have Chief Financial Officer to appoint or designate a Chief Human Capital Officer to: (1) advise and assist agency officials in selecting, developing, training, and managing a high-quality, productive workforce in accordance with merit system principles; and (2) implement the rules and regulations of the President and the Office of OPM and civil service laws.

Requires such Officer's functions to include: (1) setting the agency's workforce development strategy; (2) assessing workforce characteristics and future needs; (3) aligning the agency's human resources policies and programs with organization mission, strategic goals, and performance outcomes; (4) developing and advocating a culture of continuous learning to attract and retain employees with superior abilities; (5) identifying best practices and benchmarking studies; and (6) applying methods for measuring intellectual capital and identifying links of that capital to organizational performance and growth.

(Sec. 1303) Establishes a Chief Human Capital Officers Council (consisting of the Director of OPM, the Deputy Director for Management of the Office of Management and Budget, and the Chief Human Capital Officers of executive departments and other members designated by the Director of OPM) to advise and coordinate the activities of the agencies of its members on such matters as modernization of human resources systems, improved quality of human resources information, and legislation affecting human resources operations and organizations.

(Sec. 1304) Directs OPM to design a set of systems, including metrics, for assessing the management of human capital by Federal agencies.

Subtitle B: Reforms Relating to Federal Human Capital Management - (Sec. 1311) Requires each agency's: (1) performance plan to describe how its performance goals and objectives are to be achieved; and (2) program performance report to include a review of the goals and evaluation of the plan relative to the agency's strategic human capital management.

(Sec. 1312) Authorizes the President to prescribe rules which grant authority for agencies to appoint candidates directly to certain positions for which there exists a severe candidate shortage or a critical hiring need.

Allows OPM to establish quality category rating systems for evaluating applicants for competitive service positions under two or more quality categories based on merit rather than numerical ratings. Requires agencies that establish a quality category rating system to report to Congress on that system, including information on the number of employees hired, the impact that system has had on the hiring of veterans and minorities, and the way in which managers were trained in the administration of it.

(Sec. 1313) Sets forth provisions governing Federal employee voluntary separation incentive payments. Requires each agency, before obligating any resources for such payments, to submit to OPM for modification and approval a plan outlining the intended use of such payments and a proposed organizational chart for the agency once such payments have been completed. Requires such plan to include the positions and functions affected, the categories of employees to be offered such payments, the timing and amounts of payments, and how the agency will subsequently operate. Limits voluntary separation incentive payments to the lesser of: (1) the amount of severance pay to which an employee would be entitled; or (2) an amount determined by the agency head, not to exceed $25,000. Sets forth provisions regarding the repayment and waiver of repayment of such incentive payments upon subsequent employment with the Government. Authorizes the Director of the Administrative Office of the United States Courts to establish a substantially similar program for the judicial branch. Continues existing voluntary separation incentives authority until expiration.

Amends Federal employee early retirement provisions to apply to employees who are: (1) voluntarily separated by an agency undergoing substantial delayering, reorganization, reductions in force, functions transfer, or workforce restructuring; or (2) identified as being in positions that are becoming surplus or excess to the agency's future ability to carry out its mission effectively; and (3) within the scope of the offer of voluntary early retirement on the basis of specific periods or such employee's organizational unit, occupational series, geographical location, and/or skills, knowledge, and other factors related to a position. Expresses the sense of Congress that the implementation of this section is intended to reshape, and not downsize, the Federal workforce.

(Sec. 1314) Includes students who provide voluntary services for the Government as "employees" for purposes of provisions authorizing agency programs to encourage employees to commute by means other than single-occupancy motor vehicles.

Subtitle C: Reforms Relating to the Senior Executive Service - (Sec. 1321) Repeals recertification requirements for senior executives.

(Sec. 1322) Changes the limitation on total annual compensation (basic pay and cash payments) from the annual rate of basic pay payable for level I of the Executive Schedule to the total annual compensation payable to the Vice President for certain senior level executive and judicial employees who hold a position in or under an agency that has been certified as having a performance appraisal system which makes meaningful distinctions based on relative performance.

Subtitle D: Academic Training - (Sec. 1331) Revises agency academic degree training criteria to allow agencies to select and assign employees to academic degree training and to pay and reimburse such training costs if such training: (1) contributes significantly to meeting an agency training need, resolving an agency staffing problem, or accomplishing goals in the agency's strategic plan; (2) is part of a planned, systemic, and coordinated agency employee development program linked to accomplishing such goals; and (3) is accredited and is provided by a college or university that is accredited by a nationally recognized body.

(Sec. 1332) Amends the David L. Boren National Security Education Act of 1991 to modify service agreement requirements for recipients of scholarships and fellowships under the National Security Education Program to provide for recipients to work in other Federal offices or agencies when no national security position is available.

Title XIV: Arming Pilots Against Terrorism –

Arming Pilots Against Terrorism Act - (Sec. 1402) Amends Federal law to direct the Under Secretary of Transportation for Security (in the Transportation Security Administration) to establish a two-year pilot program to: (1) deputize volunteer pilots of air carriers as Federal law enforcement officers to defend the flight decks of aircraft against acts of criminal violence or air piracy (Federal flight deck officers); and (2) provide training, supervision, and equipment for such officers.

Requires the Under Secretary to begin the process of training and deputizing qualified pilots to be Federal flight deck officers under the program. Allows the Under Secretary to request another Federal agency to deputize such officers.

Directs the Under Secretary to authorize flight deck officers to carry firearms and to use force, including lethal force, according to standards and circumstances the Under Secretary prescribes. Shields air carriers from liability for damages in Federal or State court arising out of a Federal flight deck officer's use of or failure to use a firearm. Shields flight deck officers from liability for acts or omissions in defending the flight deck of an aircraft against acts of criminal violence or air piracy, except in cases of gross negligence or willful misconduct.

Declares that if an accidental discharge of a firearm results in the injury or death of a passenger or crew member on the aircraft, the Under Secretary: (1) shall revoke the deputization of the responsible Federal flight deck officer if such discharge was attributable to the officer's negligence; and (2) may temporarily suspend the pilot program if the Under Secretary determines that a shortcoming in standards, training, or procedures was responsible for the accidental discharge.

Prohibits an air carrier from prohibiting a pilot from becoming a Federal flight deck officer, or threatening any retaliatory action against the pilot for doing so.

Declares the sense of Congress that the Federal air marshal program is critical to aviation security, and that nothing in this Act shall be construed as preventing the Under Secretary from implementing and training Federal air marshals.

(Sec. 1403) Directs the Under Secretary, in updating the guidance for training flight and cabin crews, to issue a rule to: (1) require both classroom and effective hands-on situational training in specified elements of self-defense; (2) require training in the proper conduct of a cabin search, including the duty time required to conduct it; (3) establish the required number of hours of training and the qualifications for training instructors; (4) establish the intervals, number of hours, and elements of recurrent training; (5) ensure that air carriers provide the initial training within 24 months of the enactment of this Act. Directs the Under Secretary to designate an official in the Transportation Security Administration to be responsible for overseeing the implementation of the training program; and (6) ensure that no person is required to participate in any hands-on training activity that such person believes will have an adverse impact on his or her health or safety.

Amends the Aviation and Transportation Security Act to authorize the Under Secretary to take certain enhanced security measures, including to require that air carriers provide flight attendants with a discreet, hands-free, wireless method of communicating with the pilot of an aircraft.

Directs the Under Secretary to study and report to Congress on the benefits and risks of providing flight attendants with nonlethal weapons to aide in combating air piracy and criminal violence on commercial airlines.

(Sec. 1404) Directs the Secretary of Transportation to study and report within six months to Congress on: (1) the number of armed Federal law enforcement officers (other than Federal air marshals) who travel on commercial airliners annually, and the frequency of their travel; (2) the cost and resources necessary to provide such officers with supplemental aircraft anti-terrorism training comparable to the training that Federal air marshals receive; (3) the cost of establishing a program at a Federal law enforcement training center for the purpose of providing new Federal law enforcement recruits with standardized training comparable to Federal air marshal training; (4) the feasibility of implementing a certification program designed to ensure that Federal law enforcement officers have completed aircraft anti-terrorism training, and track their travel over a six-month period; and (5) the feasibility of staggering the flights of such officers to ensure the maximum amount of flights have a certified trained Federal officer on board.

(Sec. 1405) Amends Federal aviation law to require the Under Secretary to respond within 90 days of receiving a request from an air carrier for authorization to allow pilots of the air carrier to carry less-than-lethal weapons.

Title XV: Transition –

Subtitle A: Reorganization Plan - (Sec. 1502) Requires the President, within 60 days after enactment of this Act, to transmit to the appropriate congressional committees a reorganization plan regarding: (1) the transfer of agencies, personnel, assets, and obligations to DHS pursuant to this Act; and (2) any consolidation, reorganization, or streamlining of agencies transferred to DHS pursuant to this Act.

(Sec. 1503) Expresses the sense of Congress that each House of Congress should review its committee structure in light of the reorganization of responsibilities within the executive branch by the establishment of DHS.

Subtitle B: Transitional Provisions - (Sec. 1511) Outlines transitional provisions with regard to assistance from officials having authority before the effective date of this Act; details of personnel and services to assist in the transition; acting officials during the transition period; the transfer of personnel, assets, obligations and functions; and the status of completed administrative actions, pending proceedings and civil actions, and Inspector General oversight. Prohibits DHS use of any funds derived from the Highway Trust Fund, the Airport and Airway Trust Fund, the Inland Waterway Trust Fund, or the Harbor Maintenance Trust Fund, with a specified exception for certain security-related funds provided to the Federal Aviation Administration.

(Sec. 1514) Provides that nothing in this Act shall be construed to authorize the development of a national identification system or card.

(Sec. 1516) Authorizes and directs the Director of OMB to make additional necessary incidental dispositions of personnel, assets, and liabilities in connection with the functions transferred by this Act.

Title XVI: Corrections to Existing Law Relating to Airline Transportation Security –

(Sec. 1601) Amends Federal aviation law to require the Administrator of the Federal Aviation Administration (FAA), along with the Under Secretary of Transportation for Security, to each conduct research (including behavioral research) and development activities to develop, modify, test, and evaluate a system, procedure, facility, or device to protect passengers and property against acts of criminal violence, aircraft piracy, and terrorism and to ensure security.

Directs the Secretary of Transportation (currently, the Under Secretary) to prescribe regulations prohibiting disclosure of information obtained or developed in ensuring security under this section if the Secretary of Transportation decides disclosing such information would: (1) be an unwarranted invasion of personal privacy; (2) reveal a trade secret or privileged or confidential commercial or financial information; or (3) be detrimental to the safety of passengers in transportation. Sets forth similar provisions requiring the Under Secretary to prescribe regulations prohibiting the disclosure of information obtained or developed in carrying out security under authority of the Aviation and Transportation Security Act (PL107-71).

(Sec. 1602) Increases the maximum civil penalty to $25,000 for a person who violates certain aviation security requirements while operating an aircraft for the transportation of passengers or property for compensation (except an individual serving as an airman).

(Sec. 1603) Revises certain hiring security screener standards to allow a national (currently, only a citizen) of the United States to become a security screener.

Title XVII: Conforming and Technical Amendments –

(Sec. 1701) Sets forth technical and conforming amendments.

(Sec. 1706) Transfers from the Administrator of General Services to the Secretary of Homeland Security law enforcement authority for the protection of Federal property.

(Sec. 1708) Establishes in DOD a National Bio-Weapons Defense Analysis Center to develop countermeasures to potential attacks by terrorists using weapons of mass destruction.

(Sec. 1714) Amends the Public Health Service Act to define "vaccine" to mean any preparation or suspension, including one containing an attenuated or inactive microorganism or toxin, developed or administered to produce or enhance the body's immune response to a disease and to include all components and ingredients listed in the vaccine's product license application and product label.

Chapter 2
Citizen-Centric E-Government

INTRODUCTION

Electronic government or e-government in this chapter can be defined as the delivery of government information and services to citizens through the Internet 24 hours a day, seven days per week. This definition has been used in other empirical studies of e-government adoption (Moon and Norris, 2005a). This chapter adds to this definition Grant and Chau's (2005) interpretation of e-government as a broad-based transformative initiative, which is consistent with creating more citizen-centric government. Gronlund (2005) reviews the various definitions of e-government and has found they share a common theme of the need for organizational transformation through technological implementation.

Citizen-centric e-government is the delivery of government services continuously to citizens, businesses, and other government agencies through the Internet (Seifert and Relyea, 2004). Citizen-centric government through e-government acts as a transformational tool that provides a new government model based on being citizen focused (Schelin, 2003). Some scholars have argued that for e-government to fully realize its capabilities, it must transform government from agency-centric to citizen-centric (Seifert and Relyea, 2004).

The term e-government emerged in the late 1990s. It was born out of the Internet boom. The literature on information technology (IT) use within government is different from e-government because it more often focuses on external use, such as services to citizens' and organizational change (Gronlund and Horan, 2004). Definitions of e-government that focus exclusively on service delivery components fail to capture the more complex aspects of government transformation because of IT (Grant and Chau, 2005).

The purpose of this chapter is to provide an overview of the e-government literature with a focus on how it influences citizens. In order to understand some of the issues associated with Homeland Secu-

DOI: 10.4018/978-1-60566-834-5.ch002

rity Information Systems (HSIS), we need to provide information on e-government and its impact on government. There is a discussion in this chapter of the evolution of the roles and responsibilities of federal CIOs. There also is a description of how the public sector CIO's environment is uniquely different from what can be found in private sector. In this chapter, we identify what it means to create a more citizen-centric government through e-government. A conceptual framework is outlined explaining what factors one would expect to be associated with creating a more citizen-centric government. This chapter articulates how these findings can be used to move e-government to higher stages of development. There also are examples of HSIS creating more citizen-centric government towards the end of the chapter.

EXISTING RESEARCH ON CIOs

The existing research on Chief Information Officers (CIO) or Information Resource Managers (IRM) has focused on the federal government (Bertot and McClure, 1997; Bertot, 1997; Westerback, 2000; Buehler, 2000; McClure and Bertot, 2000), state governments (Ugbah and Umeh, 1993), local governments (Fletcher, 1997), and comparisons between the public and private sectors (Ward and Mitchell, 2004). There have been few scholarly studies that examine public sector CIOs and their opinions on e-government issues and effectiveness. This is most likely attributed to the Internet being a relatively new research area in the public sector. In general, the management of IT in private sector organizations has long been a focus of Information Systems (IS) research, but the extent of diffusion has not been as extensively explored in public sector organizations (Fletcher, 1997).

This study empirically focuses on the connection between e-government and creating a more citizen-centric federal government. The existing research has started to explore the relationship between e-government and increasing citizen-initiated contacts with government, and this study fits into that research area (Thomas and Streib, 2003; West, 2004). However, much needs to be done to identify the key attributes of CIOs, which enable them to create more citizen-centric organizations.

CITIZEN-CENTRIC E-GOVERNMENT ADOPTION

In a survey of state and federal government CIOs and an analysis of their Websites, West (2004) arrived at the conclusion that e-government has fallen short of its potential to transform government service delivery and trust in government - that is, creating a more citizen-centric government. E-government does have the possibility of enhancing the responsiveness of government by making it more efficient and effective. There is also evidence that e-government increases citizen-initiated contact with public officials (Thomas and Streib, 2003). The potential of the Internet to improve citizens' access to government and involvement in policy-making is well articulated in the literature. However, citizen-centric government is difficult to achieve in the public sector since governments need to provide universal access to its services (Mahler and Regan, 2002).

Citizen-centric e-government is consistent with the four-stage model of e-government adoption, in that governments can reach higher levels of adoption if they become more citizen-centric. Layne and Lee (2001) proposed a "stages of e-government growth model" that begins first with cataloging online information, second moving to online transactions, and then third to vertical integration in which local systems are linked to the national systems. The fourth stage of adoption is horizontal integration across different functions leading to one-stop shopping for citizens. Citizen-centric federal government would involve the fourth stage of the Layne and Lee model of horizontal integration - where citizens use Web portals to attain services rather than get information from individual departments or agencies.

This chapter focuses on e-government adoption at its highest stages of development of creating a citizen-centric government. Most of the existing empirical research that examines e-government adoption primarily explores the first two stages of providing online information and municipal e-service delivery (Ho and Ni, 2004; Moon and Norris, 2005b). In addition, Andersen and Henriksen (2005) argue that the role of government in technological diffusion is studied the least of all in the literature.

A study of e-government over two years found that as local government Websites mature they will become more sophisticated, becoming transactional, and more integrated vertically and horizontally (Moon and Norris, 2005a). These authors and others found that e-government adoption is progressing rapidly if measured by the deployment of Websites. However, a movement toward integrated and transactional e-government is progressing much more slowly in more of an incremental fashion (West, 2004). Therefore, it is imperative to understand the impact of e-government on transforming change in government. HSIS is one technology that can be used to facilitate this organizational change.

CLINGER-COHEN ACT AND CIOs

The *Information Technology Management Reform Act* (ITMRA) of 1996 (P.L. 104-106), also known as the *Clinger-Cohen Act*, established the position of CIO in executive branch agencies. This Act requires agency heads to designate CIOs to lead reforms to help control system development risks, better manage technology spending, and achieve measurable improvements in agency performance through management of information resources (GAO, 2004b). However, the Government Accountability Office (GAO) reports that almost a decade after the passage of this Act, and despite the government's expenditure of billions of dollars annually on IT, its management of these resources has produced mixed results (GAO, 2004b)

The *Clinger-Cohen Act* is consistent with the *Government Performance and Results Act* (GPRA) of 1993 (P.L. 103-62) that requires agencies to establish clear and measurable objectives, to implement a process to report on the degree to which those objectives are accomplished, and to report regularly to Congress on their progress in establishing and meeting performance objectives (McClure and Bertot, 2000). Together the *Clinger-Cohen Act* and the *Paperwork Reduction Act* (P.L. 10413) of 1995 (which deals with the strategic acquisition and management of information resources by federal agencies) ushered in a new era of IT management practices in the federal government (Westerback, 2000; Relyea, 2000).

With the passage of the *Clinger-Cohen Act,* federal department and agencies now have the authority and responsibility to make measurable reforms in performance and service delivery to the public through the strategic use of IT (Bertot and McClure, 1997). Prior to this Act the majority of agencies and departments had an IRM official as their top information person who was viewed as an administrative overhead function. IRMs were far removed from the agencies' strategic decision-making and program offices that they served, with little or no access to senior agency officials. As a solution, the *Clinger-Cohen Act* states that federal CIOs will report and work directly with agency directors. As a result, the CIOs were raised to the executive level and were expected to ask the tough questions about strategic planning, outsourcing, and attaining economy and efficiency for their organization (Buehler, 2000).

The importance that CIOs place on strategic planning for their department or agency can be found in existing survey research. A survey of senior IT officers and managers of federal departments and agencies revealed that their top priority was aligning IT with strategic goals (AFFIRM, 2004). Existing research on Federal CIOs has examined whether proper management of information resources can lead to more effective, efficient, and strategic organizations (Bertot, 1997). Evidence was found for a connection between federal agency strategic planning and agency mission attainment, which face different environmental constraints compared with private sector organizations. Essentially, there is evidence that strategic planning matters in government and this should be reflected the environmental constraints that CIOs face in their job.

THE ENVIRONMENTAL CONTEXT OF PUBLIC SECTOR CIOs

In their seminal work Bozeman and Bretchneider (1986) argued that Management Information Systems (MIS) developed for business administration are not altogether appropriate for public administration. Essentially, the different environmental context of the public organization is an important constraint, which makes public MIS diverge from business. Public sector MIS differs from the private sector because of the greater accountability, procedural delays, and red tape associated with government (Bretschneider, 1990). Budget and other constraints on purchasing make it impossible for comprehensive approaches to work well such as strategic planning (Rocheleau and Wu, 2002).

In a survey of state agencies concerning the ability of public organizations to control and manage information resources the following was found: (1) public agencies find their programs and sources of information externally oriented; (2) recruiting and retaining a technically competent workforce in public agencies to manage information resources effectively was found to be a problem; and (3) public agencies are constrained by fiscal crisis and a political climate in which they must operate (Ugbah and Umeh, 1993). These unique challenges make public sector Internet use especially worthy to explore to understand the environmental context of HSIS.

CITIZEN-CENTRIC FEDERAL GOVERNMENT AND E-GOVERNMENT

The *E-Government Act of 2002* (H.R. 2458) defines electronic government as the use by the government of Web-based Internet application and other information technologies. The E-Government Act is one of the most important pieces of federal legislation with respect to IT and government information and service delivery, therefore, Appendix A provides a summary of the main provisions of this Act. This Act established an Office of Electronic Government within the OMB to oversee implementation of its provisions. This *E-government Act* was enacted with the general purpose of promoting better use of the Internet and other information technologies to improve government services for citizens, internal government operations, and provide opportunities for citizen participation in government (GAO, 2004a). According to the GAO, the OMB and federal agencies have taken many positive steps towards implementing the provisions of the *E-government Act* (GAO, 2004a).

Creating a more citizen-centric government can be found in President George W. Bush's management document the *President's Management Agenda* (PMA) of 2002. The PMA states that the "...administration's goal is to champion citizen-centered electronic government that will result in a major improvement in the federal government's value to the citizen" (EOP, 2002a: 23). In evaluating the PMA, the GAO showed that the results in terms of e-government implementation were mixed with many only being partially achieved or no significant progress being made (GAO, 2005a).

Citizen-centric e-government is further elaborated upon in the Bush administration's document *E-government Strategy* (EOP, 2002b). President Bush has made expanding e-government part of a five-part management agenda for making government more focused on citizens and results. According to the Bush administration, the three main aspects of expanding e-government are to make it easier for citizens to obtain service and interact with the federal government, improve government efficiency and effectiveness, and improve government's responsiveness to citizens. E-government is "...critical to meeting today's citizen and business expectations for interaction with government" (EOP, 2002b, p. 3).

Although the PMA does not specifically define citizen-centric government in its application to the federal government, one can discern from reading the document that it implies a focus on citizen expectations driving government responses rather than the other way around. Citizen-centric government essentially focuses on providing citizens with the services and information they require from their government. What follows is a conceptual framework that can be used to illustrate citizen-centric e-government.

CONCEPTUAL FRAMEWORK

The conceptual framework demonstrated in Figure 1 shows the relationship between six factors that are predicted to create more citizen-centric federal government. Each of these factors are discussed along with their respective literatures.

MANAGEMENT CAPACITY

The literature in public administration on e-government has often advocated that effective management is a critical catalyst for its advancement (Brown and Brudney, 1998; Ho and Ni, 2004). The benefits of IT, expressed in the public administration literature, are often associated with the efficiency and rationality of service provision (Danziger and Andersen, 2002). For instance, putting a strong CIO in place can be used to address the federal government's IT and management challenges (GAO, 2005b). The literature on management capacity and its impact on federal e-government initiatives is not as well developed as the local e-government literature. For instance, has e-government made the federal CIO a more effective manager? Empowering employees to make more decisions on their own is a desirable trait according to the Total Quality Management (TQM) literature. Has e-government facilitated the empowerment of employees in the federal government? Finally, the literature in public administration also mentions that performance measures are of critical importance in both public and private sectors. Have federal departments or agencies been able to achieve greater results because of e-government? These three management factors are expected to have an impact on creating a more citizen-centric federal government. Indeed, in a survey of all three levels of government public sector IS managers attached more importance to managerial issues than technical ones (Swain et al., 1995). Figure 1 shows the predicted impact of management capacity on creating a more citizen-centric federal government.

Figure 1. Conceptual framework of factors that create citizen-centric government

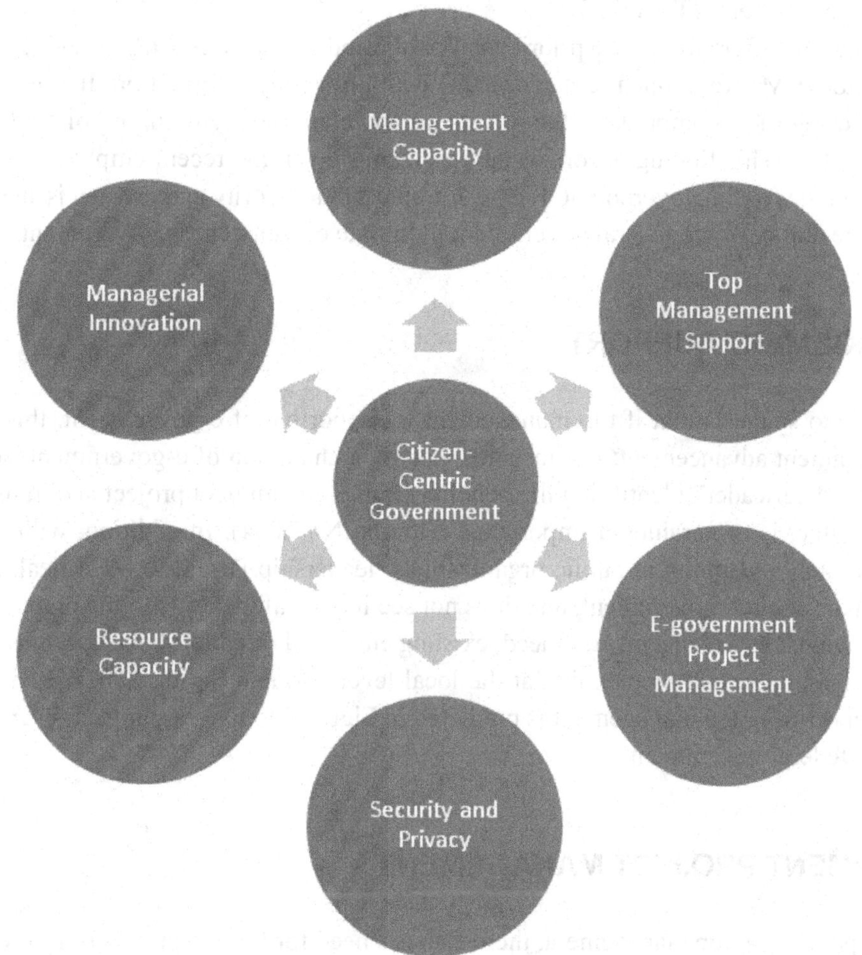

SECURITY AND PRIVACY

Besides the importance of management capacity outlined in the literature there also is a growing trend to think about e-government in light of security and privacy concerns. Since the terrorist attacks of September 11, 2001, there has been an emphasis on homeland security and emergency preparedness as it relates to information systems (Dawes et al., 2004). One of the crucial and growing issues for the near future of e-government is the security of information infrastructure and government information applications (Stowers, 2004). This trend is consistent with security and privacy of digital information. For instance, threats or attacks on information systems could compromise national security. In addition, privacy of citizens' personally identifiable information (PII) is of paramount importance with increased incidence of identity theft. The federal government must make sure that it has safe and secure information systems. IT security remained a top priority for federal CIOs in President Bush's second term in office (ITAA, 2005). Federal CIOs continued to focus on security and authentication as key building blocks for the advancement of e-government (ITAA, 2004). According to federal government CIOs, in the age of terrorism and identity theft, a clear authentication protocol is necessary for creating a more citizen-centric government (ITAA, 2004).

In past studies on differences in the priorities of public and private sector IRMs, evidence has shown that public sector IRMs were much less concerned with protecting information. It was ranked almost last (out of 23 categories) compared to the private sector relatively high ranking of sixth place (Ward and Mitchell, 2004). This finding is somewhat perplexing given the recent emphasis on privacy and security issues in the federal government. Figure 1 predicts that security and privacy issues should have an impact on the ability of the federal government to initiate citizen-centric government.

TOP MANAGEMENT SUPPORT

The literature also suggests that if top management is supportive of e-government, this provides for greater e-government advancement. For instance, having a champion of e-government, someone who is essentially a "cheerleader" identifying the benefits of an e-government project and translating it into something of value, is of paramount importance (Ho and Ni, 2004). In addition, with the increased emphasis on strategic planning in public organizations, leadership is said to be critical. If a manager is not enthusiastic about e-government, and does not see its overall benefits to the organization, this is likely to wear against its advancement. Indeed, existing empirical research shows a connection between top management support and IT planning at the local level (Ho and Smith, 2001; Ho and Ni, 2004). Therefore, support from top management is predicted in Figure 1 to have an impact on creating a more citizen-centric federal government.

E-GOVERNMENT PROJECT MANAGEMENT

Along with support from top management, there also is a need for finding and recruiting well-qualified project managers for e-government projects. Project managers are in short supply, especially for government agencies, which must compete with the higher paying jobs these professionals could get in the private sector (ITAA, 2004). How widely and quickly have e-government projects been adopted in a department or agency is said to be the barometer of project management success. Can e-government projects be seen through from start to finish on time and on budget? CIOs were unanimous in the belief that attracting and retaining qualified project management personnel remains a significant challenge for moving e-government forward (ITAA, 2005).

How have e-government projects changed the interaction of a department or agency with its clients or customers? Ideally, one would assume that e-government has increased citizen and business interaction with government and has provided for more satisfaction with these contacts (Thomas and Streib, 2003). Therefore, good project management should have an impact on creating a more citizen-centric federal government (Figure 1).

MANAGERIAL INNOVATION

The transformation agenda of e-government has been promoted under the label of "new public management' which calls for reinvention of government as an institutional reform (Grant and Chau, 2005). This managerial innovation has been one of the major thrusts of the theoretical work on e-government. Scholars have argued that e-government is associated with a more decentralized, flexible, efficient, and effective public sector (Ho, 2002; Moon and Norris, 2005b). Research shows that public agencies do indeed face higher levels of formalization and red tape than the private sector (Rainey and Bozeman, 2000).

Existing work has also argued that e-government will break down the silos of information dissemination in government; it will decentralize government allowing it to run more efficiently and effectively. Agencies will share information more readily and there will be a greater amount of teamwork towards reaching a common goal. Departments and agencies will collaborate more on projects and look at IT not as part of a functional unit, but in terms of serving customers.

An example of the managerial innovation having an influence on e-government is the www.firstgov.gov Web portal, where instead of listing departments the federal government lists services that a citizen most often uses. A number of CIOs also believed that the process of working together across departments, agencies, and in some cases levels of government, had resulted in a new model of collaboration through e-government (ITAA, 2005). However, CIOs have started to raise significant concerns about the difficulty of changing ingrained cultural attitudes in order to manage change (ITAA, 2004). Existing research suggests a connection between the managerial innovation and e-government at the local level (Ho, 2002; Moon and Norris, 2005b), but there is little empirical work in this area on the federal government and the creation of a more citizen-centric government.

LACK OF RESOURCE CAPACITY

One area that should also have an impact on creating a more citizen-centric government is whether the federal government has adequate resources to fulfill its e-government mandates. Lack of resources capacity is a perennial problem that federal CIOs face in IT implementation (ITAA, 2005). Is the budget Congress appropriates to an agency adequate to provide for e-government services? Has the government been able to save resources by eliminating manual processes through e-government? Does the department or agency have an adequate amount of IT infrastructure to fulfill its e-government mandates? What kind of outsourcing relationship does the agency have? Does the department or agency fit into the Office of Management and Budget's (OMB), the chief agency responsible for federal e-government, vision of e-government project management? CIOs have expressed frustration with the difficulty of securing budget deliberations from Congress to fund e-government initiatives (ITAA, 2004).

Existing empirical research does not show that resource capacity is a major constraint on public sector IT planning (Ho and Smith, 2001; Ho and Ni, 2004). However, this factor was viewed as being important in focus group discussions with CIOs (ITAA, 2005). We make a prediction that resource capacity should have an impact on creating a more citizen-centric federal government (Figure 1). These six factors are used to explain e-government creating more citizen-centric government through survey evidence provided in the following sections.

CHARACTERISTICS OF FEDERAL CIOs

A survey of federal government CIOs was administered during June and July 2005. The contact information for the CIOs was taken from the CIO Council Website at www.cio.gov. This Website provides the most comprehensive listing of contact information for CIOs employed by the federal government. There were 115 federal departments and agencies which had a CIO designated official. All of them were sent a survey. In total, 38 CIOs responded to the survey, which indicates a response rate of 33 percent. This is a slightly lower response rate than West's (2004) study of CIOs and e-government service delivery.

The survey protocols were to first send a cover letter to each of the CIOs indicating that in a few days they were going to receive a survey. The survey was seeking their opinions on e-government issues and effectiveness. Second, a formal survey and a cover letter with instructions were sent to the CIOs. This was an anonymous survey to maximize candor of responses. The majority of ideas for questions on the survey were taken from the series of ITAA focus group discussion with federal CIOs and their views on IT planning and management (ITAA, 2004; 2005).

Table 1 provides the characteristics of CIOs who responded to the survey and their department/agency's size. The majority of CIOs who responded were from large departments/agencies that employed 5,000 or more Full Time Equivalent (FTE) employees. Large-sized departments represented 56 percent of CIOs surveyed. Smaller agency CIOs employing 99 or less FTE, composed only 14 percent of the sample. Therefore, this survey is more representative of larger department CIOs than smaller agencies.

Table 1 also indicates that the typical age range of CIOs was between 45 and 54 years, representing around half of those surveyed. A third of respondents were between 55 and 64 years of age. The smallest numbers of CIOs surveyed were between the ages of 35 and 44 years, representing around 17 percent of the sample.

According to Table 1, almost half of the CIOs have worked for the federal government for more than a quarter of a century. Therefore, their tenure in the federal government is very substantial. However, those surveyed have not acted as CIOs for long. According to the survey results, three quarters of CIOs have been in that position for 10 years or less. This finding is most likely attributed to the *Clinger-Cohen Act* of 1996, which established a new position of CIO for most federal government departments/agencies.

The highest level of academic attainment for the CIOs was typically a master's degree, with just over half of them holding this advanced degree. Only a quarter of CIOs hold a bachelors degree as their highest level of academic achievement. This finding is what one would expect, the requirement of an advanced degree when working at an executive level position in the federal government.

The characteristics of CIOs and their departments and agencies generally show that they are from large agencies, they tend to be baby boomers, are male, have many years of experience in the federal government, but fewer years of experience as a CIO, and most of them are well educated. The survey results are more representative of large-sized federal department and agencies than smaller ones, and this should be kept in mind when interpreting the findings presented in the following section.

CIOs OPINIONS ON E-GOVERNMENT

In this section, this chapter explores the opinions of federal government CIOs on e-government. It also examines the views of CIOs on whether they agree that e-government has created a more citizen-centric federal government. This chapter outlines the issues of management capacity, security and privacy,

Table 1.Characteristics of CIOs and their department's/agency's

	Frequency	Percent
How many FTE employees are employed in your department/agency?		
99 or less	5	13.9
100 to 499	3	8.3
500 to 999	2	5.6
1,000 to 4,999	6	16.7
5,000 or more	20	55.6
What is your age range?		
35-44	6	16.7
45-54	18	50.0
55-64	12	33.3
What is your gender?		
Female	9	25.0
Male	27	75.0
How many years have you worked for the federal government?		
Less than 5 years	5	13.9
5 to 10 years	4	11.1
11 to 15 years	4	11.1
16 to 20 years	2	5.6
21 to 25 years	5	13.9
26 years or more	16	44.4
How many years have you worked as a CIO?		
Less than 5 years	14	38.9
5 to 10 years	13	36.1
11 to 15 years	3	8.3
16 to 20 years	4	11.1
21 to 25 years	1	2.8
26 years or more	1	2.8
What is your highest level of academic attainment?		
High school diploma	2	5.6
2 year college degree	2	5.6
4 year college degree	9	25.0
Master's degree	19	52.8
Law degree	3	8.3
Doctorate degree	1	2.8

support from top management, project management, managerial innovation, and resource capacity and their influence on e-government.

Table 2 presents the impact of e-government on creating a more citizen-centric federal government. Over 60 percent of CIOs agree that e-government has indeed created a more citizen-centric federal gov-

Table 2. Perceptions of CIOs on e-government creating citizen-centric government

E-government in my federal department/ agency...	*Strongly Agree (%)*	*Agree (%)*	*Neither Agree/Disagree (%)*	*Disagree (%)*	*Strongly Disagree (%)*
Has created a more citizen-centric federal government.	13.9	47.2	25	11.1	2.8

Table 3. Perceptions of CIOs on the impact of e-government on management

E-government in my federal department/ agency...	*Strongly Agree (%)*	*Agree (%)*	*Neither Agree/ Disagree (%)*	*Disagree (%)*	*Strongly Disagree (%)*
Has made me a more effective manager.	13.2	28.9	47.4	10.5	0
Has empowered employees to make more decisions on their own.	5.3	42.1	23.7	26.3	2.6
Has enabled us to achieve greater performance milestones and results.	10.5	55.3	23.7	7.9	2.6

ernment. However, 14 percent disagree that e-government has created a more citizen-centric government. A quarter of respondents indicated that they neither agree nor disagree with this statement. However, only 40 percent of CIOs either disagree or are uncertain of its impact on e-government.

Table 3 shows the impact of management capacity on e-government. Has e-government made the CIO a more effective manager? First, around forty percent of CIOs agree that e-government has made them more effective managers. Second, almost half of CIOs agreed e-government had empowered employees to make more decisions on their own. Third, nearly two-thirds of CIOs believed that the performance of their agency had improved because of e-government. Overall, the management capacity findings revealed that e-government had a major impact on the federal government.

Security and privacy issues are of paramount importance for federal government IT management (Table 4). This issue is evident in the CIOs' opinions on security and privacy issues. Almost all CIOs believed that secure storage of citizen and business PII was the most important concern for the future advancement of e-government. In addition, 92 percent of the CIOs believed that security and authentication was the key building blocks of e-government advancement. Finally, according to 95 percent of CIOs, information

Table 4. Perceptions of CIOs on the impact of e-government on security and privacy

In my federal department/agency...	*Strongly Agree (%)*	*Agree (%)*	*Neither Agree/Disagree (%)*	*Disagree (%)*	*Strongly Disagree (%)*
Secure storage of citizen and business Personally Identifiable Information (PII) is one of the most pressing concerns for e-government advancement.	45.9	48.6	2.7	2.7	0
Information assurance/security is one of the most important concerns for e-government adoption.	40.5	54.1	2.7	2.7	0
Security and authentication are the key building blocks for the advancement of e-government.	35.1	56.8	5.4	2.7	0

Table 5. Perceptions of CIOs on the impact of e-government on top management support

In my federal department/agency ...	Strongly Agree (%)	Agree (%)	Neither Agree/Disagree (%)	Disagree (%)	Strongly Disagree (%)
Having a champion of e-government is one of the most important critical success factors for e-government advancement.	52.8	36.1	11.1	0	0
Top management has a vision and strategic direction for e-government for my department/agency.	22.2	50	13.9	11.1	2.8
Top management is very supportive of my department/agency's participation in the decision-making process for e-government.	27.8	44.4	16.7	8.3	2.8

assurance/security was one of the most pressing concerns for e-government adoption. Not surprisingly, very few CIOs disagreed with these three above-mentioned security and privacy statements.

Table 5 shows support from top management for e-government adoption, which is one of the critical success factors noted in the literature (Ho and Ni, 2004). Does having a champion of e-government, someone who will spearhead the implementation of e-government efforts, make a difference towards attaining greater levels of adoption? Nearly 90 percent of CIOs believe that having a champion of e-government is one of the most important critical success factors. Top management, according to over 70 percent of CIOs surveyed, has a vision and strategic direction for e-government. In addition, top management is supportive of CIOs in the e-government decision-making process, according to over 70 percent of CIOs. There is general agreement that the OMB has a vision and strategic direction for e-government and has been inclusive in the decision-making process.

This survey outlines the level of adoption of e-government projects in the federal government (Table 6). Project management has been identified as one of the most critical success factors for a department or agency to possess according to the ITAA's (2005) survey. E-government projects have been adopted widely and quickly according to over half of CIOs. Over 60 percent of CIOs believed that e-government projects had increased citizen and business interaction with the federal government. E-government projects are a top priority of departments or agencies according to almost 60 percent of CIOs. Seventy

Table 6. Perceptions of CIOs on the impact of e-government on project management

E-government in my federal department/ agency...	Strongly Agree (%)	Agree (%)	Neither Agree/Disagree (%)	Disagree (%)	Strongly Disagree (%)
Has been adopted quickly and widely.	13.2	42.1	28.9	13.2	2.6
Have increased citizen and business interaction with my department/agency.	22.2	38.9	22.2	13.9	2.8
Are a top-priority of my department/ agency.	13.9	44.4	19.4	19.4	2.8
Recruitment and retention of qualified e-government project management and support staff is one of the most critical issues.	41.7	27.8	25	2.8	2.8

percent of CIOs believed that recruitment and retention of qualified e-government project management staff was of critical importance.

Has e-government been influenced by managerial innovation? The existing literature in this area argues that this has been the case (Ho, 2002; Moon and Norris, 2005b). E-government has allowed for a greater level of information sharing among departments according to 70 percent of CIOs (Table 7). In addition, e-government had created more teamwork in federal departments and agencies, according to 42 percent of respondents. Two-thirds of CIOs believed that e-government had created a new level of collaboration among departments and agencies.

Lack of resource capacity of a department or agency is also said to have an impact on e-government advancement (Table 8). Does the CIO's department or agency lack the requisite IT infrastructure, which would inhibit e-government adoption? Only 20 percent of CIOs agreed with this statement of not having adequate IT infrastructure. However, around half of CIOs agreed that they did not have an adequate budget to fund e-government in their department or agency. Only 28 percent of CIOs agreed that they have not seen manual processes being eliminated because of e-government. Finally, there is a movement in the federal government to holistically and competitively outsource IT. Around 22 percent of CIOs agreed that they do not take a holistic view when it comes to outsourcing e-government projects. The resource capacity findings provided evidence that key e-government infrastructure was available, but not surprisingly, the greater issue was not having adequate budgetary resources to fund e-government. The resource capacity issue is also addressed in the open-ended question.

Table 7. Perceptions of CIOs on the impact of e-government on managerial innovation

In my federal department/agency...	*Strongly Agree (%)*	*Agree (%)*	*Neither Agree/Disagree (%)*	*Disagree (%)*	*Strongly Disagree (%)*
E-government has allowed a greater degree of information sharing among departments/agencies.	19.4	50	19.4	11.1	0
E-government has fostered greater teamwork in employees.	5.6	36.1	38.9	19.4	0
E-government has developed a new level of collaboration among departments/agencies.	13.9	52.8	16.7	16.7	0

Table 8. Perceptions of CIOs on the impact of e-government on resource capacity

My department/agency ...	*Strongly Agree (%)*	*Agree (%)*	*Neither Agree/Disagree (%)*	*Disagree (%)*	*Strongly Disagree (%)*
Lacks Information Technology (IT) infrastructure which inhibits e-government adoption.	2.8	16.7	16.7	44.4	19.4
Does not have adequate budgetary resources to fund e-government projects.	13.9	33.3	22.2	22.2	8.3
Has not seen manual processes being eliminated as a result of e-government.	5.6	22.2	19.4	47.2	5.6
Does not take a holistic view of e-government when competitively outsourcing e-government projects.	5.6	16.7	33.3	27.8	16.7

OPEN ENDED RESPONSES

An open-ended question was also asked of federal government CIOs on their opinions concerning e-government issues and effectiveness. The most common responses, not surprisingly, were that CIOs had issues with lack of budgetary resources, the OMB dictating e-government projects, and neglible role for smaller agencies in federal e-government initiatives.

For instance, in the budgetary resources issue, one CIO believed that the most significant hindrance to implementing e-government is OMB's practice of mandating implementation schedules that are shorter than the budget cycle. This CIO argued that agency budgets were developed two years in advance. Consequently, OMB needs to either provide planning guidance that announces e-government initiatives or mandates two years in advance of their issuance or allow at least two years for implementation of initiatives. Another CIO stated that e-government project managers spend far too much time begging for money from reluctant agency partners. Finally, a CIO said that lack of funding is the biggest obstacle for e-government advancement.

A second common theme was reaction from some CIOs about the role of top management being either the chief executive of the department/agency or OMB. A CIO stated that he/she personally has not seen much value in the e-government policies promulgated by OMB. According to another CIO, $60 billion in federal IT spending is simply too large to be managed on a top-down basis. According to another CIO, "e-government is very important to my agency, but has sometimes been stymied by OMB." A CIO commented that executive leadership must really understand e-government opportunities. Thus, they must want and know how to leverage technology for successful e-government outcomes.

A third common response was the role of small agencies in federal e-government initiatives. Scalability of e-government initiatives presents problems for very small agencies according to one CIO, in which one size does not fit all agencies. E-government needs to address the needs of the very small agencies (10 employees or less) as well as the larger agencies, according to another CIO comment.

Less common responses indicated by CIOs were that too many silos of information and information technologies exist in the federal government. According to a CIO, departments/agencies are finding it difficult to keep up with new government regulations. A CIO commented that governments must close the digital divide for e-government to reach its full potential. One response that is consistent with creating a more citizen-centric federal government was the comment by a CIO that e-government initiatives are very worthwhile in giving citizens a participatory role in government and providing easy access to information. The following section presents examples of HSIS influencing citizens and their behavior in a disaster.

EXAMPLES OF CITIZEN-CENTRIC GOVERNMENT AND HSIS

Research indicates that citizens are the most effective emergency management personnel (Helsloot and Ruitenberg, 2004). Indeed, disaster evaluations show that the most lives are actually saved by the average citizen. However, citizens are difficult to work with in disaster preparedness, unless they perceive that they are personally at risk. In essence, citizens calculate rationally the benefits of preparation versus the costs.

Local citizens are often the true first responders on the scene in emergency situations (Palen, Hiltz, and Liu, 2007). Citizens are generally very organized and provide assistance when at a disaster scene. With the Internet online forms have emerged that allow people to share information and coordinate citizen led efforts. These online groups could become virtual communities with their own membership policies and norms. There have been several online forms that have emerged after Hurricane Katrina. For example, Scipionuis.com was created to share location-specific information about the storm and the damage. In summary, the involvement of the public as a result of the Internet through online discussion forums during and after disasters is just beginning to come to fruition. The reach of the Internet greatly expands the opportunities for public involvement where individuals are geographically removed from the disaster.

The Report from the Committee on Using Information Technology to Enhance Disaster Management in 2007 advocated, among other things, better citizen engagement in emergency management through IT (National Research Council, 2007). The Committee believed that there are two ways to better engage citizens through the use of IT. First, there is the use of early warning systems and broadcast alerts of information to the public on actions that they can do to protect themselves from in the event of a major disaster. Second, is the ability to use the public as a resource to help with the disaster recovery though devices such as mobile phones. IT such as mobile phones can be easily used by citizens in a disaster to provide a visual account of the emergency for first responders.

There are several communications channels that can be used to communicate with the public in the event of an emergency. Wang and Kapucu (2008) found during Hurricane Charley in Florida evidence that radio stations, local TV, hurricane flyers, websites, situation reports, and press conferences reduced public complacency, while local newspapers, public meetings, and electronic roadway signs increased public complacency. More dynamic real-time media reduced the level of public complacency during a disaster. In addition, their survey results showed that more media channels are better than fewer to reduce complacency. Essentially, effective communication strategies through multiple channels should reduce public complacency and enhance public preparedness in response to disasters, according to Wang and Kapucu (2008).

Public libraries have become an integral resource for citizens affected by disasters. There are essentially four functions of public libraries and their provision of public access computing and internet access in communities affected by disasters like hurricanes (Bertot, Jaeger, Langa, and McClure, 2006). First, they serve a purpose of finding and communicating with family members and friends who have been displaced, evacuated to other cities, or were missing. Second, libraries provide Internet access to complete FEMA forms and insurance claims online. Third, libraries provide the ability of the disaster victims to search for news about conditions in their area from which they had been evacuated. Fourth, public libraries have Internet access which can help displaced individuals find information about the condition of their home and place of work through checking online news, maps, and satellite photos.

In a discussion of government information policy McClure and Jaeger (2008) believe that homeland security concerns have influenced the degree to which libraries can successfully deliver a range of government information and services to its citizens. This has been noticeably impacted government information policy since the terrorist attacks of 9/11. Since these attacks, all levels of government, including private sector entities, have been much more cautious in scrutinizing information that might influence national security, making sure that such information is not released to the public. For example, the USA PATRIOT Act of 2001 had a direct impact on public libraries and their provision of e-government services and resources. Libraries may restrict access to records they keep in fear that federal agents will demand access to user logs and other personal information regarding their use of e-government services in a particular library. Under the PATRIOT Act, Federal agents could potentially wiretap communications going into and out of a library to obtain information on suspected terrorists.

Community Response Grids (CRG) make use of the Internet and mobile communication devices that allow citizens and first responders to communicate, share, and coordinate activities during a major disaster (Jaeger, Shneiderman, Fleischmann, Preece, Qu, and Wu, 2007). The combination of mobile communications and the Internet provide a greater capacity of first responders to effective prepare and manage a disaster than without this technology. In addition, CRGs can enable citizens to help each other out before, during, and after a major disaster.

There are several website available that provide preparedness information for citizens in the event of a terrorist attack or natural disaster. Figure 2 shows a screen shot of the Department of Homeland Security's website that focuses on services that can be used by citizens for preparedness (http://www.dhs.gov/xcitizens). This website provides a range of information and services from providing links for disaster victims that need assistance to more general information on the DHS. There is a citizen guide to homeland security and information for travelers. There also is the color-coded homeland security advisory system that can be found at this website.

Figure 3 shows a screen short of the DHS's (http://www.Ready.gov) website. The Department of Homeland Security launched an emergency preparedness website Ready.gov in July 2006, which is to provide citizens with information on preparedness for natural disasters and terrorist attacks. The purpose of the website is to educate citizens about the steps that citizens can take to get ready for an emergency. For example, on the website there is information on what citizens need to have in an emergency supply

Figure 2. Department of Homeland Security's services focused on citizens (Source: http://www.dhs.gov/xcitizens)

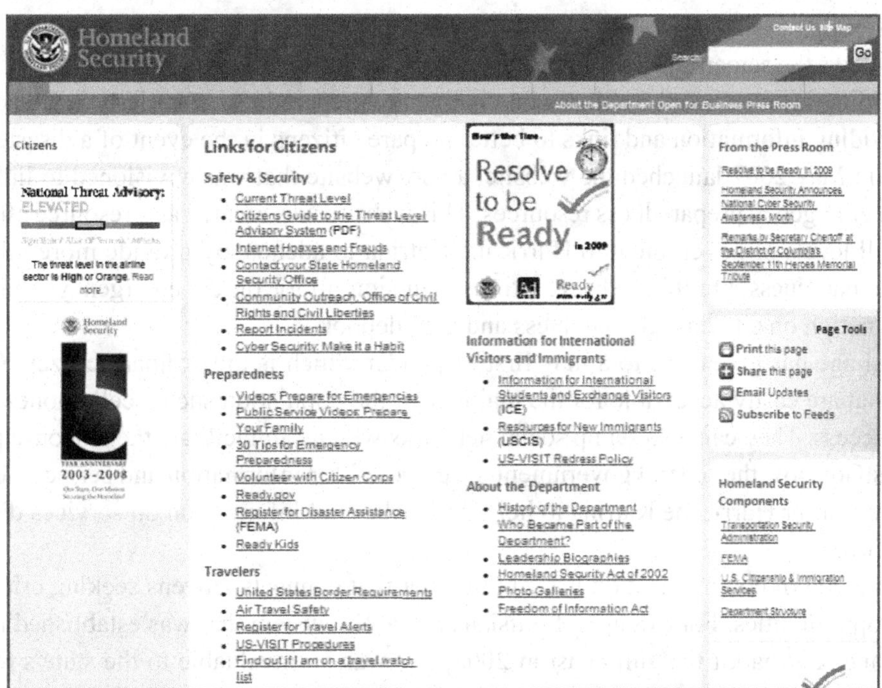

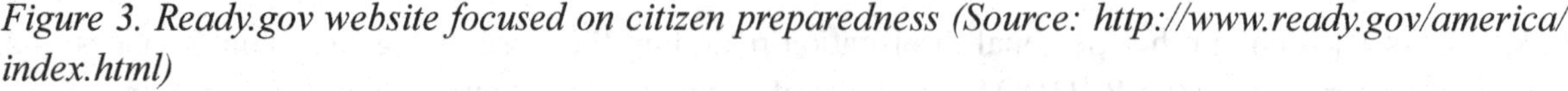

Figure 3. Ready.gov website focused on citizen preparedness (Source: http://www.ready.gov/america/index.html)

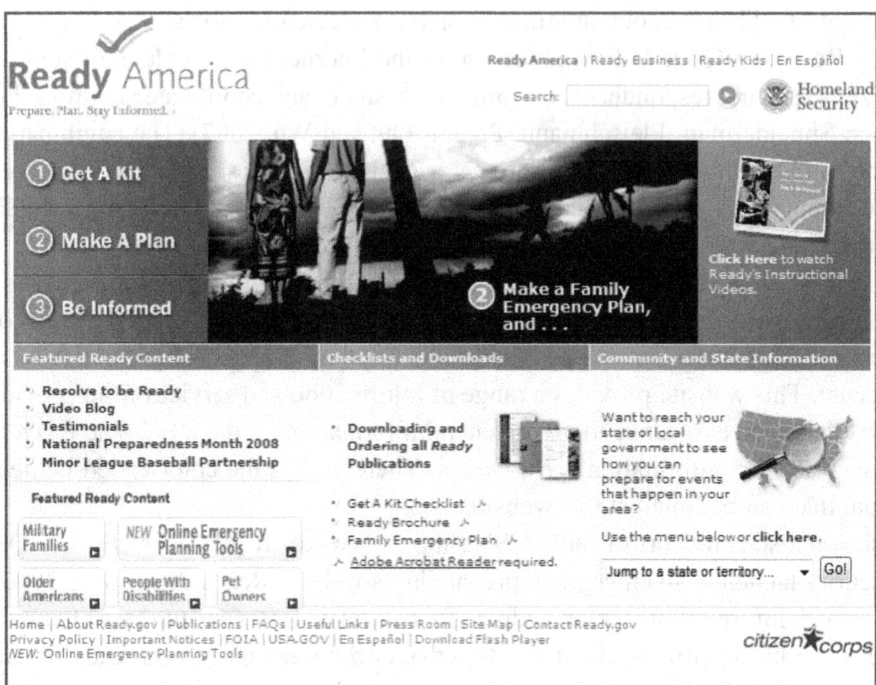

kit. There is also information for special needs population, pet owners, and senior citizens. Similarly, to the previous website, this one focuses on disaster preparedness and what citizens can do in the event of a disaster. For example, information on Ready.gov enables citizens to create plans in case of a disaster through disaster kits.

Figure 4 shows the screen short for http://emergency.louisiana.gov which is the State of Louisiana's website providing information for citizens on emergency preparedness. Similarly, to Ready.gov it focuses on providing information and links to better prepare citizens in the event of a disaster. The State of Louisiana in May 2007 launched the website, a new website that was envisioned to link citizens in the state with emergency preparedness resources. This website was created as a resource after the failed response of all levels of government to Hurricane Katrina to adequately provide more information to citizens on preparedness. On this website, citizens can sign up for timely emergency email alerts and there is information on citizens' preparedness and a guidebook.

The digital age has given rise to a new first responder which is the ordinary citizen. Citizens can use devices that are easily accessible for the majority of the population such a cell phones, computers, and internet access. They can also set up social networks which can facilitate the response process. For example, FirstGov.gov, the federal government's web portal for information and services, enhanced its search functions after Hurricane Katrina to help the public find information on services distributed by federal agencies.

Another method of communication is a 211 number that connects citizens seeking critical services or volunteer opportunities. For example, Louisiana has a 211 system that was established in 2003, and when Hurricane Katrina hit the gulf coast in 2005, this was an invaluable to the state's response and

Figure 4. The State of Louisiana's emergency management citizen-centric website (Source: http://emergency.louisiana.gov/)

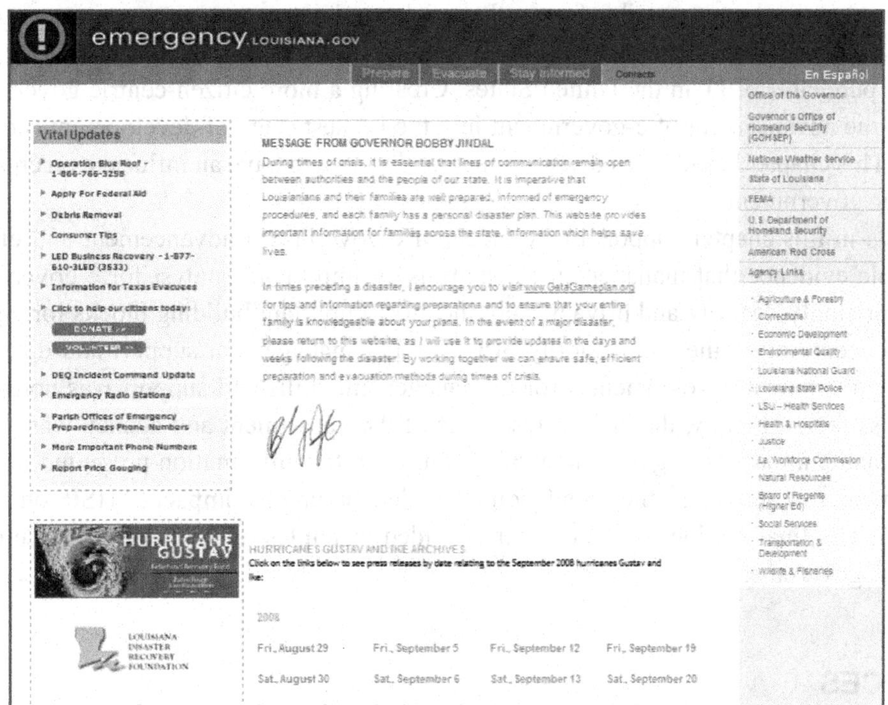

recovery efforts. The issue before 211 was that many victims have called 911 with questions, which has put tremendous pressure on the emergency response system. The 211 system was designed to offload the non-emergency questions about city services to take some pressure off 911 operators.

As mentioned, after Hurricane Katrina many displaced residents and their relatives used the Internet for information about a home that they believed was damaged or destroyed in the storm. For instance, many used Google Earth (http://earth.google.com/) where users can zoom in and see an aerial shot from satellite photos. Google along with National Aeronautics and Space Administration (NASA) had nearly 4000 images from the post hurricane destruction loaded into the Google Earth database for public use. This has become an invaluable tool for residents worried about what they are going to come back to in the aftermath of Hurricane Katrina. The Red Cross and other nonprofits have sent more computers into emergency shelters such as cell phones and other communication equipment hit by Hurricane Katarina. The use of this equipment should help victims get in touch with their families and friends.

A final example of citizens use of HSIS was in Texas in 2007 the state launched an effort to keep track of evacuees and their families in the event of a disaster by using Radio Frequency Identification (RFID) technology. In an event of an emergency, evacuees would be registered on site and issued a bar coded RFID wristband. This technology can be used to keep track of displaced citizens and allow the state to know how many victims are out there to keep track of resources needed to facilitate response.

CONCLUSION

This study has examined some possible factors that might explain creating a more citizen-centric federal government. This is an important area of information systems research given that the federal government is the largest purchaser of IT in the United States. Creating a more citizen-centric government is one indication of the advancement of e-government into the highest stage of development (i.e., horizontal integration). This chapter has identified several factors that should have an influence on creating a more citizen-centric government.

The results in this chapter support many facets of e-government advancement and effectiveness. There is ample evidence that management capacity is an important catalyst for e-government adoption. Not surprisingly, security and privacy were the most important building blocks for e-government advancement according to the vast majority of CIOs. Top management support and direction is also crucial for e-government development. Project management skills and support was noted as being a critical success factor. Finally, the lack of resources of the department and agency was also found to have a discernable impact on e-government adoption. With this information presented in this chapter on e-government, this should lay the foundation for understanding the impact of HSIS on public sector organizations. The final section of this chapter provided examples of the use of HSIS creating more citizen-centric government.

REFERENCES

AFFIRM. (2004). *The Federal CIO - Ninth Annual CIO Challenges Survey*. Retrieved July 30, 2005, from http://www.affirm.org/

Andersen, K. V., & Henriksen, H. Z. (2005). The first leg of e-government research: Domains and application areas 1998-2003. *International Journal of Electronic Government Research, 1*(4), 26–44.

Bertot, J. C. (1997). The impact of Federal IRM on agency missions: Findings, issues, and recommendations. *Government Information Quarterly, 14*(3), 235–253. doi:10.1016/S0740-624X(97)90003-4

Bertot, J. C., Jaeger, P. T., Langa, L. A., & McClure, C. R. (2006). Public Access Computing and Internet Access in Public Libraries: The Role of Public Libraries in E-Government and Emergency Situations. *First Monday, 11*(9), 1–25.

Bertot, J. C., & McClure, C. R. (1997). Key issues affecting the development of federal IRM: A view from the trenches. *Government Information Quarterly, 14*(3), 271–290. doi:10.1016/S0740-624X(97)90005-8

Bozeman, B., & Bretschneider, S. (1986). Public management information systems: Theory and prescription. *Public Administration Review, 46*, 475–487. doi:10.2307/975569

Bretschneider, S. (1990). Management information systems in public and private organizations: An empirical test. *Public Administration Review, 50*(5), 536–545. doi:10.2307/976784

Brown, M. M., & Brudney, J. L. (1998). Public sector information technology initiatives: Implications for programs of public administration. *Administration & Society, 30*(4), 421–442. doi:10.1177/0095399798304005

Buehler, M. (2000). U.S. Federal government CIOs: Information technology's new managers – preliminary findings. *Government Information Quarterly, 27*, 29–45. doi:10.1016/S1352-0237(99)00154-9

Danziger, J. N., & Andersen, K. V. (2002). The impacts of information technology on public administration: An analysis of empirical research from the "golden age" of Transformation. *International Journal of Public Administration, 25*(5), 591–627. doi:10.1081/PAD-120003292

Dawes, S. S., Cresswell, A. M., & Cahan, B. B. (2004). Learning from crisis: Lessons in human and information infrastructure from the World Trade Center response. *Social Science Computer Review, 22*(1), 52–66. doi:10.1177/0894439303259887

EOP. (2002a). *The President's Management Agenda*. Retrieved July 30, 2005, from http://www.whitehouse.gov/omb/

EOP. (2002b). *Implementing the President's Management Agenda for E-Government: E-Government Strategy*. Retrieved July 30, 2005, from http://www.whitehouse.gov/omb.

Fletcher, P. D. (1997). Local governments and IRM: Policy emerging from practice. *Government Information Quarterly, 14*(3), 313–324. doi:10.1016/S0740-624X(97)90007-1

General Accountability Office. (2004a). *Electronic government: Federal agencies have made progress implementing the e-government act of 2002*. (GAO Publication No. GAO-05-12). Washington, DC: U.S. Government Printing Office.

General Accountability Office. (2004b). *Federal chief information officers: Responsibilities, reporting, relationships, tenure, and challenges*. (GAO Publication No. GAO-04-823). Washington, DC: U.S. Government Printing Office.

General Accountability Office. (2005a) *Management reform: Assessing the President's Management Agenda*. (GAO Publication No. GAO-05-574T). Washington, DC: U.S. Government Printing Office.

General Accountability Office. (2005b). *Chief information officers: Responsibilities and information and technology governance at leading private-sector companies*. (GAO Publication No. GAO-05-986). Washington, DC: U.S. Government Printing Office.

Grant, G., & Chau, D. (2005). Developing a generic framework for e-government. *Journal of Global Information Management, 13*(1), 1–30.

Gronlund, A. (2005). State of the art in e-gov research: Surveying conference publications. *International Journal of Electronic Government Research, 1*(4), 1–25.

Gronlund, A., & Horan, T. (2004). Introducing e-gov: History, definitions, and Issues. *Communications of the Association for Information Systems, 15*, 713–729.

Helsloot, I., & Ruitenberg, A. (2004). Citizen Response to Disasters: A Survey of Literature and Some Practical Implications. *Journal of Contingencies and Crisis Management, 12*(3), 98–111. doi:10.1111/j.0966-0879.2004.00440.x

Ho, A. T.-K. (2002). Reinventing local government and the e-government initiative. *Public Administration Review, 62*(4), 434–444. doi:10.1111/0033-3352.00197

Ho, A. T.-K., & Ni, A. Y. (2004). Explaining the adoption of E-government Features: A Case Study of Iowa County Treasurers' Offices. *American Review of Public Administration, 34*(2), 164–180. doi:10.1177/0275074004264355

Ho, A. T.-K., & Smith, J. F. (2001). Information technology planning and the Y2K problem in local governments. *American Review of Public Administration, 31*(2), 158–180. doi:10.1177/02750740122064901

ITAA. (2004). *CIO: Catalyst for Business Transformation 2004 Survey of Federal Chief Information Officers*. Retrieved July 30, 2005, from http://www.grantthornton.com

ITAA. (2005). *Issues in Leadership: 2005 Survey of Federal Chief Information Officers.* Retrieved July 30, 2005, from http://www.grantthornton.com.

Jaeger, P.T., Shneiderman, B., Fleishmann, K.R., Preece, J., Qu, Y., & Wu, P.F. (2007). Community Response Grids: E-Government, Social Networks, and Effective Emergency Management. *Telecommunications Policy, 31*(10-11), 592.604.

Layne, K., & Lee, J. (2001). Developing Fully Function E-Government: A Four Stage Model. *Government Information Quarterly, 18*(1), 122–136. doi:10.1016/S0740-624X(01)00066-1

Mahler, J., & Regan, P. M. (2002). Learning to govern online: Federal agency Internet use. *American Review of Public Administration, 32*(3), 326–349. doi:10.1177/0275074002032003004

McClure, C. R., & Bertot, J. C. (2000). The Chief Information Officer (CIO): Assessing its Impact. *Government Information Quarterly, 17*(1), 7–12. doi:10.1016/S0740-624X(99)00021-0

McClure, C. R., & Jaeger, P. T. (2008). Government Information Policy Research: Importance, Approaches, and Realities. *Library & Information Science Research, 30*(4), 257–264. doi:10.1016/j.lisr.2008.05.004

Moon, M. J., & Norris, D. F. (2005a). Advancing e-government at the grassroots: Tortoise or Hare? *Public Administration Review, 65*(1), 64–75. doi:10.1111/j.1540-6210.2005.00431.x

Moon, M. J., & Norris, D. F. (2005b). Does managerial orientation matter? The adoption of reinventing government and e-government at the municipal level. *Information Systems Journal, 15*, 43–60. doi:10.1111/j.1365-2575.2005.00185.x

National Research Council. (2007). *Improving Disaster Management: The Role of IT in Mitigation, Preparedness, Response, and Recovery.* Committee on Using Information Technology to Enhance Disaster Management. Retrieved January 26, 2009 from www.nap.edu/catalog/11824.html

Palen, L., Hiltz, S. R., & Liu, S. B. (2007). Online Forums Supporting Grassroots Participation in Emergency Preparedness and Response. *Communications of the ACM, 50*(3), 54–58. doi:10.1145/1226736.1226766

Rainey, H. G., & Bozeman, B. (2000). Comparing public and private organizations: Empirical research and the power of the a priori. *Journal of Public Administration: Research and Theory, 10*(2), 447–469.

Relyea, H. C. (2000). Paperwork Reduction Act reauthorization and government information management issues. *Government Information Quarterly, 17*(4), 367–393. doi:10.1016/S0740-624X(00)00048-4

Rochelleau, B., & Wu, L. (2002). Public versus private information systems do they differ in important ways? A Review and Empirical Test. *American Review of Public Administration*, *32*(4), 379–397. doi:10.1177/027507402237866

Schelin, S. H. (2003). E-government an overview. In G.D. Garson (ed.) *Public Information Technology: Policy and Management Issues*. Hershey, PA: Idea Group Publishing.

Seifert, J. W., & Relyea, H. C. (2004). Considering E-government from the U.S. federal perspective: An evolving concept, a developing practice. *Journal of E-Government*, *1*(1), 7–15. doi:10.1300/J399v01n01_02

Stowers, G. (2004). Issues in e-commerce and e-government service delivery. In A. Pavlichev, & G.D. Garson. *Digital Government: Principles and Best Practices*. Hershey, PA: Idea Group Publishing.

Swain, J. W., White, J., & Hubbert, E. D. (1995). Issues in public management information systems. *American Review of Public Administration*, *25*(3), 279–296. doi:10.1177/027507409502500305

Thomas, J. C., & Streib, G. (2003). The New Face of Government: Citizen-Initiated Contacts in the Era of E-Government. *Journal of Public Administration: Research and Theory*, *13*(1), 83–102. doi:10.1093/jpart/mug010

Ugbah, S. D., & Umeh, O. J. (1993). Information resource management: An examination of individual and organizational attributes in state government agencies. *Information Resources Management Journal*, *6*(1), 5–13.

Wang, X., & Kapucu, N. (2008). Public Complacency under Repeated Emergency Threats: Some Empirical Evidence. *Journal of Public Administration: Research and Theory*, *18*(1), 57–78. doi:10.1093/jopart/mum001

Ward, M. A., & Mitchell, S. (2004). A comparison of the strategic priorities of public and private sector information resource management executives. *Government Information Quarterly*, *21*, 284–304. doi:10.1016/j.giq.2004.04.003

West, D. M. (2004). E-government and the transformation of service delivery and citizen attitudes. *Public Administration Review*, *64*(1), 15–27. doi:10.1111/j.1540-6210.2004.00343.x

Westerback, L. K. (2000). Toward best practices for strategic information technology management. *Government Information Quarterly*, *17*(1), 27–41. doi:10.1016/S0740-624X(99)00023-4

APPENDIX A: CONGRESSIONAL RESEARCH SERVICE SUMMARY OF THE *E-GOVERNMENT ACT* OF 2002

H.R. 2458

Title: To enhance the management and promotion of electronic Government services and processes by establishing a Federal Chief Information Officer within the Office of Management and Budget, and by establishing a broad framework of measures that require using Internet-based information technology to enhance citizen access to Government information and services, and for other purposes.
Sponsor: Rep Turner, Jim [TX-2] (introduced 7/11/2001)
Related Bills: S.803
Latest Major Action: Became Public Law No: 107-347
House Reports: 107-787 Part 1
SUMMARY AS OF: 11/15/2002--Passed House amended.
E-Government Act of 2002 –

Title I: Office of Management and Budget Electronic Government Services –

(Sec. 101) Establishes in the Office of Management and Budget (OMB) an Office of Electronic Government, headed by an Administrator appointed by the President. Requires the Administrator to assist the Director and Deputy Director for Management and work with the Administrator of the Office of Information and Regulatory Affairs in setting strategic direction for implementing electronic Government under relevant statutes, including the Privacy Act, the Government Paperwork Elimination Act, and the Federal Information Security Management Act of 2002. Defines "electronic Government" (E-Government) as the use by Government of web-based Internet applications and other information technologies, combined with processes that implement these technologies, to: (1) enhance the access to and delivery of Government information and services; or (2) bring about improvements in Government operations.

Directs the Administrator to work with offices within OMB to oversee implementation of E-Government in areas including: (1) capital planning and investment control for information technology (IT); (2) the development of enterprise architectures; (3) information security; (4) privacy; (5) access to, dissemination of, and preservation of Government information; and (6) accessibility of IT for persons with disabilities.

Directs the Administrator to assist the Director by performing E-Government functions, including: (1) advising on the resources required to develop and effectively administer E-Government initiatives; (2) recommending changes relating to government-wide strategies and priorities for E-Government; (3) providing overall leadership and direction to the executive branch on E-Government; (4) promoting innovative uses of IT by agencies; (5) overseeing the distribution of funds from, and ensuring appropriate administration and coordination of, the E-Government Fund (established by this Act); (6) coordinating with the Administrator of General Services regarding programs undertaken by the General Services Administration (GSA) to promote E-Government and the efficient use of information technologies by agencies; (7) leading the activities of the Chief Information Officers Council (established by this Act) on behalf of the Deputy Director for Management (who shall chair the council); (8) assisting in establishing policies which shall set the framework for Government IT standards developed by the National Institute of Standards and Technology (NIST) and promulgated by the Secretary of Commerce; (9) coordinating with the Administrator for Federal Procurement Policy to ensure effective implementation of electronic procurement initiatives; and (10) assisting Federal agencies in implementing accessibility standards under the Rehabilitation Act of 1973 and ensuring compliance with those standards.

Establishes in the executive branch a Chief Information Officers Council. Designates the Council as the principal interagency forum for improving agency practices related to the design, acquisition, development, modernization, use, operation, sharing, and performance of Federal Government information resources.

Requires the Council to perform functions that include: (1) developing recommendations for the Director on Government information resources management policies and requirements; (2) sharing experiences, ideas, best practices, and innovative approaches related to information resources management; (3) assisting the Administrator in the identification, development, and coordination of multi-agency projects and other innovative initiatives to improve Government performance through the use of IT; (4) promoting the development and use of common performance measures for agency information resources management; (5) working with NIST and the Administrator to develop recommendations on IT standards; (6) working with the Office of Personnel Management (OPM) to assess the hiring, training, classification, and professional development needs of the Government related to information resources management; and (7) working with the Archivist of the United States on how the Federal Records Act can be addressed effectively by Federal information resources management activities.

Establishes in the U.S. Treasury the E-Government Fund to support projects to expand the Government's ability to conduct activities electronically, including efforts to: (1) make Government information and services more readily available to members of the public; (2) make it easier for the public to conduct transactions with the Government; and (3) enable Federal agencies to take advantage of IT in sharing information and conducting transactions with each other and with State and local governments.

Requires the Administrator to: (1) establish procedures for accepting and reviewing proposals for funding; and (2) assist the Director in coordinating resources that agencies receive from the Fund with other resources available to agencies for similar purposes. Sets forth provisions regarding procedures the Administrator shall incorporate, criteria to be considered in determining which proposals to recommend for funding, and permissible uses of funds.

Directs the Administrator to: (1) establish a Government-wide program to encourage contractor innovation and excellence in facilitating the development and enhancement of E-Government services and processes, under which the Administrator shall issue announcements seeking unique and innovative solutions to facilitate such development and enhancement; and (2) convene a multi-agency technical assistance team to assist in screening solution proposals.

Requires the Director to submit an annual E-Government status report.

(Sec. 102) Requires the Administrator of General Services to consult with the Administrator of the Office of Electronic Government on programs undertaken by GSA to promote E-Government and the efficient use of IT by Federal agencies.

Title II: Federal Management and Promotion of Electronic Government Services –

(Sec. 202) Makes the head of each agency responsible for: (1) complying with the requirements of this Act, the related information resource management policies and guidance established by the Director of OMB, and the related IT standards promulgated by the Secretary of Commerce; (2) communicating such policies, guidance, and related IT standards to all relevant agency officials; and (3) supporting the efforts of the Director and the Administrator of GSA to develop, maintain, and promote an integrated Internet-based system of delivering Government information and services to the public.

Requires agencies to: (1) develop performance measures that demonstrate how E-Government enables progress toward agency objectives, strategic goals, and statutory mandates; (2) rely on existing data collections in measuring performance under this section; (3) link performance goals to key groups, including citizens, businesses, and other governments, and to internal Government operations; and (4) work collectively in linking performance goals to such groups and to use IT in delivering Government information and services to those groups. Includes customer service, agency productivity, and adoption of innovative IT as areas of performance measurements that agencies should consider.

Requires: (1) agency heads, when promulgating policies and implementing programs regarding the provision of Government information and services over the Internet, to consider the impact on persons without Internet access; (2) all actions taken by Federal departments and agencies under this Act to comply with the Rehabilitation Act; and (3) agencies to sponsor activities that use IT to engage the public in the development and implementation of policies and programs.

Makes the Chief Information Officer (CIO) of each of the designated agencies responsible for: (1) participating in the functions of the Chief Information Officers Council; and (2) monitoring the implementation of IT standards promulgated by the Secretary of Commerce, including common standards for interconnectivity and interoperability, categorization of Government electronic information, and computer system efficiency and security.

Requires each agency to submit to the Director an annual E-Government status report.

Makes this title inapplicable to national security systems, with exceptions.

(Sec. 203) Requires: (1) each executive agency to ensure that its methods for use and acceptance of electronic signatures are compatible with the relevant policies and procedures issued by the Director; and (2) the Administrator of General Services to support the Director by establishing a framework to allow efficient interoperability among executive agencies when using electronic signatures.

(Sec. 204) Requires the Director to work with the Administrator of GSA and other agencies to maintain and promote an integrated Internet-based system of providing the public with access to Government information and services, based on specified criteria.

(Sec. 205) Directs the Chief Justice of the United States, the chief judge of each circuit and district and of the Court of Federal Claims, and the chief bankruptcy judge of each district to cause to be established and maintained a court website that contains specified information or links to websites, including location and contact information for the courthouse, local rules, access to docket information, access to the substance of all written opinions issued by the court, access to documents filed with the courthouse in electronic form, and other information deemed useful to the public. Requires the information and rules on each website to be updated regularly.

Requires each court to make any document that is filed electronically publicly available online, with exceptions (such as sealed documents). Directs the Supreme Court to prescribe rules to protect privacy and security concerns relating to electronic filing of documents and their public availability, providing for uniform treatment of privacy and security issues throughout the Federal courts, taking into consideration best practices in Federal and State courts, and meeting requirements regarding the filing of an unredacted document under seal.

Sets forth provisions regarding the issuance by Judicial Conference of the United States of interim and final rules on privacy and security. Directs the Judicial Conference to explore the feasibility of technology to post online dockets with links allowing all filings, decisions, and rulings in each case to be obtained from the docket sheet of that case.

Amends the Judiciary Appropriations Act, 1992 to authorize (currently, requires) the Judicial Conference to prescribe reasonable fees for collection by the courts for access to information available through automatic data processing equipment.

Requires the websites to be established within two years of this title's effective date, except that access to documents filed in electronic form shall be established within four years.

Authorizes the Chief Justice, a chief judge, or a chief bankruptcy judge to submit a notification to the Administrative Office of the United States Courts to defer compliance with any requirement of this section with respect to that court, subject to specified requirements. Sets forth reporting requirements regarding notifications.

(Sec. 206) Requires that each agency, subject to a specified timetable and limitations: (1) ensure that a publicly accessible Government website includes all information about that agency required to be published in the Federal Register under the Freedom of Information Act; (2) accept submissions by electronic means; (3) ensure that a publicly accessible Government website contains electronic dockets for rule-makings.

(Sec. 207) Requires the Director to establish the Interagency Committee on Government Information to: (1) engage in public consultation, including with interested communities such as public and advocacy organizations; (2) conduct studies and submit recommendations to the Director and Congress; and (3) share effective practices for access to, dissemination of, and retention of Federal information.

Requires the Committee to submit recommendations to the Director on: (1) the adoption of standards to enable the organization and categorization of Government information in a way that is searchable electronically and in ways that are interoperable across agencies; (2) the definition of categories of Government information which should be classified under the standards; and (3)determining priorities and developing schedules for initial implementation of the standards by agencies. Requires the Director to issue policies to effectuate such recommendations.

Requires the Committee to submit recommendations to the Director and the Archivist of the United States on, and directs the Archivist to require, the adoption by agencies of policies and procedures to ensure that specified Federal statutes are applied effectively and comprehensively to Government information on the Internet and to other electronic records Requires the Director to promulgate guidance for agency websites that includes: (1) requirements that websites include direct links to descriptions of the mission and statutory authority of the agency, information made available under the Freedom of Information Act, information about the organizational structure of the agency, and the strategic plan of the agency; and (2) minimum agency goals to assist public users to navigate agency websites, including goals pertaining to the speed of retrieval of search results, the relevance of the results, tools to aggregate and dis-aggregate data, and security protocols to protect information.

Requires each agency to: (1) solicit public comment; (2) establish a process for determining which Government information the agency intends to make available to the public on the Internet and by other means; (3) develop priorities and schedules for making Government information available and accessible; (4) make such final determinations available for public comment; (5) post such final determinations on the Internet; and (6) report such final determinations, to the Director.

Requires the Director and each agency to: (1) establish a public domain directory of public Government websites; and (2) post the directory on the Internet with a link to the integrated Internet-based system. Requires the Administrator of the Office of Electronic Government to update the directory at least every six months and solicit interested persons for improvements to the directory.

Requires the Director of OMB to ensure the development and maintenance of: (1) a repository that fully integrates information about research and development (R&D) funded by the Federal Government; and (2) one or more websites upon which all or part of the repository of Federal R&D shall be made available to and searchable by Federal agencies and non-Federal entities, including the general public, to facilitate the coordination of Federal R&D activities, collaboration among those conducting Federal R&D, the transfer of technology among Federal agencies and between Federal agencies and non-Federal entities, and access by policymakers and the public to information concerning Federal R&D activities.

Authorizes appropriations.

(Sec. 208) Requires each agency to conduct a privacy impact assessment, ensure the review of that assessment by the Chief Information Officer or equivalent official, and make such assessment publicly available, before: (1) developing or procuring IT that collects, maintains, or disseminates information that is in an identifiable form; or (2) initiating a new collection of information that will be collected, maintained, or disseminated using IT and that includes any information in an identifiable form permitting the physical or online contacting of a specified individual if identical questions have been posed to, or identical reporting requirements have been imposed on, ten or more persons other than Federal agencies, instrumentalities, or employees.

Sets forth provisions regarding modifying or waiving requirements of this section for security reasons or to protect classified, sensitive, or private information.

Requires the Director to issue guidance to agencies specifying the required contents of a privacy impact assessment. Requires the guidance to: (1) ensure that a privacy impact assessment is commensurate with the size of the information system being assessed, the sensitivity of information that is in an identifiable form, and the risk of harm from unauthorized release of that information; and (2) require that such assessment address what information is to be collected, why it is being collected, the intended use of the information, with whom it will be shared, what notice or opportunities for consent would be provided to individuals, how the information will be secured, and whether a system of records is being created under the Privacy Act. Requires the Director to: (1) develop policies and guidelines on conducting such assessments; (2) oversee implementation of the assessment process throughout the Government; and (3) require agencies to conduct assessments of existing information systems or ongoing collections of information that is in an identifiable form.

Requires the Director to develop guidance for privacy notices on agency websites used by the public.

(Sec. 209) Requires the Director of OPM to: (1) analyze, on an ongoing basis, the personnel needs of the Government related to IT and information resource management; (2) identify where current IT and information resource management training do not satisfy such needs; (3) oversee the development of curricula, training methods, and training priorities that correspond to the projected needs; and (4) assess the training of Federal employees in IT disciplines to ensure that information resource management needs of the Government are addressed.

Requires each agency head to establish and operate IT training programs that: (1) have curricula covering a broad range of IT disciplines corresponding to the specific IT and information resource management needs; (2) are developed and applied according to rigorous standards; and (3) are designed to maximize efficiency through the use of self-paced courses, on-the-job training, and the use of remote instructors.

Requires the Director of OPM to: (1) issue policies to promote the development of performance standards for training and uniform implementation of this section by executive agencies; and (2) evaluate implementation.

Sets forth provisions regarding chief information officer authorities and responsibilities, IT training reporting, authority to detail employees to non-Federal employers, and employee participation. Authorizes appropriations.

Authorizes an agency head to arrange for the assignment of an agency employee to a private sector organization or of an employee of such an organization to the agency. States that an eligible employee is one who works in the IT management field, is considered an exceptional performer by the individual's current employer, is expected to assume increased IT management responsibilities in the future, and is employed at the GS-11 level or above. Sets forth provisions regarding assignment agreements, termination and duration of assignments, assistance in maintaining lists of potential candidates, and considerations in exercising authority under this section.

Authorizes the Chief Technology Officer of the District of Columbia to arrange for such an assignment in the same manner as the head of an agency.

Sets forth provisions regarding reporting requirements, regulations prescribed by the Director of OPM, and ethics provisions (including restrictions on the disclosure of confidential communications, contract advice by former detailees, and the disclosure of procurement information).

(Sec. 210) Authorizes an agency head to enter into a share-in-savings contract for IT in which the Government awards a contract to improve mission-related or administrative processes, or to accelerate the achievement of its mission, and to share with the contractor savings achieved through contract performance. Limits such a contract to a five year period, with exceptions. Sets forth reporting requirements by the Director of OMB and by the Comptroller General regarding such contracts. Repeals the share-in-savings pilot program.

(Sec. 211) Authorizes the Administrator to provide for the use by State or local governments of Federal supply schedules of GSA for automated data processing equipment, software, supplies, support equipment, and services.

(Sec. 212) Requires the Director to: (1) oversee a study and report to specified congressional committees on progress toward integrating Federal information systems across agencies; and (2) designate a series of no more than five pilot projects that integrate data elements.

(Sec. 213) Directs the Administrator to: (1) ensure that a study is conducted to evaluate the best practices of community technology centers that have received Federal funds; (2) work with other relevant Federal agencies and other interested persons to assist in the implementation of recommendations and to identify other ways to assist community technology centers, public libraries, and other institutions that provide computer and Internet access to the public; and (3) develop an online tutorial that explains how to access Government information and services on the Internet and that provides a guide to available online resources. Authorizes appropriations.

(Sec. 214) Directs the Administrator to: (1) ensure that a study is conducted on using IT to enhance crisis preparedness, response, and consequence management of natural and manmade disasters; and

(2) initiate and cooperate with other agencies and appropriate State, local, and tribal governments in initiating pilot projects or report to Congress on other activities aimed at maximizing the utility of IT in disaster management.

(Sec. 215) Directs the Administrator of GSA to request that the National Academy of Sciences, acting through the National Research Council, enter into a contract to conduct a study on disparities in Internet access for online Government services.

(Sec. 216) Requires the Administrator to facilitate the development of common protocols for the development, acquisition, maintenance, distribution, and application of geographic information.

Title III: Information Security –

Federal Information Security Management Act of 2002 - Requires the Director of OMB to oversee agency information security policies and practices, including by: (1) developing and overseeing the implementation of policies, principles, standards, and guidelines on information security; (2) requiring agencies to identify and provide information security protections commensurate with the risk and magnitude of the harm resulting from the unauthorized access, use, disclosure, disruption, modification, or destruction of information or information systems used or operated by an agency or by a contractor on behalf of an agency; (3) coordinating the development of standards and guidelines under the National Institute of Standards and Technology Act with agencies exercising control of national security systems to assure that such standards and guidelines are complementary with those developed for national security systems; (4) overseeing agency compliance with this Act; (5) reviewing at least annually, and approving or disapproving, agency information security programs; (6) coordinating information security policies and procedures with related information resources management policies and procedures; (7) overseeing the operating of the Federal information security incident center; and (8) reporting to Congress by March 1 of each year on agency compliance with this Act.

Sets forth provisions regarding delegation of the Director's authority regarding certain systems operated by the Department of Defense and by the Central Intelligence Agency.

Directs the head of each agency to: (1) be responsible for providing information security protections commensurate with the risk and magnitude of the harm resulting from unauthorized access and for complying with information security standards and guidelines; (2) ensure that senior agency officials provide information security for the information and information systems that support operations and assets; (3) delegate to the agency CIO the authority to ensure compliance with the regulations imposed under this Act; (4) ensure that the agency has trained personnel sufficient to assist the agency in complying with Act requirements; and (5) ensure that the agency CIO reports annually on the effectiveness of the agency information security program.

Requires each agency to develop, document, and implement an agency-wide information security program to provide information security for the information and information systems that support operations and assets. Requires such program to include: (1) periodic risk assessments; (2) policies and procedures that ensure that information security is addressed throughout the life cycle of each agency information system; (3) subordinate plans for providing adequate information security for networks, facilities, and systems or groups of information systems; (4) security awareness training; (5) periodic testing and evaluation of the effectiveness of information security policies, procedures, and practices; (6) a process for planning, implementing, evaluating, and documenting remedial action to address deficiencies; (7) procedures for detecting, reporting, and responding to security incidents; and (8) plans and procedures to ensure continuity of operations for information systems that support the operations and assets of the agency.

Requires each agency to: (1) report annually to the Director, specified congressional committees, and the Comptroller General on the adequacy and effectiveness of information security policies, procedures, and practices and on compliance with this Act; (2) address such adequacy and effectiveness in plans and reports relating to annual agency budgets, information resources management, IT management, program performance, financial management, financial management systems, and internal accounting and administrative controls; and (3) report any significant deficiency.

Sets forth requirements regarding performance plans, and public notice and comment. Requires each agency to have performed an annual independent evaluation.

Requires the Director to: (1) summarize the results of the evaluations and report to Congress; and (2) ensure the operation of a central Federal information security incident center. Requires each agency exercising control of a national security system to share information about information security incidents, threats, and vulnerabilities with the center to the extent consistent with standards and guidelines for national security systems).

(Sec. 302) Directs that standards and guidelines for national security systems be developed, prescribed, enforced, and overseen as otherwise authorized by law and as directed by the President.

Requires the Secretary to make standards prescribed for Federal information systems compulsory and binding as necessary to improve the efficiency of operation or security of such systems. Requires that the decision by the Secretary regarding the promulgation of standards under this section occur within six months of submission of the proposed standard by NIST.

(Sec. 303) Amends the National Institute of Standards and Technology Act to provide that NIST shall: (1) have the mission of developing standards, guidelines, and associated methods and techniques for information (currently, computer) systems; (2) develop standards and guidelines, including minimum requirements, for information systems used or operated by an agency or by a contractor on behalf of an agency, other than national security systems; and (3) develop standards and guidelines, including minimum requirements, for providing adequate information security for all agency operations and assets.

(Sec. 304) Renames the Computer System Security and Privacy Advisory Board as the Information Security and Privacy Advisory Board. Includes among its duties to advise the Director (currently limited to the Institute and the Secretary) on information security and privacy issues pertaining to Government information systems.

(Sec. 305) Amends the Paperwork Reduction Act to require each agency head to develop and maintain an inventory of major information systems (including major national security systems) operated or under the control of such agency, including an identification of the interfaces between each such system and all other systems or networks. Requires such inventory to be: (1) updated at least annually; (2) made available to the Comptroller General; and (3) used to support information resources management.

Title IV: Authorization of Appropriations and Effective Dates –

(Sec. 401) Authorizes appropriations to carry out titles I and II for FY 2003 through 2007.

Title V: Confidential Information Protection and Statistical Efficiency –

Confidential Information Protection and Statistical Efficiency Act of 2002 - (Sec. 503) Authorizes agencies to promulgate rules to implement this title. Requires the Director to: (1) coordinate and oversee the confidentiality and disclosure policies established by this title; and (2) review any rules proposed by an agency pursuant to this title. Sets forth reporting requirements.

(Sec. 504) Prohibits data or information acquired by the Energy Information Administration under a pledge of confidentiality and designated by that Administration to be used for exclusively statistical purposes from being disclosed in identifiable form for non-statistical purposes under specified energy statutes.

Subtitle A: Confidential Information Protection - (Sec. 512) Directs that data or information acquired by an agency under a pledge of confidentiality and for exclusively statistical purposes be used by officers, employees, or agents of the agency exclusively for statistical purposes.

Bars the use of data or information acquired by an agency under a pledge of confidentiality for exclusively statistical purposes from being disclosed by an agency in identifiable form for use other than an exclusively statistical purpose, except with the respondent's informed consent.

Requires a statistical agency or unit to clearly distinguish data or information it collects for non-statistical purposes (as authorized by law) and provide notice to the public, before it is collected, that it could be used for non-statistical purposes.

Allows a statistical agency or unit to designate agents who may perform exclusively statistical activities, subject to specified limitations and penalties.

(Sec. 513) Sets penalties for willfully disclosing information to a person or agency not entitled to receive it.

Subtitle B: Statistical Efficiency - Requires the head of each of the Designated Statistical Agencies (DSA) (defined as the Bureau of the Census and the Bureau of Economic Analysis of the Department of Commerce and the Bureau of Labor Statistics of the Department of Labor) to: (1) identify opportunities to eliminate duplication and otherwise reduce reporting burden and cost imposed on the public in providing information for statistical purposes; (2) enter into joint statistical projects to improve the quality and reduce the cost of statistical programs; and (3) protect the confidentiality of individually identifiable information acquired for statistical purposes by adhering to safeguard principles.

(Sec. 524) Allows a DSA to provide business data in an identifiable form to another DSA under the terms of a written agreement.

(Sec. 525) Requires: (1) business data provided by a DSA pursuant to this subtitle to be used exclusively for statistical purposes; and (2) publication of data acquired by a DSA in a manner whereby the data furnished by any particular respondent are not in identifiable form.

Chapter 3
Collaboration and E-Government

INTRODUCTION

Collaboration is an important element in the advancement of e-government (Hu et al., 2006). This chapter examines the level of collaboration among state governments to see how advanced they are in e-government. Collaboration is critical in homeland security because it is one of the often cited challenges in the time of a crisis (Reddick, 2008). In order to understand Homeland Security Information Systems (HSIS), one must delve into the impact of collaboration and e-government.

There is a growing body of research on e-government and its impact on managerial effectiveness; with collaboration being an important area of management effectiveness (Yang and Paul, 2005; Reddick 2007). This chapter examines how state governments measure up against some noted principles of effective collaboration. The role of citizens in the collaborative process is examined, with citizens arguably being the key to more effective collaborative efforts through e-government (Vigoda-Gadot, 2002). Indeed, research shows that citizen involvement in the decision-making process through collaborative efforts will enhance democracy and accountability of governments (Vigoda-Gadot, 2003).

In order to examine collaboration and e-government this chapter first outlines several key principles of effective collaboration and relates them to e-government. Second, this chapter provides a conceptual framework of collaboration and e-government. Third, there is a data analysis of a survey of Chief Information Officers (CIO) opinions on collaboration and e-government. The conclusion of this chapter summarizes and examines the impact of collaboration on HSIS.

DOI: 10.4018/978-1-60566-834-5.ch003

BACKGROUND

There are many definitions of e-government discussed in Chapter 2. Some look at e-government exclusively as it relates to the Internet adoption in governments (Moon, 2002). Other definitions of e-government examine it in relation to information technology's (IT) impact on the governance of organizations (Gronlund, 2005). The definition, provided by the Government Accountability Office (GAO), used in this chapter takes into account collaboration. The term e-government refers to the use of IT, particularly Web-based Internet applications, to enhance the access to and delivery of government information and services to citizens, to business partners, to employees, and among agencies at all levels of government (GAO, 2003b). This definition takes into account the Internet as one of the main vehicles for e-government, but also leaves room for other types of IT. More importantly, it also considers the interrelationship between different stakeholders and the e-government process, something that is supposed to influence collaboration (Sharma, 2004).

There are also many definitions of collaboration. One common definition offered by Bardach (1998) defines collaboration as any joint activity by two or more agencies that can be used to increase the public value by working together rather than working separately. Agranoff and McGuire (2003) further believe that collaboration can occur both vertically across different levels of government such as federal, state, and local and horizontally with players representing different interests in the community. Therefore, collaborative efforts can involve intra-agency and/or inter-agency dimensions.

The definition of collaboration that is used in this chapter is also taken from the GAO. In the context of e-government, collaboration can be defined as a mutually beneficial and well-defined relationship entered into by two or more organizations to achieve common goals (GAO, 2003b). This definition takes into account the important dimensions of Bardach's (1998) work, but sets collaboration in the context of e-government. The following question should be asked, why would governments want to engage in collaboration? Huxham and Vangen (2005) provide some reasons for collaboration that should be briefly mentioned:

1. Organizations often collaborate if they are unable to achieve their objectives with their own resources;
2. Sharing of risk is a reason often cited for collaboration;
3. Governments sometimes believe that commercial organizations are more efficient providers of services than public entities, arguing for collaboration on efficiency grounds;
4. There is a belief by some that the provision of public services will become seamless and coordinated as a result of successful collaboration;
5. There is the argument of learning more about a process because of some joint activity; and
6. There is the argument of the moral dimension of collaboration. For instance, the really important issues of society cannot be tackled by an organization acting alone.

What does collaboration mean in the context of e-government? There are three public administration arguments for the study of collaboration and e-government. According to Allen, Juillet, Paquet, and Roy (2005), e-government requires an important shift in the nature of collaborative governance according to three dimensions. First, technology applications create new opportunities to link together organizations. Second, policy changes require a growing level of collaboration across levels of government and sectors.

Third, improving performance in the public sector requires an increasingly interconnected society and also the alignment of those to potential business partners, citizens, and other key stakeholders.

Finally, why is it important to understand collaboration in the context of HSIS? HSIS can influence the level of collaboration and facilitate achieving homeland security-related objectives in the different levels of government and across the same government. Essentially, collaboration will be promoted by the use of HSIS and, therefore, should be discussed in the context of e-government. In order to understand the impact of HSIS on government, one must understand the extent of collaboration as a result of e-government. An important element of collaboration and HSIS is information sharing between governments as the next section will examine.

INFORMATION SHARING

In order to discern the context of information sharing, a survey in 2007 by the National Governors Association (NGA) of 56 state government homeland security advisors found that public safety interoperability communication was at the top of the list of homeland security advisors' concerns (NGA, 2007). Their survey indicated that almost all states have a statewide interoperability communications governance structure in place. There were around 70 percent of states that have a full-time interoperability coordinator at the state level.

One of the major issues in emergency management is that the majority of command and control activities for emergencies depend upon communications based on analogue technologies using radio waves (Ryoo and Choi, 2006). This technology can be effective when a small number of first responders are working in the vicinity of each other. However, this technology deteriorates when there are multiple groups of responders using different types of equipment. There also is a greater likelihood of distortion with analog technology and it does not leave an audit trail like digital technology. As a result, analog technology can impede information sharing during a disaster.

Wybo and Lonka (2002) believe that IT has the great potential to improve organizational performance during an emergency. This can be done by providing correct and timely information to anticipate situations and take the appropriate actions, by providing reliable communication channels, by providing tools and applications that can simulate the problem, monitor situations, and track resources.

One of the key recommendations of the 9/11 Commission Report was better information sharing among departments and agencies and levels of government (9/11 Commission Report, 2004). Specifically, the 9/11 Commission Report stated (p. 416-417):

The U.S. government has access to a vast amount of information. When databases not usually thought of as "intelligence," such as customs or immigration information, are included, the storehouse is immense. But the U.S. government has a weak system for processing and using what it has. In interviews around the government, official after official urged us to call attention to frustrations with the unglamorous "back office" side of government operations... In the 9/11 story, for example, we sometimes see examples of information that could be accessed—like the undistributed NSA [National Security Administration] information that would have helped identify Nawaf al Hazmi in January 2000. But someone had to ask for it. In that case, no one did.

The 9/11 Commission found that information is being distributed, but it is compartmentalized located within a specific agency and not shared. The Commission found that there was a mentality of the "need to know" before sharing of information could occur. The Commission calls this a Cold War assumption of weighing the risk of disclosure against the benefits of wider information sharing. The Commission made a recommendation of changing the culture of federal agencies from ownership of information to sharing the information to help protect the homeland. This is a common theme identified in state and local governments, where it is difficult to get actionable information from the federal government.

In a GAO (2003a) survey on homeland security information sharing among federal, state, and city officials, survey results revealed certain information was important for them to receive, but they were not routinely getting this information. Officials that completed the survey indicated that they are typically receiving less than 50% of the categories of information they actually need. Some of this information they thought they needed was broad threat information, specific and actionable threat information, movement of Weapons of Mass Destruction (WMD), movement of know terrorists, and so forth. For example, there was between 90% to 98% of state and large and small cities that reported they needed specific and actionable threat information, but only 21% to 33% of them reported that they received this information. However, more than 50% of respondents were receiving broad threat information. The information that these governments received was not viewed as being very timely, accurate, or relevant to their preparedness efforts.

NATIONAL INFORMATION EXCHANGE MODEL

One example of using HSIS to share information is the National Information Exchange Model (NIEM). This project was designed to develop, disseminate, and support enterprise-wide information sharing and standards through justice, public safety, emergency management, intelligence, and homeland security through all levels of government (NIEM, 2007). One of the criticism as noted of the 9/11 commission report, was the inability of agencies to share information. NIEM is envisioned to provide an enterprise architecture that is able to share information across levels of government. NIEM is designed to provide for the development of an enterprise-wide information exchange standards, which can be uniformly developed and maintained.

The NIEM was established in February 28, 2005, through a partnership between federal Chief Information Officers (CIO), the Department of Homeland Security, and the Department of Justice. The NIEM uses the data standards implemented through the Department of Justice's Global Justice Information Sharing Initiative and uses the eXtensible Markup Language (XML) data model. The NIEM is taken from Homeland Security Presidential Directive 5 of managing domestic incidents through a national incident management system. Sharing information is done through XML is an initiative that allows information and services to be encoded with meaningful structure and semantics. NIEM should have an impact on HSIS given that one of the common criticisms leveled against emergency response is the lack of common communication standards; NIEM could go part way towards addressing this problem.

ENTERPRISE ARCHITECTURE AND HSIS

In order to understand collaboration in HSIS one must understand enterprise architecture. An enterprise architecture generally connects an organization's strategic plan with its information systems. An enterprise architecture as defined by the GAO (2007) is a corporate blueprint that serves as an authoritative guide for IT development. The enterprise architecture provides a clear picture of the organizations and where IT fits into the organization. The GAO (2004) believes that a well defined enterprise architecture is essential for the organization's success because it eliminates duplication, promotes interoperability, reduces costs, and optimizes the performance of the organization. GAO (2004) has criticized the DHS for not having an effective enterprise architecture in place.

Enterprise architecture is part of e-government reform effort (Hjort-Madsen, 2007). According to the GAO (2004), enterprise architecture is the trademark of an effective public and private sector organizations. The Clinger-Cohen Act of 1996 mandates that an agency's CIO develop, maintain, and facilitate the implementation of an IT architecture. Furthermore, the E-Government Act of 2002 requires the OMB to oversee the development of enterprise architectures within and across federal agencies.

Interoperability between information systems can be defined as the ability to exchange information and use information which has been exchanged (Guijarro, 2006). An interoperability framework would enable communication between different agencies to respond to disasters in an integrated fashion. Enterprise architecture is the comprehensive mapping of all key information system elements of the organization. Enterprise architecture attempts to align the business processes and goals of the organization with its applications and technical infrastructure. Both enterprise architecture and interoperability can be viewed in tandem since you would need both for the organization to function effectively and be able to exchange information among all parties.

There are some criticisms leveled at the enterprise architecture approach as advocated for federal information systems. Peled (2007) believes that enterprise architecture approach is flawed since it encourages bureaucrats and consultants to ignore the information systems achievements of the past. This author advocates for a more moderate approach to information systems development focusing on incremental change from past systems. Peled advocates that systems of the past that work should be kept and new systems can be placed on top of old systems. This is very applicable to the DHS, where there is a great emphasis on an effective enterprise architecture system, perhaps ignoring the information systems that have worked well in the past.

COLLABORATIVE MANAGEMENT PRINCIPLES AND E-GOVERNMENT

The New Public Management (NPM) literature argues for the responsiveness to citizens as clients, while collaborative management argues for the more effective use of partnerships with citizens, moving away from the focus on responsiveness (Vigoda-Gadot, 2002). Critics of responsive-oriented thinking of NPM have called for a theoretical and practical shift towards increased collaboration in public administration (Vigoda-Gadot, 2004). Therefore, the collaborative management literature argues for the movement from responsiveness to collaboration, treating citizens as partners in government rather than clients.

NPM potentially breeds passivism among citizens as clients by overstating the idea of responsiveness (Vigoda-Gadot, 2004). NPM typically treats citizens as clients, by asking them about their needs and demands. However, it asks citizens to keep their distance from the administrative work and decision-making centers (Vigoda-Gadot, 2004). A criticism of NPM and e-government is about its application of citizen-centric government using a rational-goal approach, which may not be suitable for the public sector (Kolsaker and Lee-Kelley, 2006; Kolsaker, 2006). Some authors suggest that there needs to be a greater emphasis on improving existing services before embarking on transformational e-government (Kolsaker and Lee-Kelley, 2007).

E-government could possibly change this relationship from being primarily responsive to citizens to collaboration, with citizens being seen as business partners. For example, a common objective of cross-agency collaborations is to provide citizen-centric online one-stop services that maximize service accessibility and user satisfaction (Ho, 2002; Hu, Cui, and Sherwood, 2006). For example, the Federal Government's Web portal Firstgov.gov (http://www.firstgov.gov) provides a gateway to government information and services. The Web portal can be viewed as more citizen-centric given its emphasis on what citizens need in terms of information and services. Therefore, as shown in Chapter 2, this citizen-centric aspect of e-government is vital for understanding collaborative efforts and e-government. In turn, enhancing the input of key stakeholders in e-government, such as citizens, should move governments more towards collaborative management.

There are several dimensions outlined in the collaborative management literature that discuss principles of effective collaboration (Agranoff and McGuire, 2003; Huxham and Vangen, 2005). The GAO (2003b) completed a study of best practices in collaborative efforts in e-government project management. Based on their review of government, private sector, and academic research they identified five recommendations that were found to have a significant impact on collaboration, namely:

- Establishing a collaborative management structure that provides shared leadership and involvement at all levels and defines roles and responsibilities so that each participating organization is accountable for the initiative's success;
- Maintaining collaborative relationships among participants within a climate of trust and respect, including mechanisms for feedback and debate, based on formal agreements that document a shared vision for the project;
- Contributing resources equitably among all participants to reinforce the shared commitment to achieving common objectives;
- Facilitating communication and outreach that provides complete and timely information for all stakeholders to promote trust and reinforce commitment to achieving common objectives; and
- Adopting a common set of standards for use by all project partners to provide a basis upon which otherwise independent entities can agree to share or integrate data or services.

Some of these best practices are also found in the examination of case studies of inter-agency IT supported collaboration (Fedorowicz, Gogan, and Williams, 2006). Other research, by Thomson and Perry (2006), similarly to the GAO study, shows that in order for public managers to collaborate efficiently they must know five dimensions of the collaborative process: governance, administration, organizational autonomy, mutuality, and norms.

The GAO (2005) also conducted a more general study of collaborative management that identified best practices that can help enhance and sustain agency collaboration. The GAO found the following eight best practices that can help federal agencies enhance and sustain their collaborative efforts.

- *Define and articulate the common outcome*: Collaborating agencies must have a clear and compelling rationale to work together;
- *Establishing mutually reinforcing or joint strategies*: Collaborating agencies need to establish strategies that work in concert with their partners or are joint in nature;
- *Identify and address needs by leveraging resources*: Collaborating agencies should identify the human, IT, physical, and financial resources needed to initiate or sustain their collaborative effort;
- *Agree on roles and responsibilities*: Collaborative agencies should work together to define and agree on their respective roles and responsibilities, including how the collaborative effort will be led;
- *Establish compatible policies, procedures, and other means to operate across agency boundaries*: To facilitate collaboration, agencies need to address the compatibility of standards, policies, procedures, and data systems that will be used in the collaborative effort;
- *Develop mechanisms to monitor, evaluate, and report on results*: Agencies engaged in collaborative efforts need to create the means to monitor and evaluate their efforts to enable them to identify areas for improvement;
- *Reinforce agency accountability for collaborative efforts through agency plans and reports*: Agencies can use their strategic and annual performance plans as tools to drive collaboration with partners for achieving collaborative results; and
- *Reinforce individual accountability for collaborative efforts through performance management systems*: Performance management systems can be used to strengthen accountability for results, specifically by placing greater emphasis on fostering the necessary collaboration both within and across organizational boundaries to achieve results.

The public administration literature on e-government and collaboration is sparse. That research indicates that the e-government paradigm has called for a more collaborative effort in local managerial innovation (Ho, 2002). A case study of the federal government's e-file program provides an example of a successful e-government collaborative management effort (Holden and Fletcher, 2005). Other research shows that in e-government there is a need to identify the key stakeholders, recognize the different interests among the stakeholders, and how the organization can cater to meet those interests for collaborative management (Tan, Pan, and Lim, 2005). The following section provides a conceptual framework which examines how these principles of effective collaboration can be applied to e-government.

COLLABORATION AND E-GOVERNMENT CONCEPTUAL FRAMEWORK

One way to express collaboration and e-government is to examine its impact on the decision-making process of government (Frey, Lohmeier, Lee, and Tollefson, 2006). Figure 1 provides a possible conceptual framework of the relationship between how decisions are made about e-government and the extent of collaboration.

The first arrow on the left-most starting point of the continuum in Figure 1 represents a situation where there is no collaboration and decisions are essentially made independently without input from citizens, other agencies within the state government, or other key stakeholders. For example, a CIO may want to implement a new e-government information security policy for the state. The CIO could possibly do this unilaterally without input from his/her stakeholders. Unilateral decisions in any government can be

Figure 1. Levels of collaboration and e-government

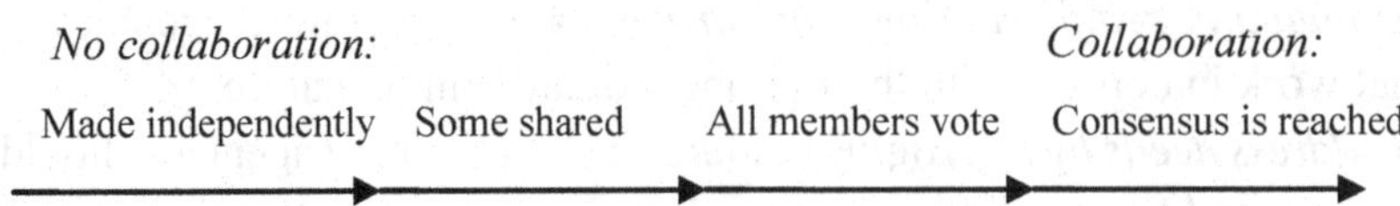

difficult, especially when it comes to e-government projects that involve many diverse interests (Garson, 2006). It seems probable that unilateral e-government decision-making would occur infrequently, given the high risk of project failure.

As we move to the right on Figure 1, there is a degree of collaboration when moving toward the second arrow with some shared decision-making occurring. Following the first example, instead of the CIO unilaterally implementing a new information security policy without key stakeholders involved in the decision-making process he/she decides to ask some other state government agencies about developing a policy. In this scenario, some shared decision-making is taking place. This approach would be the one occurring most frequently in state government because with any e-government project, there is a desire for some level of input in the decision-making process from key stakeholders (Garson, 2006).

The third arrow to the right in Figure 1 shows that all members have a vote in e-government project decision-making. Following the information security policy example, the CIO might decide to set up a meeting to include all stakeholders in the project; a vote is taken on whether to adopt the project from the stakeholders. Given the wide reaching scope of e-government projects it is unlikely that many current project partners will have a vote in its implementation. However, this stage would reach a higher level of collaboration given that key stakeholders would be more involved in the process.

Finally, Figure 1 shows the highest level of collaboration where consensus is reached on all decisions. Again, following the information security policy example the CIO instead of taking a vote tries to include all stakeholders in the project and attempts to move forward on the initiative that gains consensus among stakeholders. The consensus approach to decision-making on an e-government project should be the least likely to be achievable given all the diverse stakeholders that need to be accommodated. However, this is a desirable stage in collaborative management because of its inclusiveness of those involved in the decision-making process. The following sections present results from a survey on e-government and collaboration to show evidence of its occurrence in state governments.

SURVEY RESULTS

In order to examine the impact of e-government and collaboration a survey of state government CIOs was conducted. Surveys in e-government research are a common method of discerning the opinions of those responsible for making important decisions in government (Reddick, 2007). Data for this study was collected during the months of September and October 2006. The survey was conducted online by state government CIOs. An email message was sent to CIOs with a Web link to the survey instrument. The mailing list of CIOs was taken from the 2006 Council of State Governments directory of administrative officials (CSG, 2006). After two emails, 23 state government CIOs chose to participate in the survey (out of 50 possible state government CIOs), which is a response rate of 46%. This is a good response rate since almost half of the state governments are represented in the sample. In order to enhance the participation rate and candor of responses, this was an anonymous survey where there was assurance to the CIOs that only summary data would be used in the analysis. The following section provides descriptive characteristics of CIOs and their state governments in order to determine how representative these results are of collaboration and e-government.

STATE GOVERNMENT CIOS AND THEIR GOVERNMENTS

The descriptive characteristics of state government CIOs and their governments are provided in Table 1. The typical CIO is between the ages of 45 and 54 years, more likely to be male, have less than five years of experience in that position, and well-educated with a graduate degree.

To examine the size of the states that responded to the survey, data was collected from the U.S. Bureau of Labor Statistics on number of employees (Chong et al., 2003). There was a fairly even split of small state governments with eight of them employing between 15,000 and 64,999 employees. There were nine states that employed 100,000 or more employees. While medium-sized states accounted for the least amount in the sample, with only six states having between 65,000 and 99,999 employees.

Both the demographic profile of CIOs and the states that responded to the survey indicate that they are fairly representative of state governments. However, the results may be under representative of medium-sized state governments, given the smaller number of states that responded to the survey.

Table 1. State CIOs and their governments

	Frequency	Percent
Age range		
35-44	3	13
45-54	12	52.2
55-64	7	30.4
65 or over	1	4.3
Gender		
Female	8	34.8
Male	15	65.2
Years worked as CIO for state government		
Less than 5 Years	18	78.3
5 to 10 Years	2	8.7
11 to 15 Years	3	13
Highest level of academic attainment		
Undergraduate Degree	8	34.8
Graduate Degree	15	65.2
Number of state government employees		
15,000 to 64,999	8	34.8
65,000 to 99,999	6	26
100,000 or greater	9	39.1

Table 2. Levels of collaboration and e-government

Indicate the extent to which you currently interact in the decision-making process with each partner in e-government:	All decisions are made independently	Some shared decision-making	All members have a vote in decision-making	Consensus is reached on all decisions
Within my state government	0	82.6	17.4	0
With our contractors/suppliers	17.4	69.6	13	0
With the business community	26.1	65.2	8.7	0
With other levels of governments	17.4	78.3	4.3	0
With citizens	34.8	65.2	0	0

LEVELS OF COLLABORATION AND E-GOVERNMENT

Table 2 provides information on the level of collaboration in e-government with the various stakeholders of state government. As previously mentioned in the conceptual framework in Figure 1, the possible levels of collaboration from least to most are: all decisions are made independently, some shared decision-making, all members have a vote in decision-making, and consensus is reached on all decisions. From Table 2, it appears that the majority of state CIOs believed that the greatest collaboration occurred within the state government when there was some shared decision-making (82.6%). This is followed by some shared decision-making with other levels of government (78.3%). The least shared decision-making was with citizens and the business community both registering 65.2% of responses.

Table 2 also showed, not surprisingly, that none of the CIOs surveyed believed that there was consensus reached on all e-government decisions. Many CIOs (34.8%) believed that e-government decisions with citizens were made independently. This lack of citizen involvement is shown by none of the responding CIOs believing that citizens have a vote in decision-making. Overall, the results in Table 2 indicated that the greatest level of collaboration was within the state government and the least was with its citizens. The following section examines the opinions of CIOs on the principles of effective collaboration and e-government.

COLLABORATION AND E-GOVERNMENT WITHIN STATE GOVERNMENTS

The results in Table 3 asked CIOs about the characteristics of collaboration and e-government within their state government. The questions consisted of the series of perceived impacts by CIOs on collaboration taken from the existing literature of effective collaborative management principles.

The greatest level of agreement, when summing the strongly agree and agree responses in Table 3, was for communication strategies facilitating two-way communication among the project teams, partners, and other stakeholders (82.6%). The second strongest level of agreement was that a climate of trust and respect is fostered through open lines of communication (78.2%). While the third highest level of agreement was that processes being in place which partners can discuss, develop, and agree to common standards needed for initiative success (73.9%).

The least agreement in Table 3 for collaboration and e-government was for the statement that formal agreements with clear purpose, common performance outputs, and realistic performance measures are

Table 3. Collaboration and e-government within state governments

Collaboration and e-government within my state government has the following characteristics:	Strongly Agree	Agree	Neutral	Disagree	Strongly Disagree
Strong leadership is present among partners.	21.7	34.8	26.1	17.4	0
Communication strategies facilitate two-way communication among the project team, partners, and other stakeholders.	21.7	60.9	8.7	8.7	0
Processes are in place which partners can discuss, develop, and agree to common standards needed for initiative success.	17.4	56.5	17.4	8.7	0
Involvement of all leadership levels is an instituted practice.	13	39.1	26.1	21.7	0
Formal processes to contribute human capital and funds, such as written agreements, ensure that needed resources are promised and delivered.	13	43.5	21.7	21.7	0
Partner/stakeholder roles and responsibilities are clearly defined, agreed to, and understood by participants.	8.7	56.5	17.4	17.4	0
Outreach programs keep those affected by the initiative informed of new developments and provide structural means for feedback and questions.	8.7	60.9	17.4	13	0
A common vision is shared among partners.	4.3	56.5	26.1	13	0
A climate of trust and respect is fostered through open lines of communication	4.3	73.9	17.4	4.3	0
Formal agreements with clear purpose, common performance outputs, and realistic performance measures are used to provide a firm management foundation.	4.3	39.1	34.8	21.7	0

used to provide a firm management foundation (43.4%). There were only 52.1% of CIOs who agreed that involvement of all leadership levels was an instituted practice.

The results in Table 3 generally show a high level of collaboration in e-government. Communication, trust, and standards are in place to enhance collaboration. However, there is less agreement on performance metrics for the state governments being in place to evaluate collaboration. This could be problematic for state governments without adequate measurement of results; this could stifle future collaborative efforts.

COLLABORATION AND STATE E-GOVERNMENT PROJECTS

The survey also asked questions about collaboration and e-government projects. This issue is important to know given that most of the wide-reaching collaborative efforts involve the implementation of e-government projects. The results in Table 4 examine the discourse by CIOs on the characteristics of e-government collaboration and project management according to some of the principles noted in the literature. The highest level of agreement (when summing up the strong agree and agree categories) was defining and articulating a common outcome for e-government projects (82.6%). The second greatest level of agreement was for identifying and addressing needs by leveraging resources (78.2%). The third highest level of agreement was for defining roles and responsibilities for e-government project collaboration (73.9%). The least agreement was for reinforced department/agency accountability for collaborative efforts (52.1%). There was also the least agreement for two questions of developing mechanisms

Table 4. Collaboration and state government e-government projects

When conducting e-government projects our state government has:	Strongly Agree	Agree	Neutral	Disagree	Strongly Disagree
Identified and addressed needs by leveraging resources.	21.7	56.5	4.3	17.4	0
Established mutually reinforcing or joint strategies.	17.4	39.1	30.4	13	0
Agreed on roles and responsibilities.	17.4	56.5	17.4	8.7	0
Defined and articulated a common outcome.	13	69.6	8.7	8.7	0
Developed mechanisms to monitor, evaluate, and report on the results.	13	43.5	30.4	13	0
Reinforced department/agency accountability for collaborative efforts.	13	39.1	26.1	21.7	0
Reinforced individual accountability for collaborative efforts.	13	47.8	21.7	17.4	0
Established compatible policies, procedures, and other means to operate across agency boundaries.	8.7	56.5	17.4	13	4.3

to monitor, evaluate, and report on results and establishing mutually reinforcing or joint strategies, both registering 56.5% of respondents.

What do these results mean for collaboration and e-government projects? Outcomes are being articulated, roles and responsibilities defined, and resources are being leveraged for e-government projects. At the same time, there appears to be a lack of mechanisms for evaluation and accountability for state e-government projects. Similarly, to the responses in Table 3 the post collaboration efforts appear to be shortchanged. The process of reaching collaboration is taking place in state governments, however, the evaluation of the processes and outcomes are not taking place. These important findings will be examined in the conclusion to this chapter as well as how collaboration fits into HSIS.

CONCLUSION

There are many reasons to collaborate in government especially in the context of homeland security preparedness. Collaboration is part of the NPM movement that has swept all levels of government. In collaboration there needs to be agreement on means and ends for it to be effective. Collaboration is shown in this chapter on a continuum and citizens seem to be the least involved in collaborative efforts.

This chapter has examined the current state of collaboration and e-government through the lens of state government CIOs. The purpose of this chapter was to set the context of collaboration because of its important influence on HSIS. The most important research results indicated that citizens were collaborated with the least in e-government, while not surprisingly the most collaboration was occurring within the state government. This finding is somewhat problematic for collaborative and e-government since the most important stakeholders of collaboration are not being included, to any great extent. This finding also has implications for both transparency and accountability of the state government to its citizens. The promising news is that there is some shared decision-making taking place in state governments to get key stakeholders involved in the process, so they will be more supportive of the project. One recommendation for governments that implement HSIS is to include citizens in the implementation of these information systems. This will lead to greater support for the project and ultimately more successful implementation.

With collaboration and e-government there is a high level of agreement that it is having an impact on communication, trust, and standards within state government. However according to CIOs, measuring the results of collaboration through performance measures is being shortchanged. Research shows that when state governments have citizens somewhat involved in the decision-making process for e-government there is a greater likelihood that more collaboration occurs. These results essentially show that communication is the key for effective collaboration and that citizens are the prime outlet to facilitate collaborative efforts within their state government. One recommendation for the implementation of HSIS is to promote more open dialogue with stakeholders when implementing these information systems. There also is the definite need for information sharing to create a more successful collaboration.

Collaborative efforts and e-government project success requires the needs of the project to be clearly defined and articulated. There is a need to leverage resources for e-government project success. There was a high level of agreement among CIOs that they were achieving the eight principles outlined for successful e-government projects. Similarly to the question about e-government collaboration in general, there is a need to provide more accountability and focus on results for project success. As with e-government projects in general, the same is applicable for the implementation of HSIS, of clearly defining and articulating the needs of the project and providing a framework that focuses on project success is vital.

REFERENCES

9/11 Commission Report (2004). *The 9-11 Commission Report Final Report of the National Commission on Terrorist Attacks upon the United States*. Retrieved January 26, 2009, from http://www.gpoaccess.gov/911/pdf/fullreport.pdf.

Agranoff, R., & McGuire, M. (2003). *Collaborative Public Management: New Strategies for Local Governments*. Washington, D.C.: Georgetown University Press.

Allen, B. A., Juillet, L., Paquet, G., & Roy, J. (2005). E-government as Collaborative Governance: Structural, Accountability, and Cultural Reform. *In Practicing E-Government: A Global Perspective*, edited by Mehdi Khosrow-Pour, 1-15. Hershey, PA: Idea Group Publishing.

Bardach, E. (1998). *Getting Agencies to Work Together: The Practice and Theory of Managerial Craftsmanship*. Washington, D.C.: Brookings Institution Press.

Chong, P. P., Chang, M., Kuo, C., & Chong, E. (2003). "City Size Analysis: A Preliminary Research for E-government Applications" Proceedings to the 2003 International Conference of Pacific Rim Management, Seattle, WA, July 31-August 2, 2003.

Council of State Governments (CSG). *State Directory III: Administrative Officials2006*. Lexington, KY: The Council of State Governments.

Fedorowicz, J., Gogan, J. L., & Williams, C. B. (2006). *The E-government Collaboration Challenge: Lessons from Five Case Studies*. IBM The Center for Business of Government. Retrieved September 24, 2008 from http://www.businessofgovernment.org

Frey, B. B., Lohmeier, J. H., Lee, S. W., & Tollefson, N. (2006). Measuring Collaboration among Grant Partners. *The American Journal of Evaluation*, *27*(3), 383–392. doi:10.1177/1098214006290356

GAO. (2003a). *Homeland Security: Efforts to Improve Information Sharing Need to be Strengthened.* (GAO Publication No. GAO-03-760). Washington, DC: U.S. Government Printing Office.

GAO. (2003b). *Electronic Government: Potential Exists for Enhancing Collaboration on Four Initiatives*. Washington, D.C.: United States Government Accountability Office. Report No. GAO-04-6.

GAO. (2004). *Homeland Security: Efforts Under Way to Develop Enterprise Architecture, but Much Work Remains*. (GAO Publication No. GAO-04-777). Washington, D.C.: U.S. Government Printing Office.

GAO. (2007). *Homeland Security: DHS Enterprise Architecture Continues to Evolve but Improvements Needed.* (GAO Publication No. GAO-07-564). Washington, D.C.: U.S. Government Printing Office.

Garson, G. D. (2006). *Public Information Technology and E-Governance: Managing the Virtual State*. Sudbury, MA: Jones and Bartlett Publishers.

Government Accountability Office. (2005). *Results-Oriented Government: Practices that can Help Enhance and Sustain Collaboration among Federal Agencies*. Washington, D.C.: United States Government Accountability Office. Report No. GAO-06-15.

Gronlund, A. (2005). State of the Art in E-Gov Research: Surveying Conference Publications. *International Journal of Electronic Government Research, 1*(4), 1–25.

Guijarro, L. (2007). Interoperability Frameworks and Enterprise Architectures in E-Government Initiatives in Europe and the United States. *Government Information Quarterly, 24*(1), 89–101. doi:10.1016/j.giq.2006.05.003

Hjort-Madsen, K. (2007). Institutional Patterns of Enterprise Architecture Adoption in Government. *Transforming Government: People . Process and Policy, 1*(4), 333–249.

Ho, A. T.-K. (2002). Reinventing Local Governments and the E-government Initiative. *Public Administration Review, 62*(4), 434–444. doi:10.1111/0033-3352.00197

Holden, S. H., & Fletcher, P. D. (2005). The Virtual Value Chain and E-Government Partnership: Non-Monetary Agreements in the IRS E-File Program. *International Journal of Public Administration, 28*(7-8), 643–664. doi:10.1081/PAD-200064223

Hu, P. J.-H., Cui, D., & Sherwood, A. C. (2006). *Examining Cross-Agency Collaborations in E-government Initiatives*. Proceedings of the 39th Hawaii International Conference on System Sciences - 2006. Retrieved September 24, 2008 from http://www.computer.org/portal/site/ieeecs/index.jsp

Huxham, C., & Vangen, S. (2005). *Managing to Collaborate: The Theory and Practice of Collaborative Advantage*. New York, NY: Routledge.

Kolsaker, A. (2006). Reconceptualising e-government as a tool of governance: the UK case. *Electronic Government: An International Journal, 3*(4), 347–355. doi:10.1504/EG.2006.010798

Kolsaker, A., & Lee-Kelly, Liz. (2006). Citizen-centric e-government: a critique of the UK Model. *Electronic Government: An International Journal, 2*(3), 127–138.

Kolsaker, A., & Lee-Kelly, L. (2007). G2C e-government modernization or transformation? *Electronic Government: An International Journal, 4*(1), 68–75. doi:10.1504/EG.2007.012180

Moon, M. J. (2002). The Evolution of E-Government among Municipalities: Rhetoric or Reality? *Public Administration Review*, *62*(4), 424–433. doi:10.1111/0033-3352.00196

NGA. (2007). *2007 State Homeland Security Directors Survey*. National Governors Association. Retrieved January 26, 2009, from http://www.nga.org/Files/pdf/0712HOMELANDSURVEY.PDF.

NIEM. (2007). *Introduction to the National Information Exchange Model (NIEM)*. Retrieved January 26, 2009, from http://www.niem.gov/files/NIEM_Introduction.pdf.

Peled, A. (2007). The Electronic Mountain: A Tale of Two Tels. *American Review of Public Administration*, *37*(4), 458–478. doi:10.1177/0275074006297996

Reddick, C. G. (2008). Collaboration and Homeland Security Preparedness: A Survey of U.S. City Managers. *Journal of Homeland Security and Emergency Management*, *5*(1), 1–19. doi:10.2202/1547-7355.1414

Reddick, C. G., & Frank, H. A. (2007). E-government and its Influence on Managerial Effectiveness: A Survey of Florida and Texas City Managers. *Financial Accountability and Management*, *23*(1), 1–26. doi:10.1111/j.1468-0408.2007.00417.x

Ryoo, J., & Choi, Y. B. (2006). A Comparison and Classification Framework for Disaster Information Management Systems. *International Journal of Emergency Management*, *3*(4), 264–279. doi:10.1504/IJEM.2006.011296

Sharma, S. K. (2004). Assessing e-government implementations. *Electronic Government: An International Journal*, *1*(2), 198–212. doi:10.1504/EG.2004.005178

Tan, C.-W., Pan, S. L., & Lim, E. T. K. (2005). Managing Stakeholder Interests in e-Government Implementation: Lessons Learned from a Singapore e-Government Project. *Journal of Global Information Management*, *13*(1), 31–53.

Thomson, A. M., & Perry, J. L. (2006). Collaboration Processes: Inside the Black Box. *Public Administration Review*, *66*(6), 20–32. doi:10.1111/j.1540-6210.2006.00663.x

Vigoda-Gadot, E. (2002). From Responsiveness to Collaboration: Governance, Citizens, and the Next Generation of Public Administration. *Public Administration Review*, *62*(5), 527–540. doi:10.1111/1540-6210.00235

Vigoda-Gadot, E. (2003). *Managing Collaboration in Public Administration: The Promise of Alliance among Governance, Citizens, and Business*. Westport, Connecticut: Praeger.

Vigoda-Gadot, E. (2004). Collaborative Public Administration: Some Lessons from the Israeli Experience. *Managerial Auditing Journal*, *19*(6), 700–711. doi:10.1108/02686900410543831

Wybo, J.-L., & Lonka, H. (2002). Emergency Management and the Information Society: How to Improve the Synergy? *International Journal of Emergency Management*, *1*(2), 183–190. doi:10.1504/IJEM.2002.000519

Yang, J., & Paul, S. (2005). E-government application at local level: issues and challenges: an empirical study. *Electronic Government: An International Journal*, *2*(1), 56–76. doi:10.1504/EG.2005.006648

Section 2
Homeland Security Information Systems in Government

The second section of this book examines the implementation of HSIS in the federal government, state emergency management, and local governments. The chapters in Section 2 provide evidence on the impact of HSIS on the different levels of government in the United States.

Chapter 4
Federal Government Homeland Security Information Systems

INTRODUCTION

This chapter focuses on Homeland Security Information Systems (HSIS) in the federal government. One definition of HSIS, in the federal government, is the application of information technology to homeland security with the aim of detecting fragmented clues, assembling them as a puzzle, then using the information to stop a terrorist attack (Nunn, 2005). Nunn's definition focuses on the use of information for data mining for deducing possible terrorist attacks and responses to these incidents. This chapter recognizes the importance of data analysis, but uses a broader definition of federal HSIS being the use of information systems to prepare for and respond to a terrorist attack or significant national emergency. This definition of HSIS covers the importance of data mining to discover how information fits together as pieces of the puzzle, but it also incorporates other elements of information technology (IT) that are used to respond and prepare for a national incident.

This chapter will first examine the Department of Homeland Security which has a tremendous influence over homeland security policy and information systems in the United States. There is an examination in this chapter of the environmental context of HSIS in the federal government, demonstrating some of the important pieces of legislation that have an influence in this area. This chapter discusses the roles and responsibilities of federal government Chief Information Officers (CIOs) to discern the scope of their responsibilities. A section of this chapter examines some principles of effective IT management in federal agencies. The final part of this chapter provides the results of a survey of CIOs in federal government departments/agencies to determine the influence of HSIS on their organizations.

DOI: 10.4018/978-1-60566-834-5.ch004

THE DEPARTMENT OF HOMELAND SECURITY

In the aftermath of the terrorist attacks of September 11, 2001, responding to potential threats to homeland security became one of the federal government's most significant challenges (GAO, 2004a). To address this challenge, Congress passed and the President signed the *Homeland Security Act* of 2002 (GAO, 2008). This act merged 22 federal agencies and organizations into the Department of Homeland Security (DHS). One of the department's most significant challenges was to integrate these 22 agencies and their IT organizations into a unified system.

In establishing the new DHS, Congress defined seven-point mission for the DHS.

- prevent terrorist attacks within the United States;
- reduce the vulnerability of the United States to terrorism;
- minimize the damage and assist in the recovery from terrorist attacks;
- carry out all functions of entities transferred to the department, including acting as a focal point regarding natural and man-made crises and emergency planning;
- ensure that the functions of the components within the department that are not directly related to securing the homeland are not diminished or neglected;
- ensure that the overall economic security of the United States is not diminished by efforts aimed at securing the homeland; and
- monitor connections between illegal drug trafficking and terrorism, coordinate efforts to sever such connections, and otherwise contribute to efforts to interdict illegal drug trafficking (GAO, 2004a).

The seven-point mission of the DHS requires that IT be adopted by this organization at each of these mission critical areas. For example, the prevention of a terrorist attack would involve looking at intelligence information and discerning patterns that predict a possible terrorist incident. Emergency planning would involve having the communications equipment to effectively communicate with first responders. Reducing the vulnerability of the United States could be done though data mining of information that terrorist might find useful to lodge an attack on the United States.

The Department of Homeland Security has the 10 principal organizations and their respective missions are shown in Table 1.

The DHS began operations in March 2003, and assumed operational control of about 209,000 civilian and military operations from 22 federal agencies. A simplified organizational chart for DHS is shown in Figure 1 (GAO, 2007).

The *National Strategy for Homeland Security* issued by President George W. Bush on July 16, 2002 has defined homeland security as "a concerted national effort to prevent terrorist attacks within the United States, reduce America's vulnerability to terrorism, and minimize the damage, and recover from attacks that do occur."(Office of Homeland Security, 2002, p. 2). The national strategy clearly recognizes the critical importance of information sharing through IT to prevent a future terrorist attack (Relyea, 2004). The National Strategy identified a plan to strengthen homeland security through the cooperation and partnering of federal, state, and private sector organizations on a number of functions (GAO, 2008).

President Bush's *National Strategy* specifically addressed HSIS in the following passage (2002, p. xi):

Table 1. DHS's principal organizations and their missions (Source: GAO, 2007)

Principal organizations	Missions
Citizenship and Immigration Services	Administers immigration and naturalization adjudication functions and establishes immigration services policies and priorities.
Coast Guard	Protects the public, the environment, and U.S. economic interests in the nation's ports and waterways, along the coast, on international waters, and in any maritime region as required to support national security.
Customs and Border Protection	Secures the nation's borders in order to prevent terrorists and terrorist weapons from entering the United States, while facilitating the flow of legitimate trade and travel.
Federal Emergency Management Agency	Prepares the nation for hazards, manages federal response and recovery efforts following any national incident, and administers the National Flood Insurance Program.
Immigration and Customs Enforcement	Investigates, identifies, and addresses vulnerabilities in the nation's border, economic, transportation, and infrastructure security.
Management Directorate	Is responsible for department budgets and appropriations, expenditure of funds, accounting and finance, procurement, human resources, IT systems, facilities and equipment, and the identification and tracking of performance measurements. This directorate includes the Offices of the Chief Financial Officer and the CIO.
National Protection and Programs Directorate	Supports the department's homeland security risk reduction mission through an integrated approach that encompasses both physical and virtual threats and their associated human elements. This directorate includes the Offices of Cyber Security and Communications and Infrastructure Protection.
Science and Technology Directorate	Serves as the primary research and development arm of the department, responsible for providing federal, state, and local officials with the technology and capabilities to protect the homeland.
Secret Service	Protects the President and other high-level officials and investigates counterfeiting and other financial crimes (including financial institution fraud, identity theft, and computer fraud) and computer-based attacks on the nation's financial, banking, and telecommunications infrastructure.
Transportation Security Administration	Protects the nation's transportation systems to ensure freedom of movement for people and commerce.

Figure 1. DHS organizational structure (simplified and partial)

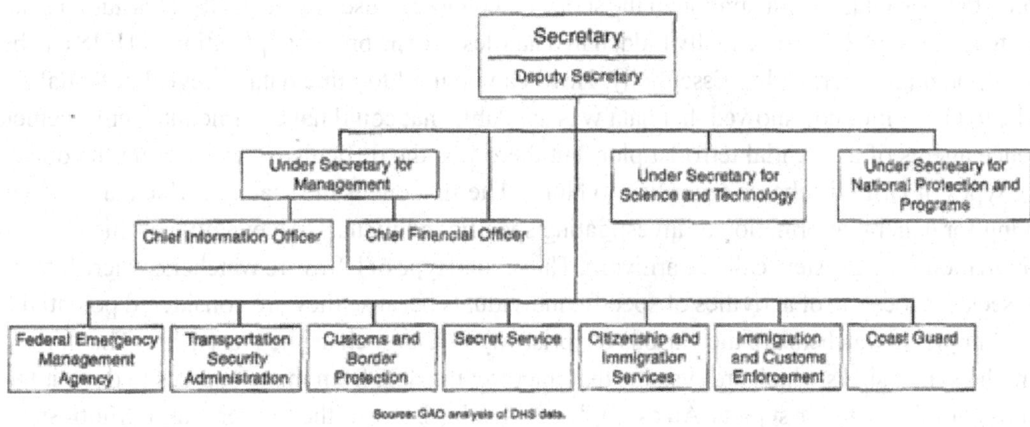

Information systems contribute to every aspect of homeland security. Although American information technology is the most advanced in the world, our country's information systems have not adequately supported the homeland security mission. Databases used for federal law enforcement, immigration, intelligence, public health surveillance, and emergency management have not been connected in ways that allow us to comprehend where information gaps or redundancies exist. In addition, there are

deficiencies in the communications systems used by states and municipalities throughout the country; most state and local first responders do not use compatible communications equipment. To secure the homeland better, we must link the vast amounts of knowledge residing within each government agency while ensuring adequate privacy.

As we can see, HSIS is one critical element of the *National Strategy* and vitally important for protecting the homeland.

INFORMATION TECHNOLOGY USED AT DEPARTMENT OF HOMELAND SECURITY

To accomplish its mission the DHS requested for fiscal year 2007 about $4.16 billion for IT to support 278 major IT programs (Table 2).

Homeland Security Presidential Directives (HSPD) were issued by the President George W. Bush on matters pertaining to Homeland Security (DHS, 2009) and are shown in Table 3.

There are several HSPDs that have a direct influence on information systems and technology in the realm of homeland security. For instance, there is HSPD 3 of a Homeland Security Advisory System (HSAS) which is a color-coded chart posted on many government websites indicating the current threat level as provided by the DHS.

Another HSPD that is directly applicable is 23, which is the National Cyber Security Initiative. All of the other HSPDs are applicable to some degree to HSIS because the delivery of the directive normally involves information technology in some capacity. For example, Biometrics for Identification and Screening to Enhance National Security (HSPD-24) is one that would not be possible without advanced information systems.

Nunn (2005) provides an illustration of the scope of technology used by the DHS. This author states that the clues to terrorist plots are essentially hidden in data files and the proper application of HSIS can be used to detect a potential terrorist plot. Essentially, HSIS can be used to mine data to reveal potential terrorist plots. The 9-11 commission showed that data was available that could have warned law enforcement and intelligence agents of a potential terrorist plot, but there was the difficulty of connecting the dots. There are three types of HSIS databases according to Nunn. The first one is the scanner, which are systems that are looking for general information or investigating specific individuals. An example of this would be the FBI's email monitoring system called Carnivore. The second type of HSIS are watchers, where information systems seek the location of activities of specific individuals because they are considered potential terrorists. An example of watchers are the various terrorist watch lists such as the No-fly list. The third type of HSIS are the synthesizers which are systems that interpret the data from many sources to draw inferences about current or future terrorist plots. An example of a synthesizer was the formerly used Multi-State Anti-Terrorism Information Exchange (MATRIX). This was a federally funded data mining system used as a tool to identify terrorist subjects; this program was shut down in 2005 due to privacy concerns.

Table 2. IT funding for fiscal year 2007 (Source:GAO, 2007)

Millions	
DHS components and investments	**Funding**
Citizenship and Immigration Services	$570.30
Coast Guard	196.7
Customs and Border Protection	546.4
Federal Emergency Management Agency	77.1
Immigration and Customs Enforcement	134
Management Directorate	
Enterprise Application Delivery[a]	20.7
Enterprise Architecture and Investment Management Program[b]	35.6
Enterprise-Geospatial System[c]	12.8
Homeland Secure Data Network[d]	32.7
Human Resources IT[e]	19.1
Information Security Program[f]	57.8
Integrated Wireless Network[g]	361.3
Watch List and Technical Integration[h]	9.9
CIO Office salaries and expenses	16.5
Other IT infrastructure[i]	954.3
Other	55.3
Preparedness Directorate[j]	213.5
Science and Technology Directorate	34.1
Secret Service	3.8
Transportation Security Administration	356.4
US-VISIT[k]	407.4
Other DHS components	45.1
Total	$4,160.80

Notes:
[a]Enterprise Application Delivery is to consolidate existing and planned Web pages and platforms of the DHS component organizations.
[b]The Enterprise Architecture and Investment Management Program is to develop the department's enterprise architecture and implement the transition strategy through the department's investment management process.
[c]The Enterprise-Geospatial System is to establish a framework, organizational structure, and requisite resources to enable departmentwide use of geographic information systems.
[d]The Homeland Secure Data Network is to merge disparate classified networks into a single, integrated network to enable, among other things, the secure sharing of intelligence and other information.
[e]Human Resources IT includes the set of DHS enterprise wide systems to support personnel regulations
[f]The Information Security Program is to establish information security policies and procedures throughout the department to protect the confidentiality, integrity, and availability of information.
[g]The Integrated Wireless Network is to deliver the wireless communications services required by agents and officers of DHS, the Department of Justice, and the Department of the Treasury.
[h]Watch List and Technical Integration is to increase effective information sharing by consolidating, re-using, and retiring applications that develop multiple terrorist watch lists being used by multiple operating entities within the government.
[i]Other infrastructure includes initiatives with the goal of creating a single, consolidated, and secure infrastructure to ensure connectivity among the department's 22 component organizations.
[j]On April 1, 2007, this Directorate was replaced by the National Protection and Programs Directorate.
[k]On April 1, 2007, US-VISIT became part of the National Protection and Programs Directorate.

Table 3. Summary of homeland security presidential directives (Source: DHS, 2009)

HSPD – 1: Organization and Operation of the Homeland Security Council. Ensures coordination of all homeland security-related activities among executive departments and agencies and promote the effective development and implementation of all homeland security policies.
HSPD – 2: Combating Terrorism Through Immigration Policies. Provides for the creation of a task force which will work aggressively to prevent aliens who engage in or support terrorist activity from entering the United States and to detain, prosecute, or deport any such aliens who are within the United States.
HSPD – 3: Homeland Security Advisory System. Establishes a comprehensive and effective means to disseminate information regarding the risk of terrorist acts to Federal, State, and local authorities and to the American people.
HSPD – 4: National Strategy to Combat Weapons of Mass Destruction. Applies new technologies, increased emphasis on intelligence collection and analysis, strengthens alliance relationships, and establishes new partnerships with former adversaries to counter this threat in all of its dimensions.
HSPD – 5: Management of Domestic Incidents. Enhances the ability of the United States to manage domestic incidents by establishing a single, comprehensive national incident management system.
HSPD – 6: Integration and Use of Screening Information. Provides for the establishment of the Terrorist Threat Integration Center.
HSPD – 7: Critical Infrastructure Identification, Prioritization, and Protection. Establishes a national policy for Federal departments and agencies to identify and prioritize United States critical infrastructure and key resources and to protect them from terrorist attacks.
HSPD – 8: National Preparedness. Identifies steps for improved coordination in response to incidents. This directive describes the way Federal departments and agencies will prepare for such a response, including prevention activities during the early stages of a terrorism incident. This directive is a companion to HSPD-5.
HSPD – 8 Annex 1: National Planning. Further enhances the preparedness of the United States by formally establishing a standard and comprehensive approach to national planning.
HSPD – 9: Defense of United States Agriculture and Food. Establishes a national policy to defend the agriculture and food system against terrorist attacks, major disasters, and other emergencies.
HSPD – 10: Biodefense for the 21st Century. Provides a comprehensive framework for our nation's Biodefense.
HSPD – 11: Comprehensive Terrorist-Related Screening Procedures. Implements a coordinated and comprehensive approach to terrorist-related screening that supports homeland security, at home and abroad. This directive builds upon HSPD – 6.
HSPD – 12: Policy for a Common Identification Standard for Federal Employees and Contractors. Establishes a mandatory, Government-wide standard for secure and reliable forms of identification issued by the Federal Government to its employees and contractors (including contractor employees).
HSPD – 13: Maritime Security Policy. Establishes policy guidelines to enhance national and homeland security by protecting U.S. maritime interests.
HSPD – 15: U.S. Strategy and Policy in the War on Terror.
HSPD - 16: Aviation Strategy. Details a strategic vision for aviation security while recognizing ongoing efforts, and directs the production of a National Strategy for Aviation Security and supporting plans.
HSPD - 17: Nuclear Materials Information Program.
HSPD – 18: Medical Countermeasures against Weapons of Mass Destruction. Establishes policy guidelines to draw upon the considerable potential of the scientific community in the public and private sectors to address medical countermeasure requirements relating to CBRN threats.
HSPD – 19: Combating Terrorist Use of Explosives in the United States. Establishes a national policy, and calls for the development of a national strategy and implementation plan, on the prevention and detection of, protection against, and response to terrorist use of explosives in the United States.
HSPD – 20: National Continuity Policy. Establishes a comprehensive national policy on the continuity of federal government structures and operations and a single National Continuity Coordinator responsible for coordinating the development and implementation of federal continuity policies.
HSPD – 20 Annex A: Continuity Planning. Assigns executive departments and agencies to a category commensurate with their COOP/COG/ECG responsibilities during an emergency.
HSPD – 21: Public Health and Medical Preparedness. Establishes a national strategy that will enable a level of public health and medical preparedness sufficient to address a range of possible disasters.
HSPD – 23: National Cyber Security Initiative.

HOMELAND SECURITY ENVIRONMENT

With the war against terrorism there has been the catalyst for shifting the focus of e-government in the federal government (Halchin, 2004). One change is the realization of the vulnerability of e-government as a possible terrorist target. The infrastructure of e-government could be potentially destroyed or damaged with a terrorist attack. Second, terrorists could use the content of federal government websites to find potential targets, identify and exploit weaknesses, and obtain and integrate information. However, on the upside e-government can link different levels of government to facilitate information sharing and provide citizens with emergency preparedness information.

The federal government has responded in several ways to the possibility of providing information on website that would aid terrorists (Halchin, 2002). Federal agencies have removed or modified information, established firewalls around information, limited access to some data, and have not provided updates.

According to Halchin (2002), one of the byproducts of having less information on websites is that information is the most important component of the American democracy. In order to have self-government citizens must be informed. If they are to vote, they will need information on issues and different programs that the government offers. In essence, less information would make it more difficult to hold government accountable for their decisions and actions. Halchin argues since the terrorist attack of September 11, 2001 the balance has shifted to an emphasis on national security rather than the right to know information about government.

One of the main lessons learned from September 11, 2001 is the need for continuity and disaster recovery planning (Seifert, 2002). Continuity and disaster recovery planning is an evolving process requiring regular practice and testing of information systems in preparation for a terrorist or emergency incident. Both public and private sector organizations need to have business continuity plans in place in the event of a major disaster to keep information systems operational.

In order to see the environmental context of HSIS one must understand the differences between the public and private sectors' CIOs. Research shows that there is a higher degree of interdependence between other public sector organizations when compared to private sector counterparts (Ward and Mitchell, 2004).

Table 4. Important federal IT legislative policies and HSIS (Adapted from Mullen, 2005)

Computer Security Act of 1987	Improve the security and privacy of sensitive information in federal computer systems
Paperwork Reduction Act of 1995	Minimize the public's paperwork burdens
	Coordinate federal information resources management
	Improve dissemination of public information
	Ensure the integrity of the federal statistical system
Clinger-Cohen Act of 1996	Improve federal programs through improved acquisition, use, and disposal of IT resources
	Established the position of CIO in executive-branch agencies
E-Government Act of 2002	Promote the use of the Internet and other IT to provide government services electronically
	Strengthen agency information security
	Define how to manage the federal government's growing IT human capital needs
	Established an Office of Electronic Government, within OMB, to provide strong central leadership and full-time commitment to promoting and implementing e-government

This was especially the case when it comes to oversight. The fragmented process of IT acquisition in the public sector makes it difficult to attain goals. There are several important pieces of federal legislation as noted in Table 4 that address IT in the federal government and have an influence on HSIS.

COMPUTER SECURITY ACT

The purpose of the *Computer Security Act* of 1987 is to improve security of sensitive information in federal information systems. Under this law all operators of federal information systems including contractors are required to establish security plans. There also is the requirement of training on security awareness and acceptable security practices (Mullen, 2005). This obviously influences HSIS given that information security is one of the critical dimensions of any information system and its development. There is another piece of federal legislation discussed below which deals with the information flow in federal agencies.

PAPERWORK REDUCTION ACT

The Paperwork Reduction Act (PRA) of 1995 focuses on reducing the government's information collection burden (GAO, 2001; Relyea, 2000). Mullen (2005) outlines the main purposes of the PRA are to: (1) minimize the public's paperwork burdens resulting from the collection of information from the federal government; (2) to coordinate agencies' information resource management policies; (3) to improve the dissemination of information; and (4) to ensure the integrity of the federal statistical system. The PRA emphasizes that agencies need to acquire and apply such resources efficiently to support the accomplishment of agency missions and delivery of services to the public (Westerback, 2000). This PRA laid the groundwork for putting more information online in order to reduce the number of forms that must be filled out and reports that have to be completed by federal agencies. However, placing more information online would have an impact on increasing the vulnerability of federal information systems to potential terrorist targets. The Clinger-Cohen Act repeats the theme of the PRA and elaborates on the specific role for CIOs in federal government.

CLINGER-COHEN ACT

As noted in Chapter 2, the *Information Technology Management Reform Act* (ITMRA) of 1996 also known as the Clinger-Cohen Act established the position of CIO in executive-branch agencies (GAO, 2004b). The previous title for the position was Information Resource Manager (IRM) with this position focusing on the proper management of information resources throughout a federal agency leading to effective, efficient, and strategic organizations (Bertot, 1997). ITMRA provides a framework for moving federal agencies in the direction of integrating IT into management and performance measures (Bertot and McClure, 1997). Congress has mandated from the Clinger-Cohen Act that CIOs should play a leadership role in ensuring that agencies manage their information functions in a coordinated and integrated fashion in order to improve efficiency and effectiveness of government programs and operations (GAO, 2006).

The Clinger-Cohen Act addresses the issue of customer service by requiring CIOs to have information systems knowledge, to focus on customer service, and to manage IT programs by tracking the success or failure of an IT program (Buehler, 2000). Previously, as noted the majority of agencies and departments had an IRM official as their top information person. They advocated IT for the organization without thinking strategically about how it would enhance the performance of the department/agency. The Clinger-Cohen Act stated that federal CIOs will report to and work directly with agency directors. The CIO raised to the executive level, would be able to ask the hard questions of how IT will enhance the performance of the organization (Buehler, 2000). This Act had an influence on HSIS given that it recognizes the important strategic role that IT plays in federal departments and agencies.

E-GOVERNMENT ACT

As mentioned in Chapter 2, the *E-government Act* of 2002 was enacted to promote the use of the Internet and other technologies to improve government services to citizens, internal government operations, and opportunities for citizen participation in government (GAO, 2005a). The E-government Act directs federal agencies to promote electronic government. This act specifically required the establishment of the Office of Electronic Government within the Office of Management and Budget (OMB) to oversee implementation of the Act's provisions and mandates. One area that is addressed in the E-government Act, with particular relevance to HSIS, is that of enhanced crisis management through advanced IT systems.

CHALLENGES, ROLES, AND RESPONSIBILITIES OF FEDERAL CIOs

The purpose of establishing the position of CIOs was to improve federal IT management. There was the establishment of the CIO Council (http://www.cio.gov) to promote government-wide the role of CIOs in the federal government. The Information Technology Association of America (ITAA) in their 18th annual survey of federal government CIOs found out during their interviews some top challenges that CIOs will face in the years to come (ITAA, 2008). This chapter will later report on a survey of CIOs on how these challenges have impacted HSIS. In priority, the federal CIOs indentified the following as their top challenges:

- IT security/cyber security
- Standardization and consolidation
- IT workforce planning
- IT governance
- Resources
- Implementing plans
- Information sharing
- Achieving results
- Acquisition and project management

The most pressing issue for CIOs in the survey, which is vital for HSIS, was IT security/cyber security. Most of the CIOs interviewed for the survey were actively engaged in efforts to enhance their IT security and believed that they were making progress in this area. However, there was some dissenting opinion that much still needs to be done in IT security.

In order to gain an understanding of the scope of federal government HSIS we must understand the responsibilities of CIOs. The Government Accountability Office (2004) identified 13 major areas of CIO responsibilities as either statutory requirements or what they labeled as critical to effective IT and management. Table 5 provides a listing of the 13 major areas along with their statutory requirements, if any. GAO administered a questionnaire and interviewed CIOs at 27 major federal departments and agencies during November 2003 through May 2004. They found that respondents were responsible for most of the 13 areas that are indentified in Table 5.

Table 5. Federal CIO roles and responsibilities

Responsibility	*Description*	*Statutory Requirement/Law/Guidance*
IT/IRM strategic planning	CIOs are responsible for strategic planning for all information and information technology management functions—thus, the term IRM strategic planning.	[44 U.S.C. 3506(b)(2)]
IT capital planning and investment management	CIOs are responsible for IT capital planning and investment management.	[44 U.S.C. 3506(h) and 40 U.S.C. 11312 & 11313]
Information security	CIOs are responsible for ensuring compliance with the requirement to protect information and systems.	[44 U.S.C. 3506(g) and 3544(a)(3)]
IT/IRM workforce planning	CIOs have responsibilities for helping the agency meet its IT/IRM workforce or human capital needs.	[44 U.S.C. 3506(b) and 40 U.S.C. 11315(c)]
Information collection/paperwork reduction	CIOs are responsible for the review of agency information collection proposals to maximize the utility and minimize public "paperwork" burdens.	[44 U.S.C. 3506(c)]
Information dissemination	CIOs are responsible for ensuring that the agency's information dissemination activities meet policy goals such as timely and equitable public access to information.	[44 U.S.C. 3506(d)]
Records management	CIOs are responsible for ensuring that the agency's information dissemination activities meet policy goals such as timely and equitable public access to information agency implements and enforces records management policies and procedures under the Federal Records Act.	[44 U.S.C. 3506(f)]
Privacy	CIOs are responsible for compliance with the Privacy Act and related laws.	[44 U.S.C. 3506(g)]
Statistical policy and coordination	CIOs are responsible for the agency's statistical policy and coordination functions, including ensuring the relevance, accuracy, and timeliness of information collected or created for statistical purposes.	[44 U.S.C. 3506(e)]
Information disclosure	CIOs are responsible for information access under the Freedom of Information Act.	[44 U.S.C. 3506(g)]
Enterprise architecture	Federal laws and guidance direct agencies to develop and maintain enterprise architectures as blueprints to define the agency mission, and the information and IT needed to perform that mission.	None
Systems acquisition, development, and integration	We have found that a critical element of successful IT management is effective control.	[44 U.S.C. 3506(h)(5) and 40 U.S.C. 11312]
E-government initiatives	Various laws and guidance direct agencies to undertake initiatives to use IT to improve government services to the public and internal operations.	[44 U.S.C. 3506(h)(3) and the E-government Act of 2002]

Some of the important areas, of the 13 identified in Table 5, for HSIS are information security and strategic planning. In information security it is critical to make sure that federal information systems are not vulnerable to a terrorist attack. Strategic planning influences how the IT architecture fits into the overall mission of the federal department or agency. Since HSIS pervades many responsibilities and functions in the federal government, recognizing its mission and developing strategic plans in conjunction with homeland security is critical.

PRINCIPLES OF EFFECTIVE MANAGEMENT AND IT

IT is a key element of management reform efforts in federal departments/agencies that can help to shape the performance and reduce costs of the federal government (GAO, 2003; GAO, 2005a). Advances in IT can influence the way that federal agencies communicate, use and disseminate information, deliver services, and conduct business. There are also significant challenges that they must overcome such as the need for integration and sharing information among agencies.

The GAO (2004d) identified seven key components of effective information technology management in an evaluation of the information systems of the DHS. These seven principles of effective IT management can be applied to HSIS. The seven principles were derived from what GAO observed as being critical for effective IT management. They are: (1) IT strategic planning; (2) enterprise architecture; (3) IT investment management; (4) systems development and acquisition management; (5) information security management; (6) information management; and (7) IT human capital management.

IT strategic planning defines what an agency seeks to accomplish and indentifies the strategies that can be used to achieve results (GAO, 2004c). The Paperwork Reduction Act requires that agencies indicate in strategic IRM plans how they are applying information resources to improve the productivity, efficiency, and effectiveness of government programs. The strategic plan serves as a roadmap for implementing effective management of IT.

The effective use of *enterprise architecture*, which is the connection of an organization's strategic plan with programs and systems, provides a clear and comprehensive picture of the agency. According to the GAO (2004c), what organizations do not want to do is have IT investments that are not well integrated, that are duplicative, making them unnecessarily costly.

IT investments can have a dramatic impact on an organization's performance. They can improve government performance and accountability (GAO, 2004c). An *IT investment management* process provides for a systematic method for agencies to minimize risks and maximize return on investment.

According to the GAO (2004c), applying rigorous management practices for the development and *acquisition management* of IT systems can improve the likelihood of delivering expected capabilities on time and within budget. Essentially, the quality of the management processes involved in developing and acquiring IT dictates better procurement and management.

Due to the integration of IT systems in federal departments and agencies with the rise of the Internet, government officials are increasingly concerned about *information security* breaches from external attacks and internal misuse of IT (GAO, 2004c). Information security has been a priority area identified in the ITAA (2008) CIO survey. Enhancing information security can also lead to more effective management of IT in the federal government.

As departments and agencies move into an operational environment that is electronic rather than paper based *information management* is a critical management function for effective IT (GAO, 2004c). This is particularly important since September 11, 2001 where there is both a need for information sharing with other state and local entities, but also the need to keep sensitive information confidential and out of the wrong hands.

The final area for effective IT management is *IT human capital management* (GAO, 2004c). This is the ability of organizations to recruit and retain staff who can effectively implement technology in a changing business environment. The challenge of the federal government faces in maintaining a high-quality workforce.

The GAO (2006) believes that these principles of effective IT and management are interdependent. If effectively established and implemented, they can go a long way towards determining how successful a department or agency can use IT to achieve its mission. In this chapter, results from a survey of federal CIOs are presented which asked these government officials about the impact of HSIS on the principles of effective management just outlined.

DATA COLLECTION METHODS

An online survey of Federal Government department and agency CIOs was conducted between the months of May and June 2008. The mailing list for this survey was found on the CIO Council website (http://www.cio.gov). There were 147 CIOs identified on the Council Website that were sent a survey. There was a reminder letter for those CIOs that did not respond to the initial request for participation. The total number of responses was 38, which represents a response rate of 26%. The CIOs were asked on the survey a series of questions about the impact of HSIS on their department or agency.

In order to get a sense of the representativeness of the survey sample, Table 6 shows the descriptive characteristics of the CIOs that responded to the survey and the size of their agencies. The highest number of responses came from large federal agencies with 11 (29.7%) of them having 5,000 or more full-time equivalent (FTE) employees. There were also many smaller agencies that responded as represented by eight (21.6%) of them with 99 or fewer FTE employees. Essentially, we can say that the survey is fairly representative of CIOs and their agencies, but there are fewer medium-sized agencies, seven in total, within the range of 500 to 2,499 FTE employees.

The age range of the federal CIOs that responded to the survey were more likely to be middle-aged males, 46 years of age and older. There was 40.5% of the sample composed of CIOs that have worked for the federal government for 26 years or more. However, holding the position of CIO was for a relatively short period of time, with 80.6% having this title for five years or less. This finding is consistent with the GAO (2004) report which showed a median tenure of federal CIOs was two years in office. Finally, there was no respondent in the sample that had less than a bachelor's degree. There was 51.4% of the sample with advanced educational credentials such as a master's degree. Therefore, the federal CIOs that were surveyed generally had an advanced level of higher education.

HSIS IMPACT ON CIO ROLES AND RESPONSIBILITIES

Table 7 examines the impact of HSIS on the roles and responsibilities of federal government CIOs. The most important impact (when summing agree and strongly agree responses) on the CIOs responsibilities was information security. The results indicated that 72.9% of CIOs agreed that information security has been impacted because of homeland security. The second most important impact on the roles and

Table 6. Information of federal CIOs and their agencies

Number of full-time equivalent (FTE) employees in federal agency	*Frequency*	*Percent*
99 or less	8	21.6
100 to 499	9	24.3
500 to 999	1	2.7
1,000 to 2,499	6	16.2
2,500 to 4,999	2	5.4
5,000 or more	11	29.7
Age range of the CIOs		
35 and below	1	2.6
36 - 40	3	7.9
41-45	5	13.2
46-50	11	28.9
51-55	11	28.9
Above 55	7	18.4
Gender		
Female	8	22.2
Male	28	77.8
How many years CIO worked for federal government		
Less than 5 years	5	13.5
5 to 10 years	4	10.8
11 to 15 years	3	8.1
16 to 20 years	3	8.1
21 to 25 years	7	18.9
26 years or more	15	40.5
Years position as CIO in department/agency		
Less than 2 years	14	38.9
2 to 5 years	15	41.7
6 to 10 years	5	13.9
11 to 15 years	2	5.6
Highest academic attainment		
4 year college degree	14	37.8
Master's degree	19	51.4
Law degree	1	2.7
Doctorate	3	8.1

responsibilities showed that 67.6% of CIOs believed that IT capital planning and investment management has been influenced because of HSIS. Also, tied for second were 67.5% of CIOs who believed that privacy had been impacted because of HSIS. Enterprise architecture (64.9%) was the third most important role and responsibility of the CIO that had changed as a result of HSIS.

Table 7. HSIS impact on CIO roles and responsibilities

In my department/agency HSIS has impacted the following roles as CIO...	*Strongly Agree %*	*Agree %*	*Neutral %*	*Disagree %*	*Strongly Disagree %*	*Median*
IT/Information Resource Management (IRM) strategic planning	18.9	43.2	24.3	13.5	0.0	2.0
IT capital planning and investment management	13.5	54.1	21.6	10.8	0.0	2.0
Information security	27.0	45.9	18.9	8.1	0.0	2.0
IT/IRM workforce planning	5.6	44.4	36.1	13.9	0.0	2.5
Information collection/paperwork reduction	5.6	33.3	41.7	16.7	2.8	3.0
Information dissemination	13.9	25.0	47.2	13.9	0.0	3.0
Records management	5.4	48.6	32.4	13.5	0.0	2.0
Privacy	18.9	48.6	21.6	10.8	0.0	2.0
Statistical policy and coordination	0.0	21.6	54.1	18.9	5.4	3.0
Information disclosure	8.1	43.2	32.4	16.2	0.0	2.0
Enterprise architecture	13.5	51.4	24.3	10.8	0.0	2.0
Systems acquisition, development, and integration	13.2	42.1	34.2	10.5	0.0	2.0
E-government initiatives	11.1	47.2	30.6	11.1	0.0	2.0
Notes: strongly agree=1, agree =2, neutral=3, disagree =4, and strongly disagree =5						

Statistical policy and coordination had the least impact on HSIS with only 21.6% of agencies agreeing to this changing (Table 7). Information dissemination and collection had changed the role of federal CIOs according to only 38.9% of respondents.

Overall, it appears that most of the roles and responsibilities of CIOs have been impacted because of HSIS. This is evident by the median statistics which showed that nine out of 13 roles indentified have been impacted, which represents 70% of CIOs responsibilities. There were, however, factors of statistical policy and coordination, information dissemination, information collection/paperwork reduction, and IT workforce planning which did not show as great an impact because of HSIS. This is not surprising given that many of these roles may not be heavily influenced by HSIS.

HSIS IMPACT ON TOP IT CHALLENGES FOR CIOs

Another series of questions on the survey asked how much of an impact HSIS had on federal departments or agencies top IT challenges. Table 8 identifies the top challenges that CIOs face according to the 2008 Gartner Group survey of federal CIOs. The table is used to show the overall impact that HSIS had on the most pressing priorities that CIOs face. IT security/cyber security was noted as the most significant impact with 18.9% of CIOs believing that this had the highest impact. The median statistic was 2.0, which indicated that moderate impact was the most common response. Examining the median statistics another important impact that HSIS had on the top challenges were standardization and consolidation, resources, and implementing plans all had median statistics of 2.0. The results from this Table 8 indicated

Table 8. Impact of HSIS on top IT challenges for CIOs

How much of an impact does HSIS have in your department/agency for the following top IT challenges:	*Highest Impact %*	*Moderate Impact %*	*Low Impact %*	*Marginal Impact %*	*No Impact %*	*Median*
IT security/cyber security	18.9	56.8	10.8	2.7	10.8	2.0
Standardization and consolidation	10.8	45.9	29.7	2.7	10.8	2.0
IT workforce development	2.7	32.4	43.2	8.1	13.5	3.0
IT governance	8.1	37.8	32.4	8.1	13.5	3.0
Resources	5.9	47.1	29.4	5.9	11.8	2.0
Implementing plans	0.0	58.3	25.0	5.6	11.1	2.0
Information sharing	8.3	36.1	38.9	5.6	11.1	3.0
Achieving results	2.9	28.6	40.0	14.3	14.3	3.0
Acquisition and project management	2.8	33.3	36.1	11.1	16.7	3.0
Notes: highest impact=1, moderate impact =2, low impact=3, marginal impact =4, and no impact =5						

that in terms of the challenges that CIOs face, HSIS fits well into what the 2008 Gartner Group survey results indicated that information security was a pressing challenge for CIOs.

There was less agreement that HSIS impacted IT workforce development, IT governance, information sharing, achieving results, and acquisition and project management. All of these top challenges had a median score of 3.0; therefore, the most common response for them was low impact.

HSIS AND IT MANAGEMENT CAPABILITIES

Another area which this survey examines is if HSIS had an impact on IT management capabilities of federal CIOs. The results from these questions are shown in Table 9 indicating that there was the most agreement that HSIS impacted the management capabilities of IT investment management, information security management, and IT strategic management. All of the median statistics for these questions were 2.0, indicating that agree was the most common response. The results here are also consistent with the previous questions indicating that information security is a driver for HSIS for federal departments/agencies. The idea of fitting HSIS into strategic and investment management is important since its shows the high priority placed on this management capability for CIOs.

The IT management capabilities of enterprise architecture, systems development and acquisition management, IT human capital management, and information management the most common response was neutral, indicating that these management capabilities were not affected as much by HSIS. This finding is consistent with the other questions on the survey where resources are being devoted to more likely influences on HSIS. According to the survey, back office management functions are not being influenced greatly from HSIS.

Table 9. HSIS impact on IT management capabilities

In my department/agency, HSIS have impacted the following IT management capabilities...	*Strongly Agree %*	*Agree %*	*Neutral %*	*Disagree %*	*Strongly Disagree %*	*Median*
Enterprise architecture management	2.7	45.9	32.4	13.5	5.4	3.0
IT investment management	2.6	55.3	26.3	10.5	5.3	2.0
System development and acquisition management	5.6	41.7	36.1	11.1	5.6	3.0
Information security management	15.8	52.6	18.4	7.9	5.3	2.0
IT human capital management	0.0	27.8	50.0	16.7	5.6	3.0
IT strategic management	8.1	45.9	32.4	8.1	5.4	2.0
Information management	13.9	33.3	36.1	11.1	5.6	3.0
Notes: strongly agree=1, agree =2, neutral=3, disagree =4, and strongly disagree =5						

HOMELAND SECURITY PREPAREDNESS AND HSIS

The final group of questions are responses from CIOs to the impact of HSIS on federal department/agency preparedness as shown in Table 10. The results of this table first indicate that CIOs are likely to agree that they are well prepared with their current HSIS (55.3%). Second, there was agreement that top management supports HSIS development with 62.1% of CIO supporting this statement.

There was a more neutral response that departments/agencies had the necessary resources to fund HSIS and had the organizational culture that values HSIS adoption. The results of Table 10 indicate that 15.8% of CIOs actually disagree that their department/agency is well prepared with its current HSIS. Also, there were 29.7% of federal CIOs who disagreed that they had the necessary resources to fund HSIS. The conclusion to this chapter summarizes some of the important research findings and discusses the significance of them for HSIS.

Table 10. Federal government homeland security preparedness and HSIS

In homeland security preparedness my department/agency...	*Strongly Agree %*	*Agree %*	*Neutral %*	*Disagree %*	*Strongly Disagree %*	*Median*
Is well prepared with its current HSIS.	13.2	42.1	28.9	15.8	0.0	2.0
Has the necessary resources to fund HSIS.	5.4	27.0	37.8	24.3	5.4	3.0
Top management supports HSIS development.	16.2	45.9	27.0	10.8	0.0	2.0
Has the organizational culture that values HSIS adoption.	13.5	35.1	32.4	18.9	0.0	3.0
Notes: strongly agree=1, agree =2, neutral=3, disagree =4, and strongly disagree =5						

CONCLUSION

This chapter has examined the impact of HSIS on federal government departments and agencies. An overview of the functions and responsibilities of the DHS was provided. Some of the interesting results indicated that HSIS has shaped the roles and responsibilities of federal government CIOs. The GAO identified 13 roles and responsibilities that are common to federal government CIOs. The survey results in this chapter showed that all 13 of them were impacted because of HSIS. The greatest impacts were the influence of HSIS on information security, IT capital and investment planning, privacy, and enterprise architecture. There was evidence that all 13 areas of roles and responsibilities of CIOs were shaped to some extent by HSIS. From the survey responses, it appears that federal government HSIS has impacted the choices that CIOs make when doing their job.

One of the top challenges that CIOs face, when doing this job, is IT security/cyber security and it had the highest impact on homeland security. The impact of HSIS on the IT management capabilities of federal agencies indicates that it had an influence on IT investment management, information security management, and IT strategic management. The results of the survey indicate that CIOs are likely to agree that they are well prepared with their current HSIS.

REFERENCES

Bertot, J. C. (1997). The Impact of Federal IRM on Agency Missions: Findings, Issues, and Recommendations. *Government Information Quarterly*, *14*(3), 235–253. doi:10.1016/S0740-624X(97)90003-4

Bertot, J. C., & McClure, C. R. (1997). Key Issues Affecting the Development of Federal IRM: A View from the Trenches. *Government Information Quarterly*, *14*(3), 271–290. doi:10.1016/S0740-624X(97)90005-8

Buehler, M. (2000). U.S. federal Government CIOs: Information Technology's New Managers-Preliminary Findings. *Journal of Government Information*, *27*(1), 29–45. doi:10.1016/S1352-0237(99)00154-9

DHS. (2009). *Homeland Security Presidential Directives*. Retrieved January 26, 2009, from http://www.dhs.gov/xabout/laws/editorial_0607.shtm.

GAO. (2007). *Information Technology: DHS Needs to Fully Define and Implement Policies and Procedures for Effectively Managing Investments*. (GAO Publication No. GAO-07-424). Washington, DC: U.S. Government Printing Office.

Government Accountability Office. (2001). *Maximizing the Success of Chief Information Officers: Learning from Leading Organizations*. (GAO Publication No. GAO-01-376G). Washington, DC: U.S. Government Printing Office.

Government Accountability Office. (2003). *Major Management Challenges and Program Risks: A Governmentwide Perspective*. (GAO Publication No. GAO-03-95). Washington, DC: U.S. Government Printing Office.

Government Accountability Office. (2004a). *Department of Homeland Security: Formidable Information and Technology Management Challenges Requires Institutional Approach.* (GAO Publication No. GAO-04-702). Washington, DC: U.S. Government Printing Office.

Government Accountability Office. (2004b). *Federal Chief Information Officers: Responsibilities, Reporting Relationships, Tenure, and Challenges*. (GAO Publication No. GAO-04-823). Washington, DC: U.S. Government Printing Office.

Government Accountability Office. (2004c). *Information Technology: Homeland Security should Better Balance Need for System Integration Strategy with Spending for New and Enhanced Systems*. (GAO Publication No. GAO-04-509). Washington, DC: U.S. Government Printing Office.

Government Accountability Office. (2005a). *Veterans Affairs: The Role of the Chief Information Officer in Effectively Managing Information Technology*. (GAO Publication No. GAO-06-201T). Washington, DC: U.S. Government Printing Office.

Government Accountability Office. (2005b). *Electronic Government: Federal Agencies Have Made Progress Implementing the E-Government Act of 2002*. (GAO Publication No. GAO-05-12). Washington, DC: U.S. Government Printing Office.

Government Accountability Office. (2006). *Homeland Security: Progress Continues, but Challenges Remain on Department's Management of Information Technology*. (GAO Publication No. GAO-06-598T). Washington, DC: U.S. Government Printing Office.

Government Accountability Office. (2008). *Department of Homeland Security: Progress Made in Implementation of Management Functions, but more work Remains*. (GAO Publication No. GAO-08-646T). Washington, DC: U.S. Government Printing Office.

Halchin, L. E. (2002). Electronic Government in the Age of Terrorism. *Government Information Quarterly, 19*(3), 243–254. doi:10.1016/S0740-624X(02)00104-1

Halchin, L. E. (2004). Electronic Government: Government Capability and Terrorist Resource. *Government Information Quarterly, 21*(4), 406–419. doi:10.1016/j.giq.2004.08.002

ITAA. (2008). *Information Technology Association of America's Eighteenth Annual Survey of Federal Chief Information Officers.* Retrieved August 1, 2008, http://www.grantthornton.com/staticfiles/GTCom/files/Industries/GlobalPublicSector/2008%20ITAA%20Survey.pdf

McClure, C. R., & Bertot, J. C. (2000). The Chief Information Officer (CIO): Assessing its Impact. *Government Information Quarterly, 17*(1), 7–12. doi:10.1016/S0740-624X(99)00021-0

Mullen, P. R. (2005). US Performance-Based Laws: Information Technology and E-Government Reporting Requirements. *International Journal of Public Administration, 28*(7&8), 581–598. doi:10.1081/PAD-200064204

Nunn, S. (2005). Preventing the Next Terrorist Attack: The Theory and Practice of Homeland Security Information Systems. *Journal of Homeland Security and Emergency Management, 2*(3), 1–28. doi:10.2202/1547-7355.1137

Office of Homeland Security. (2002). *National Strategy for Homeland Security*. Retrieved August 1, 2008, http://www.whitehouse.gov/homeland/book/

Relyea, H. C. (2000). Paperwork Reduction Act Reauthorization and Government Information Management Issues. *Government Information Quarterly, 17*(4), 367–393. doi:10.1016/S0740-624X(00)00048-4

Relyea, H. C. (2004). Homeland Security and Information Sharing: Federal Policy Considerations. *Government Information Quarterly, 21*(4), 420–438. doi:10.1016/j.giq.2004.08.007

Seifert, J. W. (2002). The Effects of September 11, 2001, Terrorist Attacks on Public and Private Information Infrastructures: A Preliminary Assessment of Lessons Learned. *Government Information Quarterly, 19*(3), 225–242. doi:10.1016/S0740-624X(02)00103-X

Ward, M. A., & Mitchell, S. (2004). A Comparison of the Strategic Priorities of Public and Private Sector Information Resource Management Executives. *Government Information Quarterly, 21*(3), 284–304. doi:10.1016/j.giq.2004.04.003

Westerback, L. K. (2000). Toward Best Practices for Strategic Information Technology Management. *Government Information Quarterly, 17*(1), 27–41. doi:10.1016/S0740-624X(99)00023-4

Chapter 5
Information Technology and Emergency Management

INTRODUCTION

This chapter examines the impact of information technology (IT) on emergency management. E-emergency management is the use of the digital means as a way of performing professional disaster-related work (Green, 2001). Some of the components of e-emergency management that are being used according to Green (2001, p 79) are:

- Use of emergency management software to communicate internally and externally and to manage data;
- Remote access to emergency operations center databases and communications;
- Access to internet sites to gather information;
- Dissemination of information on the internet both to official response organizations and for public access; and
- Linking dispersed individuals to perform emergency operations center functions remotely

Section 214 of the E-Government Act of 2002 called on the Office of Management and Budget (OMB) in consultation with the Federal Emergency Management Agency (FEMA) to ensure that IT is studied to enhance crisis preparedness and response as a consequence of natural and manmade disasters (Rao, Eisenberg, and Schmitt, 2007). This important e-government legislation demonstrates the vital role of IT in emergency management. E-emergency management is especially critical to understand given the important role that the different levels of government play in disasters.

This chapter will show that there is a need to be comprehensive in IT and emergency management. For effective emergency planning there is a need to use IT to leverage planning efforts. Federalism mat-

DOI: 10.4018/978-1-60566-834-5.ch005

ters when doing emergency planning and should be taken into account in these efforts. Citizens play a critical role in emergency management. Information that is timely, and of high quality, is essential for emergency management. The digital divide matters in planning for emergency management and there is an importance of public libraries in the event of a disaster to serve those populations impacted from the disaster.

This chapter first examines the four functions of emergency management to determine how these functions relate to IT. Emergency planning and its application to IT adoption is discussed in this chapter. The intergovernmental aspects of emergency management are discussed to set the context of the environment that emergency responders work under. The role that citizens play in emergency management is discussed to determine the important influence they have over the process. The chapter also examines the impact of management information systems on emergency management. This chapter examines the important organizational, societal, and technology issues of IT and emergency management. There are results from a survey of state government directors of emergency management to determine what impact that IT has had on their departments. Finally, a conclusion summarizes the important findings of this study.

FUNCTIONS EMERGENCY MANAGEMENT

The emergency management activities of the different levels of government are based on an emergency management model (Waugh, 1994). This four phase model was a product of a National Governors Association study of state emergency management in the late 1970s (McLoughlin, 1985). This model divides emergency management into four phases, which are:

1. **Mitigation:** Activities undertaken in the long term, before disaster strikes, that are designed to prevent emergencies and reduce the damage that results from those that occur, including modifying the causes of hazards, reducing vulnerability to risk, and diffusing potential losses;
2. **Preparedness:** Activities undertaken in the shorter term, before disaster strikes, that enhance the readiness or organizations and communities to respond to disasters effectively;
3. **Response:** Activities undertaken immediately following a disaster to provide emergency assistance to victims and remove further threats; and
4. **Recovery:** Short term and long term activities undertaken after a disaster that are designed to return the people and property in an affected community to at least their pre-disaster condition of well being (Donahue and Joyce, 2001, p. 730).

This model is generally accepted by emergency managers and researchers as appropriate for the policy implementation process. These four phases are all of the necessary components of emergency management. However, in practice they are not always linear or clearly delineated (Col, 2007). Towards the end of this chapter, there is survey evidence presented on the extent to which IT has influenced the four phases of emergency management.

A strategic management approach is necessary to establish effective emergency management actions and plans to prepare for disasters (Choi, 2008). The strategic management perspective is characterized by long-term process for developing a continual commitment to the vision of the organization. A comprehensive strategic management approach is a potential tool that emergency managers should be able to apply to their government. As shown in Chapter 4, IT is often incorporated as one important element of the strategic plan for organizations.

EMERGENCY PLANNING

Emergency preparedness refers to the readiness of jurisdictions to react constructively to threats from the environment, and minimizes the negative consequences of impact on the health and safety of individuals in that jurisdiction (Perry and Lindell, 2003). There are several guiding principles of emergency planning indentified by Lindell and Perry (2007, pp. 115-116).

1. Anticipate both active and passive resistance to the planning process, and develop strategies to manage these obstacles;
2. Address all hazards to which the community is exposed;
3. Include all response organizations, seeking their participation, commitment, and clearly defined agreement;
4. Base pre-impact planning on accurate assumptions about the threat, about the typical human behavior in disasters, and about likely support from external sources such as state and federal agencies;
5. Identify the types of emergency response actions that are most likely to be appropriate but encourage improvisation based on continuing emergency assessment;
6. Address the linkage of emergency response to disaster recovery;
7. Provide training and evaluation of the emergency response organization at all levels, individual, team, department, community; and
8. Recognize that emergency planning is a continuing process.

We use these guiding principles to determine the impact that planning has on IT adoption in state government emergency management agencies.

Alexander (2005) believes that there are several reasons why the quality of emergency planning is in need of improvement. First, there is a general consensus that emergency management is not a full-fledged profession; it is still common to find emergency planners without adequate training and specialized knowledge. There is inefficiency in emergency planning because of poor quality emergency planning. Third, emergency planning is often considered as a static process, there is not a continuous feedback loop after the incident happens. Fourth, planning oftentimes is informal where responsibilities and procedures are inadequately defined. Firth, emergency planning should not be viewed in isolation since there are many actors involved from different levels of government and nonprofit entities and as a result collaboration is essential. This intergovernmental aspect of emergency management is of critical importance to understand. There is a definite need for IT to improve the emergency management function; IT should help with collaboration, training, and process improvement of agencies.

INTERGOVERNMENTAL AND COLLABORATION

The federal system itself does not promote a coherent and comprehensive disaster preparedness effort (Waugh, 1988). Vertical fragmentation because of the dividing of powers between the federal government and state governments and the limited powers given to local governments makes decision making and program coordination awkward. There also is horizontal fragmentation due to jurisdictional issues involved and the number of agencies involved.

There has traditionally been unwillingness of the federal government and state governments to assume the lead in disaster preparedness and response (Waugh, 1988). Most disasters produce much localized damage without mass causalities or high levels of property damage. Therefore, most of the preparedness and planning for disasters belong to local governments. Some of these intergovernmental aspects that Waugh indentifies may have changed as a result of the response by the federal government to Hurricane Katrina. After the inadequate federal government response to Katrina, there has been more effort to respond more quickly to disasters.

Information management is crucial to any efforts to mitigate the effects of a disaster such as a Hurricane (Ryoo and Choi, 2006). During Hurricane Katrina, there were the federal government agencies such as FEMA and the Department of Homeland Security, all of the branches of the armed forces, state and local governments, the American Red Cross among other nonprofit agencies involved. After Hurricane Katrina the problem was the lack of collaboration to help the victims; one could envision that IT could have helped with coordination efforts.

The recent disasters such as the December 2005 Tsunami and Hurricane Katrina show the need for improvements in crisis response and management information systems (Jefferson, 2006). There was evidence that the existing systems were both inadequate and overwhelmed to respond to the magnitude of these events. In order for disaster management efforts to succeed, there needs to be a link between information collection and analysis and decision making and action. Therefore, IT plays a key role in collaboration and emergency management as the literature demonstrates. The following section will examine the important role that citizens play in emergency management.

CITIZENS AND EMERGENCY MANAGEMENT

Research examining the cities of Grand Forks, North Dakota and East Grand Forks, Minnesota success of recovery from a disastrous flood demonstrates the importance of citizens and emergency management (Kweit and Kweit, 2004). Research shows that cities that attempted to get citizens involved had a substantial effect on the overall evaluation of the success of recovery. Public officials must take seriously their responsibility to include citizen input in their decision making and to be responsive to their input.

Research shows that citizens in western societies act rationally in disaster situations (Helsloot and Ruitenberg, 2004). They tend not to panic and make rational decisions based on the available information at the time. However, when citizens have inadequate information to assess during a disaster, the choices that they make may be suboptimal. Citizens effectively bring themselves to safety and evacuations of disasters shows that citizens oftentimes save their fellow citizens. Therefore, it is important for first responders to take advantage of citizen response capabilities. Helsloot and Ruitenberg believe that citizens will prepare for situations of which they have the perception that preparation for the disaster is useful and where there is a reasonable chance that a disaster might occur. These authors argue that information is critical for the successful management of citizens in a disaster.

There is a great potential for public involvement in our digital world in the case of disasters (Palen, Hiltz, and Liu, 2007). The reach of the internet expands the opportunities for public involvement for those especially geographically removed from the situation and can provide information and help. Online forms create a means of sharing and learning from personal stories, experience, and the knowledge for preparation of future events. For example, Katrina.com (www.Katrina.com) was a Website previously used to advertise for a small consulting business run by Katrina Blankenship. After Hurricane Katrina, Blankenship converted her webpage to serve as a resource to help locate missing people.

Research indicates that information is more useful to the decision maker in a disaster if it is specific and is delivered in a timely manner (Wang and Kapucu, 2007). Public complacency increases under repeated threat warnings, suggesting that information that is not specific or timely may be more harmful than helpful for the public's decision because it could make them less alert and more reluctant to take actions because of the threat. This is shown in Hurricane Katrina, where certain groups such as the poor and the elderly are at greater risk throughout the disaster, specific and timely information would be of great help to them. Governments should determine the public's need for information and develop proper channels for information delivery. For instance, new information channels such as the internet and other digital means should be used in addition to more traditional channels such as public meetings and television.

In the United States, public libraries have become the unofficial place to access e-government for those that cannot otherwise reach this information (Jaeger, et al., 2007). During a major emergency, access to FEMA and other governments websites provided by public libraries can be essentially for recovery. Therefore, for certain population group's public libraries play a key role in providing access in times of emergencies.

MANAGEMENT INFORMATION SYSTEMS

There are three common management information systems used by emergency management which are knowledge management systems, decision support systems, and geographic information systems. Each of these will be briefly discussed in relation to emergency management.

According to Chua, Kaynak, and Foo (2007) knowledge management systems (KMS) in disaster preparation and response phases can be viewed along three dimensions of knowledge creation, knowledge transfer, and knowledge use. In the preparation stage, knowledge creation is the system of capturing, analyzing, and transmitting timely disaster information into action. Knowledge transfer is the clear lines of control to disseminate information about the disaster's imminence. While knowledge reuse is a system for accurately evaluating disaster situations to invoke appropriate disaster plans.

While in the response phase, knowledge creation is the encouragement of effective communication for the ground rescue operations (Chua, Kaynak, and Foo, 2007). In the knowledge transfer stage there is clear lines of control to support the rescue operations. In the knowledge reuse stage there is the implementation of disaster procedures in response to difficulties faced from the initial response.

Decision Support Systems (DSS) support operational, tactical, and strategic decisions in organizations (Wallace and Balogh, 1985; French and Turoff, 2007). DSS are designed to affect the decision making process and behavior of organizations. DSS are the information technologies such as computer hardware, software, telecommunications, that are designed to complement the cognitive processes of humans in their decision making. These systems may be built on large databases and/or models of which they share results that can be communicated with decision makers in emergency situations.

There also is Geographic Information Systems (GIS), another important technology in the emergency management function. The experience with Hurricane Andrew in 1992 demonstrates both the importance of GIS to disaster management and the development of GIS capabilities (Waugh, 1995). According to Waugh, there are several lessons learned from GIS as a result of Hurricane Andrew that hit South Florida. First, a strong GIS capability could have made the response more effective and speeded the recovery; second, databases need to be created beforehand rather than pieced together during the disaster; and third, emergency managers and other public officials need to understand the capabilities of GIS based analysis to improve planning and disaster management. There are several other socio-technical issues on the impact of IT and emergency management that are discussed in the next section of this chapter.

EMERGENCY MANAGEMENT TECHNOLOGIES

Information technologies are an integral component of emergency preparedness and planning. Emergency preparedness can be defined as a community's ability to react constructively to threats from its environment and minimize the impact of these threats to the health and safety of the community (Perry and Lindell, 2003). Written plans do not guarantee a level of preparedness for government, because preparedness is an ongoing process which is contingent upon the process that takes place, it is not merely the outputs of the planning process. Perry and Lindell believe that preparedness is the ability of the community to respond to these environmental threats and change their response as the threat changes. With IT communities can have the ability to use technology to change as the threat increases.

There are two important element of emergency preparedness that should be noted and are applicable to IT (Perry and Lindell, 2003). Emergency planning is shaped by both hazard assessment and risk reduction. Hazard assessment involves not only identifying threats in the community, but leveraging technology that leads to the identification of new threats. Once the hazards are identified by the emergency planning agency, there should be a formal assessment of their risk to the community. Emergency planning secondly involves risk reduction through an examination of actions that decrease threats. Risk reduction is the implementation of activities that involve the four phases of emergency management, namely, mitigation, preparedness, response, and recovery.

Stephenson and Anderson (1997) have indentified four phases and their application of IT to emergency management. I have added and additional phase of mobile communication that is relevant to current emergency management. The early period was until the 1970s and this was a time when many users shared the same large mainframe computer. The most common ways that the mainframe computer was used in the 1970s was operational research and mathematical simulations mostly for defense-related civil emergencies. One early simulation was the SPLASH model, and its successor was the SLOSH used for storm surge and mitigation planning. The second phase was great improvement in accessibility and experimentation in the first half of the 1980s. During this phase there was the growth of internet in academic settings using email, for example, to transfer large data files. There was the rise of thousands of amateur radio operators setting up essentially wireless networks for emergency management. The late 1980s was a period of maturing applications and communications innovations and standards. The growth of local area networks gave more control of information resources to departments rather than centralized management information services. Desktop computer equipment became more common and portable, more independent than the traditional mainframe computer. This period saw the emergency of GIS technology to support emergency management. Software packages such as ARC-Info, MapInfo, and Intergraph were used to support mitigation activities, response, and recovery planning. The fourth phase is networking and it had a tremendous impact on contemporary emergency management. In this phase, the Internet blossomed in the late 1990s and has been able to connect up many useful emergency management applications. One phase Stephenson and Anderson did not discuss in their paper, written in the late 1990s, was the rise of mobile communications and this should be the fifth phase. Mobile digital communications such as cellular phones have enabled current emergency responders to be at any location and receive and transmit information during a disaster.

There are numerous important broad types of technologies that are used in emergency management as illustrated by Pine (2007). This author identifies seven technologies that are universal for emergency management: the Internet, wireless technology, GIS, direct and remote sensing, emergency management decision support systems, hazard analysis and modeling, and warning systems. Each of these technologies will be briefly discussed, outlining their relevance to emergency management.

The Internet, as mentioned, can provide useful information about emergencies and disasters to the public and first responders (Liu, 2008). The Internet enables first responder to work well with others due to its ability to communicate quickly and share resources (Pine, 2007). The Internet provides a low cost approach to exchanging information on specialized topics. It also allows small and rural communities access to information that may not be available to these communities (Bertot, et al., 2006; Palen, Hiltz, and Liu, 2007).

Wireless technology, including global positioning systems (GPS), allows disaster response to change quickly with updated information (Cutter, et al., 2007). Wireless technology ranges from doing simple tasks such as communicating with first responders remotely. It also allows more complex tasks such as collecting digital data using, for example, wireless tools such as personal digital assistants (PDAs).

As mentioned, geographic Information Systems (GIS) use geographic location to relate otherwise disparate data and provide a systemic way of collection and managing location specific information (Waugh, 1995). Because of its ability to gather, manipulate, query, and display geographic information quickly, and present it in an understandable format, this makes GIS critical for the emergency management function (Cutter et al., 2007).

Remote sensing uses image sensors over an area of interest, collecting optical and radar-based imagery and transforming it into spatial information that can be used to gain an understanding of disaster conditions (Cutter, et al., 2007). This makes remote sensing valuable for hazard monitoring and assessment of the damages.

Emergency management decision support systems are critical for emergency management since they enable officials to record, select, sort, and save population, chemical, or weather data about a community (Wallace and Balogh, 1985; French and Turoff, 2007; Pine, 2007). Individual facilities can use information systems to comply with or monitor federal or state requirements, and to determine the level of risk to the community and appropriate response on the basis of the risk. Computer Aided Management Emergency Operations (CAMEO), which is commonly used for chemical emergency planners and first responders, is an example of an emergency management decision support system (Clarke, 2006).

Hazard analysis and modeling is the simulation of real systems of a potential hazard event (Pine, 2007). Modeling hazards provides a means of measuring the nature and extent of a disaster. For example, one model used for hurricanes is Sea, Lake, and Overland Surges from Hurricanes (SLOSH) used by the National Weather Service (NWS) to calculate potential surge heights from hurricanes.

Finally, warning systems provide a means of getting information about an impending emergency and communicating that information to those in need (Pine, 2007). The NWS has detection systems and warning systems through local and regional weather centers. Emergency management officials receive the information and broadcast this information to warn communities.

There are six IT-based capabilities listed by the Committee on Using Information Technology to Enhance Disaster Management in Table 1 that are believed to improve disaster management (National Research Council, 2007). These capabilities span hazard mitigation, disaster preparation, disaster response, and disaster recovery and are listed along with an example of technology that could potentially address this issue. The Committee noted that technology is only part of the solution for better and more effective disaster management capabilities since there are many social aspects that must be brought into the equation. These capabilities were selected since they first have the ability to address major problems in current disaster management and second they represent the potential for significant improvement in the current state of the art.

Table 1 shows the first IT capability that can be used to enhance disaster management is more robust, interoperable, and priority-sensitive communications (National Research Council, 2007). Common examples of this technology are mobile devices that enable the first responder to effectively communicate with one another in the response to a disaster. There must be simply availability of communications at the disaster scene. Many communications problems at the scene of a disaster are caused by destruction of communication devices and lines; Hurricane Katrina is an often cited example of the failure of communications. There needs to be improvements in hardening technology for worst case events. Promising technology in this capability of disaster management is push-to-talk capabilities, text messaging, and web access.

The second capability of disaster management noted in Table 1 is improved situation awareness and common operating picture (National Research Council, 2007). Situational awareness focuses on providing operators and decision makers with information relevant to what they want to accomplish,

Table 1. Six issues to improve disaster management and related IT capabilities (Source: Adapted from National Research Council, 2007)

More robust, interoperable, and priority-sensitive communications	Cellular
	Wireless networking
	Redundant and resilient infrastructure
	Internet/IP-based networking
Improved situational awareness and a common operating picture	Radio-frequency identification for resource tracking and logistics
Improved decision support and resource tracking and allocation	Online resource directories
	Commercial collaboration software and file sharing
Greater organizational agility for disaster management	Computer-mediated exercises
	Portable unmanned aerial vehicles and robots
Better engagement of the public	Automated, multimodal public notification and resource contact systems
	Multimodal public reporting capabilities
	Validated online information sources
	Reverse 911 capability (i.e., two-way emergency reporting)
Enhanced infrastructure survivability and continuity of societal functions	Mobile power generators
	Redundant radio systems
	Dynamic stockpiled supply management
	Wikis

by helping them understand and assess the characteristics and consequences of alternative courses of action. Improved situation awareness is the degree to which the situation reflects reality. By leveraging IT, to enhance the ability of the first responder, this will improve disaster management. One example of a technology that could be used to improve situation awareness and operating picture is radio-frequency identification tags to track the whereabouts of disaster victims.

The third capability to enhance disaster management is improved decision support and resource tracking and allocation (National Research Council, 2007). Decision support involves analyzing actions taken to monitor the effectiveness of these actions. For example, technology could be used such as online resource directories which will provide rapid information for emergency responders on the scene.

The fourth capability for improved disaster management is greater organizational agility (National Research Council, 2007). During disasters organizations must be able to work well together. The tragic events of September 11, 2001 showed that precious hours have an impact on the ability of first responders to save lives. An example of technology that could be used to improve organizational agility is computer mediated exercises. Disaster management is an area where there is a potential for organizational learning. The Department of Homeland Security has created the Lessons Learned Information Sharing website (http://www.llis.gov) as a mechanism for distributing lessons learned information to emergency management officials.

The fifth capability of enhancing disaster management with IT is better engagement of the public (National Research Council, 2007). Citizens are normally the first on the scene of a disaster and can greater help the recovery process if informed of the situation. Two types of potentially promising technology for this area is reverse 911 capability and online information sources for disaster victims, families, and their friends.

The sixth and final capability for enhanced disaster management is enhancing infrastructure survivability and continuity of societal functions (National Research Council, 2007). Hurricane Katrina is an example of having displaced much of the metropolitan population of New Orleans, with its residents being dispersed across the country. There is the potential of IT to reconnect people that have been displaced because of a hurricane or other disaster. Hurricane Katrina showed that people can come together with the Internet and other IT. One example is using wikis that enabled volunteers to connect with victims. Some of the functions of the wikis during Hurricane Katrina were to list online helpline numbers, posting offers of temporary housing, identifying where and how donations can be made, and offering health and safety information.

There are a number of new and emerging technologies that have surfaced in recent years to enable better emergency management coordination (Chen, Sharman, Rao, and Upadhyaya, 2008). Some notable ones are wireless mesh networks (A wireless mesh network is a communications network made up of radio nodes organized in a mesh topology. The coverage area of the radio nodes working as a single network is sometimes called a mesh cloud. Access to this mesh cloud is dependent on the radio nodes working in harmony with each other to create a radio network. A mesh network is reliable and offers redundancy. When one node can no longer operate, the rest of the nodes can still communicate with each other, directly or through one or more intermediate nodes), sensor networks (wireless sensor network is a wireless network consisting of spatially distributed autonomous devices using sensors to cooperatively monitor physical or environmental conditions, such as temperature, sound, vibration, pressure, motion or pollutants, at different locations), knowledge management systems, GIS, communication standards, incident forecast and analysis, peer-to-peer communication platforms, collaborative work systems, and command and control systems.

Another emerging technology are Community Disaster Information Systems (CDIS), which automates the identification of and access to information on local and national suppliers of disaster-related goods and services (Troy, Carson, Vanderbeek, and Hutton, 2007). It provides access both online and offline to a central server and data repository over the Internet. Typically entry is through a web-based system using an Internet browser. This local resource database would provide information on, for example, construction equipment and operators, medical facilities and personnel, transportation, food, housing and shelter, and animal shelters. An example of the potential use of a CDIS would be Red Cross workers come from around the United States to a disaster scene. These workers are not familiar with the community and the services that it provides. CDIS has the ability to provide information on physical, information, and human resources to help workers assist victims. The old way of doing it would be through a paper-based system. The problem with this system is that information is not uniformly available to workers, can be outdated, and may not be properly indexed for an easy search among emergency management personnel. In addition, CDIS can be made available not just on the Internet; they can be uploaded into an independent software program such as handheld PDAs or laptops that can be taken directly to the disaster scene.

There are several barriers indentified in surveys of e-government adoption that could possibly impact the implementation of IT and emergency management. Coursey and Norris (2008) believe that the common barriers to e-government implementation are technical, political and organizational, legal, and financial. Hurdles to the implementation of e-government can have a significant impact on its success of adoption (Brown, 2007). The barriers that have seen the greatest impact on local e-government adoption in a 2004 survey were lack of financial resources and lack of technology web staff (Coursey and Norris, 2008). Both of these findings are not surprising, given that the public sector has traditionally faced very tough resource constraint issues. What was not found to be a significant barrier to the adoption of e-government in this survey was lack of support from elected officials?

IT ISSUES AND EMERGENCY MANAGEMENT

There are several challenges and issues associated with the adoption of IT in emergency management. There are three communications challenges which are necessary to address for effective disaster communications systems; they are technological, sociological, and organizational (Manoj and Baker, 2007). For example, technological challenges in communications are radio interoperability issues by creating dual use technology which enables both normal and emergency situation modes. The social challenge is the sharing of information is both critical and problematic because of issues of trust and privacy. Organizational challenges are prevalent in disasters, especially when groups that are used must be coordinated in a flatter, more dynamic organization that occurs during a disaster. There are communications technologies such as webmail, mobile communications, and wireless that can aid in these situations.

There are several issues that IT presents for emergency management as summarized by Quarantelli (1997) and discussed further by Fisher (1999). There first is the issue of rich-poor dichotomy which essentially means the difference between those that can go online for information and use IT and those that do not have access during an emergency. Information technology access normally revolves around age, race and socioeconomic status; where those of minorities, the elderly and poorer populations have less access to technology. This digital divide translates into differences in access to emergency management information on websites and other means of communication in preparation for a disaster.

Second, Quarantelli (1997) also believes that technology is viewed as an ends rather than the means for emergency management. Some emergency planning agencies need more sophisticated information systems than other jurisdictions. There should be a match when purchasing information systems with organizational needs. Therefore, technology for emergency management should fit into the strategic plan for the organization.

Third, there is information overload with the Internet for example being able to locate a lot of valuable information to aid in emergency planning and management. The issue becomes how the emergency planner effectively uses this information. With all of the information the emergency manager could be overwhelmed with choices and may make suboptimal decisions.

A fourth issue is outdated and lost information for the emergency management function. For example, information that is used in a GIS database, if not updated, will not provide accurate assessment. It is critical to regularly update databases that support GIS.

The fifth issue becomes the diffusion of inappropriate information. The internet provides citizens with quick access to information and greater volumes of information, there also is an additional burden placed upon the consumer of such information.

Sixth, there is often non-verbal communication issue. For example, with email the information is static distributed at one point in time. This information may change or become outdated or misread by the user. As a result, technology can only go so far in solving problems in emergency management because of social behavior of people.

Seventh, there is the issue of group communication that must be addressed. Does IT in emergency management facilitate group communication? An often cited example of technology interoperability is Hurricane Katrina, where the different levels of government were unable to effectively communicate with each another.

Eight, there also is fashions and fads in IT in emergency management. Many organizations want to have the cutting edge technology to prepare for disasters, but there should to be some assessment of the actually use and value of the new technology for the organization.

Ninth, information systems may create their own disaster. For example, the blackouts experienced in several urban areas such as New York City in 2004 can create serious economic disruptions because of these tightly coupled information systems.

Tenth, there is an issue of the IT outpacing our existing cultural and social structure. One must determine the extent to which technology would be functional rather than dysfunctional to the existing society.

The following section presents the survey results of an assessment of IT and state government emergency management. This is followed by information on IT used in the day-to-day operations of FEMA, and illustrates two examples of technology that is currently used by FEMA, namely expedited assistance and the emergency alert system.

INFORMATION TECHNOLOGY AND FEMA

FEMA is part of the Emergency Preparedness and Response (EP&R) Directorate of the Department of Homeland Security. Figure 1 shows the organizational chart of FEMA in relation to EP&R in the Department of Homeland Security. This agency is responsible for coordinating the disaster relief efforts for the federal, state, and volunteer organizations such as the Red Cross (OIG, 2005). FEMA relies on various IT

Figure 1. EP&R/FEMA organization

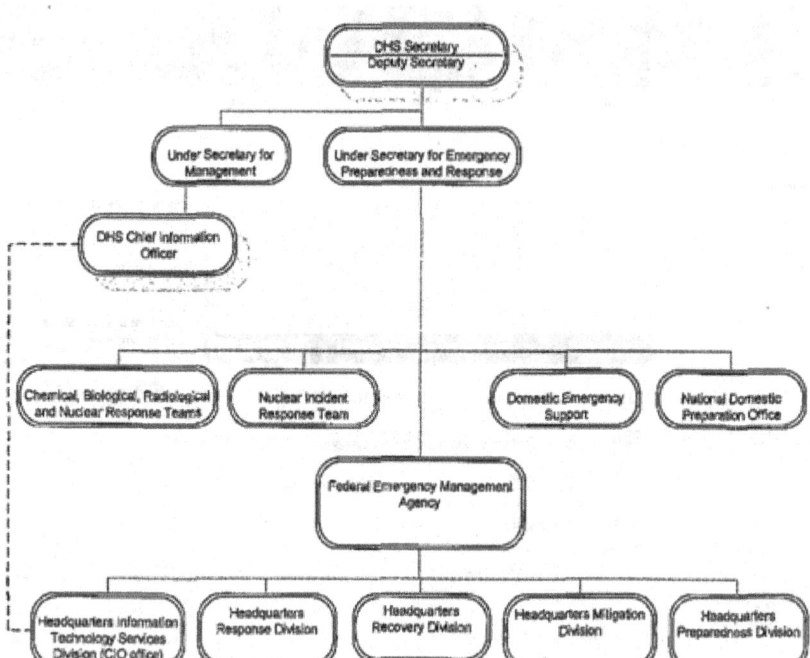

systems that are used to implement response and recovery efforts. As a result, strategic management of these assets is critically important in order for first responders to work effectively with one another during and after a disaster. The Stafford Act of 2000 gives FEMA the authority to lead the disaster response and recovery operations of 28 major federal agencies and departments, the American Red Cross, and other volunteer organizations. FEMA in addition provides financial assistance to individuals that sustained damage to their personal property. FEMA has 10 regional offices located throughout the United States to assist states in disaster management effort.

Figure 2 shows a screen shot for the FEMA website's (http://www.fema.gov). From FEMA's website one can notice that there is information on the organization in general, information on disaster preparedness and response, and information on the type of disasters that this agency would deal with. The website is very user friendly, and has the appearance of a web portal or gateway to information and services that FEMA provides.

EP&R has many emergency and IT support capabilities to help manage disasters. FEMA has four National Processing Service Centers which handle telephone registration and process victims' claims for disaster assistance. FEMA has five Mobile Emergency Response Support operations which provide initial support for on-site disaster management. This mobile support includes voice, data, and video for emergency managers. In 2005, the EP&R directorate's CIO had a budget of approximately $80 million and a total of 400 full-time and temporary employees. The CIOs office is charged with designing, developing, testing, implementing, and maintaining the operation of FEMA's systems. It has the following four applications that are critical to its IT systems.

Figure 2. Federal emergency management (FEMA) website (Source: http://www.fema.gov)

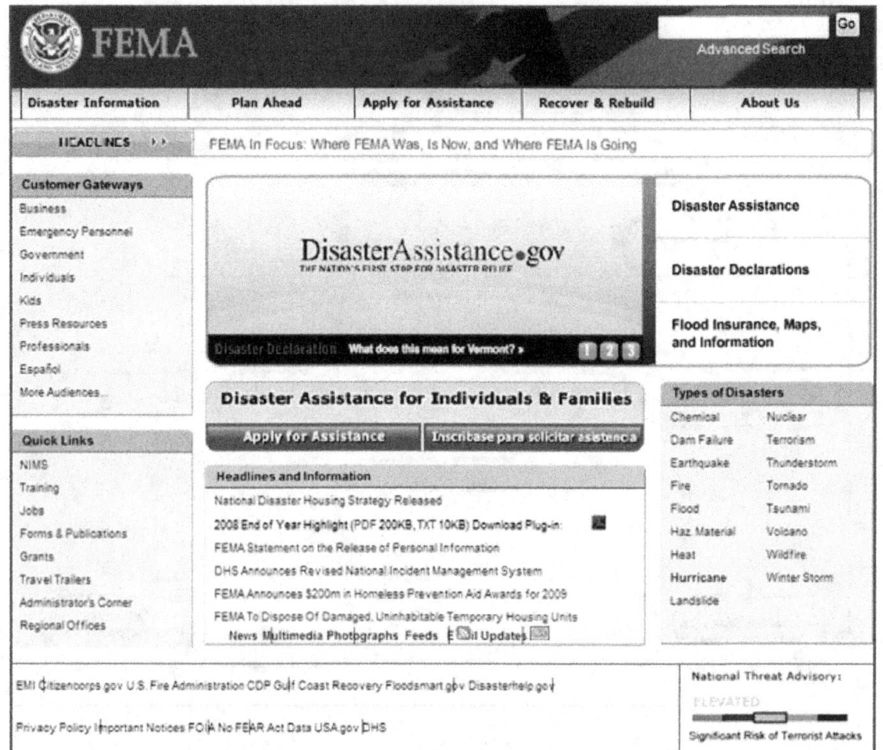

- *National Emergency Management Information System* (NEMIS) is the backbone IT system for response and recovery operations. FEMA uses NEMIS to electronically enter, record, and manage information regarding registered applicants for disaster assistance, obligations and payments, mission assignments, and grants.
- *Integrated Financial Management Information System* (IFMIS) forwards financial information to the Department of Treasury for payment of disaster assistance claims.
- *Logistics Information Management System III* (LIMS III) maintains the inventory of equipment and supplies.
- *Automated Deployment Database* (ADD) is used to identify and deploy personnel to disaster sites (OIG, p. 5).

The CIO for EP&R office maintains and manages the IT infrastructure such as the networks, databases, desktops, telephone systems to support operations. The CIO is also responsible for providing the IT infrastructure for support of emergency operations at disaster field offices and recovery centers, which involves running cable, establishing networks, supplying wireless connectivity, and installing equipment for information processing and communications. In addition, there is the national helpdesk which assists users by providing accounts, ensuring remote access, troubleshooting problems, and making referrals to engineers to fix problems.

The Office of Inspector General (OIG), in the Department of Homeland Security, in a 2005 report provided the following IT recommendations for EP&R (OIG, 2005). Some of the issues that OIC noticed were that EP&R's IT approach has been able to meet disaster challenges to date, with four major hurricanes since 2004, however, there are a number of information technology and management issues that limit the directorate's effectiveness. For example, the strategic plan for IT in FEMA does not reflect integration into the Department of Homeland Security's strategic goals. In addition, EP&R systems are not well integrated and do not effectively support information exchange during response and recovery operations. As a result, during the 2004 Hurricane season, IT systems cannot effectively handle increased workloads, are not adaptable to change, and lack needed real-time reporting.

OIG (2005) provided an example of IT support during the very busy hurricane season that struck Florida and the Gulf Coast in 2004. These hurricanes pushed FEMA's IT capabilities to the limit. Hurricanes Charley, Frances, Ivan, and Jeanne all category three or stronger storms hit the region within two weeks of each other. These hurricanes collectively cause an estimated $42 billion worth of damage. The EP&R CIO IT support staff provided significant support during this hurricane season. For example, FEMA IT was asked to establish a 200,000 square foot disaster field office within seven days, the largest of its history. Significant IT resources were needed to set up phone, networks, and computer stations to manage these information systems. For example, the NEMIS handled more than one million requests for disaster assistance in just six weeks. The NEMIS automation enabled individual assistance to be generally provided in 7 to 10 days. NEMIS staff at one point supported 18 call centers, which was well beyond the design requirement of three call centers and 20,000 calls per day. The overall satisfaction with call center service was about 85%, despite these very large volumes of calls. Another example of IT used in emergency management is FEMA's expedited assistance program.

EXPEDITED ASSISTANCE

During Hurricane Katrina, FEMA experimented with the use of debt cards to expedite payments of $2000 to about 11,000 disaster victims at three Texas shelters (GAO, 2006). FEMA stated that these victims had difficulty accessing bank accounts. The debit card was an effective means of distributing aid quickly to those in need. Some of the problems that GAO found in an audit of the expedited assistance program was that FEMA did not validate the identify of debit card recipients who registered over the phone. In addition, FEMA did not provide instructions on how to use the debt cards, that they should only be used for necessary expenses and serious needs related to disasters when the cards were distributed. In isolated instances, debit cards were used for adult entertainment, to purchase weapons, for purchases at a massage parlor.

The process for expedited assistance during Hurricane Katrina shows the dangers of not have correction validation of identify in place when using information systems. The GAO (2006) found weaknesses in the process that FEMA used to review registrations for disaster relief and approve assistance payments. The GAO found that individuals could apply for disaster relief via the Internet or telephone. FEMA's Internet registrations used credit card and other information to validate the identity of the individual. Individuals who failed to register via the Internet were advised to contact FEMA by telephone. FEMA did not have an identity verification process when 1.5 million registrants called over the phone. In fact, GAO officials tested the system and used falsified information and actually received $2,000 of disaster assistant. The following final example of IT and emergency management is the modernization of the emergency alert system.

EMERGENCY ALERT SYSTEM

Hurricane Katrina and the terrorist attacks on September 11, 2001 showed the need for timely, accurate emergency information. The Emergency Alert System (EAS) relies primarily on broadcast media, and is one tool to warn the public of potential emergencies such as Hurricanes or other disasters (GAO, 2007). The EAS remains a tool for the President can use to issue messages preempting all other broadcast programming.

There is concern over the ability of the current alert system to effectively warn the public about natural disasters or terrorist attacks as well as providing information on how to respond in the event of an emergency (GAO, 2007). The current EAS is not able to alert the public on devices other than radios or televisions. In essence the EAS does not provide messages over other common media that the public uses such as cell phones, personal digital assistants, and the Internet. In addition, the EAS does not transmit alerts in a language other than English, and its alerts are not accessible to some members of the disabled community. A final challenge is that most emergencies originate at the state and local levels, but EAS broadcasts at these levels are voluntary.

FEMA has developed an implementation plan visioning the EAS as being integrated into different communication media and distributed to the public (GAO, 2007). FEMA's plan outlines an integrated alert and warning system that are designed that the President can alert people under all conditions. With this proposed integrated alerting system, FEMA believes that messages will travel over more channels to reach the public through multiple devices, including cell phones, pagers, road signs, and the Internet as well as existing EAS technologies. The following section of this chapter presents the results of a survey of state emergency management officials on the use of IT in their operations.

SURVEY METHODS AND SUMMARY RESULTS

A online survey of state government directors of emergency management was conducted during the months of July and August 2008. Listed below are the results of this survey. Each of the 50 state government directors of emergency management were sent a copy of the survey, of which 27 responded, which represents a response rate of 54%. The process for administering the survey was to send an initial email invitation to directors of emergency management to fill out the survey; this was followed by another email to those directors that did not respond to the request for participation.

The demographic characteristics and state directors of emergency management are provided on Table 2. The descriptive statistics in this table indicate that 36% of emergency management departments or divisions had over 100 full-time equivalent (FTE) employees. There was only 12%, or three state governments, that had emergency management departments with between 11 to 24 FTE employees.

Table 2 also indicates that the age range of the directors of emergency management typically falls between 45 and 54 years old (44%). Given the nature of the experience level needed, there were not surprisingly very few emergency management directors less than 45 year old (20%). There were many more males (92%) than females (8%) directors of emergency management. As with many executive positions in government, the average tenure for a director of emergency management was less than 5 years (64%). There were only 24% of directors that hold tenure between 5 and 10 years. Having more than 10 years in this position was very rare. Finally, directors of emergency management typically had a

Table 2. Demographics and state government emergency management information

How many full-time equivalent (FTE) employees work for your emergency management department?	*Frequency*	*Percent*
11 to 24	3	12.0%
25 to 50	6	24.0%
51 to 100	7	28.0%
Over 100	9	36.0%
Age Range of Director of Emergency Management		
25-34	1	4.0%
35-44	4	16.0%
45-54	11	44.0%
55-64	9	36.0%
Gender of Director of Emergency Management		
Female	2	8.0%
Male	23	92.0%
How many years have you worked as a Director of Emergency Management (or equivalent position) for your state government?		
Less than 5 Years	16	64.0%
5 to 10 years	6	24.0%
16 to 20 years	1	4.0%
21 to 25 years	1	4.0%
26 years or more	1	4.0%
Highest level of Academic Attainment of Director of Emergency Management		
High school diploma	1	4.2%
2 year college degree	2	8.3%
4 year college degree	14	58.3%
Master's degree	7	29.2%

4 year college degree (58.3%). There were 29.2% of the responding directors that held a more advanced academic credential such as a master's degree.

The results in Table 2 indicated that in the survey sample, directors of emergency management were typically between the ages of 45 and 54, were male, had less than 5 years of tenure, and held a four year college degree. These directors came from departments that were typically small to medium-sized, just over a third had more than 100 FTE employees. With this background information on directors of emergency management, the following section of the chapter provides further information on the environment that they face in state government.

THE ENVIRONMENTAL CONTEXT OF EMERGENCY MANAGEMENT AND PREPAREDNESS

Table 3 provides information on the environmental context of emergency management. There are five questions that ask directors of emergency management to provide their views on the level of preparedness of their state government. The first question asks directors to respond using Likert scales, ranging from agree to disagree, if there is a high risk of their state being a potential terrorist target. Only 16% of directors strongly agreed that there was a high level of risk of their state being a possible terrorist target. The survey results revealed that 36% of respondents actually disagreed with the statement about risk. The second question asked directors to indicate if there was a high level of risk of a natural disaster occurring in their state. A vast majority of respondents strongly agreed that their state had a high level of risk of a natural disaster occurring (80%). The results show that there is not much faith by directors of emergency management that their state will be a terrorist target, there is much stronger agreement that a natural disaster will occur in their state.

There was 36% of directors of state emergency management that strongly agreed that there was a high level of emergency management preparedness in their state, and 52% of directors agreed to this statement. There was not a lot of agreement that there is a high level of public complacency of a natural disaster actually occurring, with only 16% of directors strongly agreeing with this statement. Only 16% of respondents, when summing the strongly agree and agree responses, believed that the color-coded homeland security advisory system is an effective source of information for emergency preparedness. There were 60% of directors that disagreed with the effectiveness of the federal homeland security advisory system.

The results in Table 3 indicated in the emergency management environment there was a not a great deal of concern that a terrorist target would actually occur. There were much stronger convictions by directors that a natural disaster will take place in their state. There is a belief that the state is well prepared for a disaster if it occurs. There is agreement that the public is complacent that a natural disaster will occur. Finally, confirming existing research at the local level, the federal government's homeland security advisory system is not regarded as being very effective.

Table 3. The environmental context of emergency management and preparedness

In my state...	*Strongly Agree %*	*Agree %*	*Neutral %*	*Disagree %*	*Strongly Disagree %*	*Median*
There is a high level of risk of being a potential terrorist target.	16.0	24.0	16.0	36.0	8.0	3.0
There is a high level of risk of a natural disaster occurring.	80.0	16.0	0.0	4.0	0.0	1.0
There is a high level of emergency management preparedness.	36.0	52.0	8.0	4.0	0.0	2.0
There is a high level of public complacency of a natural disaster actually occurring.	16.0	28.0	32.0	20.0	4.0	3.0
The color-coded Federal Homeland Security Advisory System is an effective information source for emergency preparedness.	4.0	12.0	24.0	40.0	20.0	4.0

Notes: strongly agree=1, agree=2, neutral=3, disagree=4, and strongly disagree=5

IT AND THE EMERGENCY MANAGEMENT FUNCTION

Table 4 provides information on the impact that IT has had on emergency management functions. The four common phases as defined earlier in the emergency management literature are mitigation, preparedness, response, and recovery. There was general agreement that IT impacted all phases of emergency management. For example, there were 56% of directors of emergency management strongly agreeing that emergency management response has been impacted by IT. The median statistics also showed a 1.0, which indicates that strongly agree was the most commonly found response. The median score indicated that strongly agree was the most commonly occurring response. There were 28% of directors strongly agreeing that IT has impacted the mitigation stage of emergency management. There were 36% of directors believing that IT has impacted the preparedness stage. Finally, 33% of directors believed that IT has impacted the recovery stage. However, when comparing all of the stages the greatest impact seems to be IT impacting the response phase. This could be attributed to the most resources by state governments for IT being devoted towards this phase of emergency management.

Table 5 shows the survey results for the impact of IT on emergency planning in state governments. The results in this table indicate that "agree" was the most likely response according to the median statistics of "2" for almost all of the planning questions. The results show that there were 33.3% of directors strongly agreeing that IT has impacted emergency planning in their state government by addressing inter-organizational coordination and collaboration among responding groups. There were 25.9% of respondents who strongly agreed that IT has helped to decide on the appropriate actions necessary to a situation. There also was the same percentage of respondents that strongly agreed that IT has emphasized response flexibility so those involved in operations can adjust to changing disaster demands. There were 19.2% of directors strongly agreeing that IT has impacted the testing of proposed response operations, and the same percentage believed that IT provided a continuous process for planning in response to the threat environment.

Generally, the results in Table 5 indicated that IT had impacted several noted principles in the literature on emergency planning. IT has addressed inter-organizational collaboration and coordination among responding groups. This is not surprising as having a good IT system is critical for an effective response to an emergency by bringing together teams of responders. One area worth noting is that of the impact of IT being used for planning in the face of conflict and resistance, where 16% of directors disagreed with this statement.

Table 6 provides the responses from directors of state emergency management on the effectiveness of IT on different technologies typically used by departments of emergency management. The listing of

Table 4. IT and the emergency management function of state governments

IT in the emergency management function of my state government has an impact on:	*Strongly Agree %*	*Agree %*	*Neutral %*	*Disagree %*	*Strongly Disagree %*	*Median*
Mitigation	28.0	60.0	12.0	0.0	0.0	2.0
Preparedness	36.0	52.0	8.0	4.0	0.0	2.0
Response	56.0	40.0	4.0	0.0	0.0	1.0
Recovery	33.3	58.3	8.3	0.0	0.0	2.0

Notes: strongly agree=1, agree=2, neutral=3, disagree=4, and strongly disagree=5

Table 5. IT and emergency planning in state governments

In my state government, IT has impacted emergency planning by:	*Strongly Agree %*	*Agree %*	*Neutral %*	*Disagree %*	*Strongly Disagree %*	*Median*
Providing accurate knowledge of the threat and likely human response through a hazard assessment and vulnerability analysis.	14.8	59.3	18.5	7.4	0.0	2.0
Helping to decide on the appropriate actions necessary to the situation.	25.9	44.4	22.2	7.4	0.0	2.0
Emphasizing response flexibility so that those involved in operations can adjust to changing disaster demands.	25.9	40.7	25.9	7.4	0.0	2.0
Addressing inter-organizational coordination and collaboration among responding groups.	33.3	51.9	7.4	7.4	0.0	2.0
Integrating plans for each individual community into a comprehensive approach for multi-hazard management.	15.4	50.0	26.9	7.7	0.0	2.0
Helping with plans that have a training component.	11.5	42.3	38.5	7.7	0.0	2.0
Testing of the proposed response operations.	19.2	50.0	23.1	7.7	0.0	2.0
Providing a continuous process for planning in response to the threat environment.	19.2	42.3	30.8	7.7	0.0	2.0
Planning in the face of conflict and resistance.	8.0	36.0	40.0	16.0	0.0	3.0
Helping with management of the plan by implementing what was discussed in the planning stage.	15.4	53.8	19.2	11.5	0.0	2.0

Notes: strongly agree=1, agree=2, neutral=3, disagree=4, and strongly disagree=5

these information technologies were compiled from the work of Pine (2007) and Cutter, et al, (2007). The responses by directors of emergency management showed that the Internet and GIS had the greatest impact on emergency planning both registering a median score of 1.0. The internet was perceived by all respondents to be effective, and 68% of respondents viewed the internet as being very effective. GIS was viewed by all respondents as effective and 60% believed it to be very effective. Wireless technologies were viewed by 48% of directors as being very effective and warning systems received 44% of directors' approval as being very effective.

IT that was viewed as moderately effective was direct and remote sensing (32%), emergency management decision support systems (24%), and hazard analysis and modeling (28%). More advanced technologies such as direct and remote sensing was not used by 8% of emergency management department. Emergency management decision support systems was not used by 12% of states. The results in Table 6 show that the Internet and GIS lead the way in providing effective technologies for state government emergency management. More complex applications are viewed as being moderately effective, possibly because their predictions are not always accurate as shown through hazard analysis and modeling technologies.

Table 7 in this chapter examines the barriers to the adoption of IT in state emergency management. The results in this table show that the lack of collaboration with other levels of government, difficulty justifying return on investment, issues regarding privacy and security, and lack of financial resources all had median scores of 2.0, indicating that there was agreement with these barriers. There was disagreement

Table 6. Effectiveness of IT on emergency management

How effective are each of the following for emergency management in your state government?	*Very Effective %*	*Effective %*	*Moderately Effective %*	*Ineffective %*	*Not used %*	*Median*
Internet	68.0	32.0	0.0	0.0	0.0	1.0
Wireless networks	48.0	44.0	4.0	4.0	0.0	2.0
Geographic Information Systems	60.0	32.0	8.0	0.0	0.0	1.0
Direct and Remote Sensing	16.0	36.0	32.0	8.0	8.0	2.0
Emergency Management Decision Support Systems	28.0	28.0	24.0	8.0	12.0	2.0
Hazard Analysis and Modeling	24.0	40.0	28.0	8.0	0.0	2.0
Warning Systems	44.0	40.0	16.0	0.0	0.0	2.0

Notes: very effective=1, effective=2, moderately effective=3, ineffective=4, and not used=5

that barriers to IT in emergency management were lack of technology for emergency management, community resistance, and technological obsolesce all having a median scores of 4.0 (or disagree). It appears from this data that state emergency management have up to date technology to respond to disasters.

With respect to the strongly agree category, lack of financial resources there were 40% of directors believing that this was a significant barrier (Table 7). In addition, there were 29% of directors believing that the lack of support from elected officials was a significant barrier. Lack of technology there was strong disagreement that this was a barrier according to 12% of directors. There was also strong disagreement by 12% of directors of staff resistance to change as a barrier to IT adoption. The results in Table 8 show that common issues generally found in public agencies such as security and privacy, collaboration and financial were also found to be significant barriers to the adoption of emergency management IT.

Table 7. Barriers to the adoption of IT in state emergency management

The following barriers have influenced the adoption of IT in emergency management:	*Strongly Agree %*	*Agree %*	*Neutral %*	*Disagree %*	*Strongly Disagree %*	*Median*
Lack of technology	4.0	20.0	16.0	48.0	12.0	4.0
Lack of technology expertise	12.0	36.0	24.0	24.0	4.0	3.0
Lack of support from elected officials	29.2	16.7	41.7	12.5	0.0	3.0
Lack of collaboration with other levels of government	12.0	44.0	8.0	32.0	4.0	2.0
Difficulty justifying return on investment	16.0	36.0	28.0	20.0	0.0	2.0
Staff resistance to change	16.0	20.0	24.0	28.0	12.0	3.0
Issues regarding privacy and security	8.0	44.0	20.0	28.0	0.0	2.0
Lack of financial resources	40.0	40.0	4.0	16.0	0.0	2.0
Community resistance	4.0	8.0	32.0	52.0	4.0	4.0
Data quality/quantity problems	4.2	41.7	20.8	33.3	0.0	3.0
Interoperability in communications systems	8.0	28.0	28.0	28.0	8.0	3.0
Technological obsolescence	8.0	28.0	36.0	24.0	4.0	3.0

Notes: strongly agree=1, agree=2, neutral=3, disagree=4, and strongly disagree=5

CONCLUSION

This chapter has examined the role of IT in emergency management. IT has a major role in the four functions of emergency management namely: mitigation, preparedness, response, and recovery. There is a prevalence of IT in planning for emergencies. Citizens play a critical role in disaster incidents. They can aid emergency responders when they have enough information to make well informed decisions on the appropriate course of action during an emergency. There also is the intergovernmental aspect of emergency management that should be considered, and the key role that information systems play here. There are several important technologies that are currently being used in emergency management; some of them discussed were knowledge management systems, geographic information systems, and decision support systems. There are organizational, technical, and social dimensions that need to be addressed in the application of IT to the emergency management function. There was a case study presented showing the day to day use of technology in FEMA.

This chapter also examined the impact of IT on emergency management through survey data on state governments in the United States. Some of the key findings of this survey of directors of emergency management indicated that IT has impacted all four phases of emergency management. There was, however, the strongest impact as a result of IT on the response phase of emergency management. There was also an impact of IT on state government emergency planning. The results indicate that IT and emergency planning had the greatest impact on collaboration among responding groups, deciding on the appropriate course of action, and adjusting response plans. In terms of the technologies used by state governments, directors of emergency management viewed GIS and the internet as very effective for emergency management operations. More advanced technologies such as emergency management decision support systems were not as commonly used by state governments. Finally, there was agreement by directors of emergency management that the greatest barriers to the adoption of IT in emergency management were lack of collaboration with other levels of government, difficulty justifying a return on investment, issues regarding security and privacy, and lack of financial resources. Overall, it appears that state emergency management departments are well prepared for a disaster, and there is a critical role for IT in their preparedness efforts.

REFERENCES

Alexander, D. (2005). Towards the development of a standard in emergency planning. *Disaster Prevention and Management, 14*(2), 158–175. doi:10.1108/09653560510595164

Bertot, J. C., Jaeger, P. T., Langa, L. A., & McClure, C. R. (2006). Public Access Computing and Internet Access in Public Libraries: The Role of Public Libraries in E-government and Emergency Situations. *First Monday, 11*(9), 1–25.

Brown, M. M. (2007). Understanding E-Government Benefits: An Examination of Leading-Edge Local Governments. *American Review of Public Administration, 37*(2), 178–197. doi:10.1177/0275074006291635

Chen, R., Sharman, R., Rao, H. R., & Upadhyaya, S. J. (2008). Coordination in Emergency Management Response Management. *Communications of the ACM, 51*(5), 66–73. doi:10.1145/1342327.1342340

Choi, S. O. (2008). Emergency Management: Implications from a Strategic Management Perspective. *Journal of Homeland Security and Emergency Management*, *5*(1), 1–21. doi:10.2202/1547-7355.1372

Chua, A. Y., Kaynak, S., & Foo, S. S. (2006). An Analysis of the Delayed Response to Hurricane Katrina through the Lens of Knowledge Management. *Journal of the American Society for Information Science and Technology*, *58*(3), 391–403. doi:10.1002/asi.20521

Clarke, W. (2006). *Emergency Management in County Government: A National Survey*. Retrieved August 10, 2008, from http://www.naco.org/Template.cfm?Section=Library&template=/ContentManagement/ContentDisplay.cfm&ContentID=21623

Col, J. M. (2007). Managing Disasters: The Role of Local Government. *Public Administration Review*, *67*(s1), 114–124.

Coursey, D., & Norris, D. F. (2008). Models of E-government: Are they Correct? An Empirical Assessment. *Public Administration Review*, *68*(3), 523–536. doi:10.1111/j.1540-6210.2008.00888.x

Cutter, S. L., Emrich, C. T., Adams, B. J., Huyck, C. K., & Eguchi, R. T. (2007). In Waugh, W.L., & Tierney, K. (eds.)., New Information Technologies in Emergency Management. *Emergency Management: Principles and Practices for Local Government*. (pp. 279-297). Washington, DC: International City/County Management Association.

Donahue, A. K., & Joyce, P. G. (2001). A Framework for Analyzing Emergency Management with an Application to Federal Budgeting. *Public Administration Review*, *61*(6), 728–740. doi:10.1111/0033-3352.00143

Fisher, H. W. (1999). Enhancing Disaster Mitigation Planning and Response through the use of Cyberspace: Suggestions and Issues to Consider. *Journal of Contingencies and Crisis Management*, *7*(1), 48–54. doi:10.1111/1468-5973.00098

French, S., & Turoff, M. (2007). Decision Support Systems. *Communications of the ACM*, *50*(3), 39–40. doi:10.1145/1226736.1226762

GAO. (2006). *Expedited Assistance for Victims of Hurricanes Katrina and Rita: FEMA's Control Weaknesses Exposed the Government to Significant Fraud and Abuse*. (GAO Publication No. GAO-06-403T). Washington, DC: U.S. Government Printing Office.

GAO. (2007). *Emergency Preparedness: Current Emergency Alert System has Limitations, and Development of a New Integrated System will be challenging*. (GAO Publication No. GAO-07-411). Washington, DC: U.S. Government Printing Office.

Green, W. G. (2001). E-emergency Management in the USA: A Preliminary Survey of the Operational State of the Art. *International Journal of Emergency Management*, *1*(1), 70–81. doi:10.1504/IJEM.2001.000511

Helsloot, I., & Ruitenberg, A. (2004). Citizen Response to Disasters: A Survey of Literature and Some Practical Implications. *Journal of Contingencies and Crisis Management*, *12*(3), 98–111. doi:10.1111/j.0966-0879.2004.00440.x

Jaeger, P. T., Shneiderman, B., Fleishmann, K. R., Preece, J., Qu, Y., & Wu, P. F. (2007). Community Response Grids: E-government, Social Networks, and Effective Emergency Management . *Telecommunications Policy, 31*(10-11), 592–604. doi:10.1016/j.telpol.2007.07.008

Jefferson, T. L. (2006). Evaluating the Role of Information Technology in Crisis and Emergency Management. *Journal of Information and Knowledge Management Systems, 36*(3), 261–264.

Kweit, M. G., & Kweit, R. W. (2004). Citizen Participation and Citizen Evaluation in Disaster Recovery. *American Review of Public Administration, 34*(4), 354–373. doi:10.1177/0275074004268573

Lindell, M. K., & Perry, R. W. (2007). Planning and Preparedness. In Waugh, W.L., & Tierney, K. (eds.), *Emergency Management: Principles and Practices for Local Government,* (pp. 113-141). Washington, DC: International City/County Management Association.

Liu, B. F. (2008). Online Disaster Preparation: Evaluation of State Emergency Management Web Sites. *Natural Hazards Review, 9*(1), 43–48. doi:10.1061/(ASCE)1527-6988(2008)9:1(43)

Manoj, B. S., & Baker, A. H. (2007). Communication Challenges in Emergency Response. *Communications of the ACM, 50*(3), 51–53. doi:10.1145/1226736.1226765

McLoughlin, D. (1985). A Framework for Integrating Emergency Management. *Public Administration Review, 45*(Special Issue), 165–172. doi:10.2307/3135011

National Research Council. (2007). *Improving Disaster Management: The Role of IT in Mitigation, Preparedness, Response, and Recovery.* Committee on Using Information Technology to Enhance Disaster Management. Retrieved January 26, 2009 from www.nap.edu/catalog/11824.html.

OIG. (2005). *Emergency Preparedness and Response Could Better Integrate Information Technology and Incident Response and Recovery.* Department of Homeland Security, Office of Inspector General, Retrieved January 26, 2009, from http://www.dhs.gov/xoig/assets/mgmtrpts/OIG_05-36_Sep05.pdf.

Palen, L., Hiltz, S. R., & Liu, S. B. (2007). Online Forums Supporting Grassroots Participation in Emergency Preparedness and Response. *Communications of the ACM, 50*(3), 54–58. doi:10.1145/1226736.1226766

Perry, R. W., & Lindell, M. K. (2003). Preparedness for Emergency Response: Guidelines for the Emergency Planning Process. *Disasters, 27*(4), 336–350. doi:10.1111/j.0361-3666.2003.00237.x

Pine, J. C. (2007). *Wiley Pathways Technology in Emergency Management.* Hoboken, NJ: John Wiley & Sons.

Quarantelli, E. L. (1997). Problematic aspects of the Information/Communication Revolution for Disaster Planning and Research: Ten non-technical issues and questions. *Disaster Prevention and Management, 6*(2), 94–106. doi:10.1108/09653569710164053

Rao, R. R., Eisenberg, J., & Schmitt, T. (2007). *Improving Disaster Management: The Role of IT in Mitigation, Preparedness, Response, and Recovery.* Washington, DC: The National Academies Press.

Ryoo, J., & Choi, Y. B. (2006). A Comparison and Classification Framework for Disaster Information Management Systems. *International Journal of Emergency Management*, *3*(4), 264–279. doi:10.1504/IJEM.2006.011296

Stephenson, R., & Anderson, P. S. (1997). Disasters and the Information Technology Revolution. *Disasters*, *21*(4), 305–334. doi:10.1111/1467-7717.00065

Troy, D. A., Carson, A., Vanderbeek, J., & Hutton, A. (2007). Enhancing Community-Based Disaster Preparedness with Information Technology. *Disasters*, *32*(1), 149–165. doi:10.1111/j.1467-7717.2007.01032.x

Wallace, W.A., & Balogh, F.D. (1985). Decision Support Systems for Disaster Management. *Public Administration Review, 45*(Special Issues), 134-146.

Wang, X., & Kapucu, N. (2008). Public Complacency under Repeated Emergency Threats: Some Empirical Evidence. *Journal of Public Administration: Research and Theory*, *18*(1), 57–78. doi:10.1093/jopart/mum001

Waugh, W. L. (1988). Current Policy and Implementation Issues in Disaster Preparedness. In L.K. Comfort, (ed.) *Managing Disaster: Strategies and Policy Perspectives*, (pp. 111-125). Durham, North Carolina: Duke University Press.

Waugh, W. L. (1994). Regionalizing Emergency Management: Counties as State and Local Government. *Public Administration Review*, *54*(3), 253–258. doi:10.2307/976728

Waugh, W. L. (1995). Geographic Information Systems: The Case of Disaster Management. *Social Science Computer Review*, *13*(4), 422–431. doi:10.1177/089443939501300403

Chapter 6
Local Government Homeland Security Information Systems

INTRODUCTION

This chapter examines homeland security information systems (HSIS) with a focus on local governments. Local governments are typically the first at the scene when responding to an emergency or a terrorist attack. The most notable incidents are Hurricane Katrina and the terrorist attacks of September 11, 2001. In both of these incidents the first responders were the local governments, which faced dual issues of communication and information sharing. It is important to understand the current level of preparedness and use of HSIS in local governments. This chapter tries to discern the relative priority of HSIS compared to other priorities of local governments in the realm of homeland security.

This chapter first outlines some background information on local governments with respect to their organizational structure and level of homeland security preparedness. The second section outlines the stages of e-government adoption, which is commonly discussed in the local e-government literature. Third, there is a discussion of homeland security information sharing between the federal, state, and local governments. There is some evidence presented from existing surveys of the impact of HSIS on local governments. Finally, there is survey results presented from a study conducted by the International City/County Management Association (ICMA) on homeland security preparedness. This survey information is used to determine where HSIS fits into local priorities on homeland security.

BACKGROUND ON LOCAL GOVERNMENTS

The federal government has strong incentives for disaster management and preparedness; local governments often lack the administrative capacity or commitment for effective policies (Gerber, Cohen, and

DOI: 10.4018/978-1-60566-834-5.ch006

Stewart, 2007). The federal system because of its conflicting incentives, lack of management coordination, and uneven resources has a difficult time providing comprehensive disaster preparedness. Local governments because they are first on the scene provide a key role in homeland security.

When examining local government HSIS, it is important to understand the type of government. The two main forms of government that cities have adopted are the council manager and mayor council structures (DeSantis and Renner, 2002). Proponents of the council-manager form of government argue that this structure centralizes administrative responsibility in the hands of one individual, normally called the city manager. However, the distinction between the different forms of government have been blurred with for example the major-council governments increasingly hiring a Chief Administrative Officer (CAO) who performs similar tasks as the city manager. In addition, many council manager governments have strengthened the role of the mayor. The literature on e-government adoption in local governments generally has found that council-manager governments have been greater innovators of e-government diffusion than other forms of government. This is attributed to the professional city manager wanting to use e-government as a way of strengthening reforms within the city.

Research results indicate that cities that are more innovate in management culture are more receptive to the adoption and advancement of e-government (Moon and Norris, 2005). The reasoning is that more innovative governments tend to be more receptive to new managerial and technical approach such as e-government. These cities tend to adopt change better because there is less administrative resistance. Governments that are strong adopters of information technology, such as e-government, should also have a capacity to use HSIS as well.

In a review of a future research agendas for counties two areas of 15 identified by Streib, Svara, and Waugh, et. al. (2007) was homeland security and IT related. With respect to the former many counties have many other pressing issues on their agenda and homeland security must be included with this. For example, as noted later in this chapter many counties do not take the threat level indicated in the homeland security advisory system very seriously, and do not increase security when the threat level rises. The second issue of IT indicates that there is optimism that IT could potentially solve many of the service issues that have plagued counties, but the greater issue is pay back, if a system is build will there be a return on investment. There are additional issues of privacy of data collected by counties and what will become of the information.

Clarke and Chenoweth (2006) make the argument that terrorism is a city-specific activity. They believe that there is a potential for non-metropolitan areas to be a terrorist target, to date terrorist attacks on the U.S. have been an urban occurrence. Cities are center of power, the focus of media, and complex enough to hide terrorist activities. Cities are tightly coupled systems which makes them especially prone to risk of a terrorist attack.

An interesting case study of IT planning for the Year 2000 (Y2K) problem in Iowa cities and counties revealed that many local governments did not have concrete plans to handle the problem of Y2K (Ho and Smith, 2001). This lack of planning was influenced mostly by the attitude of senior management toward the Y2K problem. Essentially, their results indicate that IT planning depends on the attitude of senior management towards the problem. The more concerned senior management is, the more likely that they will participate in IT planning.

STAGES OF LOCAL E-GOVERNMENT DEVELOPMENT

This section of the chapter reviews some of the most important studies on the adoption of e-government in local governments. This information is used to see what are the issues associated with the adoption of local e-government as a way of understanding the challenges faced by HSIS. In a longitudinal study of the ICMA surveys on local e-government, Brown (2007) found that the maturity of e-government has been typically described in stages of development. Where one stage leads to another and local governments would follow this linear progression to maturity. Brown (2007) makes the argument showing that it is much more complicated than the maturity model suggests; where local governments adapt and change because of some environmental pressure and may proceed or skip stages of development.

In an assessment of the stages of e-government development, Moon (2002) and Holden, Norris, and Fletcher (2003) found that municipal size and form a government had an impact on development. This author found that larger-sized local governments were more proactive and strategic in the advancement of e-government. There was also evidence that council-manager governments seemed to pursue e-government more readily than mayor-council government. Moon found that local governments are essentially just posting information online, indicating that the current state of e-government is very primitive in many municipal governments (Norris and Moon, 2005).

Horizontal integration is the ability of e-government to break down the silos of information dissemination so that citizens can focus on getting information rather than navigating local government departments. In an examination of horizontal integration of e-government in a local council in the United Kingdom, Choudrie and Weerrakody (2007) found that there were still integration issues that need to be addressed before services can be offered to citizens through a one-stop shop. Essentially, for a one-stop shop to take place parties involved must give up some powers to reach horizontal integration.

In local governments, IT and especially the Internet, has been envisioned to transform government (Ho, 2002; McLoughlin and Cornford, 2006; Yang and Rho, 2007). The traditional bureaucratic model, public managers focus on internal efficiency, functional departments, hierarchy, control, and rules based management. According to Ho (2002), with the e-government model, public managers focus now on user satisfaction, results, flexible service delivery, and a networked relationship with constituents and clients. There is a movement from departments to "one-stop service centers," where citizens focus on services provided by government. There is evidence from a content analysis of municipal websites, some movement in the direction of one-stop customer service (Ho, 2002).

INFORMATION AND HOMELAND SECURITY

This section of the chapter reports on the provision of information on homeland security by different levels of government. Homeland security information provided by the federal government is viewed more negatively than information provided by state governments. This raises questions about the level of competency of the federal government to provide the information needed for local governments for homeland security preparedness (Scavo, Kearney, and Kilroy, 2007).

The GAO (2003) reports in a survey of information sharing among federal, state, and local governments that the current process of information sharing was not considered being effective (Figure 1). The three levels of government indentified three problems that account for this perception. First, no level of government was satisfied that they received enough information. Typically, governments were reporting that they were receiving less than 50% of specified categories of information that they perceived they needed to support their homeland security goals. Second, no level of government was satisfied with the timeliness, accuracy, or relevance of the information they received, this was especially the case for states and cities. Third, the federal government still perceives the fight against terrorism to generally be a federal responsibility. The federal government has not created comprehensive policies and procedures to effectively integrate state and city governments into the information sharing process. Many of the local governments expressed concerns that they were not given the opportunity to participate in a national policy for homeland security information sharing.

There is an oral history archive compiled by the New York City Fire Department asking first responders to provide an accounting of their experiences with 9/11. An analysis of this archive revealed that with the role of information (Dearstyne, 2006, p. 34):

1. Coordination and communication were serious problems;
2. Securing information early in the emergency was difficult;
3. Commanders lacked solid information to direct efforts;
4. Information was contradictory and difficult to interpret;
5. The collapse of the buildings was difficult to conceptualize;
6. Improvisation was common; and
7. False information compounded confusion.

The research results indicated that the information on homeland security received by the state and local governments was not viewed very positively. In addition, the analysis of the 9/11 archive also revealed that information was not used very effectively. It seems that in order to respond effectively to a terrorist attack, information is the key element for the most effective response. There is not much evidence that the current information provided is working effectively for the different levels of government.

Figure 1. GAO survey that information sharing with federal agencies is effective or very effective (Source: GAO, 2003)

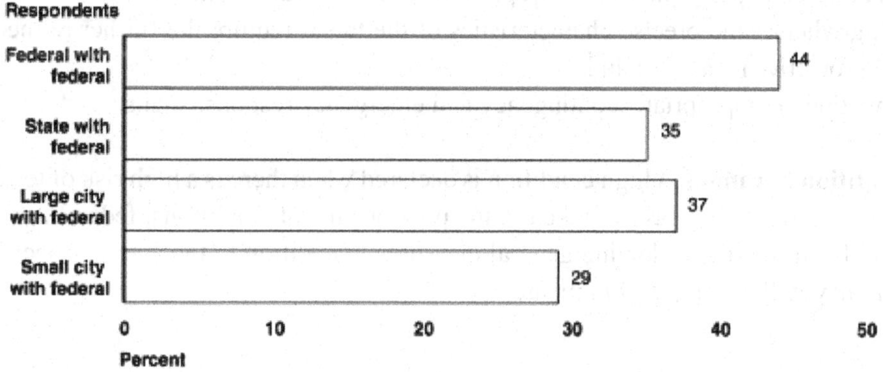

HOMELAND SECURITY ADVISORY SYSTEM

The Homeland Security Advisory System (HSAS) was established in 2002 to inform all levels of government and local authority, as well as the public, to the current risk of terrorist acts. The HSAS involves a five-level, color-coded threat condition indicator to correspond to the current situation as shown in Figure 2 (DHS, 2009). Specifically, each of the five categories are outlined on the DHS (2009) website below:

Low Condition (Green). This condition is declared when there is a low risk of terrorist attacks. Federal departments and agencies should consider the following general measures in addition to the agency-specific protective measures they develop and implement:

- Refining and exercising as appropriate preplanned protective measures;
- Ensuring personnel receive proper training on the HSAS and specific preplanned department or agency protective measures; and
- Institutionalizing a process to assure that all facilities and regulated sectors are regularly assessed for vulnerabilities to terrorist attacks, and all reasonable measures are taken to mitigate these vulnerabilities.

Guarded Condition (Blue). This condition is declared when there is a general risk of terrorist attacks. In addition to the protective measures taken in the previous Threat condition, federal departments and agencies should consider the following general measures in addition to the agency-specific protective measures that they will develop and implement:

- Checking communications with designated emergency response or command locations;
- Reviewing and updating emergency response procedures; and
- Providing the public with any information that would strengthen its ability to act appropriately.

Elevated Condition (Yellow). An elevated condition is declared when there is a significant risk of terrorist attacks. In addition to the protective measures taken in the previous Threat conditions, federal departments and agencies should consider the following general measures in addition to the protective measures that they will develop and implement:

- Increasing surveillance of critical locations;
- Coordinating emergency plans as appropriate with nearby jurisdictions;
- Assessing whether the precise characteristics of the threat require the further refinement of preplanned protective measures; and
- Implementing, as appropriate, contingency and emergency response plans.

High Condition (Orange). A high condition is declared when there is a high risk of terrorist attacks. In addition to the protective measures taken in the previous threat conditions, federal departments and agencies should consider the following general measures in addition to the agency-specific protective measures that they will develop and implement:

Figure 2. Homeland security advisory system (Source: DHS, 2009)

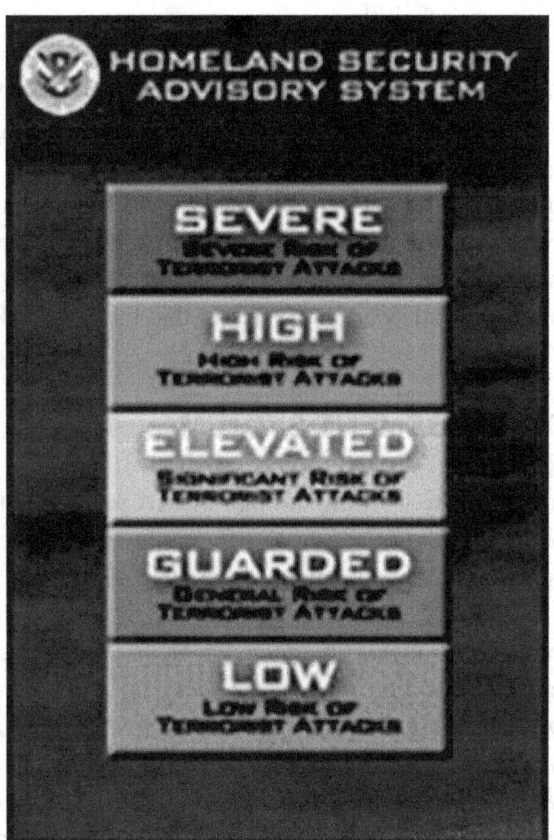

- Coordinating necessary security efforts with federal, State, and local law enforcement agencies or any National Guard or other appropriate armed forces organizations;
- Taking additional precautions at public events and possibly considering alternative venues or even cancellation;
- Preparing to execute contingency procedures, such as moving to an alternate site or dispersing their workforce; and
- Restricting threatened facility access to essential personnel only.

Severe Condition (Red). A severe condition reflects a severe risk of terrorist attacks. Under most circumstances, the protective measures for a severe condition are not intended to be sustained for substantial periods of time. In addition to the protective measures in the previous Threat conditions, federal departments and agencies also should consider the following general measures in addition to the agency-specific protective measures that they will develop and implement:

- Increasing or redirecting personnel to address critical emergency needs;
- Assigning emergency response personnel and pre-positioning and mobilizing specially trained teams or resources;

- Monitoring, redirecting, or constraining transportation systems; and
- Closing public and government facilities.

In an evaluation of the effectiveness of the federal government's HSAS MacManus and Caruson (2006) found through their Florida survey that the information provided may have more relevance to the federal government than local governments. State and local governments would prefer more specific information than what is currently provided with the HSAS. MacManus and Caruson found that local officials do not give the HSAS very high marks, and these officials tend to rely on other information sources than the federal government for threat data. Essentially, they tend to believe that other sources of information from state and local outlets are more useful that the HSAS (Reddick, 2007).

NATIONAL INCIDENT MANAGEMENT SYSTEM

The Department of Homeland Security working through FEMA developed the National Incident Management System (NIMS) to facilitate coordination of different levels of government (Lester and Krejci, 2007). The NIMS according to the policy document of the DHS (2008, p. 1):

Provides a systematic, proactive approach to guide departments and agencies at all levels of government, nongovernmental organizations, and the private sector to work seamlessly to prevent, protect against, respond to, recover from, and mitigate the effects of incidents, regardless of cause, size, location, or complexity, in order to reduce the loss of life and property and harm to the environment. NIMS works hand in hand with the National Response Framework (NRF). NIMS provides the template for the management of incidents, while the NRF provides the structure and mechanisms for national-level policy for incident management.

NIMS was designed to coordinate the response of local, state, and federal responders by establishing an Incident Command System, standardizing communications, working for joint preparedness, creating a joint information system, and setting up a National Integration Center to guide the process of coordination. The rationale for the NIMS was that traditionally first responders were uncoordinated and often late and issues of jurisdictions and resources were worked out as the disaster was unfolding. This was supposed to change with the NIMS.

Lester and Krejci (2007) use the example of the failure of the NIMS showing the federal, state, and local governments in their ineffective response to Hurricane Katrina. These authors believed that some of the failure can be attributed to the power struggle between federal and state governments, the NIMS was designed to provide collaboration among these governments, but the system failed during Hurricane Katrina. There are several surveys addressing, in part, local efforts in HSIS that are discussed in the following section.

SURVEYS ON LOCAL HSIS

In a survey of city governments with populations of 100,000 residents or greater in the U.S., Reddick (2007) showed some interesting impacts of IT on local government homeland security efforts. In a question on rating the possible terrorist threats that the city could have, there were 63% of cities reporting cyber-terrorism as a concern for them as a potential threat. This was a greater concern than a radiological, nuclear, and airplane used as a bomb as possible terrorist threats. The survey also revealed that information technology has been purchased to complete city government homeland security goals according to 63% of cities. What was most interesting was the assessment by city officials of the effectiveness of information received from the state and federal governments. There were 25% of cities that believed the homeland security advisory system was effective. However, there were 32% of cities that believed this was an ineffective source of information for their preparedness efforts. A broader question on the current information received from federal and state agencies on terrorists' threats did much better with 47.7% of cities believing that this was effective. A much smaller portion, at only 23.8%, believed the information provided by federal and state governments was ineffective.

In a survey of counties conducted in 2006, the National Association of Counties (NACo) found that 80% of U.S. counties use Geographic Information Systems (GIS) technology, but only 14% have this capacity within their emergency management agency (Clarke, 2006). This could be problematic for the county since emergency management would have to rely on another department for their GIS information. The planning department or other central government unit was the most common agency to perform GIS work (60%). GIS was used most often in the Northeast (91%), and the least in the Southern U.S. counties (74%). NACo survey data shows that GIS is most commonly used for the following three things: the identification of persons or facilities to notify them about potential disasters (57.6%), as a means of risk assessment (54.9%), and dispatch resources (50.1%).

In the NACo survey there was also other technologies that are used for emergency management. The most common technology used by counties was Ham/shortwave radio (61.1%), followed by interoperable communications equipment (53.7%), and Cameo/Aloha/MARPLOT software at 46.3% of counties (these software packages have been around the longest and integrates a chemical database, an air dispersion model, and mapping capability) (Clarke, 2006). There was only 21.1% of counties that used WebEOC, which is an Internet application that provides meteorological and mapping information, satellite images, and a resource management capability.

Gerber, Cohen, and Stewart (2007) examine homeland security preparedness in cities and found that as administrative resources increase, municipal governments are better at performing preparedness tasks. These authors also found that as local financial conditions are more positive, local government officials take a more optimistic view of how their city is committed to homeland security preparedness. Essentially, what this means for HSIS is that preparedness is related to the financial status and the administrative capacity of the city government, which translates into more capacity to prepare and use IT.

In a survey of Florida city and county officials, Caruson and MacMansus (2007) examine regional differences in homeland security preparedness. For instance, the concern for cyber terrorism varies among the regions of this state. The greatest concern for this security threat is in Southeast (Miami) (33%) and East Central (Orlando) (30%). The least amount of concern for cyber terrorism can be found in Northwest (Pensacola). There are also regional variations in officials that reported about the unmet security needs of software and technology for homeland security. The survey results indicate the Southwest (Miami) (45%) and North Central (Tallahassee) (42%) had the greatest need for software and technology for homeland security.

In a survey of Texas county government officials Reddick and Frank (2006) found that with respect to homeland security funding only 24% of counties purchased IT for homeland security goals. The most common type of equipment purchased, not surprisingly, was communications equipment (76%). There was very little grant funding as well for IT, with only 8% of Texas counties reporting that they received this and fewer received cyber security technology (2%). The following section of the chapter provides information from a survey of local governments to examine the influence of HSIS on local priorities.

DATA AND METHODS

A homeland security survey of local governments was conducted by the ICMA during the spring and summer of 2005. The survey was sent to Chief Administrative Officers (CAO) of municipalities with populations of 2,500 residents and over and to CAOs of counties with council-administrator and council-elected executive forms of government. Of the 7,968 municipalities and counties that received surveys 2,786 local governments responded (35.0%). The survey results presented in this chapter are a subsample that only include the Southern region of the United States. There were 2,472 surveys sent out with 868 responding local governments, indicating a response rate of 35.1%.

Table 1 shows information on local governments in the South of the United States that responded to the survey. This information will provide us with a view of how representative the survey sample is of the general population. Most of the local governments that responded to the survey, 63.7% in fact, were serving 24,999 or less residents. Therefore, most of the cities that responded were of a smaller size. There were only 12 cities that had populations of 500,000 or more. Overall, the population groupings in Table 1 indicate that American small cities are the most highly represented group in the sample.

Table 1 also provides information on the form of government of the local governments surveyed. The most common form of government was the council-manager, with 51.6% of the local governments having this structure. The second most common form of government was the mayor-council, with 25.8% of local governments having this governance structure.

Finally, the metro status of the survey sample is shown in Table 1. The results indicated that central cities were only represented by 18.2% of the survey sample. There were many suburban and independent districts as show both by around 81.8% of respondents. Examining the summary statistics on population groupings, form of government, and metro status we can say that the results of the survey are fairly representative of the population of local governments in the South given that most of them would be small, having a council-manager form of government, and are outside of the central city.

HOMELAND SECURITY INFORMATION SYSTEMS INITIATIVES

Table 2 provides information on two important HSIS initiatives that local governments have undergone. The first initiative was to develop local response plans based on changes to the Homeland Security Advisory System. There were 323 or 37.9% of local governments that have developed response plans based on the advisory system. The majority (56.5%) did not base their plans on this advisory system, which is consistent with the literature, which argues that many state and local governments are having difficulty interpreting the information on the advisory system.

The National Incident Management System (MIMS) is another information resource that makes sure that local government first responders are operating under the same plan. The results of the survey indicate that 536 or 64.7% of local governments have adopted the NIMS. There is some movement to work under the same plan and use IT to accomplish this goal.

Table 1. Characteristics of local government surveyed

Population Group	Frequency	Percent
Over 500,000	12	1.3
100,000 to 499,000	91	10.5
25,000 to 99,999	212	24.4
5000 to 24,999	368	42.4
Under 5,000	185	21.3

Table 2. Since September 11, 2001, have local governments undertaken the following homeland security initiatives?

Developed local response plans based on changes to the Homeland Security Advisory System (color-codes bases on treat assessment)	Frequency	Percent
Yes	323	37.9
No	482	56.5
Don't know	48	5.6

FEDERAL/STATE FUNDING FOR HOMELAND SECURITY RELATED PROGRAMS

A question on the ICMA survey asked about the level of funding for homeland security related programs. Table 3 shows the low priority of homeland security IT for local governments compared with other types of priorities. Equipment was the first priority that received funding from federal and state sources, with 57.5% of grant funding coming from state sources, and 63.4% of grant funding coming from the federal government. Information security, a top priority of HSIS, was close to the bottom of the list of grant funding for homeland security. There were only 42 local governments, or 9.1% of the sample that received a state grant for information security. Only 68 local governments, or 14.3% of the sample received a federal grant for information security. In addition, cyber security had only 20 local governments, or 4.2% received state funding for homeland security. There were only 26 local governments, or 5.6% that received federal funding for homeland security related cyber security initiatives. Overall, the results in Table 3 indicate that two common elements of HSIS preparedness of having both secure information systems and cyber security were a relative low priority for local governments. The top priorities for grant funding from state and federal sources were the more traditional areas of homeland security preparedness such as for purchasing equipment and disaster mitigation/preparedness measures.

LOCAL GOVERNMENT OWN-SOURCE FUNDING FOR HOMELAND SECURITY INITIATIVES

Table 4 shows the use of own source funding for homeland security related programs and initiatives. The results in this table indicate that similarly to grant funding from state and federal sources, there is

Table 3. Local government received federal/state funding for homeland security related programs and needs

	Frequency	*Percent*	*Frequency*	*Percent*
	State		*Federal*	
Equipment	357	57.5	408	63.4
Disaster mitigation/preparedness	248	44.5	225	42.7
Disaster response	235	43.8	273	49.8
Drills and training exercises	190	35.4	175	33.4
Physical surveillance/security systems	127	24.4	148	27.9
Public education	96	19.1	102	20.7
Medical/public health surveillance systems	56	11.8	60	12.7
Information security	42	9.1	68	14.3
Staffing	42	8.6	56	11.5
Cyber security	20	4.2	26	5.6
Other	9	3.7	16	6.7

not a lot of own source funding for information security and cyber security. The number one own-source funded area was equipment with 67.1% of local governments spending picking up the tab for this. There were 44% of local governments spending their own money on information security and 28.5% for cyber security. The results in Table 4 indicate that local governments are taking information security very seriously and are spending to fund these initiatives, despite receiving very little from grant funding for these initiatives.

Table 4. Local government used its own funds (not from state and federal grants) to pay for homeland security activities

Program	*Frequency*	*Percent*
Equipment	527	67.1
Disaster mitigation/preparedness	479	64.1
Disaster response	467	62.2
Drills and training exercises	456	60.6
Staffing	350	48.4
Physical surveillance/security systems	345	47.7
Public education	337	46.6
Information security	317	44.0
Cyber security	194	28.5
Medical/public health surveillance systems	102	15.1
Other	25	8.0

Table 5. Quality of homeland security information received from state and federal government

	Strongly agree %	*Somewhat agree %*	*Neutral %*	*Somewhat disagree %*	*Strongly disagree %*
The information I receive from the state government is easily understood	20.4	44.9	21.9	8.7	4.2
The information I received from the state government is timely	14.8	40.1	25.5	13.1	6.4
The information I receive from the federal government is easily understood	13.1	39.3	27.8	14.7	5.1
The information I receive from the federal government is timely	11.8	33.4	32.6	14.9	7.3

QUALITY OF HOMELAND SECURITY INFORMATION RECEIVED FROM FEDERAL AND STATE GOVERNMENTS

As shown in the previous chapter, one of the major issues that local governments face in homeland security is the quality of information received from federal and/or state sources. Table 5 provides an assessment of the quality of information received from state and federal governments in terms of being easily understood and timely. Information is critical in the "War on Terror" since it directly aids preparedness plans for local governments. The results indicated that information received from state government is more easily understood and timely than from the federal government. For instance, information received from the state government, 20.4% of local governments strongly agreed that it was easily understood, compared with information received from the federal government, having 13.1% of local governments strongly agreeing that this information was easily understood. While the timeliness of information was viewed as being better for the state government (14.8% strongly agree) compared with the federal government at 11.8% strongly agreeing. There was also greater disagreement about the quality of information between both levels of government. According to CAOs, the federal government essentially scored lower on the quality of information.

LOCAL GOVERNMENT TRAINING AND TECHNICAL ASSISTANCE AND HSIS

Table 6 shows the areas that local governments believed they needed help in training or technical assistance. The top areas were biohazards awareness/identification, emergency planning, and critical infrastructure protection all showing 74% of local governments needed training in these areas. Cyber security there was 68.5% of local governments or 541 that believed this was an area they needed training. It appears from Table 6 that there is a great need for training in cyber security analysis, a critical component of HSIS.

TRAINING METHODS THAT LOCAL GOVERNMENTS PREFER

Table 7 outlines the training methods that local governments prefer and where IT fits into these priorities. Onsite training was the most often cited training method that local governments prefer for homeland

Table 6. Local government need for training or technical assistance in the following areas

	Frequency	*Percent*
Biohazard awareness/identification	610	74.8
Emergency planning, preparedness, response	609	74.0
Critical infrastructure protection	604	74.8
Chemical, biological, radiological, nuclear, high-yield explosives attacks/responses	594	73.9
Grant development and writing	579	71.8
Cyber security	541	68.5
Coordination of volunteer efforts/donations	490	62.3
Media communications	423	54.2
Other	84	36.8

security. Webcasting/online training was a preferred method of training according to 36.9 percent of CAOs. Online training makes a lot of sense especially for more remote rural communities to learn the latest homeland security methods.

CONCLUSION

This chapter has examined the influence of HSIS on local governments in the United States. There is evidence that information sharing, especially from the federal government, is not viewed very positively. Generally, the information that local governments receive from the federal government is viewed less favorably than information from state governments. Only around one third of local governments have developed their local response to homeland security on the basis of the color-coded HSAS. However, there are almost two-thirds of local governments that have adopted the NIMS. Information security does not fare well with respect to grant funding from federal and state sources, where it was one of the last areas to receive funding. Information security was funded by just over 40 percent of local governments using their own source revenue. There was over two-thirds of local government indicating that cyber security training was a needed area for them to get training on.

Table 7. Preferred training methods for local governments

	Frequency	*Percent*
Onsite training designed for your local government	726	83.6
Webcast/online training	320	36.9
Workshops held at several locations within the state so that staff from other local governments can attend	500	57.6
Regional training, so that staff in neighboring states can attend	310	35.7
Table top exercises	400	46.1
Other	30	3.4

Notes: N=868

The results of this chapter indicated that the federal government should make more of an effort to address information sharing with local governments. This makes a lot of sense since local governments, as mentioned at the beginning of the chapter, are normally the first to respond to major terrorist incidents or national emergencies. Also, there needs to be more funding for HSIS related activities at the local level. The survey evidence showed that grant funding in this area is virtually non-existent; but it remains an important area and these local governments have to tap into their own coffers to provide funding for these initiatives. Generally, this chapter shows that HSIS is one of the priorities, among many others, that local governments must deal with post 9/11.

REFERENCES

Brown, M. M. (2007). Understanding E-Government Benefits: An Examination of Leading-Edge Local Governments . *American Review of Public Administration, 37*(2), 178–197. doi:10.1177/0275074006291635

Caruson, K., & MacManus, S. A. (2007). Designing Homeland Security Policy within a Regional Structure: A Needs Assessment of Local Security Concerns. *Journal of Homeland Security and Emergency Management, 4*(2), 1–23. doi:10.2202/1547-7355.1243

Choudrie, J., & Weerrakody, V. (2007). Horizontal Process Integration in E-Government: The Perspective of a UK Local Authority. *International Journal of Electronic Government Research, 3*(3), 22–39.

Clarke, S. E., & Chenoweth, E. (2006). The Politics of Vulnerability: Constructing Local Performance Regimes for Homeland Security. *Review of Policy Research, 23*(1), 95–114. doi:10.1111/j.1541-1338.2006.00187.x

Clarke, W. (2006). *Emergency Management in County Government: A National Survey*. Retrieved August 10, 2008, from http://www.naco.org/Template.cfm?Section=Library&template=/ContentManagement/ContentDisplay.cfm&ContentID=21623

Dearstyne, B. (2007). The FDNY on 9/11: Information and Decision Making in Crisis. *Government Information Quarterly, 24*(1), 29–46. doi:10.1016/j.giq.2006.03.004

DeSantis, V. S., & Renner, T. (2002). City Government Structures: An Attempt at Clarification. *State and Local Government Review, 34*(2), 95–104.

DHS. (2008). *National Incident Management System*. Retrieved January 26, 2009, from http://www.fema.gov/pdf/emergency/nims/NIMS_core.pdf.

DHS. (2009). *Homeland Security Advisory System*. Retrieved January 26, 2009, from http://www.dhs.gov/xinfoshare/programs/Copy_of_press_release_0046.shtm.

GAO. (2003). *Homeland Security: Efforts to Improve Information Sharing Need to be Strengthened*. (GAO Publication No. GAO-03-760). Washington, DC: U.S. Government Printing Office.

Gerber, B. J., Cohen, D. B., Cannon, B., Patterson, D., & Stewart, K. (2005). On the Front Line: American Cities and the Challenge of Homeland Security Preparedness. *Urban Affairs Review, 41*(2), 182–210. doi:10.1177/1078087405279900

Gerber, B. J., Cohen, D. B., & Stewart, K. (2007). U.S. Cities and Homeland Security: Examining the Role of Financial Conditions and Administrative Capacity in Municipal Preparedness Efforts. *Public Finance and Management*, *7*(2), 152–188.

Ho, A. T.-K. (2002). Reinventing Local Governments and the E-Government Initiative. *Public Administration Review*, *62*(4), 434–444. doi:10.1111/0033-3352.00197

Ho, A. T.-K., & Smith, J. F. (2001). Information Technology Planning and the Y2K Problem in Local Governments. *American Review of Public Administration*, *31*(2), 158–180. doi:10.1177/02750740122064901

Holden, S. H., Norris, D. F., & Fletcher, P. D. (2003). Electronic Government at the Local Level: Progress to Date and Future Issues. *Public Performance & Management Review*, *26*(4), 325–344. doi:10.1177/1530957603026004002

Lester, W., & Krejci, D. (2007). Business "Not" as Usual: The National Incident Management System, Federalism, and Leadership. *Public Administration Review*, *67*(s1), 84–93.

MacManus, S. A., & Caruson, K. (2006). Code Red: Florida City and County Officials Rate Threat Information Sources and the Homeland Security Advisory System. *State and Local Government Review*, *38*(1), 12–22.

McLoughlin, I., & Cornford, J. (2006). Transformational Change in the Local State? Enacting E-government in English Local Authorities. *Journal of Management & Organization*, *12*(3), 195–208.

Moon, M. J. (2002). The Evolution of E-Government among Municipalities: Rhetoric or Reality? *Public Administration Review*, *62*(4), 424–433. doi:10.1111/0033-3352.00196

Moon, M. J., & Norris, D. F. (2005). Does Managerial Orientation Matter? The Adoption of Reinventing Government and E-Government at the Municipal Level. *Information Systems Journal*, *15*(1), 43–60. doi:10.1111/j.1365-2575.2005.00185.x

Norris, D. F., & Moon, M. J. (2005). Advancing E-Government at the Grassroots: Tortoise or Hare? *Public Administration Review*, *65*(1), 64–75. doi:10.1111/j.1540-6210.2005.00431.x

Reddick, C. G. (2007). Homeland Security Preparedness and Planning in US City Governments: A Survey of City Managers. *Journal of Contingencies and Crisis Management*, *15*(3), 157–167. doi:10.1111/j.1468-5973.2007.00518.x

Reddick, C. G., & Frank, H. A. (2006). Homeland Security Administration and Finance: A Survey of Texas County Officials. *Journal of Homeland Security and Emergency Management*, *3*(3), 1–21. doi:10.2202/1547-7355.1255

Scavo, C., Kearney, R. C., & Kilroy, R. J. (2008). Challenges to Federalism: Homeland Security and Disaster Response. *Publius: The Journal of Federalism*, *38*(1), 81–110. doi:10.1093/publius/pjm029

Yang, K., & Rho, S.-Y. (2007). E-Government for Better Performance: Promises, Realities, and Challenges. *International Journal of Public Administration*, *30*(11), 1197–1217. doi:10.1080/01900690701225556

Section 3
Emerging Issues

The final section of this book examines some emerging issues in the realm of HSIS. These important issues discussed in Section 3, faced by governments, are citizens' use of terrorism information for preparedness, information security, and an assessment of information on emergency management websites. The conclusion summarizes the main findings of the book and provides recommendations for future research on this important subject matter.

Chapter 7
Citizens, the Internet, and Terrorism Information

INTRODUCTION

This chapter examines the role that citizens play when using the internet for gathering information. It is vital to understand the use of the Internet by citizens to address the issue of access to homeland security information. This chapter also provides information on how terrorism information is presented online and citizens' use of this information is discussed. Jones, Hackney, and Irani (2007) believe that the key to the successful development of e-government is its citizens. There needs to be efforts to engage citizens in the adoption of e-government. These authors believe that this engagement will truly create a transformation of e-government that was envisioned by earlier writers in the field. This chapter discusses this level of engagement and shows that citizens are the least likely to use Internet for homeland security information if a terrorist attack occurs.

Existing research on the adoption of e-government tends to focus on the supply of e-government in terms of the breadth and sophistication of government Websites. However, Streib and Navarro (2006) have examined the role the internet plays in public organizations using public opinion data, examining the demand for e-government. There is a need for more research on the demand for e-government and that is the focus of this chapter. The argument made in this chapter is that you need to understand citizens, and why they go online, to more effectively cater homeland security information to their needs.

This chapter first discusses the important issue of the digital divide, the disparity between those that have Internet access and those that do not. This is followed by a discussion of citizen trust and satisfaction with e-government Websites. Followed this, there is a discussion of the citizen-initiated contacts literature as a framework that helps us understand why citizens contact government for information and services. There also is data presented in this chapter from the Pew Internet and American Life Project on the influence of the Internet on individuals for getting information and solving a problem. This is

DOI: 10.4018/978-1-60566-834-5.ch007

followed by an examination of Pew data on sources of information citizens would use in the event of a terrorist attack. The conclusion summarizes the results of the chapter.

DIGITAL DIVIDE

Understanding the digital divide, and possible ways of mitigating the divide, are crucial to know in order to provide homeland security information to citizens. According to empirical findings in the United Kingdom, there are several constraints on the adoption on e-government from the perspective of the citizen (Weerakkody and Choudrie, 2005). They are lack of internet access, disparities in computer knowledge, generation gap, lack of awareness, language barriers, security and privacy, and lack of user friendliness of websites. These factors impede citizens from taking advantage of e-government services. These differences in access from individuals that have access and do not have access to information technology such as the Internet is often referred to as the digital divide.

There are several limitations of internet-based applications:

- Difficulty in searching for and locating the right information;
- Low ownership and availability of personal computers to various segments of a population;
- High cost of maintenance of public information kiosks; and
- Low access to the Internet to various segments of a population (Singh and Sahu, 2007: p. 479).

Because citizens have differing abilities looking for information online this can be a challenge for many. In addition, access to technology varies with population group because of the digital divide. As a result, the Internet may not be the ideal medium for providing e-government to all citizens in the world, particularly in developing nations. Therefore, governments should explore other channels of communication, which are able to bridge the digital divide (Singh and Sahu, 2007).

There are three alternatives to Internet-based strategies that Singh and Sahu (2007) identify: (1) Mobile Government; (2) Interactive Voice Response System; (3) Public Information Kiosks; and (4) Government Call Centers. Mobile phones have emerged as the most popular medium for communication during the last decade. Mobile phones have the potential to bridge the digital divide, because they are not restricted to those on the higher socioeconomic status and are more accessible to the general population.

Second, interactive voice response system are found in structured questions such as information about bank account balances, authorizing a transaction, and knowing the position of an application. This provides a method which can bridge the digital divide since telephone access is much higher than Internet access.

Third, public information kiosks are computer-based devices that provide an interface medium between users and a service or information provider. Kiosks in public places provide a convenient place to interact with government agencies and bridge the digital divide by providing access to those that do not have internet access.

Finally, citizens can get information or access services by calling a government call center and choose from a standard menu of options or talk to an operator if they cannot find an answer to their question. Singh and Sahu (2007) conclude that the integration of the Internet, phones, and call centers can enable governments to deliver e-government to all citizens and help them bridge the digital divide.

Australian governments have developed initiatives to enhance community access to the Internet. Survey research shows that the young, lower income, unemployed, and indigenous individuals are the largest users of community internet access points (Dugdale, Daly, Papandrea, and Maley, 2005). This demonstrates the importance of providing these services in public places to bridge the digital divide for these populations, such as public libraries.

There are several strategies that Bertot, Jaeger, and McClure (2008) advise in creating more citizen-centered e-government. First, a comprehensive plan is needed for user-centric e-government service design. This involves indentifying the goals of that service, ways which the service supports other government goals, the managerial structure, and identifying the target audience of the service. Second, governments need to understand how users seek information on a particular topic or issue in a user information needs assessment. This knowledge allows government to know how users find and use information as well as the sources they use. Third, there is a need to understand user information and communication technology availability, expertise, and preference by citizens. Web-based e-government development requires a broadband connection, high-end computing, and other advanced technology that will exclude a significant portion of the population. Fourth, there is a need to engage users as a strategy for citizen-centered e-government. There is a range of tools that can be used to engage the public on e-government services such as focus groups and user testing. Fifth, there is a need to evaluate e-government services for continued improvement. Governments need to conduct ongoing evaluations of their e-government services in order to improve them. A final strategy for creating citizen-centered e-government services is to form community-based partnerships such as public libraries and other community centers to help address the issue of the digital divide. The following section examines trust and satisfaction, an important issue that influences citizens' use of e-government.

TRUST AND SATISFACTION

There are several studies that examine the level of citizen trust and satisfaction with the Internet for e-government information and services. This part of the chapter reviews the level of trust in government as a means of understanding why some citizens go online for e-government information. In a survey conducted by the University of Michigan's E-government Satisfaction Index for the first quarter of 2008 there was a satisfaction score of 72.4 (American Customer Satisfaction Index, 2008). This is the lowest e-government satisfaction score in three years. As a benchmark, the highest level since this statistic has been recorded in the third quarter of 2003 was 74%. When comparing the federal e-government to private sector e-commerce satisfaction there was 81.6% (e-tailers, online travel, online brokerage) and e-business satisfaction was 75.2% (news/information sites, search engines, and portals), showing that e-government was below these indexes. However, when comparing overall satisfaction with the federal government at 67.8%, the E-government Satisfaction Index scored much higher. As a result, there is more satisfaction from individuals with their government when they go online to get information or services than offline contacts.

One of the first studies that examined citizen trust and e-government was by West (2004). This author made the argument that e-government has fallen short of its potential to have an impact on public trust in government. This author found when examining public opinion data that e-government users were no more likely than nonusers to be trusting or confident about government or to believe the government is effective in solving problems.

The University of Michigan's National Election Studies (NES) longitudinal data on Government trust shows that this has been declining in the last three decades, since Watergate during the Nixon Presidency. In general, Americans are losing confidence and trust in their government. Welch, Hinnant, and Moon (2004) in an examination of public opinion data, found that trust in government is strongly associated with e-government satisfaction. Their findings indicate that citizens believe that e-government is doing a relatively good job with transactions and transparency, but it has not addressed interactivity dimensions. E-government appears to be doing well with providing information, and much of the existing research confirms this finding. There is less satisfaction with more transactions-based services that e-government could potentially offer.

Tolbert and Mossberger (2006) examined whether e-government improved citizens attitudes towards government. They use public opinion data to evaluate the impact of e-government on citizens' attitudes about government. Their results indicate that users of local government Websites are more likely to trust local government, controlling for other demographic factors, and the use of government Website is associated with other positive attitudes, especially for federal and local governments. This finding of increased trust with local governments could be its relative proximity to citizens, compared with federal and state governments. The information received on local websites might be especially useful for citizen's daily lives such as mass transit schedules, local services, and neighborhood information.

There is other research that shows individuals with prior trust in government will have this reinforced by e-government interaction (Parent, Vandebeek, and Gemino, 2005). Furthermore, individuals that are distrustful will not increase their level of trust with e-government interaction. For policy makers to increase trust, it might be better to focus on non Internet based services at the expense of improving web-based services.

In two surveys of bureaucrats and citizens a study compares the perspectives of each group on aspects of e-government (Moon and Welch, 2005). The results tend to show that citizens and bureaucrats differ on their orientations towards e-government. Citizens are less enthusiastic about e-government, less interested in great convenience and more information, and more concerned about security and privacy issues. Bureaucrats on the other hand are more enthusiastic about e-government and are drawn by the promise of e-government. However, bureaucrats realize that structural constraints exist, which may reduce the speed of its implementation.

Another study showed multiple factors besides trust such as perceived ease of use, compatibility and trustworthiness were significant predictors of citizens' intention to use e-government services (Carter and Belanger, 2005). For the factor perceived ease of use it is imperative that online government services be intuitive for the user. A government website should be easy to navigate. Information should be organized and presented based on citizens' needs. If a user becomes frustrated this will decrease his or her intention to adopt the e-government services. With respect to compatibility and trustworthiness citizens will be more willing to use online services if these services are congruent with the way they like to interact with others. For example, citizens that use web socially or economically are more likely to adopt this technology to contact government. In addition, higher levels of trustworthiness are positively associated with citizens' intention to use an e-government service as existing research shows. There also is the citizen-initiated contacts literature that is examined in the following section to determine why citizens contact government for information or services.

CITIZEN-INITIATED CONTACTS

As a way of understanding why citizens go online for e-government information this can be explained by the citizen-initiated contacts literature. Citizens that use government websites for information and services represents a new form of citizen-initiated contacts as opposed to more traditional contacts such as a public meeting or telephoning a government office (Thomas and Streib, 2003). The reason for citizen-initiated contacts is a specific need for information or service. Citizens' use of Websites represents a new form of citizen-initiated contacts. The results from Thomas and Streib indicate that government websites are emerging as an increasingly important vehicle for citizen-initiated contacts with government. There are some caveats showing that citizens who are upset about inadequate public services, may not be satisfied with venting their anger via email or using a website for emergency information.

One way to examine citizen-initiated contacts is to explore survey evidence on types of contacts. Reddick (2008) conducted a survey of IT directors during the summer of 2007 of the perceived effectiveness of different service channels for citizen-initiated contacts with government. This survey was sent to cities with populations of 75,000 residents or greater in the United States. Table 1 provides a picture of the extent to which citizens contact government through different service channels. This question was used to determine the usage of e-government in cities compared with other more traditional service channels. The telephone is the most common way for citizens to contact city government (30.8%). The second most common method was in person at a government office as represented by 24.2% of respondents. The least used service channel for citizens was through the mail according to 11.7% of IT directors. When combining Website contacts (20.7%) and email contacts (12.6%), there were 33.3% of citizens using these service channels to contact government.

Table 2 provides the views of IT directors in the level of perceived effectiveness of different service channels used by citizens to contact their city government (Reddick, 2008). These questions are divided into the different methods of contact through a Website, email, telephone, and in person visit at a government office. The effectiveness of each of these service channels is rated according to the task of citizens of accessing information, solving a problem, and accessing services.

Table 2 shows that the citizens ability to access information the Website was viewed by IT directors as the most effective method, with 92% believing this was the case (when adding the "very effective" and "effective" responses). Email was viewed by 83% of IT directors as effective for accessing information. The telephone was viewed by 88.4% of respondents as effective for accessing information. Finally, an in person visit at a government office had 84.9% of IT directors believing this was effective for access-

Table 1. Percent citizens' contact with government through different service channels (Source: Adapted from Reddick, 2008)

Service Channel	Percent
Telephone	30.8
In Person at City Government Office	24.2
Website	20.7
Email	12.6
Mail	11.7
E-government Usage (Website and Email)	**33.3**

Table 2. The level of perceived effectiveness of service channels in city government (Source: Adapted from Reddick, 2008)

	Very Effective %	Effective %	Neutral %	Ineffective %	Very Ineffective %
Effectiveness of the following service channels for citizens' ability to *access information*					
Website	31.3	60.7	4.5	2.7	0.9
Email	25.9	57.1	12.5	4.5	0.0
Telephone	20.5	67.9	8.0	3.6	0.0
In Person at City Government Office	28.6	56.3	11.6	3.6	0.0
Effectiveness of the following service channels for citizens' ability to *solve a problem*					
Website	14.3	51.8	21.4	8.0	4.5
Email	17.9	64.3	12.5	5.4	0.0
Telephone	25.0	67.0	5.4	2.7	0.0
In Person at City Government Office	39.3	50.9	8.0	1.8	0.0
Effectiveness of the following service channels for citizens' ability to *access services*					
Website	27.7	49.1	13.4	8.0	1.8
Email	19.6	43.8	26.8	8.0	1.8
Telephone	17.9	63.4	14.3	4.5	0.0
In Person at City Government Office	33.0	55.4	8.9	2.7	0.0

ing information. Overall, it appears that all of the service channels are rated as effective for accessing information, but the city Website had a slight edge.

As shown in Table 2, for solving a problem the service channel that was viewed as being the most effective was the telephone (92%). The least effective service channel for solving a problem was the city government Website (66.1%). While the effectiveness for solving a problem with email (82.2%) and in person at a government office (90.2%) were in between the phone and Website contacts in regards to effectiveness.

Finally, IT directors were asked to rate the service channels in terms of citizens' ability to access services (Table 2). The highest rated service channel for accessing services was in person at a government office (88.4%). The lowest rated service channel in terms of effectiveness was email according to 63.4% of IT directors. Accessing services by citizens through a Website was effective according to 76.8% of IT directors. Finally, the telephone was viewed by 81.3% of directors as an effective service channel for citizen access to services.

The overall results in Table 2 indicate that Websites were the most effective service channel for getting information; the telephone was the most effective service channel for solving a problem; while in person at a government office was most effective channel for citizens to access city services. These findings are also consistent with public opinion data on e-government use by citizens (Reddick, 2005).

A Pew Internet and American Life (2004) survey also showed how e-government is faring by placing it into the context of other communication channels that citizens use to initiate contact with their government such as telephone calls, in-person visits, and writing letters. Americans with internet access are more likely to contact the government than non-internet users. The results of this survey indicated that many people do not prefer to contact government with the Web or email. For real-time interaction with government the telephone or in person visits are preferred when people have urgent or complex problems to sort out with the government. For example, when the problem is very complex and urgent the telephone is preferred by 46% of respondents compared to only 14% for website and 10% for email. By contrast, when citizens contact government for information the telephone is preferred by 41%, Website 33%, and 10% for email. Therefore, as policy makers look to expanding e-government offerings, they should upgrade existing service channels as well to complement e-government.

The citizen-initiated contacts with government research shows that habit is one of the most important factors that influence contacts (Perterson and Dijk, 2007). People use different service channels because they have used them before and because they are satisfied with the experience. When the problem is more complex and ambiguous, the influence of habit declines and people are more willing to use different methods depending on the task. Citizens generally use the phone for complex problems compared to Websites.

Wang, Bretschneider, and Gant (2005) believe that citizens' activities on Websites are either looking for information or completing a transaction. One way to look at this is with respect to a problem solving process. A citizen is always trying to complete a task such as accessing services online. By trying to achieve a goal a citizen is trying to use information to reduce uncertainty. Accessing e-government services can be understood as an information seeking activity, which involves a problem solving process. The performance of citizens' information seeking activities can be seen as a measure of e-government performance and ultimately satisfaction.

Research shows that individuals contact e-government much less for policy or public concerns than for a personal reason such as filing taxes or finding information online (Cohen, 2006). For example, survey evidence indicates that 20% of individuals contacted government to express an opinion. When citizens contact government they are highly satisfied with their experience.

There is a tradeoff with citizen involvement in e-government implementation between responsiveness through citizen engagement and preserving an efficient government operation (Chen, Huang, and Hsiao, 2006). The more citizens get involved with their government the more costly it is to govern according to Chen, Huang, and Hsiao. For example, after constructing a citizen complaint mechanism in Taiwan there was a greater willingness for citizens to file complaints through digital means, rather than through other service channels. Therefore, public managers need to devote more resources to process mounting emails.

The perceived risk of a terrorist attack does not increase the citizens' intention to use an e-government website significantly (Lee and Rao, 2007). Citizens tend to focus on day to day activities that are occurring to them in the present time. In addition, Lee and Rao found that citizens will not depend on e-government websites for terrorism information unless the information provided has demonstrated a high level of competence in protecting citizens from a terrorist attack compared to alternative channels such as television.

The following section of this chapter presents public opinion survey data that examines the digital divide, the use of the Internet by citizens for finding information and solving a problem, and the use by citizens of online homeland security information.

SURVEY RESULTS OF CITIZEN ONLINE ACCESS

Table 3 provides information on U.S. Internet access by demographic group. This information is presented to learn about the type of individuals that typically go online. This data is compiled from the Pew Internet and American Life Project (2007) survey on the use of information for searching and solving problems. The results of this survey were from telephone interviews conducted between the months of June and September 2007 among a sample of 2,796 adults 18 years of age and older.

The information in Table 3 showed that 76% of adults age 18 and over had access to the Internet. There were a marginally higher number of men (78%) than women (75%) having Internet access. Whites are the most likely race to have internet access (78%), while blacks have the least Internet access (68%). In terms of the different age groupings, generation Y, those in the age range of 18-30, have the highest percentage of adults online (91%), while those who are over 71 years of age are the least likely to go online (29%).

Socio-economic status indicates that households earning less than $40,000 a year are less likely to go online (61%), while those households earning more than $40,000 are more likely to go online (91%) (Table 3). Education level also had an impact on Internet access. The least amount of Internet access was for individuals that had less than a high school diploma (41%). The most Internet access was found in

Table 3. Internet access by demographic groups (As percent of adults in each group with internet access) (Source: Data compiled from Pew, 2007)

Demographic Group	*Percent*
Adults (18 and over)	76
Men	78
Women	75
Whites	78
Blacks	68
English-speaking Latinos	75
Gen Y (age 18-30)	91
Gen X (31-42)	90
Boomers (43-61)	79
Matures (62-71)	56
After work (71+)	29
Household earns less than $40,000	61
Household earns more than $40,000	91
Less than high school diploma	41
High school diploma	69
Some College	86
College Degree +	93
Rural	66
Suburban	80
Urban	76

Table 4. Sources of help in dealing with a specific problem (Source: Data compiled from Pew, 2007)

Source	*Used Source %*
Ask friends and family members	45.0
Ask professional advisors such as doctors, lawyers, or financial experts	52.6
Use the Internet	**57.9**
Use newspapers, magazines, and books	35.7
Use television and radio	16.3
Go to the public library	12.8
Go to a local place where you can use a computer for free	9.2
Contact a government office or agency	33.6
Use another source not mentioned already	10.8

respondents that had at least a college degree (93%). Finally, individuals located in suburban areas had the most Internet access (80%) and citizens in rural areas had the least Internet access (66%).

The survey results in Table 3 show that there is a digital divide in individuals that have Internet access and those that do not have access. This digital divide runs across race, age, household income, education, and geography. The results showed that black and Hispanic, senior citizens, poor, and less educated have the least Internet access. These results are vital to know in order to understand what information governments can place online about emergencies. Indeed, placing information online may not be accessed by a significant portion of the population because of the digital divide. Therefore, providing emergency management and homeland security information online may not be of great advantage to those vulnerable populations that simply do not have Internet access.

Table 4 provides information on the sources of help that individuals use when dealing with a specific problem that they face. The number one source for citizens to get help on a specific problem was the Internet according to 57.9% of respondents. What is not shown in Table 4, is that individuals have a very successful experience when they go online to solve a problem (63%). The second most common source for help was to ask a professional advisor such as doctor, lawyer, or financial expert for information at 52.6%. The third choice was to ask friends and family members at 45% of respondents. Only 12.8% of individuals polled would go to a library to get help with a problem. What is not shown in Table 4, is that young adults in the age range of 18-29 are the heaviest users of libraries for problem solving. Most of these young adults are very satisfied with what they found at the library. Libraries because they typically provide free access to the internet would provide a good source of information in case of emergencies.

What is most interesting from the results presented in Table 4 is that the Internet was the first choice for getting information to deal with problems. This is important to know as this medium can be used as an important source to transmit information to citizens in case of an emergency.

Table 5 provides information on the preferred methods of contacting government by citizens for different issues that may arise in their daily lives. A preferred method of contacting government for a personal tax issue was the telephone (57.2%). The preferred contact method for getting a license or permit for your car was some other way (53.4%), which is a combination of methods. When exploring government benefits the preferred method of contact was the Internet (45.5%). For doing research for school or work, the preferred method was the Internet (65.9%). For accessing programs that different

Table 5. Preferred way of contacting government (Source: Data compiled from Pew, 2007)

Method of Contact	*Telephone*	*Internet*	*Some other way*	*Don't know/refused*
Personal tax issue	57.2	16.7	23.1	3.0
Getting a license or permit for your car	12.6	30.9	53.4	3.2
Exploring government benefits for yourself or someone else	25.9	45.5	24.7	3.9
Doing research for school or work	9.9	65.9	15.4	8.9
The kinds of programs different government agencies offer	21.7	54.8	18.2	5.4
Community issues such as education, crime, traffic	26.4	35	32.4	6.1

government agencies offer, the preferred contact method was the Internet (54.8%). Finally, for community issues such as education, crime, traffic, the Internet was the preferred method according to 35% of respondents.

Essentially, e-government was most commonly used for getting information and conducting research on government programs as other research indicates (Pew Internet and American Life, 2002). More complicated tax issues were more likely to be conducted over the phone. This result is important for emergency management and homeland security since the Internet may not the preferred method to get forms filled out, it is mostly an informational source. This bolds well for placing information on emergency management websites since this is preferred choice for citizens to conduct research.

EMERGENCIES AND THE INTERNET

In addition to more general information on the Internet and access to online information, the Pew Internet and American Life (2003) project also conducted a public opinion survey on emergencies and the Internet. This poll of 1001 adults was conducted in August 2003. This survey assessed public sentiment about America's emergency preparedness and warning systems two years after the 9/11 terrorist attacks.

The results in Table 6 demonstrate some public opinion data on the impact of the Internet on emergencies. There were 33.5% of citizens indicating that they were "somewhat" and "very worried" about themselves or someone in your family becoming a victim of a terrorist target. There was 71.2% of individuals polled that believed they were "very confident" and "somewhat confident" if there was a terrorist attack in their community the federal government would quickly provide accurate information. There were only a small percentage of individuals who believed that government should notify Americans on their cell phone and pagers if there was a terrorist attack (22%). Only 11.5% of respondents believed that government should notify Americans via email if there is a terrorist attack. Survey results indicated that there was a great deal and some useful information on government Websites about protecting families against a terrorist attack (69.3%). The federal government's color-coded homeland security advisory system was viewed by 56.6% of respondents as providing useful information to citizens.

Generally, the results in Table 6 indicate that most Americans do not believe that they will be a victim of a terrorist attack; there is not much of a demand for terrorist attack notification through digital means such as email and cell phones; and most individuals have not looked online for information to protect themselves or their family members from a terrorist attack. The good news is there is some faith that

Table 6. Homeland security and the Internet (Source: Data compiled from Pew, 2003)

Public opinion responses to questions about homeland security and the Internet	*Percent*
"Somewhat worried" and "very worried" about you or someone in your family might become a victim of a terrorist attack	33.5
"Very confident" and "somewhat confident" if there was a terrorist attack on your community the federal government would quickly provide accurate information	71.2
Government should notify Americans on their cell phones and pagers if there is a terrorist attack	22.0
Government should notify Americans via email if there is a terrorist attack	18.0
Looked online on government websites for information to protect yourself and your family in case of a terrorist attack	11.5
A "great deal" and "some" useful information on the government website about protecting your family against a terrorist attack	69.3
Federal Government's Homeland Security Advisory Systems provided provides useful information	56.6

the homeland security advisory system and government Websites do provide some useful information to prepare for a terrorist incident.

Finally, Table 7 provides information on the first and second choices of getting information on a terrorist attack. Respondents indicated that their first choice for information was television at 56.7%. This was distantly followed by the radio at 15% of respondents for getting information on a terrorist attack. Government websites was viewed by a mere 2.9% of respondents as their first choice for getting information about a terrorist attack. Given U.S. citizens' high Internet usage rate and dependency on the Internet for government information and services the low acceptance rate of government websites for information on national emergencies indicates a problem (Lee and Rao, 2007). As a second source of information, 3.7% of respondents would get information on a terrorist attack from government Websites. What is interesting, and is not shown in Table 5, the young (those in the age range of 18-29) are the most likely to say that the Internet would be a key news source for them in an emergency situation. More than half of them would go to Websites as one of their primary or secondary sources of information. Essentially the data in Table 7 indicate that government Websites would not have much of an impact at all as a source of information for citizens about a terrorist attack. In fact, government Websites are about the last place citizens would turn to get this important information. Their primary source of information not surprisingly was television. This was seen most vividly after September 11, 2001 of the visual images of the events of this tragic day unfolding on television.

CONCLUSION

This chapter has examined the use by citizens of e-government information as a way of understanding the challenges of placing homeland security information online. There is a digital divide in Internet access with individuals that are minorities, less educated, have lower household income, and seniors are less likely to go online. This translates into governments having to use alternative methods to reach these individuals with homeland security information. This represents a serious challenge of addressing access to homeland security information to these especially vulnerable populations in the event of a disaster.

This chapter reviewed the citizen-initiated contacts literature to understand why citizens contact their government. Contacts are generally driven by needs that citizens have for information. This chapter also

Table 7. Preferred methods of getting information on a terrorist attack (Source: Data compiled from Pew, 2003)

	Percent first choice to get information	*Percent second source for information*
Television	56.7	23.0
Radio	15.0	26.1
Newspapers	1.3	10.6
News websites	6.0	12.1
Government websites	2.9	3.7
Friends and family	5.7	12.0
Government officials (including law enforcement)	8.8	8.9
Don't know/refused	3.6	3.6

showed that as citizens trust their government more, they are more likely to go online for e-government information. The more citizen trust of government, the greater likelihood of going online for homeland security information.

The Internet is the number one source for citizens to get help when dealing with a specific problem. This is important for the provision of homeland security information online, since it represents a good source for citizens to access. However, the preferred method of contacting government varies by the type of issue at hand. For example, the preferred method for exploring government benefits and programs is the Internet. For a personal tax issue the preferred method is to initiate contact with government over the phone. This bolds well for putting homeland security information online since citizens prefer this method for contact. However, citizens generally would not go online for homeland security information in the event of a terrorist attack since a mere 3% would do so. Citizens believe they would get homeland security information on television in the event of a terrorist attack. Possibly the Internet is not dynamic enough to provide updated information in the event of a terrorist attack, this was seen on September 11, 2001, where many media websites crashed because of the overload of requests for information.

REFERENCES

American Customer Satisfaction Index. (2008).*E-Government Satisfaction Index*. Retrieved August 30, 2008 from www.foreseeresults.com.

Bertot, J. C., Jaeger, P. T., & McClure, C. R. (2008). Citizen-Centered E-government Services: Benefits, Costs, and Research Needs. *ACM International Conference Proceeding Series, 289*, 137-142. Retrieved August 30, 2008 from http://portal.acm.org.

Carter, L., & Belanger, F. (2005). The Utilization of E-government Services: Citizen Trust, Innovation and Acceptance Factors. *Information Systems Journal, 15*(1), 5–25. doi:10.1111/j.1365-2575.2005.00183.x

Chen, D.-Y., Huang, T.-Y., & Hsiao, N. (2006). Reinventing Government through On-line Citizen Involvement in the Developing World: A Case Study of Taipei City Mayor's E-mail Box in Taiwan. *Public Administration and Development, 26*(5), 409–423. doi:10.1002/pad.415

Cohen, J. E. (2006). Citizen Satisfaction with Contacting Government on the Internet. *Information Polity, 11*(1), 51–65.

Dugdale, A., Daly, A., Papandrea, F., & Maley, M. (2005). Accessing E-government: Challenges for Citizens and Organizations. *International Review of Administrative Sciences, 71*(1), 109–118. doi:10.1177/0020852305051687

Jones, S., Hackney, R., & Irani, Z. (2007). Towards E-government Transformation: Conceptualizing "Citizen Engagement" A Research Note. *Transforming Government: People, Process and Policy, 1*(2), 145-152.

Lee, J., & Rao, H. R. (2007). Citizen-Centric Analysis of Anti/Counter-Terrorism e-Government Services. *ACM International Conference Proceeding Series, 228*, 258-259. Retrieved August 30, 2008 from http://portal.acm.org/

Lee, J., & Rao, H. R. (2007). Perceived Risks, Counter-Beliefs, and Intentions to use Anti/Counter-Terrorism Websites: An Exploratory Study of Government-Citizens Online Interactions in a Turbulent Environment. *Decision Support Systems, 43*(4), 1431–1449. doi:10.1016/j.dss.2006.04.008

Moon, M. J., & Welch, E. W. (2005). Same Bed, Different Dreams? A Comparative Analysis of Citizen and Bureaucrat Perspectives on E-government. *Review of Public Personnel Administration, 25*(3), 243–264. doi:10.1177/0734371X05275508

Parent, M., Vandebeek, C. A., & Gemino, A. C. (2005). Building Citizen Trust through E-government. *Government Information Quarterly, 22*(4), 720–736. doi:10.1016/j.giq.2005.10.001

Pew Internet and American Life. (2002). *The Rise of the E-Citizen: How People use Government Agencies' Web Sites*. Retrieved August 30, 2008 from www.pewinternet.org.

Pew Internet and American Life. (2003). *Survey with Federal Computer Week Magazine about Emergencies and the Internet*. Retrieved August 30, 2008 from www.pewinternet.org.

Pew Internet and American Life. (2004). *How Americans get in Touch with Government*. Retrieved August 30, 2008 from www.pewinternet.org.

Pew Internet and American Life. (2007). *Information Searches that Solve Problems*. Retrieved August 30, 2008 from www.pewinternet.org.

Pieterson, W., & Dijk, J. (2007). Channel Choice Determinants: An Exploration of the Factors that determine the Choice of a Service Channel in Citizen Initiated Contacts. *ACM International Conference Proceeding Series, 228*, 173 – 182, Retrieved August 30, 2008 from http://portal.acm.org.

Reddick, C. G. (2005). Citizen-Initiated Contacts with Government: Comparing Phones and Websites. *Journal of E-Government, 2*(1), 27–53. doi:10.1300/J399v02n01_03

Reddick, C. G. (2008). Perceived Effectiveness of E-Government and its Usage in City Governments: Survey Evidence from Information Technology Directors. *International Journal of Electronic Government Research, 4*(4), 89–104.

Singh, A., & Sahu, R. (2008). Integrating Internet, Telephones, and Call Centers for Delivering Better Quality E-governance to all Citizens. *Government Information Quarterly, 25*(3), 477–490. doi:10.1016/j.giq.2007.01.001

Streib, G., & Navarro, I. (2006). Citizen Demand for Interactive E-government: The Case of Georgia Consumer Services. *American Review of Public Administration, 36*(3), 288–300. doi:10.1177/0275074005283371

Thomas, J. C., & Streib, G. (2003). The New Face of Government: Citizen-Initiated Contacts in the Era of E-government. *Journal of Public Administration: Research and Theory, 13*(1), 83–102. doi:10.1093/jpart/mug010

Tolbert, C. J., & Mossberger, K. (2006). The Effects of E-government on Trust and Confidence in Government. *Public Administration Review, 66*(3), 354–369. doi:10.1111/j.1540-6210.2006.00594.x

Wang, L., Bretschneider, S., & Gant, J. (2005). Evaluating Web-based E-government Services with a Citizen-Centric Approach. *Proceedings of the Proceedings of the 38th Annual Hawaii International Conference on System Sciences, 5*, 129-131. Retrieved August 30, 2008 from http://portal.acm.org.

Weerakkody, V., & Choudrie, J. (2005). Exploring E-government in the UK: Challenges, Issues and Complexities. *Journal of Information Science and Technology, 2*(2), 25–45.

Welch, E. W., Hinnant, C. C., & Moon, M. J. (2005). Linking Citizen Satisfaction with E-government and Trust in Government. *Journal of Public Administration: Research and Theory, 15*(3), 371–391. doi:10.1093/jopart/mui021

West, D. M. (2004). E-government and the Transformation of Service Delivery and Citizen Attitudes. *Public Administration Review, 64*(1), 15–27. doi:10.1111/j.1540-6210.2004.00343.x

Chapter 8
Information Security in Government

INTRODUCTION

This chapter examines the important issue of the impact of information security in government. Information security is one of the critical issues of Homeland Security Information Systems (HSIS). As we know from Chapter 4, information security is one of the leading concerns of Chief Information Officers (CIO) in the realm of homeland security. This chapter explores the impact of information security on government similarly to a framework provided by Straub and Welke (1998) who believe that the organizational environment, individual characteristics, the information systems environment, and level of threats are related to management perceptions of information security risk. The argument is that the stronger the correlation between changes in these four factors this would have an influence on the perception of management of information security risk. Therefore, the more the organizational culture supports information security the greater the managerial concern. In this chapter there is an argument made that there needs to be more knowledge of the leading issues facing information security in order to influence the organizational culture.

The first part of this chapter focuses on several information security issues that have been identified in the literature. These issues deal with management, policy, and end users of IT and their impact on information security. The second part of this chapter provides evidence from several information security surveys. The last part of this chapter deals with survey results from an information security survey of Texas state agencies.

DOI: 10.4018/978-1-60566-834-5.ch008

INFORMTION SECURITY ISSUES

Seven issues in information security management have been identified in the literature as being important. They are management and information security, organizational culture, information security threats, information security policy, education, deterrence and prevention, and users and information security. Each of these issues are indentified and later examined through results from a survey of state government CIOs. The factor that belies all of these issues is having an organizational culture that believes in the importance of information security (Rainey and Steinbauer, 1999).

MANAGEMENT AND INFORMATION SECURITY

With the advancement of IT at a fast pace, it is critical to address the issue of information security in this type of interconnected environment (Chang and Ho, 2006). Chang and Ho argue that management attention to information security has been low compared to other information systems issues. Since IT plays such an integral role in modern governments, information security has to be a key component in modern enterprise planning and management. Survey results indicate that security problems are often caused by the negligence of workers, rather than external attacks. Information security is not just a technical problem; it involves important managerial issues requiring special resources and expertise to address this issue.

Research shows that top management support is a significant predictor of an organization's security culture and level of policy enforcement (Knapp, Marshall, Rainer, and Ford, 2006). Therefore, for the successful adoption of most IT projects, including information security, top management should support its implementation.

ORGANIZATIONAL CULTURE AND INFORMATION SECURITY

Chang and Lin (2007) believe that technical aspects of information security are managed by people; therefore, the technical solution cannot protect the organization without a good security management policy. Their research shows that enterprises should conduct an integrated strategy combining both information security and organizational culture. Successful information security implementation requires a combination of favorable organizational culture, competent information security technology, and management's support towards information security. Similarly to top management support, the organizational culture should be supportive of information security for its successful adoption. There should be an emphasis, not just on the technical aspect of information security, but its impact on the organization and its people.

INFORMATION SECURITY POLICY

Whitman (2004) argues that a good information security policy is the number one recommended action an organization can take to safeguard its systems. A good information security policy should outline individual responsibilities, define authorized and unauthorized uses of the systems, provides venues for employee reporting of threats, and define penalties for violators. An information security policy according to Whitman can define the tone of the how seriously management takes on this issue. Organizational culture has a significant bearing on how seriously employees practice information security policy. If the tone is supportive from top management, of the importance of the information security policy, this should have an impact on the success of its implementation.

EDUCATION

Besides having a good information security policy, another area that needs to be addressed is education (Whitman, 2004). Education is needed to prepare future employees to work in a secure computing environment. This will go much further for the organization because it brings with it awareness, which means spending less money on deterrence. Providing education of the information security issues faced by an organization is critical for the successful implementation of an information security policy.

DETERRENCE AND PREVENTION

Kankanhalli, Teo, Tan, and Wei (2003) believe that information security practices can be classified into deterrent or prevention measures. Deterrent measures are attempts to dissuade people from criminal behavior through fear of sanctions. Deterrent efforts will correspond to the certainty that there will be sanctions for violators of security policy. Typically this can involve policy statements and guidelines for legitimate use of information systems.

The second common information security practice is preventative measures which attempts to ward off criminal behavior through controls. Some examples of using prevention are security software to prevent unauthorized access. What route an organization takes in information security is usually a function of its organizational culture. An organizational culture that is trusting of employees may rely more on prevention, and a culture that is not as trusting might rely on deterrence through threat of sanctions.

USERS AND INFORMATION SECURITY

Research shows that the success of information systems security depends upon end user behavior and awareness (D'Arcy and Hovav, 2007). Research shows that user awareness of security policies, security awareness programs, and preventative security software countermeasures significantly reduced information security misuse. The significance of these findings is that strategies to combat information security are often reactive, but these results show that a combination of prevention and deterrence is the best approach. D'Arcy and Hovav argue that fostering a security culture that encourages compliance with security policy is the best overall solution.

One of the primary objectives of an information security policy is to define the users' rights and responsibilities in an organization (Hong, Chi, Chao, and Tang, 2006). Therefore, an effective information security policy would help the user know what is acceptable and unacceptable behavior with regards to information resources. Management should set a clear policy direction and demonstrate support for the commitment of information security throughout the organization.

A majority of information security incidents are usually caused by employees. They are typically caused by employees failing to observe work procedures according to information security guidelines. Chan, Woon, and Kankanhalli (2005) make the argument that information security will require a multifaceted approach having both social and technical components.

INFORMATION SECURITY THREATS

Whitman (2004) found that information security attempts to identify the dominant threats facing organizational information security and ranking these threats to allow organizations to direct priorities towards them. Some of the common information security threats identified by Whitman are acts of human error or failure such as accidents and employee mistakes; deliberate hardware/software attacks and failures; technological obsolescence; forces of nature; and acts of vandalism. There are many threat protection mechanisms deployed to prevent these threats. The most common threat protection mechanisms are username/password access controls, media backup, employee education, and virus protection software.

Foltz (2004) combines several definitions of cyber terrorism and suggests that it is an attack or threat of an attack, politically motivated and intended to: (1) interfere with the political, social, or economic functioning of society or organization; or (2) introduce either physical violence; or (3) unjust use of power; or in conjunction with a more traditional terrorist attack.

Table 1 lists the sources of emergent cyber security threats as identified by the GAO (2005a). These threats range from hackers to more complicated attacks through bot-network operators. There are threats from insiders or the disgruntled employees who may have knowledge of the information systems.

Figure 1 shows the number of cyber incidents as reported by federal department/agencies (GAO, 2008a). We notice that there has been a steady rise of cyber incidents from 2005 to 2007. United States Computer Emergency Readiness Team (US-CERT) reports that the number of these information security incidents have increased dramatically in federal agencies from 3,634 incidents reported in fiscal year 2005 to 13,209 incidents reported in fiscal year 2007, which is about a 259 percent increase.

In order to protect the critical infrastructure in the United States, the Department of Homeland Security has established US-CERT. US-CERT is the lead agency that deals with cyber-related analysis, warning, and information sharing, major incident response, and national-level recovery efforts. It has the charge of improving warning of and response to incidents. The GAO (2008a) has criticized US-CERT since it believes that it does not have a comprehensive understanding of the nation's critical information infrastructure operations, does not monitor all critical infrastructure information system, and does not consistently provide actionable and timely warnings, and lacks the capacity to assist in mitigation and recovery in the event of incidents of national significance.

Incidents are categories by US-CERT in the following manner (GAO, 2008a, pp. 20-21):

- **Unauthorized access:** In this category, an individual gains logical or physical access without permission to a federal agency's network, system, application, data, or other resource.
- **Denial of service:** An attack that successfully prevents or impairs the normal authorized functionality of networks, systems, or applications by exhausting resources. This activity includes being the victim or participating in a denial of service attack.
- **Malicious code:** Successful installation of malicious software (e.g., virus, worm, Trojan horse, or other code-based malicious entity) that infects an operating system or application. Agencies

Table 1. Sources and descriptions of cybersecurity threats (Source: GAO, 2005b)

Threat	Description
Bot-network operators	Bot-network operators are hackers; however, instead of breaking into systems for the challenge or bragging rights, they take over multiple systems in order to coordinate attacks and to distribute phishing a schemes, spam, and malware attacks. The services of these networks are sometimes made available on underground markets (e.g., purchasing a denial-of-service attack, servers to relay spam or phishing attacks, etc.).
Criminal groups	Criminal groups seek to attack systems for monetary gain. Specifically, organized crime groups are using spam, phishing, and spyware/malware to commit identity theft and online fraud. International corporate spies and organized crime organizations also pose a threat to the United States through their ability to conduct industrial espionage and large-scale monetary theft and to hire or develop hacker talent.
Foreign intelligence services	Foreign intelligence services use cyber tools as part of their information-gathering and espionage activities. In addition, several nations are aggressively working to develop information warfare doctrine, programs, and capabilities. Such capabilities enable a single entity to have a significant and serious impact by disrupting the supply, communications, and economic infrastructures that support military power—impacts that could affect the daily lives of U.S. citizens across the country.
Hackers	Hackers break into networks for the thrill of the challenge or for bragging rights in the hacker community. While remote cracking once required a fair amount of skill or computer knowledge, hackers can now download attack scripts and protocols from the Internet and launch them against victim sites. Thus, while attack tools have become more sophisticated, they have also become easier to use. According to the Central Intelligence Agency, the large majority of hackers do not have the requisite expertise to threaten difficult targets such as critical U.S. networks. Nevertheless, the worldwide population of hackers poses a relatively high threat of an isolated or brief disruption causing serious damage.
Insiders	The disgruntled organization insider is a principal source of computer crime. Insiders may not need a great deal of knowledge about computer intrusions because their knowledge of a target system often allows them to gain unrestricted access to cause damage to the system or to steal system data. The insider threat also includes outsourcing vendors as well as employees who accidentally introduce malware into systems.
Phishers	Individuals, or small groups, that execute phishing schemes in an attempt to steal identities or information for monetary gain. Phishers may also use spam and spyware/malware to accomplish their objectives.
Spammers	Individuals or organizations that distribute unsolicited e-mail with hidden or false information in order to sell products, conduct phishing schemes, distribute spyware/malware, or attack organizations (i.e., denial of service).
Spyware/malware authors	Individuals or organizations with malicious intent carry out attacks against users by producing and distributing spyware and malware. Several destructive computer viruses and worms have harmed files and hard drives, including the Melissa Macro Virus, the Explore.Zip worm, the CIH (Chernobyl) Virus, Nimda, Code Red, Slammer, and Blaster.
Terrorists	Terrorists seek to destroy, incapacitate, or exploit critical infrastructures in order to threaten national security, cause mass casualties, weaken the U.S. economy, and damage public morale and confidence. Terrorists may use phishing schemes or spyware/malware in order to generate funds or gather sensitive information.

are not required to report malicious logic that has been successfully quarantined by antivirus software.

- **Improper usage:** A person violates acceptable computing use policies.
- **Scans/probs/attempted access:** This category includes any activity that seeks to access or identify a federal agency computer, open ports, protocols, service, or any combination of these for later exploit. This activity does not directly result in a compromise or denial of service.
- Unconfirmed incidents that are potentially malicious or anomalous activity deemed by the reporting entity to warrant further review.

Figure 2 shows the most common cyber security incidents found in federal departments and agencies (GAO, 2008a). There were 31% of cyber incidents that were investigations of websites. The second most

Figure 1. Number of cyber incidents reporting by federal departments/agencies, FY 2005-2007 (Source: GAO, 2008a)

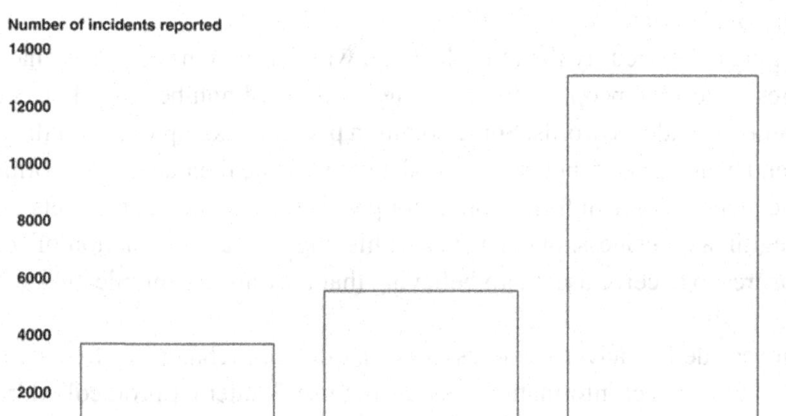

common cyber incident was improper use (26%). The third most common cyber incident was unauthorized access to federal government websites (18%).

Table 2 provides some definitions of the types of cyber attacks that typically occur. These range from the commonly known viruses and worms to lesser known exploit tools and logic bombs. There are several emerging cybersecurity threats to federal agencies as identified by the GAO (2005b). Spam, phishing, and spyware are some examples of these emerging cyber threats that are becoming more prominent. For instance, the distribution of unsolicited commercial email is commonly referred to as spam has been a problem for organizations which get inundated with email advertisements for products

Figure 2. Percentage of federal information security incidents reported to US-CERT in FY07 (Source: GAO, 2008a)

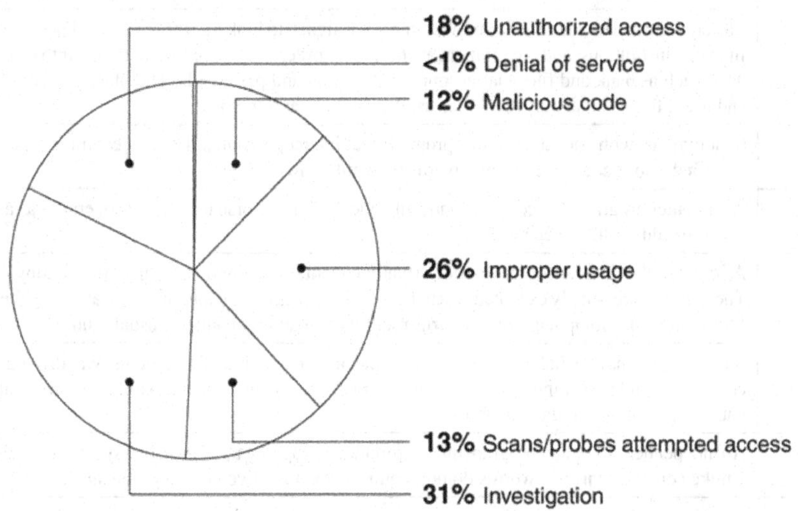

and services. The spam incidence is recent years has become significantly worse, given both the large quantity and nature of the material received by public organizations. Some estimates show that spam makes up over 60% of all email.

A second emerging cybersecurity threat is phishing, which is a high-tech scam that often uses spam or pop-up messages to deceive people into disclosing credit card numbers, bank account information, Social Security numbers, and passwords. Some common phishing examples are an illegitimate business sending an email and claiming that they need to update or validate their account information, and might threaten dire consequences if this information is not provided. The message directs users to a website that looks like a legitimate business, but is a fraud. Phishing uses a combination of social engineering and technical measures to deceive users into believing that they are communicating with an authorized organization.

Finally, spyware can deliver advertisements to users, often in exchange for free use of an application or service. Spyware can collect information such as the user's internet protocol address, web surfing history, online buying habits, email address, software and hardware specifications. Other spyware is used for surveillance and is designed specifically to steal information or monitor information access. This spyware could come in the form of key loggers to software packages that capture and transmit records into another information system.

Table 2. Types of cyber attacks (Source: GAO, 2005b)

Type of attack	Description
Denial of service	A method of attack from a single source that denies system access to legitimate users by overwhelming the target computer with messages and blocking legitimate traffic. It can prevent a system from being able to exchange data with other systems or use the Internet.
Distributed denial of service	A variant of the denial-of-service attack that uses a coordinated attack from a distributed system of computers rather than from a single source. It often makes use of worms to spread to multiple computers that can then attack the target.
Exploit tools	Publicly available and sophisticated tools that intruders of various skill levels can use to determine vulnerabilities and gain entry into targeted systems.
Logic bombs	A form of sabotage in which a programmer inserts code that causes the program to perform a destructive action when some triggering event occurs, such as terminating the programmer's employment.
Phishing	The creation and use of e-mails and Web sites—designed to look like those of well-known legitimate businesses, financial institutions, and government agencies—in order to deceive Internet users into disclosing their personal data, such as bank and financial account information and passwords. The phishers then take that information and use it for criminal purposes, such as identity theft and fraud.
Sniffer	Synonymous with packet sniffer. A program that intercepts routed data and examines each packet in search of specified information, such as passwords transmitted in clear text.
Trojan horse	A computer program that conceals harmful code. A Trojan horse usually masquerades as a useful program that a user would wish to execute.
Virus	A program that infects computer files, usually executable programs, by inserting a copy of itself into the file. These copies are usually executed when the infected file is loaded into memory, allowing the virus to infect other files. Unlike the computer worm, a virus requires human involvement (usually unwitting) to propagate.
War dialing	Simple programs that dial consecutive telephone numbers looking for modems. War driving A method of gaining entry into wireless computer networks using a laptop, antennas, and a wireless network adaptor that involves patrolling locations to gain unauthorized access.
Worm	An independent computer program that reproduces by copying itself from one system to another across a network. Unlike computer viruses, worms do not require human involvement to propagate.

As shown, it is critical to understand the information security threats which could either be internal (e.g., employees), external (e.g., hackers), or technological (e.g., technological obsolesce). It is important to do an information security audit to get a reading of the most common threats that may occur for the organizations and develop a policy in support of combating these threats. The following section examines one of the most important issues for HSIS of cyber security and cyber terrorism.

CYBERSECURITY AND CYBERTERRORISM

Cybersecurity and cyberterrorism are two important issues for HSIS. Cyberterrorism has to be treated differently than the traditional information security model which focuses on deterrents, preventives, and detectives (Foltz, 2004). There must be certainty and severity of punishment for the success of deterrents. If there is a low probability of punishment for the crime than deterrents will not be effective. Cyber terrorists, for example, are outside of the organization and the probability of them being punished is low. This implies that deterrents will essential not have an impact on the actions of cyber terrorists. As a result, governments should focus on preventives, which are used to defend against an attack, such as viruses.

There are four potential cyber threats to e-government as identified by Haugen (2005). First, hacktivism are politically motivated attacks on web pages or email to send political damaging messages. Second, terrorists are groups that use information technology to formulate plans, raise funds, and spread propaganda. Third, foreign intelligence services can use cyber tools to conduct espionage with another nation. Fourth, information warfare is foreign militaries attack critical infrastructure as a serious threat to a nation's national security.

Cavelty (2007) believes that cyber terrorism has not materialized as a true national security threat. Research has shown that vicious attacks that wreak havoc by paralyzing an entire nation seem to not be practical given the logistics needed to carry out such a widespread operation. Essentially, there are too many uncertainties concerning the scope of the threats, experts are not able to conclude whether this is actually going to happen in the first place.

The GAO (2008b) identified 13 key cybersecurity responsibilities as shown in Table 3 from federal government policy and law of the Homeland Security Act of 2002, the Homeland Security Presidential Directive -7, and the National Strategy for a Secure Cyberspace.

The GAO (2008b) indentified four key capabilities of cyber analysis and warning which are monitoring, analysis, warning, and response (Table 4). Monitoring system and communication networks includes activities to detect cyber threats, attacks, and vulnerabilities. The analysis capability involves taking the information gathered from monitoring and speculating about what the threat might be, investigating it, and identifying any impact. Warning in cyber analysis is alerting individuals and organizations about a potential or imminent attack. In cyber analysis, response is containing and recovering from cyber incidents that occur.

The GAO identifies some occurrences of cyber incidents that have caused serious damage (GAO, 2008b, pp. 8-9) to public and private sector organizations.

- In June 2003, the U.S. government issued a warning concerning a virus that specifically targeted financial institutions. Experts said the BugBear.b virus was programmed to determine whether a victim had used an e-mail address for any of the roughly 1,300 financial institutions listed in the

Table 3. DHS's key cybersecurity responsibilities (Source: GAO, 2008a)

Responsibilities	Description of responsibilities
Develop a national plan for CIP that includes cybersecurity	Developing a comprehensive national plan for securing the key resources and critical infrastructure of the United States, including information technology and telecommunications systems (including satellites) and the physical and technological assets that support such systems. This plan is to outline national strategies, activities, and milestones for protecting critical infrastructures.
Develop partnerships and coordinate with other federal agencies, state and local governments, and the private sector	Fostering and developing public/private partnerships with and among other federal agencies, state and local governments, the private sector, and others. DHS is to serve as the "focal point for the security of cyberspace."
Improve and enhance public/private information sharing involving cyber attacks, threats, and vulnerabilities	Improving and enhancing information sharing with and among other federal agencies, state and local governments, the private sector, and others through improved partnerships and collaboration, including encouraging information sharing and analysis mechanisms. DHS is to improve sharing of information on cyber attacks, threats, and vulnerabilities.
Develop and enhance national cyber analysis and warning capabilities	Providing cyber analysis and warnings, enhancing analytical capabilities, and developing a national indications and warnings architecture to identify precursors to attacks.
Provide and coordinate incident response and recovery planning efforts	Providing crisis management in response to threats to or attacks on critical information systems. This entails coordinating efforts for incident response, recovery planning, exercising cybersecurity continuity plans for federal systems, planning for recovery of Internet functions, and assisting infrastructure stakeholders with cyber-related emergency recovery plans.
Identify and assess cyber threats and vulnerabilities	Leading efforts by the public and private sector to conduct a national cyber threat assessment, to conduct or facilitate vulnerability assessments of sectors, and to identify cross-sector interdependencies.
Support efforts to reduce cyber threats and vulnerabilities	Leading and supporting efforts by the public and private sector to reduce threats and vulnerabilities. Threat reduction involves working with the law enforcement community to investigate and prosecute cyberspace threats. Vulnerability reduction involves identifying and remediating vulnerabilities in existing software and systems.
Promote and support research and development efforts to strengthen cyberspace security	Collaborating and coordinating with members of academia, industry, and government to optimize cybersecurity-related research and development efforts to reduce vulnerabilities through the adoption of more secure technologies.
Promote awareness and outreach	Establishing a comprehensive national awareness program to promote efforts to strengthen cybersecurity throughout government and the private sector, including the home user.
Foster training and certification	Improving cybersecurity-related education, training, and certification opportunities.
Enhance federal, state, and local government cybersecurity	Partnering with federal, state, and local governments in efforts to strengthen the cybersecurity of the nation's critical information infrastructure to assist in the deterrence, prevention, preemption of, and response to terrorist attacks against the United States.
Strengthen international cyberspace security	Working in conjunction with other federal agencies, international organizations, and industry in efforts to promote strengthened cybersecurity on a global basis.
Integrate cybersecurity with national security	Coordinating and integrating applicable national preparedness goals with its National Infrastructure Protection Plan.

virus's code. If a match was found, the software attempted to collect and document user input by logging keystrokes and then provide this information to a hacker, who could use it in attempts to break into the banks' networks.

- In August 2006, two Los Angeles city employees hacked into computers controlling the city's traffic lights and disrupted signal lights at four intersections, causing substantial backups and delays. The attacks were launched prior to an anticipated labor protest by the employees.
- In October 2006, a foreign hacker penetrated security at a water filtering plant in Harrisburg, Pennsylvania. The intruder planted malicious software that was capable of affecting the plant's water treatment operations.

Table 4. Attributes of cyber analysis and warning (Source: GAO, 2008b)

Capability	Attribute
Monitoring	Establish a baseline understanding of network assets and normal network traffic volume and flow
	Assess risks to network assets
	Obtain internal information on network operations via technical tools and user reports
	Obtain external information on threats, vulnerabilities, and incidents
	Detect anomalous activities
Analysis	Verify that an anomaly is an incident (threat of attack or actual attack)
	Investigate the incident to identify the type of cyber attack, estimate impact, and collect evidence
	Identify possible actions to mitigate the impact of the incident
	Integrate results into predictive analysis of broader implications or potential future attack
Warning	Develop attack and other notifications that are targeted and actionable
	Provide notifications in a timely manner
	Distribute notifications using appropriate communications methods
Response	Contain and mitigate the incident
	Recover from damages and remediate vulnerabilities
	Evaluate actions and incorporate lessons learned

- In May 2007, Estonia was the reported target of a denial-of-service cyber attack with national consequences. The coordinated attack created mass outages of its government and commercial Web sites.
- In March 2008, the Department of Defense reported that in 2007 computer networks operated by Defense, other federal agencies, and defense-related think tanks and contractors were targets of cyber warfare intrusion techniques. Although those responsible were not definitively substantiated, the attacks appeared to have originated in China.

The Federal Information Security Management Act (FISMA) of 2002 requires federal agencies to implement and enterprise-wide risk based approach to protecting federal information systems against cyber attacks (GAO, 2005a). FISMA requires federal agencies to protect and maintain the confidentiality, integrity, and availability of their information systems. FISMA requires that each federal agency develop, document, and implement agency-wide information security programs. Some of the specific provisions of FISMA are (GAO, 2005b, pp. 15-16):

- periodic assessments of the risk and magnitude of harm that could result from the unauthorized access, use, disclosure, disruption, modification, or destruction of information or information systems;
- risk-based policies and procedures that cost-effectively reduce information security risks to an acceptable level and ensure that information security is addressed throughout the life cycle of each information system;
- subordinate plans for providing adequate information security for networks, facilities, and systems or groups of information systems;

- security awareness training for agency personnel, including contractors and other users of information systems that support the operations and assets of the agency;
- periodic testing and evaluation of the effectiveness of information security policies, procedures, and practices, performed with frequency depending on risk, but no less than annually, and that includes testing of management, operational, and technical controls for every system identified in the agency's required inventory of major information systems;
- a process for planning, implementing, evaluating, and documenting remedial action to address any deficiencies in the information security policies, procedures, and practices of the agency;
- procedures for detecting, reporting, and responding to security incidents; and
- plans and procedures to ensure continuity of operations for information systems that support the operations and assets of the agency.

FISMA requires that each agency report annually to the Office of Management and Budget (OMB). FISMA, the OMB, and the Department of Homeland Security share the responsibility for the federal government's capability to detect, analyze, and respond to cyber security incidents (GAO, 2005b).

There are five major federal laws and policies that establish a need for a national cyber analysis and warning system, namely (1) the Homeland Security Act of 2002; (2) the National Strategy to Secure Cyberspace; (3) Homeland Security Presidential Directive 7; (4) the National Response Framework; and Homeland Security Presidential Directive 23 (GAO, 2008b).

As reported by GAO (2008b) the Homeland Security Act assigned the Department of Homeland Security a number of critical infrastructure protection responsibilities including gathering threat information, including cyber-related information. The DHS is also responsible for disseminating information that it analyzes to different levels of government and private sector entities to assist in the deterrence and prevention of a potential terrorist attack. The National Strategy for Cyberspace states that cyber analysis includes both tactical support during a cyber incident and strategic analyses of the threat. Tactical support includes the analysis of computer virus delivery mechanisms to help prevent damage. Strategic analysis involves indentifying long term vulnerability and threat trends that provide advanced warnings of increased attack. The Homeland Security Presidential Directive 7 directs DHS to serve as a focal point for securing cyberspace. In addition, DHS is to develop national indicators and warning architecture for infrastructure protection. The National Response Framework issued by DHS in 2008 provides guidance to coordinate cyber incident response among federal entities and other levels of government. This directive brings together officials from all agencies that have responsibility for cybersecurity. Finally, the Homeland Security Presidential Directive 23 issues in 2008 by President George W. Bush having provisions that includes protection against intrusion attempts and to better anticipate future threats. The directive requires federal agencies to implement a centralized monitoring tool and that the federal government reduce the number of connections to the Internet. As discussed the federal government is taken steps in the realm of information security. There also is progress at addressing information security at the state level as well. The following section summarizes some of the most important findings of these surveys.

INFORMATION SECURITY SURVEYS

The National Association of State Chief Information Officers (NASCIO) conducted a survey of the 50 state governments during the summer of 2006 (NASCIO, 2006). NASCIO had 41 out of 50 states that responded to their survey. The results of this study indicate that 83% of responding states have a Chief Information Security Officer (CISO) or equivalent position. The majority of the CISOs reported to the state CIO (53.8%). There were 69% of responding states indicating that they have both policy-side duties and responsibilities (planning, business strategy, enterprise architecture, policy formulation, budgeting) and the operational-side duties and responsibilities (network monitoring, perimeter defense, threat analysis, and training). The top three items/resources needed to do the job of state CISO were adequate staffing/personnel, adequate funding, and support of the state CIO (or equivalent).

The National Association of State Chief Information Officers (NASCIO) survey in 2006 found that there has been an increased need for state IT security policy and leadership in state government (NASCIO, 2006). There is a general belief that IT security should evolve strategically at the enterprise level in state government. Since the majority of CISOs report to the CIO, this shows that this position has been elevated to provide an enterprise-wide view of IT security. As a result, CIOs at this level of state government need to establish important relationships with key stakeholders such as homeland security and emergency management. With this elevation of the CISO position in state government, there are more policy-related duties of developing enterprise policies to help protect the state in IT security. The survey results showed that 70.7% of state CISOs had authority to enforce compliance of enterprise IT policies. There were 60% of states that had a defined budget to support CISOs duties, indicating that they are viewed as being important players in the state government. The survey also showed that CISOs had both depth and breadth of authority over IT security in their state government. CISOs normally had the authority over the executive branch of government (60%) and 35% of them have authority over the entire state government. With respect to their skills, state CISOs had a balance of technical, policy, and business skills that they bring to their job. This is very important since they have to be able to communicate effectively with key stakeholders. State CISOs priorities are having adequate staffing, adequate funding, and support from key stakeholders such as the governor, the CIO, state agencies, and other leaders. There are a number of surveys conducted on the impact of information security in public and private sector organizations.

Another interesting study of information security was a survey of nearly 500 state and local *Government Technology* magazine subscribers who responded to a reader poll in late 2007 (Towns, 2008). Respondents ranked information security as their top priority in 2007, placing it above other issues such as homeland security, work force retention and IT consolidation. Most of the organizations that the poll respondents worked for have a formal security policy (80%). Survey results indicated a fair amount of complacency among respondents towards information security problems. Security awareness is up, but security funding and training is generally not increased. Finally more than 75% of respondents rate the cyber-security preparedness of their organizations as good or fair.

NASCIO also conducted a cyber security survey in August 2005 (NASCIO, 2005). The CIO or CISO was invited to respond for each state. The survey had 27 responses, representing 57% of state governments. The results of this survey showed that there were only 18 states that reported on cyber-incidents from CISOs. Eight state CISOs reported between one and five information security incidents per week. Five state CISOs reported between 20 and 100 incidents per week. Three state CISOs reported between 200 and 500 incidents per week. Only one CISO reported 3,000 incidents per week. It would be hard to get an accurate read of incidents since there may be a hesitancy on the part of agencies to report their occurrence, essentially exposing the vulnerabilities of their organization.

In terms of risk assessment, awareness, and continuity plans, a large number of state CISO (73%) reported that they have conducted a risk assessment for information systems that are homeland security assets (NASCIO, 2005). There were 81% of state CISOs that reported developing an IT business continuity plan to help maintain and to deliver essential services within their jurisdictions in the event of a major cyber attack or disaster.

In a survey by Ernst & Young (2007) of all industries, both public and private, of their information security reported that there were three drivers that impacted information security practices in organizations. They are compliance with regulations (64%), privacy and data protection (58%), and meeting business objectives (45%). The issue of privacy and data protection is also borne out in the e-government literature which argues that addressing this issue is critical for its future advancement (Belanger and Hiller, 2006).

The top three security breaches indentified in a survey conducted by Deloitte (2007) were viruses and worms, e-mail attacks, e.g., spam, and phishing/pharming were prevalent. All of these breaches are penetrated through the customer, for example, this person receives an email requesting information from a clone of the businesses. The following section provides evidence for the occurrence of information security in a survey of Texas state agencies. Texas state agencies were chosen as a case study of information security and survey evidence is presented in the following section.

TEXAS STATE AGENCY INFORATION SECURITY SURVEY

A survey of Texas state agency Information Resource Managers (IRM) was conducted during the months of June and July 2008. This survey asked a series of questions on the impact that information security had on Texas state agencies. In order to see how representative the sample is we have provided in Table 5 demographic information on the IRMs that have responded to the survey. With regards to the size of the Texas state agencies there were 32.0% of them that had 500 or more FTE employees. State agencies that had fewer than 50 FTE employees was represented by 28% of respondents. There was essentially a higher proportion of small and large-sized agencies in the survey sample.

The typical age range of Texas state IRMs was over 45 years of age, which is not surprising given this type of executive level position. Most Texas state agency IRMs were male with 62.5% being of this gender. There was no predominate years of service that these IRMs worked for the Texas state government. There were, however, 20.7% of them working 26 or more years for their state government. Similarly to federal CIOs, the majority of IRMs held that position for less than 5 years (60%). The highest level of academic attainment was a four year college degree, with 54.2% of them holding this level of educational attainment. This was followed by having a master's degree, with 29.2% of IRMs having this academic credential.

The results in Table 5 essentially show that IRMs that have responded to this survey were more likely to come from small to large state agencies, were middle-aged men, have less than five years of experience as being an IRM, and have a least a bachelors degree.

Table 5. Information on IRMs in Texas state agencies

Full-time equivalent (FTE) employees	Frequency	Percent
10 or less	1	4.0
11 to 49	6	24.0
50 to 99	1	4.0
99 or 249	4	16.0
250 to 499	5	20.0
500 or more	8	32.0
Age range of the IRMs		
25 to 34	2	8.0
35 to 44	5	20.0
45 to 54	10	40.0
55 to 64	6	24.0
Over 65	2	8.0
Gender of IRMs		
Female	9	37.5
Male	15	62.5
Years IRM worked for Texas state government		
Less than 5 Years	3	12.0
5 to 10 years	4	16.0
11 to 15 years	4	16.0
16 to 20 years	4	16.0
21 to 25 years	4	16.0
26 years or more	6	20.7
Years IRM held this title and position in the state agency		
Less than 2 years	3	12.0
2 to 5 years	12	48.0
6 to 10 years	7	28.0
11 to 15 years	2	8.0
16 to 20 years	0	0.0
21 years or more	1	4.0
Highest level of academic attainment of the IRM		
2 year college degree	2	8.3
4 year college degree	13	54.2
Master's degree	7	29.2
Law degree	2	8.3

Table 6. Causes of information security incidents

In my state agency, information security incidents are usually caused by...	*Strongly Agree %*	*Agree %*	*Neutral %*	*Disagree %*	*Strongly Disagree %*	*Median*
Employee end user error	3.8	53.8	19.2	11.5	11.5	2.0
Lack of knowledge by employees of the state government's (or agency's) acceptable use policy	3.8	30.8	19.2	38.5	7.7	3.0
The inability of firewalls, intrusion detection software, and antivirus software to stop unauthorized access	3.8	11.5	26.9	38.5	19.2	4.0
The lack of organizational culture that values the importance of information security	0.0	26.9	11.5	50.0	11.5	4.0
The lack of access controls in place such as password protections	0.0	15.4	15.4	46.2	23.1	4.0
The lack of employee training on information security policy	0.0	30.8	26.9	26.9	15.4	3.0
Hackers trying to enter agency information systems	3.8	34.6	42.3	15.4	3.8	3.0
Suppliers or vendors	0.0	7.7	26.9	50.0	15.4	4.0
Computer crime	0.0	19.2	30.8	30.8	19.2	3.5
Notes: strongly agree=1, agree =2, neutral=3, disagree=4, strongly disagree=5						

CAUSES OF INFORMATION SECURITY INCIDENTS

Table 6 provides a listing of the most likely causes of information security incidents for Texas state agencies. The greatest agreement was for employee end user error with 57.6% of state agencies believing this was a cause of information security incidents. There was disagreement that firewalls, intrusion detection software, and antivirus software had the inability to stop unauthorized access. There was also disagreement that there was the lack of organizational culture that values the importance of information security. The lack of access controls in place that have caused information security incidents such as password protection, there was disagreement to this statement as well. Issues regarding suppliers and vendors there was disagreement that this created information security incidents. Generally, the results in Table 6 showed that employee end user error caused the greatest number of information security incidents. There was disagreement that virus protection software and lack of organizational culture had an impact on information security incidents.

There was some information that supported the notion that lack of knowledge by employees of the state government's acceptable use policy had caused incidents, 34.6% of IRMs agreed to this statement. Also, 30.8% of IRMs believed that lack of training on information security policy had caused some of the incidents. Both areas could be easily remedied through employee training on the state government's information security policy.

Table 7. Information security and the internal and external environment

In my state agency...	Strongly Agree %	Agree %	Neutral %	Disagree %	Strongly Disagree %	Median
Top management supports information security policy and awareness	34.6	53.8	3.8	7.7	0.0	2.0
There is an emphasis on information security	26.9	53.8	7.7	11.5	0.0	2.0
There is a constant evaluation of information security effectiveness	20.0	52.0	12.0	16.0	0.0	2.0
There is a strict enforcement of written state government (or agency) information security policy	11.5	50.0	26.9	11.5	0.0	2.0
Information security policy focuses on deterrents through threat of sanctions	11.5	11.5	50.0	23.1	3.8	3.0
Information security policy focuses on prevention through controls (e.g., access controls, security software controls)	26.9	73.1	0.0	0.0	0.0	2.0
There is a high level of information security risk compared to other state agencies	3.8	19.2	23.1	42.3	11.5	4.0
Notes: strongly agree=1, agree =2, neutral=3, disagree=4, strongly disagree=5						

INFORMATION SECURITY AND THE INTERNAL AND EXTERNAL ENVIRONMENT

Table 7 presents information on the internal and external environment that Texas state agencies face with respect to information security. There is strong agreement from IRMs that top management supports information security policy and awareness with 88.4% agreeing to this statement. There also was strong support and agreement that there was an emphasis on information security in state agencies (80.7%). There is also agreement that there is a constant evaluation of information security effectiveness with 72% of IRMs believing this was the case. Texas state agencies believe that there is strict enforcement of written state government or agency information policy (61.5%). There was also agreement that information security policy focuses on prevention through controls such as access controls, security software controls, and so forth, with all IRMs agreeing to this statement. What was most interesting from the questions on Table 5 is that 53.8% of IRMs disagree that there is a high level of information security risk in their state agency compared to other agencies. Essentially, many of the state agencies in Texas believe that they are not at a great risk in information security. They are of the opinion that the infrastructure and support is there, but there is not a high level of risk that an incident will actually occur in their state agency.

INFORMATION SECURITY SUPPORT, RESOURCES, AND PREPAREDNESS

Table 8 provides information on the support for, resources, and level of preparedness as a result of information security. There was strong agreement that top management has a willingness to invest in information security (65.4%). There was also agreement that there is a high level of information security preparedness, with 57.7% of IRMs agreeing to this statement. There was 46.1% of IRMs agreeing that there was adequate training for employees on information security policy.

Table 8. Information security support, resources, and preparedness

In my state agency, there is...	*Strongly Agree %*	*Agree %*	*Neutral %*	*Disagree %*	*Strongly Disagree %*	*Median*
Adequate staffing for information security development	7.7	23.1	19.2	46.2	3.8	3.5
Top management's willingness to invest in information security	23.1	42.3	23.1	11.5	0.0	2.0
Adequate budget resources devoted towards information security	7.7	26.9	23.1	38.5	3.8	3.0
Information security taking precedence over other state IT budget priorities	0.0	23.1	34.6	34.6	7.7	3.0
Adequate training for employees on information security policy	3.8	42.3	38.5	15.4	0.0	3.0
A high level of information security preparedness	7.7	50.0	23.1	19.2	0.0	2.0
Notes: strongly agree=1, agree =2, neutral=3, disagree=4, strongly disagree=5						

There was disagreement that state agencies had adequate staffing for information security development (50%). In addition, 42.3% of IRMs disagreed that they had adequate budget resources devoted towards information security. There were 42.3% of state agencies that responded who disagreed that information security was taking precedence over other state IT budget priorities.

THREATS TO INFORMATION SECURITY

Table 9 provides a listing of the most common threats to information security as noted by Texas state agency IRMs. The top threat was technical hardware failures or errors such as equipment failures with 76.9% of respondents saying this had occurred. Tied for second at 73.1% were deliberate software attacks such as viruses, worms, macros, and denial of service attacks and technical software failures or errors from bugs, code problems, and unknown loopholes. The third most common threats to information security were acts of human error or failure such as employee accidents and mistakes at 65.4%. There were 42.3% of agencies reporting that technological obsolesce was a threat to information security.

A threat that occurred only in two state agencies were deliberate acts of sabotage or vandalism. There were only a few agencies reporting that there were deliberate acts of espionage or trespass occurred in their state agency (19.2%).

EFFECTIVENESS OF THREAT PROTECTION MECHANISMS

Table 10 provides an evaluation of common threat protection mechanisms for information security. Texas state agency IRMs were asked to indicate whether they agreed that commonly used threat protection mechanism were effective for their organizations. The median statistics indicated that media backup, virus protection software, and firewall protection were the most effective tools. There was less agreement that employee education, security policy, information security audits, reporting of information security violations, and auto account logoff were effective threat protection mechanisms. The results

Table 9. Threats to information security

In my state agency, there have been the following threats to information security	*Percent*	*Frequency*
Acts of human error or failure (accidents, employee mistakes)	65.4	17
Deliberate acts of espionage or trespass (unauthorized access and/or data collection)	19.2	5
Deliberate acts of sabotage or vandalism (destruction of systems or information)	7.7	2
Deliberate acts of theft (illegal confiscation of equipment or information)	34.6	9
Deliberate software attacks (viruses, worms, macros, denial of service)	73.1	19
Forces of nature (fire, flood, earthquake, lightning)	23.1	6
Technical hardware failures or errors (equipment failures)	76.9	20
Technical software failures or errors (bugs, code problems, unknown loopholes)	73.1	19
Technological obsolesce (antiquated and outdated machines)	42.3	11

Notes: N=26

Table 10. Effectiveness of threat protection mechanisms for information security

In my state agency, the following threat protection mechanisms for information security are very effective:	*Strongly Agree %*	*Agree %*	*Neutral %*	*Disagree %*	*Strongly Disagree %*	*Median*
Use of passwords	50.0	34.6	11.5	3.8	0.0	1.5
Media backup	57.7	26.9	11.5	3.8	0.0	1.0
Employee education	26.9	34.6	30.8	7.7	0.0	2.0
Security policy	26.9	57.7	11.5	3.8	0.0	2.0
Virus protection software	53.8	46.2	0.0	0.0	0.0	1.0
Information security audits	28.0	48.0	12.0	8.0	4.0	2.0
Reporting of information security violations	26.9	42.3	23.1	7.7	0.0	2.0
Firewall protection	57.7	38.5	3.8	0.0	0.0	1.0
Auto account logoff	24.0	28.0	36.0	12.0	0.0	2.0
Notes: strongly agree=1, agree =2, neutral=3, disagree=4, strongly disagree=5						

essentially show that more active technologies work better than employee education and awareness of a security policy.

CONCLUSION

This chapter has examined the impact of information security with a focus on Texas state governments as a case study. Information security is the most often cited issue that governments face in HSIS. In this chapter, we first outlined seven factors that have an influence on information security which are: management and information security, organizational culture, information security threats, information security policy, education, deterrence and prevention, and users. The overriding issue for the successful adoption of information security is having the organizational culture that supports its implementation.

If the organization does not have top management support for information security, it will not be as effective for the organization. There also was an analysis of the most common information security threats that governments face.

The survey results of Texas state agency IRMs and their views on information security are very telling. The greatest agreement among IRMs was that employee end user error caused the most information security incidents. There was agreement that top management supported information security policy and awareness in Texas state agencies. There was less of the threat of sanctions to enforce information security policy and more of the use of preventions in state agencies. There is a belief by IRMs that top management is willing to invest in information security. There also is a belief that there is a high level of information security preparedness in state agencies. Equipment failures was the most common threat to information security in state agencies, this was followed by deliberate software attacks and technical software failures. The best threat protection mechanisms, according to IRMs, were media backup, virus protection software, and firewall protection.

The chapter showed that organizational culture matters in information security. Access to websites is critical for government transparency, but this opens governments up to information security risks. Deterrence and prevention are important elements in the information security framework. There is regulation going on in this area, but given that information security has become a more prevalent problem regulations are slow to catch up to the latest trends. Human error is one of the most common causes of information security issues; therefore, employee training is essential. Management should be proactive with information security, and identify threats before they become major issues for the public organization.

REFERENCES

Belanger, F., & Hiller, J. S. (2006). A Framework for E-government Privacy Implications. *Business Process Management Journal, 12*(1), 48–60. doi:10.1108/14637150610643751

Cavelty, M. D. (2007). Cyber-Terror - Looming Threat or Phantom Menace? The Framing of the US Cyber-Threat Debate. *Journal of Information Technology & Politics, 4*(1), 19–36. doi:10.1300/J516v04n01_03

Chan, M., Woon, I., & Kankanhalli, A. (2005). Perceptions of Information Security in the Workplace: Linking Information Security Climate to Compliant Behavior. *Journal of Information Privacy & Security, 1*(3), 18–41.

Chang, S. E., & Ho, C. B. (2006). Organizational Factors to the Effectiveness of Implementing Information Security Management. *Industrial Management & Data Systems, 106*(3), 345–361. doi:10.1108/02635570610653498

Chang, S. E., & Lin, C.-S. (2007). Exploring Organizational Culture for Information Security Management. *Industrial Management & Data Systems, 107*(3), 438–458. doi:10.1108/02635570710734316

D'Arcy, J., & Hovav, A. (2007). Deterring Internal Information Systems Misuse. *Communications of the ACM, 50*(10), 113–117. doi:10.1145/1290958.1290971

Deloitte. (2007). *2007 Global Security Survey: The Shifting Security Paradigm*. Retrieved August 10, 2008, from http://www.deloitte.com/dtt/cda/doc/content/rs_Deloitte_Global_Security_Survey_2007.pdf

Ernst & Young. (2007). *10th Annual Global Information Security Survey: Achieving a Balance of Risk and Performance*. Retrieved August 10, 2008, from http://www.ey.com/global/Content.nsf/International/Assurance_&_Advisory_-_Technology_and_Security_Risk_-_Global_Information_Security_Survey_2007

Foltz, C. B. (2004). Cyberterrorism, computer crime, and reality. *Information Management & Computer Security*, *12*(2), 154–166. doi:10.1108/09685220410530799

GAO. (2005a). *Critical Infrastructure Protection: Department of Homeland Security Faces Challenges in Fulfilling Cybersecurity Responsibilities*. (GAO Publication No. GAO-05-434). Washington, DC: U.S. Government Printing Office.

GAO. (2005b). *Information Security: Emerging Cybersecurity Issues Threaten Federal Information Systems*. (GAO Publication No. GAO-05-231). Washington, DC: U.S. Government Printing Office.

GAO. (2008a). *Information Security: Although Progress Reported, Federal Agencies Need to Resolve Significant Deficiencies*. (GAO Publication No. GAO-08-496T). Washington, DC: U.S. Government Printing Office.

GAO. (2008b). *Cyber Analysis and Warning: DHS Faces Challenges in Establishing a Comprehensive National Capability*. (GAO Publication No. GAO-08-588). Washington, DC: U.S. Government Printing Office.

Haugen, S. (2005). E-government, Cyber-Crime and Cyber-Terrorism: A Population at Risk. *Electronic Government*, *2*(4), 403–412. doi:10.1504/EG.2005.008331

Hong, K.-S., Chi, Y.-P., Chao, L. R., & Tang, J.-H. (2006). An Empirical Study of Information Security Policy on Information Security Evaluation in Taiwan. *Information Management & Computer Security*, *14*(2), 104–115. doi:10.1108/09685220610655861

Kankanhalli, A., Teo, H.-H., Tan, B. C. Y., & Wei, K.-K. (2003). An Integrative Study of Information Systems Security Effectiveness. *International Journal of Information Management*, *23*(2), 139–154. doi:10.1016/S0268-4012(02)00105-6

Knapp, K. J., Marshall, T. E., Rainer, K., & Ford, F. N. (2006). Information Security: Management's Effect on Culture and Policy. *Information Management & Computer Security*, *14*(1), 24–36. doi:10.1108/09685220610648355

NASCIO. (2005). *Findings from NASCIO's Strategic Cyber Security Survey*. Retrieved August 10, 2008, from http://www.nascio.org/publications/documents/NASCIO-CyberSec_Survey_Findings.pdf

NASCIO. (2006). *A Current View of the State CISO: A National Survey Assessment*. Retrieved August 10, 2008, from http://www.nascio.org/publications/documents/NASCIO-CISOsurveyReport.pdf

Rainey, H. G., & Steinbauer, P. (1999). Galloping Elephants: Developing Elements of a Theory of Effective Government Organizations. *Journal of Public Administration: Research and Theory*, *9*(1), 1–32.

Straub, D. W., & Welke, R. J. (1998). Coping with Systems Risk: Security Planning Models for Management Decision Making. *MIS Quarterly*, *22*(4), 441–469. doi:10.2307/249551

Towns, S. (2008). IT Security Survey Shows Government's Progress on Safeguarding Data. *Government Technology*. Retrieved August 10, 2008, from http://www.govtech.com/gt/277653

Whitman, M. E. (2004). In Defense of the Realm: Understanding the threats to Information Security. *International Journal of Information Management*, *24*(1), 43–57. doi:10.1016/j.ijinfomgt.2003.12.003

Chapter 9
Emergency Management Websites

INTRODUCTION

This chapter examines the provision of emergency management information on government websites. E-government websites can be an effective tool for communicating with residents of a community on preparedness measures that they can take, and provides information for those that have been impacted by disasters. This chapter demonstrates that there is much variability in the content provided on emergency management websites. This chapter focuses on the role of websites in emergency management through a content analysis of their websites.

There chapter will first provide a rationale for studying e-government through emergency management websites. It will then examine the commonly found e-government growth models indentified in the literature. The factors that influence the adoption of government websites are also examined in this chapter. The most commonly found studies of the content provided on websites are benchmarking reports, which are discussed. Accessibility and transparency are two important issues in the advancement of e-government websites, and are also mentioned in this chapter. The main thrust of this chapter is a content analysis of state government emergency management websites. The conclusion to this chapter summarizes the main research findings of the chapter.

DOI: 10.4018/978-1-60566-834-5.ch009

WEBSITES AND EMERGENCY MANAGEMENT

The Paperwork Reduction Act of 1995 allows federal agencies to maintain and provide government information through the Internet. This Act has produced a large amount of government information that has been placed online to be made publically available. This was not considered to be a great concern until the terrorist attacks of September 11, 2001 (Chau, Fang, and Sheng, 2007). After 9/11, federal government agencies have been more concerned about what information was placed online. After 9/11 there was a lot of sensitive information that was removed from websites including information on the vulnerabilities related to plants, maps of power plans or water systems, emergency response plans, and so forth. For example, the Department of Energy removed detailed maps and descriptions of nuclear facilities after the terrorist attacks of 9/11 (Schelin, 2007). The belief was that if a terrorist had access to such infrastructure information, this could potentially facilitate a terrorist attack. Essentially, after 9/11 governments have been more careful about what information they place online, this has had an impact on the adoption of e-government.

Websites can also be an effective tool to communicate with residents of a community about hazard risks and preparedness (Basolo, Steinberg, and Gant, 2006). However, research results show that disasters of the 2005 Hurricane season that greatly impacted the Gulf Coast had little effect on the content of municipal websites. Even knowing government websites could be a valuable resource for citizens to access information and get services related to homeland security preparedness, they have essentially been underutilized (Basolo, Steinberg, and Gant, 2006). As mentioned in the following section, there are several stages of e-government adoption that are relevant when examining websites.

E-GOVERNMENT GROWTH MODELS

Moon (2002) modifies an e-government growth model presented by Hiller and Bélanger (2001) and applies their framework to an analysis of e-government using International City/County Management Association (ICMA) survey data. Moon's stages of growth are, (1) simple information dissemination or one way communication, (2) two-way communication through request and response, (3) service and financial transactions, (4) integration through the organization both vertically and across different agencies, and (5) political participation. Moon found evidence that most local governments are in stage one and some are in the early parts of stage two of e-government development. More recent research has reexamined the ICMA dataset and their subsequent surveys and found similar evidence to Moon, that local e-government is mainly informational with few transactions taking place (Coursey and Norris, 2008). While political participation is virtually nonexistence on e-government websites (Norris, 2007).

Premkumar, Ho, and Chakraborty (2006) make the argument that information systems development in the public and private sector evolves into three discernable stages. These authors provide perhaps the most simplified, but all encompassing e-government growth model. At stage one, the content phase is where the website is used as a one-way communication device to provide information to citizens and customers. In stage two, citizens or customers can make online requests for specific information and conduct e-transactions with the government or private sector entity. The third stage is the virtual community phase in which the web site helps build a virtual community by providing a platform for citizens and customers to conduct business or to make collective decisions online. These authors found that in comparison to the private sector, most cities lag on e-commerce transactions and virtual community building because of political, economic, and organizational barriers. Governments are much more interested in delivering content and less focused on commerce, which is different from the private sector. The stages presented by Premkumar, Ho, and Chakraborty (2006) are similar to Moon (2002) and Hiller and Bélanger's (2001) research, but are more relevant to what one might witness in organizations in general.

One of the greatest criticisms of the e-government growth models are that they are linear interpretations that proceed in a progressive and stepwise fashion (Coursey and Norris, 2008). These models are normative of what ought to take place. These models advocate for technology driving change in organizations, rather than the organization adopting technology as a critical component of change. These models assume that achieving higher levels of adoption is better and improves citizen interaction and service delivery. Coursey and Norris go even further and criticize the growth models as being purely speculative; being not actually models based on reality, but best guesses about how e-government might evolve.

According to Andersen and Henriksen (2006) the frequently cited Layne and Lee (2001) model of e-government adoption reinforces the technology bias advocated by government, business, and much of information systems research. This technology bias is seen though the idea that e-government will promote information quality, efficiency, and effectiveness in organizations. The technology bias of existing e-government literature has led to a focus on failing to understand the power of organizations and social institutions and its impact on the adoption of e-government. There are numerous studies which try to discern what stage governments are in the adoption of websites.

LEVELS OF ADOPTION OF E-GOVERNMENT WEBSITES

In one of the first content analyses of municipal web pages Musso, Weare, and Hale (2000) showed that Web pages were superficial, at the time, with regard to the substance and did not exploit the Internet to any great extent. The websites according to these authors do not support information and communication required for reform of government. These websites were designed to facilitate routine interactions between service providers and recipients. In fact, the authors found that most of the websites just mimicked existing communications systems such as telephone books or brochures. In addition, websites tended to support the concept of "good management" rather than "good democracy". Municipal websites were not designed to improve communication with city officials (Stowers, 1999). This early finding of e-government supporting management rather than democracy is also found in other more recent studies (Norris, 2007).

In an analysis of 33 websites of some of the most populous European Union (EU) cities showed that almost all of city governments were shifting from the traditional bureaucratic model to an e-government model (Torres, Pina, and Acerete, 2005). The traditional bureaucratic model has the website that tends to be administratively oriented, where information is organized primarily according to the administrative structure of the government and does not reflect a rethinking of the bureaucratic process. In the e-government model, there are two approaches which are the information-oriented and the user oriented. The authors of this study make the case that most EU cities have moved from the traditional bureaucratic model to the e-government model with differing levels of development. There are similar findings examining cities in the United States, demonstrating a movement from a traditional bureaucratic models to an e-government model (Ho, 2002)

There is evidence in an analysis of e-government Websites in EU cities that e-government is no more than a government billboard (Torres, Pina, and Royo, 2005). E-government initiatives are predominately non-interactive. E-government is not likely to reshape e-governance because e-democracy initiatives are not front and center of the EU agenda. Overall, there seems to be evidence that e-government has changed governments, but the change is more incremental than transformative (West, 2004). Most governments are now posting information online, with less interactive services are taking place.

FACTORS OF E-GOVERNMENT WEBSITE ADOPTION

There are several important factors that can facilitate the adoption of e-government websites. In discussing the future of e-government, West (2005) in an analysis of thousands of government websites believes that greater progress needs to be made in creating websites that have uniform, integrated, and standardized navigation features. First, most government websites have a disjointed quality that impedes communication and citizen usage. Second, there needs to be greater cooperation on the part of government agencies, such as having a one-stop portal where cross agency offerings are integrated. Portal sites that integrate information regardless of agency are convenient for citizens and help them avoid the problem of not knowing where to find particular services or information. Third, agencies need to publicize their existence, since many citizens do not know about the existence of online information and services that they can take advantage of. Fourth, governments need to appoint a high-level administrator in charge of electronic governance. For instance, most state governments have a Chief Information Officer (CIO) which provides greater leadership in the development and implementation of e-government efforts. Finally, the literature emphasizes transformative change as a result of e-government, but this may not be possible since incremental change has been identified in the literature (West, 2004). On a brighter note, e-government has been consistently rated in public opinion surveys as providing a very positive experience for citizens, and this bodes well for more transformative change in the near future.

In a content analysis of city government websites and a national survey of city officials in Korea the findings of a study by Lim and Tang (2007) indicated that IT leadership was key in e-government development. These authors also found that website development was driven by the capability of the city to support its website. For instance, the better the quality of its official website, the more city government obtains useful information for decision making to enhance decision quality. Their analysis underscores the critical role of IT leadership for the success of e-government adoption.

Through an examination of state government websites and the public policy analysis McNeal, Tolbert, Mossberger, and Dotterweich (2003) showed that the professionalism of the legislature was an important factor determining whether states innovated in e-government. States that have more professional governments were more likely to be leaders in offering state residents government services online. Another factor that explained the diffusion of policy innovation and e-government was states that had Republican-controlled legislatures. Republicans may be more susceptible to believe in small government and e-government could be a method to reduce the level of bureaucracy and cut the budget. A trend in the analysis of websites, are benchmarking studies, which will be discussed next.

BENCHMARKING E-GOVERNMENT WEBSITES

According to Melitski and Holzer (2007) content on a government Website is critical for the development of e-government. If its content is not current, if there is a difficulty navigating, or the information provided is not correct and updated then it is not fulfilling its purpose. In addition, a government Website can contain out dated information which is problematic especially in emergency management since the website can be used to alert the public to a terrorist incident or severe weather so they can make informed choices in case of an emergency.

Bertot and Jaeger (2006) describe three methods of evaluating e-government websites. First, the functionality of the website assesses whether the website actually works in the manner that was intended and provides the results that it was meant to deliver for the user. Second, usability assesses how users react to and interact with the website. Does the website allow the user to believe the website was helpful and to accomplish their task? Finally, accessibility assesses how the website allows users with disabilities to have equal use of information and services. There should be functionality testing to see whether website actually lives up to these three standards.

One of the most common areas of e-government research have been studies that benchmark best practices in the adoption of e-government through an analysis of websites. Kaylor, Deshazo, and Van Eck (2001) were one of the first scholars to benchmark e-government adoption. These authors tried to discern what set of e-government features constituted leading edge cities. Their goal was to determine the status quo of municipal e-government so that the city could structure a strategic plan with a clear understanding of both what is technologically feasible and what is commonly found. Many other authors have followed in this tradition of developing e-scores of the features that governments have on their websites to see which governments are most digitally enabled (Holzer and Kim, 2008; West, 2008).

In one of the most comprehensive analyses of municipal e-government worldwide, Holzer and Kim (2008) used almost 100 measures with five distinct categories of e-government websites. The five components they examined on local government websites were (1) privacy/security, (2) Usability, (3) Content, (4), Services, and (5) Citizen Participation. Out of the highest possible score for digital governance the results showed that the average score throughout the world in 2007 was 33.4, which is a modest increase from 2005 of 33.1. The average score for municipalities in Organization for Economic Cooperation and Development (OECD) countries was 45.0 and non OECD countries it was 27.5. The results show that there is a digital divide between developed and developing countries with respect to digital governance.

A content analysis of Websites has two advantages with regards to doing research on e-government (Baker, 2008). The first reason is that it provides a structured method of quantifying the content of websites for analysis. A content analysis is an easily replicable since the scorer typically uses a rubric to assess the website according to this very structured method. The second reason is that a content analysis of websites is very unobtrusive. The researcher is able to study attributes of websites in anonymity. The scorer examines the government website in a similar fashion as the actual user of the website.

There are some criticisms of the e-government benchmarking studies as noted by Sharma (2004). First, the most striking criticism is these studies only measure the "supply" of e-government. These benchmarking studies mainly count the number of services offered online by government to citizens. Therefore, they do not account for the "demand" or the actual use of e-government by citizens. Second, these studies do not analyze the quality of service and the amount of citizen engagement in using e-government. Essentially, there is no measure of citizen satisfaction with e-government websites. Finally, the benchmarking studies do not measure the back-end office integration to offer services to citizens. According to e-government research, there should be a change in business processes of government, and these benchmarking studies cannot account for this important internal organizational change.

TRANSPARENCY AND ACCESSIBILITY AND E-GOVERNMENT WEBSITES

There are two important issues that need to be addressed in the provision of government websites. The first is promoting transparency of government through websites which ultimately leads to increased accountability to citizens. The second concern is that of the accessibility to websites for those individuals who have disabilities, or do not have access because of the digital divide.

Government transparency is defined as the ability to find out what is going on inside public sector organizations through open meetings, access to records, posting of information on websites, and so forth (Piotrowski and Van Ryzin, 2007). The release of information promotes accountability and trust with government. However, as previously noted governments are more hesitant since September 11, 2001 to release information online. Websites are a tool for governments to better communicate with their residents while increasing transparency and openness. As will be shown in this chapter, many of the state government emergency management websites are not very transparent in providing usable content for citizens. There also is a lot of variability in quality and quantity of emergency management websites.

In an examination of the 50 state government legislatures websites in 2002 Fagan and Fagan (2004) found that although some state have made efforts to provide equal access to its citizens, there are numerous examples of inaccessible websites. As the amount of information placed online continues to grow, adopting accessibility guidelines will become more crucial.

FEMA DISASTER DECLARATIONS

In order to provide the context for our examination of state government websites, the following section examines what states are more prone to natural disasters. As shown in Table 1, FEMA (2009) collects data on declared disaster declarations by both total number per year and by state declared disasters. This will provide information on what states face in disasters. The average number of declared disasters per year was 32 over the 1953 to 2009 period. The year that had the most declared disasters was 2008 with a total of 75. One can notice that there have been more disasters declared since the mid to late 1990s. The state that has declared the most disasters was Texas, this was followed by California, and in third it was Florida. The following section presents the results of a content analysis of state government emergency management websites to provide a baseline of what content is currently available on these websites.

EMERGENCY MANAGEMENT WEBSITE CONTENT ANALYSIS

During August 2008 there was a content analysis done by this author of state government departments or divisions emergency management websites. The listing of emergency management websites was found on the FEMA website (www.fema.gov), which keeps an accurate listing of all state government departments/divisions of emergency management. There was an analysis of all 50 state governments and the features of their websites. The six areas examined were access to employees, citizen participation, and information on types of disasters, information for special needs populations, links to other agencies and nonprofits, and public relations. There were two graduate research assistants that did the scoring for all 50 states. Both scorers' results were compared to ensure accuracy.

Table 1. FEMA declared disasters by year and state (Source: FEMA, 2009)

Year		State		
Year	Number of Disaster Declarations	Ranking	State	Number of disaster declared
2009	5	1	Texas	83
2008	75	2	California	74
2007	63	3	Florida	61
2006	52	4	Oklahoma	59
2005	48	5	New York	56
2004	68	6	Louisiana	55
2003	56	7	Kentucky	48
2002	49	8	Alabama	48
2001	45	9	Missouri	47
2000	45	10	Illinois	46
1999	50	11	Arkansas	46
1998	65	12	Mississippi	45
1997	44	13	Ohio	44
1996	75	14	Pennsylvania	42
1995	32	15	West Virginia	41
1994	36	16	Washington	41
1993	32	17	Minnesota	41
1992	45	18	Virginia	39
1991	43	19	Tennessee	39
1990	38	20	Nebraska	39
1989	31	21	Kansas	39
1988	11	22	Iowa	39
1987	23	23	North Dakota	36
1986	28	24	North Carolina	36
1985	27	25	Indiana	36
1984	34	26	Maine	34
1983	21	27	Georgia	33
1982	24	28	Wisconsin	32
1981	15	29	Alaska	32
1980	23	30	South Dakota	30
1979	42	31	Vermont	28
1978	25	32	Oregon	25
1977	22	33	Michigan	25
1976	30	34	New Jersey	24
1975	38	35	Hawaii	24
1974	46	36	Federated States of Micronesia	24
1973	46	37	New Hampshire	23

continued on following page

Table 1. continued

Year		State		
1972	48	38	Massachusetts	22
1971	17	39	Puerto Rico	21
1970	17	40	New Mexico	21
1969	29	41	Idaho	21
1968	19	42	Arizona	20
1967	11	43	Montana	18
1966	11	44	Maryland	18
1965	25	45	Nevada	17
1964	25	46	Colorado	16
1963	20	47	South Carolina	15
1962	22	48	US Virgin Islands	14
1961	12	49	Northern Mariana Islands	14
1960	12	50	Connecticut	13
1959	7	51	Guam	12
1958	7	52	Delaware	12
1957	16	53	American Samoa	10
1956	16	54	Wyoming	7
1955	18	55	Utah	7
1954	17	56	Rhode Island	7
1953	13	57	Marshall Islands	7
		58	District of Columbia	7
		59	Palau	1
Total Disaster Declarations	1814			
Average Number of Disasters	32			

The framework for analyzing state government emergency management websites was taken from Liu (2008). This study was the first to provide a benchmark of what was offered on state government emergency management websites in March 2005. Liu analyzed these websites, similarly to what has been done in this chapter. The factors that Liu examined were democratic outreach, information content, special needs, and intergovernmental relations. These categories are similar to what is examined in this chapter. Emergency management websites are important to analyze since they are easily accessible to most of the public, and could provide valuable information for citizens to use when preparing for an emergency.

Table 2 provides information on the features that emergency management Websites use to promote direct access by individuals that visit their sites. The most common feature found was a general phone number to the emergency management department (96%). This was followed by having a departmental address on the website, which is normally located at the bottom of the homepage (94%). However, when it came to more specific contact information for state government emergency management employees there was much less of this type of information placed online. For instance, having a specific phone number to staff in the emergency management department was found in 62% of states. Specific email addresses to staff members were also not as common, found in only 56% of state websites. A general email to contact someone in the agency was also found on 56% of state emergency management websites. While providing directions to the department was very rare with only 26% of states proving this type of information on their websites. The results show that less than two thirds of states, through a specific phone number, provide direct access to their employees in emergency management departments. What was particularly striking was three states that did not even provide their department address on their website.

Table 3 provides information on the features that emergency management websites use to provide opportunities for citizen participation. There were many opportunities on websites to volunteer (80%). A number of states have a link to Citizen Corps (www.citizencorps.gov), which helps to coordinate volunteer activities for preparation in the event of an emergency. There were 50% of states that have a comment function on their website. In addition, only 24% of websites have an email updates function to notify interested individuals of important information updates. There were only a few states that had a survey feature on their website to encourage citizen participation (22%). Essentially, the content analysis of emergency management websites showed very limited features that promote citizen engagement. There were very few options for citizens to express their opinion.

Table 4 provides information on the types of disaster information on state government emergency management websites. Several common disasters were found on these websites. Information on flooding was found on 84% of state emergency management websites. Information found on these websites ranged from the causes of flooding and what to do if it occurs in a community. Terrorism was the second most commonly found information on emergency management websites (76%). This was followed by hazardous/radiological materials and winter weather information, both at 66% and 68% respectively, of state government websites. Information on earthquakes was found in 60% of state emergency management websites and for fires it was 54% of websites. There were only 40% of websites that had information on

Table 2. Emergency management websites having direct access to employees

Website Feature	*Percent of States*
General Phone Number	96
Address	94
Specific Phone Number	62
Specific Email	56
General Email	56
Directions to Office	26

Table 3. Emergency management websites having citizen participation

Website Feature	*Percent of States*
Citizen volunteer opportunities	80
Comment function	50
Email updates	24
Survey	22

Table 4. Emergency management websites having information by disaster type

Website Feature	*Percent of States*
Floods	84
Terrorism	76
Winter weather	68
Hazardous/ radiological material	66
Lightning/thunder storms	66
Fires	64
Earthquakes	60
Tornados	58
Excess heat	50
Diseases	46
Other Disaster Information	44
Technological failures	42
Droughts	42
Hurricanes	40

Table 5. Emergency management websites having information for special needs population

Website Feature	*Percent of States*
Info for families	72
Website accessibility policy	66
Info for children	60
Info for people with disabilities	54
Info for the pet owners	52
Foreign language access	26
TTY/TTD phone access	22
Info for the elderly	16

hurricanes. Also, there were several state specific responses in the category of other disaster information (44%), ranging from tsunami to volcanoes and dam failures. Essentially, the results vary by state since some states would be more susceptible to natural disasters than others; therefore, they would most likely devote less information to certain disasters. For example, hurricanes are more common on the east coast and earthquakes are more common on the west coast of the United States.

Table 5 provides information on emergency management websites and their use of features that aid individuals with special needs. Information for families was found on 72% of state emergency management websites. This was followed by information for children on 60% of websites and information for pet owners on 52% of websites. Information to help individuals with disabilities in case of a natural disaster was found on 54% of websites. Foreign language access on a state emergency management websites was almost nonexistent (26%). While features such as website policies were found on 66% of the websites, TTY/TTD (Enables those who are deaf and hard of hearing to use a special text device with

Table 6. Emergency management websites having links to other agencies/nonprofits

Website Feature	*Percent of States*
Links to FEMA	96
Link to state agencies	86
Link to federal agencies	82
Links to local government	82
Links to National Weather Channel	80
Links to Department of Homeland Security	64
Link to Non- profits	62
www.ready.gov/disasterhelp.gov	54
Link for Center for Disease Control	24

digital service) phone access information was found on only 22% of sites. Information for the elderly, in case of a natural disaster, was not very common found in only 16% of websites. The results in Table 4 indicated that only 54% of emergency management websites provided information for people with disabilities to prepare for a natural disaster or a terrorist attack. This is somewhat surprising since this would be a good source of information for families to prepare for natural disasters.

Table 6 provides information on emergency management websites which have links to other levels of governments and nonprofit organizations. Having a link to FEMA was most common with 96% of websites having this link. A link to state agencies was found on a large number of emergency management websites (86%). Links to federal and local governments were found on 82% of websites. In addition, links to nonprofits organization such as the Red Cross were found in 62% of emergency management websites. There were 80% of websites that had a link to the National Weather Service and 64% of emergency management websites had links to the Department of Homeland Security. Links to the Center for Disease Control was not very common with only 24% of the websites having this link. In addition, links to www.DisasterHelp.gov / www.ready.gov were found in 54% of emergency management websites. What was somewhat surprising is that there were fewer links to nonprofit organizations, such as the Red Cross, where citizens could potentially volunteer or donate money.

Table 7 provides information of what kind of public relations media was found on state emergency management websites. Most (88%) of the websites had access to the emergency plans. To keep the media and public informed, press releases were found in the majority of websites (86%). There were 82% of websites having reports generated by the emergency management department. While links to the color-coded federal government homeland security advisory system were found only in 60% of emergency management websites. Some less commonly found public relations information on these websites were media links to a public information officer (44%). Online newsletters were only found in 42% of these emergency management departments. More high level features such as a photo archive (26%) and video archive (10%) were found in very few departments. Essentially, the websites of the state emergency management departments had very limited public relations options. There was not much information found on these websites that would engage the public such as a photo or video archive, brochures, and fact sheets.

Table 8 sums up all of the responses to the six outlined areas of information on state emergency

Table 7. Emergency management websites used for public relations

Website Feature	*Percent of States*
Emergency Plans	88
Press releases	86
Reports	82
Homeland Security Advisory Level	60
Media Links	44
Newsletters	42
Calendar of Events	36
Library	34
Fact sheets	28
Brochures	26
Photo Archive	26
Video Archive	10

management websites. This provides a rough measure of the ranking of the 50 state governments and their emergency management websites. There were a total of 53 features examined on state emergency management websites. In Table 8 there are also links to the website corresponding to its ranking.

The top five websites and their scores were Virginia (49), Maine (41), Florida (40), New Jersey (40), and Louisiana (40). Two of these states, Florida and Louisiana, have experienced notable natural disasters recently through hurricanes. Surprisingly, New York was not in the top five (it ranked eighth), even though it was the site of the terrorist attacks September 11, 2001 and the blackout of 2003 that crippled the city. At the bottom of the list were Mississippi (12), Nevada (15), and Ohio (16). What was

Table 8. State ranking of emergency management website features

Ranking	*Score (out of 53)*	*Name of State*	*Link to Emergency Management Website*
1	**49**	**Virginia**	http://www.vdem.state.va.us/
2	**41**	**Maine**	http://www.maine.gov/mema/mema_ema.shtml
3	**40**	**Florida**	http://www.floridadisaster.org/
4	**40**	**New Jersey**	http://www.state.nj.us/njoem/index.html
5	**40**	**Louisiana**	http://www.ohsep.louisiana.gov/
6	39	Maryland	http://www.mema.state.md.us/MEMA/index.jsp
7	37	Georgia	http://www.gema.state.ga.us/
8	36	New York	http://www.semo.state.ny.us/
9	36	Montana	http://dma.mt.gov/des/
10	36	Washington	http://www.emd.wa.gov/
11	35	Kansas	http://www.accesskansas.org/kdem/
12	35	Wisconsin	http://emergencymanagement.wi.gov/
13	34	New Mexico	http://www.nmdhsem.org/

continued on following page

Table 8. continued

Ranking	*Score (out of 53)*	*Name of State*	*Link to Emergency Management Website*
14	34	Connecticut	http://www.ct.gov/demhs/site/default.asp
15	34	Indiana	http://www.in.gov/dhs/
16	32	Texas	http://www.txdps.state.tx.us/dem/pages/index.htm
17	32	Arizona	http://www.dem.azdema.gov/
18	32	Missouri	http://sema.dps.mo.gov/semapage.htm
19	31	California	http://www.oes.ca.gov/
20	31	Colorado	http://dola.colorado.gov/dem/index.html
21	31	New Hampshire	http://www.nh.gov/safety/divisions/bem/
22	31	North Carolina	http://www.nccrimecontrol.org/index2.cfm?a=000003,000010
23	30	South Dakota	http://oem.sd.gov/Default.asp
24	30	Massachusetts	www.state.ma.us/mema
25	29	Alabama	ema.alabama.gov/
26	29	South Carolina	http://www.scemd.org/
27	29	Arkansas	http://www.adem.arkansas.gov/
28	28	Hawaii	http://www.scd.hawaii.gov/
29	27	Nebraska	http://www.nema.ne.gov/
30	27	Delaware	http://dema.delaware.gov/
31	27	Minnesota	http://www.hsem.state.mn.us/
32	26	West Virginia	http://www.wvdhsem.gov/
33	26	Alaska	http://www.ak-prepared.com/
34	26	Wyoming	http://wyohomelandsecurity.state.wy.us/main.aspx
35	25	Rhode Island	http://www.riema.ri.gov/
36	25	Pennsylvania	http://www.pema.state.pa.us/
37	25	North Dakota	http://www.nd.gov/des/
38	25	Utah	http://www.des.utah.gov/homelandsecurity/index.html
39	25	Vermont	http://www.dps.state.vt.us/vem/
40	24	Michigan	http://www.michigan.gov/msp/0,1607,7-123-1593_3507---,00.html
41	23	Illinois	http://www.state.il.us/iema/
42	23	Iowa	http://www.iowahomelandsecurity.org/
43	23	Tennessee	http://www.tnema.org/
44	23	Kentucky	http://kyem.ky.gov/
45	22	Idaho	http://www.bhs.idaho.gov/
46	19	Oregon	http://www.oregon.gov/OMD/OEM/
47	19	Oklahoma	http://www.ok.gov/OEM/
48	16	Ohio	http://ema.ohio.gov/ema.asp
49	15	Nevada	http://dem.state.nv.us/
50	12	Mississippi	http://www.msema.org/

surprising was Mississippi's ranking, since this state was greatly impacted from Hurricane Katrina, one would expect to have a more sophisticated website as a result.

When comparing West's (2008) overall state e-government rankings to the top five ranked emergency management websites indentified in this chapter some interesting results surfaced. West's rankings showed that for our top five Virginia ranked 27, Maine ranked 6, Florida ranked 3, New Jersey ranked 22, and Louisiana ranked 42. West's results showed that there was not a direct impact if a state was e-government enabled overall and having a well developed emergency management website. The finding in this chapter is not surprising, West found that states had websites that were completely inconsistent from one agency to the next and there seemed to be an independent entity from each other although in the same government. The following section summarizes the key findings of this chapter.

CONCLUSION

Websites are an effective tool to communicate with residents of a community about hazard risks and preparedness. There are several growth models of e-government adoption that attempt to explain the evolution of websites. The common stages are providing content, transactional services, and community building. The major criticisms of these models are that they are linear and proceed in a progressive stepwise fashion and do not allow for deviations on website progression. Another criticism is that they have a technology bias, advocating adopting technology as a way of advancing e-government, but do not examine alternative methods of service delivery. The existing literature shows that e-government is proceeding incremental, with most of the government websites providing information and less transaction based services. The literature shows that leadership is one important factor that facilitates development of e-government websites.

There are many benchmarking studies of e-government adoption; however, these studies are criticized because they only measure the "supply" of e-government and do not indicate the level of demand and satisfaction with e-government websites. Transparency and accessibility has challenged the content placed on e-government websites, where certain disadvantaged groups do not have the same level of access and there is less security sensitive information being placed on websites since 9/11.

In a content analysis of the 50 state government public utility commission websites the results found by Bernt, Wood, and Ting (2007) mimic what was found in this analysis of state emergency management websites. State governments are not taking advantage of the opportunity of providing citizens with information online. Similarly to these authors this study found that there was a tremendous variability among the states on the level and quality of content placed on emergency management websites.

The content analysis of 50 state government emergency management websites revealed that general access to emergency management departments is very common, with most of the websites providing an address and general phone number. However, more specific information for a citizen to get in direct contact with a state official was not very common. There is information on volunteer opportunities available on these emergency management websites. However, when it comes to more specific information of citizen participation it was very rare, for instance, for a state website to have an online survey. Information on floods and terrorism were the most commonly found on websites. Surprisingly, the least commonly found information was on hurricanes. With respect to special needs populations there appears to be ample information for families, however, there was very little information on websites for the elderly and foreign language conversion. It is very common to find links to other levels of government and nonprofit agencies; this is an area where websites excel. With regards to public relations on emergency management websites many sites have press releases and reports, but few sites had photo and video archives. Finally, Louisiana and Florida were very e-government enabled in emergency management and have experienced notable natural disasters. However, there were other states such as Maine and Virginia that rated really high, but have not experienced as many notable natural disasters.

REFERENCES

Andersen, K. V., & Henriksen, H. Z. (2006). E-government Maturity Models: Extension of the Layne and Lee Model. *Government Information Quarterly, 23*(2), 236–248. doi:10.1016/j.giq.2005.11.008

Baker, D. L. (2008). Advancing E-government Performance in the United States through enhanced Usability Benchmarks. *Government Information Quarterly*. Retrieved October 1, 2008 from http://www.sciencedirect.com/science/journal/0740624X

Basolo, V., Steinberg, L., & Gant, S. (2006). E-Government and the Preparation of Citizens for Disasters. *Proceedings of the 2006 International Conference on Digital government Research*. Retrieved October 1, 2008 from http://portal.acm.org/

Bernt, P., Wood, L., & Ting, C. (2007). The Telecommunications Content of State Public Utility Commission Web Sites: Remaining Relevant in a Changing Marketplace. *Government Information Quarterly, 24*(3), 539–553. doi:10.1016/j.giq.2006.10.003

Bertot, J. C., & Jaeger, P. T. (2006). User-Centered E-government: Challenges and Benefits for Government Web sites. *Government Information Quarterly, 23*(2), 163–168. doi:10.1016/j.giq.2006.02.001

Chau, M., Fang, X., & Sheng, O. R. (2007). What are People Searching on Government Web Sites? A Study of Search Activity at the Utah.gov Web Site. *Communications of the ACM, 50*(4), 87–92. doi:10.1145/1232743.1232753

Coursey, D., & Norris, D. F. (2008). Models of E-government: Are they Correct? An Empirical Assessment. *Public Administration Review, 68*(3), 523–536. doi:10.1111/j.1540-6210.2008.00888.x

Fagan, J. C., & Fagan, B. (2004). An Accessibility Study of State Legislative Web Sites. *Government Information Quarterly, 21*(1), 65–85. doi:10.1016/j.giq.2003.12.010

FEMA. (2009). *Declared Disasters by Year or State*. Retrieved January 26, 2009, from http://www.fema.gov/news/disaster_totals_annual.fema.

Hiller, J. S., & Belanger, F. (2001). *Privacy Strategies for Electronic Government*. Retrieved October 1, 2008 from http://www.businessofgovernment.com

Holzer, M., & Kim, S.-T. (2008). *Digital Governance in Municipalities Worldwide (2007): A Longitudinal Assessment of Municipal Websites throughout the World*. Retrieved October 1, 2008 from http://andromeda.rutgers.edu/~egovinst/Website/PDFs/100%20City%20Survey%202007%20(Full%20Report).pdf

Kaylor, C., Deshazo, R., & Eck, D. (2001). Gauging E-government: A Report on Implementing Services among American Cities. *Government Information Quarterly*, *18*(4), 293–307. doi:10.1016/S0740-624X(01)00089-2

Layne, K., & Lee, J. (2001). Developing Fully Functional E-government: A Four Stage model. *Government Information Quarterly*, *18*(2), 122–136. doi:10.1016/S0740-624X(01)00066-1

Lim, J. H., & Tang, S.-Y. (2007). Urban E-Government Initiatives and Environmental Decision Performance in Korea. *Journal of Public Administration: Research and Theory*, *18*(1), 109–138. doi:10.1093/jopart/mum005

Liu, B. F. (2008). Online Disaster Preparation: Evaluation of State Emergency Management Web Sites. *Natural Hazards Review*, *9*(1), 43–48. doi:10.1061/(ASCE)1527-6988(2008)9:1(43)

McNeal, R. S., Tolbert, C. J., Mossberger, K., & Dotterweich, L. J. (2003). Innovating in Digital Government in the American States. *Social Science Quarterly*, *84*(1), 52–70. doi:10.1111/1540-6237.00140

Melitski, J., & Holzer, M. (2007). Assessing Digital Government at the Local Level Worldwide: An Analysis of Municipal Web Sites throughout the World. In D.F. Norris (Ed.), *Current Issues and Trends in E-government Research*. Hershey, PA: Cybertech Publishing.

Moon, M. J. (2002). The Evolution of E-government Among Municipalities: Rhetoric or Reality? *Public Administration Review*, *62*(4), 424–433. doi:10.1111/0033-3352.00196

Musso, J., Weare, C., & Hale, M. (2000). Designing Web Technologies for Local Governance Reform: Good Management or Good Democracy? *Political Communication*, *17*(1), 1–19. doi:10.1080/105846000198486

Norris, D. F. (2007). Electronic Democracy at the American Grassroots. In D.F. Norris (Ed.), *Current Issues and Trends in E-government Research*. Hershey, PA: Cybertech Publishing.

Piotrowski, S. J., & Van Ryzin, G. (2007). Citizen Attitudes Toward Transparency in Local Government. *American Review of Public Administration*, *37*(3), 306–323. doi:10.1177/0275074006296777

Premkumar, G., Ho, A. T., & Chakraborty, P. (2006). E-government Evolution: An Evaluation of Local Online Services. *International Journal of Electronic Business*, *4*(2), 177–190.

Schelin, S. H. (2007). E-Government: An Overview. In G.D. Garson (Ed.), *Modern Public Information Technology Systems: Issues and Challenges*. Hershey, PA: IGI Global.

Sharma, S. K. (2004). Assessing E-Government Implementations. *Electronic Government . International Journal (Toronto, Ont.)*, *1*(2), 198–212.

Stowers, G. (1999). Becoming Cyberactive: State and Local Governments on the World Wide Web. *Government Information Quarterly*, *16*(2), 111–127. doi:10.1016/S0740-624X(99)80003-3

Torres, L., Pina, V., & Acerete, B. (2005). E-government Developments on Delivering Public Services among EU Cities. *Government Information Quarterly*, *22*(2), 217–238. doi:10.1016/j.giq.2005.02.004

Torres, L., Pina, V., & Royo, S. (2005). E-government and the Transformation of Public Administrations in EU Countries: Beyond NPM or just a Second Wave of Reforms? *Online Information Review*, *29*(5), 531–553. doi:10.1108/14684520510628918

West, D. M. (2004). E-government and the Transformation of Service Delivery and Citizen Attitudes. *Public Administration Review*, *64*(1), 15–27. doi:10.1111/j.1540-6210.2004.00343.x

West, D. M. (2005). *Digital Government: Technology and Public Sector Performance*. Princeton, NJ: Princeton University Press.

West, D. M. (2008). *State and Federal Electronic Government in the United States, 2008*. Retrieved October 1, 2008 from http://www.brookings.edu/reports/2008/0826_egovernment_west.aspx

Chapter 10
Conclusion

INTRODUCTION

This book examined Homeland Security Information Systems (HSIS) and how this technology has influenced IT at all levels of government. The first part of the book provided background information on homeland security preparedness, e-government, and collaboration. The second part examined the impact of HSIS on federal, state, and local governments in the United States. The final part of this book examined some emerging issues in HSIS of citizens and their interaction with homeland security, information security, and online emergency management information. This chapter summarizes the key findings of the book and provides future research recommendations.

The results in this book show that there is a need for homeland security preparedness and planning at all levels of government and HSIS are one critical component of planning efforts. The results demonstrate that top management support is critical for effective planning in order to ensure that these managers are fully on board with HSIS. Scarce resources at all levels of governments means that there is a priority setting process taking place, when choosing which HSIS should be incorporated. Citizen involvement is a key component to HSIS since citizens are normally the first on the disaster scene and their use of technology can help response efforts.

DOI: 10.4018/978-1-60566-834-5.ch010

THE ENVIRONMENTAL CONTEXT OF HOMELAND SECURITY

This book first outlined the environmental context of HSIS; examining both homeland security and e-government research. The purpose of Part I was to show the issues associated with homeland security preparedness, to provide an analysis of e-government to set the context of implementing HSIS, and collaboration and e-government was discussed.

Chapter 1 provides background information by providing research on homeland security preparedness to set the context of the book. There was a discussion of the government response to emergencies being normally influenced by operational, administration and sociological aspects (Carroll, 2001). Therefore, in order to understand HSIS one must take into account these important institutional dimensions. Analyzing institutions is the method that we have chosen to understand HSIS in government.

One of the critical dimensions of the HSIS is the sharing of information between federal, state, and local governments. All levels of government do not believe the current sharing of information is effective because they are not receiving information they believe is essential for homeland security preparedness. In addition, the information they receive is not very useful, timely, or accurate (GAO, 2003).

In Chapter 1 presented the adaptive management theory, where decision makers change their strategies and continuously learn for organizational survival (Wise, 2006). This entails collaboration with the various stakeholders that are impacted from a crisis. There was a high level of collaboration in homeland security supporting the adaptive management model, but there was much less measurement of results of accomplishing homeland security goals of local governments.

Survey evidence on homeland security in local governments indicated that the top three terrorist concerns were individual/suicide bomb, car or truck bomb, and biohazard/biological. HAZMAT or hazardous material suits were the most frequently purchased homeland security item and communications equipment was the second most commonly purchased item. The most common way of paying for homeland security was through the existing budget of the local government. There were almost one third of city managers who believed that the homeland security advisory system was ineffective tool for them when making homeland security decisions. The greatest management concern for city managers was lack of money available to pay for homeland security. Over a third of city managers believed that their community has a low probability of being a future terrorist target, but these officials believed that their city is well prepared for a terrorist attack.

Chapter 2 examined electronic government or e-government literature, and focuses on the impact of e-government on citizens by creating a more citizen-centric government. This study was based on melding the homeland security and e-government literatures, e-government is essential to know in order to understand HSIS. Creating a more citizen centric government is addressed in President's George W. Bush's President's Management Agenda, which has e-government as one of the pillars of the Agenda (EOP, 2002).

There are six e-government factors that were anticipated to create more citizen-centric government through e-government, namely management capacity, security and privacy, top management support, e-government project management, managerial innovation, and resource capacity. These factors were found to be important in a survey of state government Chief Information Officers (CIOs) on e-government and their organizations.

The majority of federal agency CIOs believed that e-government has created a more citizen-centric federal government. There is a strong belief that the performance of federal agencies has improved because of e-government. CIOs are of the opinion that privacy and security are critical components for e-government advancement. Almost all CIOs believe that having a champion of e-government is one of the most critical success factors. E-government has allowed for a greater degree of information sharing among departments. The majority of CIOs believed that they did not have an adequate budget for e-government initiatives and e-government projects had increased citizen and business interaction with government. There are numerous examples of e-government impacting emergency management. The Internet, for instance, enables disaster victims to reconnect with their families and friends after the disaster takes place.

In Chapter 3 there was a discussion about collaboration and e-government, which can be defined as the mutually beneficial relationship entered into by two or more organizations using digital means to achieve common goals. In order to understand HSIS, one must have a grasp of the major issues faced in collaboration and homeland security which is a major challenge often cited in the literature (Reddick, 2007). New Public Management (NPM) literature argues for government to be responsive to citizens and treating them as clients, which has been criticized as breeding passivism among citizens. While collaborative management literature believes that citizens are important stakeholders that should be included in the decision-making process of government (Vigoda-Gadot, 2004).

In a survey of state government CIOs and e-government and collaboration, the major findings show that the greatest collaboration was with the state government in e-government projects and the least collaboration was with citizens and business community. There was a high level of collaboration occurring in e-government, with communication, trust, and standards have been enhanced as a result. However, there has been less performance metrics taking place to evaluate collaborative efforts. Overall, collaboration in e-government is taking place, but the evaluation of these efforts is not frequently occurring.

PREVALENCE OF HSIS IN GOVERNMENTS

In Part II there was an examination of how HSIS has impacted federal, state, and local governments in the United States. In Chapter 4 there was a discussion of the impact of HSIS on federal government departments and agencies. The *National Strategy for Homeland Security* issued by President George W. Bush in 2002 advocated that information technology would be a critical component of the *National Strategy* (Office of Homeland Security, 2002). There is a movement since September 11, 2001 to emphasize information security rather than the right to know information about government, as seen through the removal of information on federal websites that might aid terrorists (Halchin, 2002; Schelin, 2007).

There are four important pieces of federal legislation namely the Computer Security Act, the Paperwork Reduction Act, the Clinger-Cohen Act, and the E-government Act that set the tone for federal information resource management and HSIS. For instance, IT security/cyber security is the top challenge for federal government CIOs, and all of these pieces of federal legislation address security of information resources.

In a survey of federal government CIOs, it appears that nine out of 13 roles indentified in federal legislation have been impacted from HSIS, representing 70% of the responsibilities of CIOs. Therefore, HSIS has impacted the roles and responsibilities of federal government CIOs to a great extent. Some areas where there was a low impact for HSIS influencing the roles of CIO was IT workforce development, IT governance, information sharing, achieving results, and acquisition and project management. The majority of federal CIOs believed that they were well prepared with their existing HSIS.

In Chapter 5 there was information provided on the impact of HSIS on emergency management functions. In emergency management, the recent response to the December 2005 Tsunami and Hurricane Katrina showed that information systems needed improvement, since they were inadequate and overwhelmed to respond to the magnitude of these events (Jefferson, 2006). The Internet expands the opportunities for public involvement in an emergency, especially for those geographically removed from the situation.

There are four phases of emergency management which are mitigation, preparedness, response, and recovery (Waugh, 1994). Through a survey of state directors of emergency management, there was general agreement that IT has impacted all phases of emergency management, but the greatest impact was on the response phase. IT has addressed inter-organizational collaboration and coordination among responding groups. The Internet and Geographic Information Systems (GIS) had the greatest impact on emergency planning as being the most effective technologies. More complex technology such as hazard analysis and modeling technologies were viewed as being less effective. The major barriers to the adoption of IT in emergency management were security and privacy, collaboration, and financial.

Chapter 6 examined how HSIS fits into the homeland security priorities of local governments. This chapter examined local governments since research indicates that they are more innovative than other governments in their management culture (Moon, 2002). As a result, they should be more likely to adapt change such as HSIS. Research shows that local governments are very primitive in e-government in that they normally only place information online and not much in the area of transactional services (Norris and Moon, 2005). Commonly used HSIS in local governments were Ham/shortwave radio, interoperable communication equipment, and Cameo/Aloha/MARPLOT software (Clarke, 2006).

There were only around a third of local governments in a survey of Southern United States' that have developed homeland security response plans on the basis of the color-coded homeland security advisory system. Even knowing information security is a top priority for government in HSIS, it was close to the bottom of the list of grant funding received for homeland security activities. Cyber security was almost dead last with regards to grant funding for local governments. Overall, it appears that HSIS are a relative low priority for grant funding since more traditional areas such as purchasing equipment and disaster preparation measures were at the top of the list.

Besides not receiving much in terms of grant funding, local governments are still taking information security and cyber security very seriously and are putting money towards these initiatives from their own source funds. Examining information shared from state and federal sources, the federal government generally scored lower than state governments on the quality of homeland security information provided. There is a great need for training on HSIS such as cyber security, and there is a preference for online training in homeland security preparedness.

CITIZENS, INFORMATION SECURITY, AND ONLINE INFORMATION

The final part of this book examined some emerging issues associated with HSIS, namely citizens and the use of terrorist information, information security, and information on emergency management websites. Chapter 7 examined the important issue of citizens, the internet and terrorism information. There is a digital divide in internet access with persons of color, senior citizens, poor, and less educated have the least internet access. There are some limitations of the internet, with individuals having difficulty finding the right information, low ownership and availability of personal computers for segments of the population, and low access to the Internet from various segments of the population (Singh and Sahu, 2007). There are alternatives to internet-based strategies that can bridge the digital divide such as mobile government, interactive voice response systems, public information kiosks, and government call centers. Any policy that addresses citizens' access to homeland security information should provide for these alternative channels to help bridge the digital divide.

Trust in government is strongly associated with e-government satisfaction (Welch, Hinnant, and Moon, 2004). Citizens use government websites as a new form of citizen-initiated contacts, compared to the traditional forms of public meetings and telephoning government (Thomas and Streib, 2003). The number one choice for citizens to get information on a problem is through the internet, and they have much success when they go online to solve a problem. The majority of citizens believe the color coded homeland security advisory system provided useful information, which is in direct contrast to governments, which generally do not find much value in the advisory system.

Public opinion data shows that citizens do not believe that they are likely to be a victim of a terrorist attack and there is not much demand for online terrorism information, compared with other communication mediums. Government websites do not provide much value for citizens to access information on a terrorist attack; in fact websites were the last place citizens would turn for information in the event of an attack. There is, however, evidence that when a disaster occurs citizens will flock to the Internet to get information.

Information security is a critical component of HSIS and was examined in chapter 8. Top management support is a significant predictor of an organization's information security culture. Research shows that the organizational culture should be supportive of information security for its successful adoption (Chang and Lin, 2007). There should not just be an emphasis on the technical aspects of information security, but its impact on employees should also be addressed since the majority of information security incidents are caused by employees (Chan, Woon, and Kankanhalli, 2005). This was evidence found in survey of Texas state agencies that end users caused the greatest number of information security incidents.

Survey evidence of Texas state agencies indicates that having an information security policy and educating employees on this policy is critical for the successful adoption of an information security policy. Management should set a clear policy direction on information security and should be committed towards it successful adoption throughout the organization. There was some evidence that lack of knowledge by employees of Texas state government's acceptable use policy caused many security incidents. There was also very strong evidence by Information Resource Managers (IRM) that top management supports information security policy and awareness. Texas state IRMs believed that they were not at great risk for an information security breach, and they believed that the infrastructure and support is there to handle a major incident.

Survey evidence from Texas state agencies indicates that the top information security threats were technical hardware failures or errors such as equipment failures and tied for second was deliberate software attacks such as viruses and worms. The top threat protection mechanisms were media backup, virus protection software, and firewall protection were viewed as being the most effective tools. The survey results show that more active technologies work better than employee education and awareness of information security, which is contrary to existing literature which argues that the former is more effective.

In Chapter 9 there was a discussion of the information placed on emergency management websites. After 9/11 the federal government became more concerned about what information was placed online (Schelin, 2007). Websites can be an effective tool to communicate with residents of a community about hazard risks and preparedness. One of the major criticisms of the e-government growth models, of which the website content analyses are based, is the linear progression of its e-government development that reinforces a technology bias in organizations (Coursey and Norris, 2008).

One of the greatest challenges is that progress needs to be made on creating websites that are uniform, integrated, and have standardized navigation features (West, 2005). One of the most common areas of e-government research has been benchmarking studies on the adoption of websites. The problem with their analysis they do not examine the "demand" or actual use of e-government by citizens, nor citizen satisfaction with websites (Sharma, 2004).

In a content analysis of the 50 state government emergency management websites, there were less than two thirds of state government emergency management departments that provided direct access to employees through direct email and specific phone numbers. There were very few options for citizens to express their opinion through an online survey or comment function. Flooding was the most commonly found online disaster information and terrorism was the second most commonly found information on state emergency management websites.

There was just over half of emergency management websites that provided information for people with disabilities and only 16% of websites provided information for the elderly, both especially vulnerable populations in the event of a disaster. There were not many links to nonprofit organizations such as the Red Cross on emergency management websites, where citizens could volunteer or donate money. The websites of departments of emergency management are very limited with regards to their public relations options such as providing photo or video archives, brochures, and fact sheets.

The findings of the content analysis of state emergency management websites are not surprising since other research found that there was much variability from one agency to another and across different governments (West, 2008). State governments are not taking full advantage of this opportunity to provide citizens with a rich array of online information for emergency management preparedness.

FUTURE RESEARCH RECOMMENDATIONS

There are several recommendations that can be gleaned from this analysis of HSIS on where future research could head. First, there is a need to examine more aspects of homeland security preparedness in relation to the technologies that governments currently use and its effectiveness. There needs to be more research that examines the effectiveness of this technology given that we are approaching a decade since the terrorist attacks of 9/11. There needs to be a more critical assessment of whether the technology that is currently being used will meet the needs of the next terrorist attack or the next major natural disaster. The literature on e-government is just now approaching the stage of providing a more critical assessment of the effectiveness of e-government, and this should provide an avenue for further investigations into HSIS.

Second, more research is needed that focuses on the role of citizens in emergency management and homeland security. This book was only able to provide a chapter discussing this important subject, but obviously much more could be done here since citizens are the key drivers of successful e-government implementation. There needs to be more public opinion surveys asking citizens what technologies they would use in the event of an emergency or a terrorist incident. There needs to be more research on how citizens can collaborate more with their government in the event of an emergency and the technology that could help to facilitate this collaboration.

Finally, there should be more work conducted on providing an inventory of homeland security and emergency management technologies that currently or potentially could be used. This book did not provide an extensive treatment of the technologies used since the purpose was to provide a baseline of knowledge of some issues associated with HSIS. This inventory could be further used to evaluate the effectiveness of HSIS for all levels of government, a definite need for future research.

REFERENCES

Carroll, J. (2001). Emergency Management on a Grand Scale: A Bureaucrat's Analysis. In A. Farazmand, (Ed.) *Handbook of Crisis and Emergency Management*. New York: Marcel Dekker, Inc.

Chan, M., Woon, I., & Kankanhalli, A. (2005). Perceptions of Information Security in the Workplace: Linking Information Security Climate to Compliant Behavior. *Journal of Information Privacy & Security, 1*(3), 18–41.

Chang, S. E., & Lin, C.-S. (2007). Exploring Organizational Culture for Information Security Management. *Industrial Management & Data Systems, 107*(3), 438–458. doi:10.1108/02635570710734316

Clarke, W. (2006). *Emergency Management in County Government: A National Survey*. Retrieved August 10, 2008, from http://www.naco.org/Template.cfm?Section=Library&template=/ContentManagement/ContentDisplay.cfm&ContentID=21623

Coursey, D., & Norris, D. F. (2008). Models of E-government: Are they Correct? An Empirical Assessment. *Public Administration Review, 68*(3), 523–536. doi:10.1111/j.1540-6210.2008.00888.x

EOP. (2002). *Implementing the President's Management Agenda for E-Government: E-Government Strategy*. Retrieved July 30, 2005, from http://www.whitehouse.gov/omb.

Halchin, L. E. (2004). Electronic Government: Government Capability and Terrorist Resource. *Government Information Quarterly, 21*(4), 406–419. doi:10.1016/j.giq.2004.08.002

Jefferson, T. L. (2006). Evaluating the Role of Information Technology in Crisis and Emergency Management. *Journal of Information and Knowledge Management Systems, 36*(3), 261–264.

Moon, M. J. (2002). The Evolution of E-Government among Municipalities: Rhetoric or Reality? *Public Administration Review, 62*(4), 424–433. doi:10.1111/0033-3352.00196

Norris, D. F., & Moon, M. J. (2005). Advancing E-Government at the Grassroots: Tortoise or Hare? *Public Administration Review, 65*(1), 64–75. doi:10.1111/j.1540-6210.2005.00431.x

Office of Homeland Security. (2002). *National Strategy for Homeland Security*. Retrieved August 1, 2008, http://www.whitehouse.gov/homeland/book/

Reddick, C. G. (2007). Homeland Security Preparedness and Planning in US City Governments: A Survey of City Managers. *Journal of Contingencies and Crisis Management, 15*(3), 158–167. doi:10.1111/j.1468-5973.2007.00518.x

Schelin, S. H. (2007). E-Government: An Overview. In G.D. Garson (Ed.), *Modern Public Information Technology Systems: Issues and Challenges*. Hershey, PA: IGI Global.

Sharma, S. K. (2004). Assessing E-Government Implementations. *Electronic Government . International Journal (Toronto, Ont.)*, *1*(2), 198–212.

Singh, A., & Sahu, R. (2008). Integrating Internet, Telephones, and Call Centers for Delivering Better Quality E-governance to all Citizens. *Government Information Quarterly*, *25*(3), 477–490. doi:10.1016/j.giq.2007.01.001

Thomas, J. C., & Streib, G. (2003). The New Face of Government: Citizen-Initiated Contacts in the Era of E-government. *Journal of Public Administration: Research and Theory*, *13*(1), 83–102. doi:10.1093/jpart/mug010

United States Government Accountability Office. (GAO) (2003). *Homeland Security: Efforts to Improve Information Sharing Need to be Strengthened.* (GAO-03-760). Washington, DC: U.S. Government Printing Office.

Vigoda-Gadot, E. (2004). Collaborative Public Administration: Some Lessons from the Israeli Experience. *Managerial Auditing Journal*, *19*(6), 700–711. doi:10.1108/02686900410543831

Waugh, W. L. (1994). Regionalizing Emergency Management: Counties as State and Local Government. *Public Administration Review*, *54*(3), 253–258. doi:10.2307/976728

Welch, E. W., Hinnant, C. C., & Moon, M. J. (2005). Linking Citizen Satisfaction with E-government and Trust in Government. *Journal of Public Administration: Research and Theory*, *15*(3), 371–391. doi:10.1093/jopart/mui021

West, D. M. (2005). *Digital Government: Technology and Public Sector Performance*. Princeton, NJ: Princeton University Press.

West, D. M. (2008). *State and Federal Electronic Government in the United States, 2008*. Retrieved October 1, 2008 from http://www.brookings.edu/reports/2008/0826_egovernment_west.aspx

Wise, C. R. (2006). Organizing for Homeland Security after Katrina: Is Adaptive Management What's Missing? *Public Administration Review*, *66*(3), 302–318. doi:10.1111/j.1540-6210.2006.00587.x

Section 4
Selected Readings from the Author

Chapter 11
Perceived Effectiveness of E-Government and its Usage in City Governments:
Survey Evidence from Information Technology Directors

ABSTRACT

This article examines the perceived effectiveness of e-government by Information Technology (IT) directors in local governments in the United States. Most of the existing empirical research has examined the level of adoption of e-government; it does not focus on what is the overall effectiveness of e-government for city governments as this study does. This is accomplished through a survey of IT directors exploring their perceptions of e-government to determine whether this is related to the overall usage of e-government in cities. Websites were the most effective service channel for getting information; the telephone was the most effective service channel for solving a problem; while in person at a government office was most effective service channel for citizens' to access city services. E-government usage was positively related to managerial effectiveness, having a champion of e-government, and perceived effectiveness of citizen access to online information.

INTRODUCTION

E-government research has proliferated since the rise of the Internet in the 1990s as a mainstream method of citizen-initiated contacts with government. The Internet was originally envisaged to be a major transformational force to empower citizens to affect major change in governments (Ho, 2002). The evolution of e-government has been noted to be incremental rather than transformational (West, 2004; Norris and Moon, 2005). The literature in public administration on e-government was written during the high point of interest in the Internet as one method to decentralize government hierarchies and focus public sector organizations on results.

Much of the e-government literature to date has examined the overall adoption of e-government in terms of its level of sophistication and breadth of information and service offerings (Ho, 2002; Norris and Moon, 2005). There is much less research that evaluates the effectiveness of e-government for public managers (Streib and Navarro, 2005). This knowledge gap in the literature is where this study fits in and where it contributes to the literature. This study is different from existing surveys on e-government because it examines effectiveness through a national survey of Information Technology (IT) directors in large-sized cities in the United States. This study uses the citizen-initiated contacts literature as a conceptual framework to discern more explicitly the effectiveness of e-government. As resources for e-government become increasingly scarce for city governments, this study attempts to address what impact e-government has actually made for city governments.

Citizen participation through e-government has been argued that it will lead to increased accountability of governments and increase citizen trust and confidence in public officials (West, 2004; Welch, Hinnant, and Moon, 2004). The Internet has been touted as one service channel that can increase trust and confidence in citizen-initiated contacts with government (Thomas and Streib, 2003). Therefore, one way of examining why citizens contact government can be found in the extensive literature on citizen-initiated contacts with government; with much of this literature essentially predating the Internet.

In order to examine the effectiveness of e-government this study covers the following. There is an examination of the citizen-initiated contacts with government literature, showing the connection between this literature and the e-government literature. There is a review of the existing e-government survey research to determine where this study fits into this body of knowledge. Following this, the hypotheses and research methods are presented. The most important part of this article is the examination of the survey results. The conclusion outlines the importance of the relationship between perceived effectiveness of e-government and its usage.

Citizen-Initiated Contacts and E-Government Literatures

The existing literature on citizen-initiated contacts examines contacts by citizens being essentially related to needs, awareness, and their socio-economic status (Thomas, 1982). There is little systematic information on the impact of the sources of citizens' contacts with bureaucracy or their satisfaction with that contact (Moon, Serra, and West, 1993; Serra, 1995). Research indicates that perceived needs for a service was the most important predictor of all forms of citizen-initiated contacts (Thomas and Melkers, 1999; Thomas and Melkers, 2000). Therefore, the need for a service with municipal government can be used to examine citizen-initiated contacts with e-government.

There are several studies that examine citizen-initiated contacts by citizens (Jones; Greenberg, Kaufman, and Drew, 1977; Vedlitz, Dyer, and Durand, 1980; Sharp, 1984; Vedlitz and Dyer, 1984;

Hirlinger, 1992; Thomas and Melkers, 1999), but there is much less research that examines administrators' receptivity to these contacts (Greene, 1982; Reddick, 2005a). Citizen-initiated contacts has been an established field of study in public administration, but as noted most of the literature predates the Internet (Thomas and Streib, 2003; Pieterson and Dijk, 2007).

E-government can link citizens to government services, thus eliminating their need to interact with government employees as a means to gain access to city services (Milward and Snyder, 1996; Snellen, 2002). The movement from street-level to system level bureaucracies has evolved because of the Internet, which has changed the traditional role of citizen-initiated contacts with government (Snellen, 1998; Bovens and Zouridis, 2002).

Citizen-initiated contacts with a government agency through the Internet are usually in the form of requesting a service or lodging a complaint about a government service (Thomas and Streib, 2003). The e-government literature shows that citizens use different channels for different purposes depending on the task at hand (Pieterson and Dijk, 2007). For instance, when citizens have a problem they prefer to contact government by phone and for information they prefer to contact government by Website (Reddick, 2005b). Therefore, this study examines the effectiveness of different service channels for citizen-initiated contacts with government.

Existing E-Government Survey Research

The existing research on public sector Chief Information Officers (CIOs) and IT directors has focused on the federal government (Bertot, 1997; Bertot and McClure, 1997; Buehler, 2000; McClure and Bertot, 2000; Westerback, 2000), state governments (Ugbah and Umeh, 1993), local governments (Fletcher, 1997), and comparisons between the public and private sectors (Ward and Mitchell, 2004). There have been few scholarly studies that examine public-sector CIOs and their opinions on e-government effectiveness, which is the goal of this research.

The existing survey research on municipal e-government adoption concentrates mainly on the International City/County Management Association (ICMA) dataset on e-government in local governments (Moon, 2002; Holden, Norris, and Fletcher, 2003; Brown, 2007). These surveys of chief administrative officers (CAO) focus on the level and sophistication of e-government adoption. This research does not examine, to any great extent, the level of effectiveness of e-government (Streib and Navarro, 2005). Most local e-government in the United States is informational, involving the one way transmission of information to citizens (Moon and Norris, 2005). There is much less transaction based e-government taking place in local governments. *Given this rather unsophisticated nature of e-government offerings, one must ask what is the overall effectiveness of e-government for local governments?* This study attempts to address this important question through the following hypotheses.

Research Hypotheses

There are four hypotheses of this article that examine the impact of the perceived effectiveness of e-government on e-government usage. The first hypothesis examines the perceived effectiveness of different service channels for citizens to access information, to solve a problem, and access city services. The most common service channels examined were the Website, email, telephone, and in person at a city government office. The existing citizen-initiated contacts literature argues that contact depends upon citizens' needs (Thomas and Melkers, 2000; Thomas and Streib, 2003). This study predicts that the greater the perceived effectiveness of a service channel would have an impact on e-government usage.

H1: *The perceived effectiveness of the service channel for citizens to access information, to solve and problem, and access services is positively related to e-government usage.*

The second hypothesis examines the perceived effectiveness of e-government and its impact on management to determine if this is related to e-government usage. Management and e-government has been studied is surveys of e-government adoption (Norris and Moon, 2005). The areas of management this study examines are leadership, governance, and performance. These different categories of management are examined to determine whether there is any relationship to e-government usage.

H2: *The perceived effectiveness of e-government on management is positively related to e-government usage.*

This article also examines through the third hypothesis the perceived effectiveness of e-government and its impact on the administration of the city government. Some of the areas covered are e-government and the workforce, e-government and resources, and e-government and administrative discretion. The administrative angle of e-government has been examined in surveys of municipal government (Moon, 2002; Holden, Norris, and Fletcher, 2003).

H3: *The perceived effectiveness of e-government on administration is positively related to e-government usage.*

The final hypothesis examines a common factor found in the literature on e-government of the size of the government. The research argues that usage of e-government would be dependent upon city size (Moon, 2002; Holden, Norris, and Fletcher, 2003). Larger cities, for instance, might have more resources to spend on e-government than smaller cities.

H4: *The number of full-time equivalent (FTE) employees of a city government is positively related to e-government usage.*

These four hypotheses are explored through an analysis of national survey data on e-government effectiveness in city governments.

Data Collection and Research Methods

This survey of IT directors was administered by the authors of this study during the summer months of 2007. A survey and cover letter introducing the project were sent to IT directors serving cities with populations of 75,000 residents or greater. In total there were 290 cities that were sent a survey, of which 112 responded, which is a response rate of 38.6%. This response rate is consistent with the ICMA surveys on e-government of city administrators (Norris and Moon, 2005). The comprehensive mailing list of IT directors was obtained from the National League of Cities (NLC).

The methods of analysis of the survey results were Chi-square statistics to test whether there was a relationship between e-government usage and different perceived factors of e-government effectiveness. This study also used Ordinary Least Squares (OLS) regression to examine the relationship between the perception of e-government effectiveness and its usage.

Characteristics of Cities and their IT Directors

Table 1 provides information on the characteristics of cities and their IT directors. The majority of IT directors in the sample were male, as represented by 79.5% of the sample. The typical age range for IT directors was over 45 to 64 years of age as represented by 80.3% of those surveyed. These city officials were well educated with 86.7% having a post secondary diploma. Typically, IT directors have not worked that long for their city government, usually less than 10 years (69.6%). In terms of full-time equivalent (FTE) employees for the cities surveyed, 39.3% of them had between 1,000 and 2,499 FTE, representing fairly large city governments in the survey sample.

Overall, the results in Table 1 are consistent with what is know about CIOs from the information systems research, they are more likely to be male, well educated, middle-aged, and do not have a long tenure in their position (Fletcher, 1997). The sample is also more representative of larger-sized city governments. This is different from existing surveys on local e-government conducted by the ICMA, which has a larger sample of small to medium-sized cities (Moon and Norris, 2005).

Citizen-Initiated Contacts through Service Channels

Table 2 provides a picture of the extent to which citizens contact government through different service channels. This question was used to determine the usage of e-government in cities compared with other service channels. The telephone is the most common way for citizens to contact city government (30.8%). The second most common method was in person at a government office as represented by 24.2% of respondents. The least used service channel for citizens was through the mail according to 11.7% of IT directors. When combining Website contacts (20.7%) and email contacts (12.6%), there were 33.3% of citizens using these service channels to contact government.

This study focuses on the combined responses of citizen-initiated contacts by Website and email to represent the variable used throughout this study of e-government usage. Of course, the e-government literature has not limited itself to these two service channels, since there are other forms of e-government such as government to government and business to government that are beyond the scope of this study.

The Perceived Effectiveness of Service Channels

Table 3 examines the level of perceived effectiveness of different service channels used by citizens to contact their city government. These questions are divided into the different methods of contact through a Website, email, telephone, and in person visit at a government office. The effectiveness of each of these service channels is rated according to the task of citizens of accessing information, solving a problem, and accessing services.

Table 3 shows that the citizens ability to access information the Website was viewed by IT directors as the most effective method, with 92% believing this was the case (when adding the "very effective" and "effective" responses). Email was viewed by 83% of IT directors as effective for accessing information. The telephone was viewed by 88.4% of respondents as effective for accessing information. Finally, an in person visit at a government office had 84.9% of IT directors believing this was effective for accessing information. Overall, it appears that all of the service channels are rated as effective for accessing information, but the city Website had a slight edge.

As shown in Table 3, for solving a problem the service channel that was viewed as being the most effective was the telephone (92%). The least effective service channel for solving a problem was the city government Website (66.1%). While the effectiveness for solving a problem with email (82.2%) and in person at a government office (90.2%) were in between the phone and Website contacts.

Finally, IT directors were asked to rate the service channels in terms of citizens' ability to access services (Table 3). The highest rated service channel for accessing services was in person at a government office (88.4%). The lowest rated service channel in terms of effectiveness was email according to 63.4% of IT directors. Accessing services by citizens through a Website was effective according to 76.8% of IT directors. Finally, the telephone was viewed by 81.3% of directors as an effective service channel for citizen access to services.

The overall results in Table 3 indicate that Websites were the most effective service channel for getting information; the telephone was the most effective service channel for solving a problem; while in person at a government office was most effective channel for citizens to access city services. These findings are consistent with public opinion data on e-government use by citizens (Reddick, 2005b).

Perceived Effectiveness of E-Government and Management

Table 4 examines the perceived effectiveness of e-government and its impact on management, leadership, and governance. There is a long history of literature that discusses the impact of IT on management (Bozeman and Bretschneider, 1986; Bretschneider, 1990; Moon and Norris, 2005). This study uses Chi-square statistics to determine whether there is a statistically significant relationship between e-government usage and several management factors. The highest level of agreement was that e-government has enabled the city government to achieve greater performance milestones and results (67%). The least level of agreement was for e-government empowering employees to make more decisions on their own (40.2%). There was agreement that e-government has made the IT director a more effective manager (51.8%), and this was statistically related to e-government usage. Overall, there was agreement that e-government has impacted management, but there was disagreement, when adding the "disagree" and "strongly disagree" responses that it has been adopted widely and quickly (29.5%).

As shown in Table 4, leadership is examined as one of the important aspects of e-government advancement in local governments. For instance, having a champion of e-government is a critical success factor for e-government advancement (91.1%) and this was statistically related to e-government usage. Another issue for leadership and e-government is top management support of the IT department's participation in the decision-making process for e-government (68.7%), which was also related to e-government usage. The least level of agreement was for top management having a vision and strategic direction for e-government, with only 46.5% of IT directions believing this was the case. This finding is somewhat problematic since cities need a vision to move e-government forward.

Table 4 examines the impact of e-government on governance in city government, specifically as it is related to e-government projects. In terms of e-government projects in city government this has increased citizen interaction with city government (80.4%). Only 43.8% of IT directors believe that e-

Table 1. Descriptive characteristics of cities and their information technology (IT) directors

	Frequency	Percent
Gender		
Male	89	79.5
Female	23	20.5
Age Range		
25-34	1	0.9
35-44	21	18.8
45-54	50	44.6
55-64	40	35.7
Highest academic attainment		
High school diploma	5	4.5
2 year college	10	8.9
4 year college	43	38.4
Master's degree	48	42.9
Doctorate degree	6	5.4
Years worked as an IT Director in current city government		
Less than 5 Years	27	24.1
5 to 10 years	51	45.5
11 to 15 years	15	13.4
16 to 20 years	7	6.3
21 to 25 years	8	7.1
26 years or more	4	3.6
Full-time equivalent (FTE) employees		
249 or less	2	1.8
250 to 499	6	5.4
500 to 999	30	26.8
1,000 to 2,499	44	39.3
2,500 to 4,999	20	17.9
5,000 or more	10	8.9

government projects are a top priority of their city government. There was a majority of city IT directors who believed that e-government projects have created a more citizen-focused government (67.9%). Finally, there was a majority of IT directors who believed that e-government project decisions rested with city government rather than key stakeholders (75.9%).

Perceived Effectiveness of E-Government and Administration

Table 5 provides information on e-government and its impact on the city government workforce, resources, and administrative discretion. The survey evidence indicates that e-government has allowed a

Table 2. Average citizens' contact with government through different service channels

Service Channel	Percent
Telephone	30.8
In Person at City Government Office	24.2
Website	20.7
Email	12.6
Mail	11.7
E-government Usage (Website and Email)	**33.3**

Table 3. The level of perceived effectiveness of service channels in city government

	Very Effective %	Effective %	Neutral %	Ineffective %	Very Ineffective %	Median Response
Effectiveness of the following service channels for citizens' ability to *access information*						
Website	31.3	60.7	4.5	2.7	0.9	2.0
Email**	25.9	57.1	12.5	4.5	0.0	2.0
Telephone	20.5	67.9	8.0	3.6	0.0	2.0
In Person at City Government Office**	28.6	56.3	11.6	3.6	0.0	2.0
Effectiveness of the following service channels for citizens' ability to *solve a problem*						
Website	14.3	51.8	21.4	8.0	4.5	2.0
Email	17.9	64.3	12.5	5.4	0.0	2.0
Telephone	25.0	67.0	5.4	2.7	0.0	2.0
In Person at City Government Office***	39.3	50.9	8.0	1.8	0.0	2.0
Effectiveness of the following service channels for citizens' ability to *access services*						
Website	27.7	49.1	13.4	8.0	1.8	2.0
Email	19.6	43.8	26.8	8.0	1.8	2.0
Telephone	17.9	63.4	14.3	4.5	0.0	2.0
In Person at City Government Office***	33.0	55.4	8.9	2.7	0.0	2.0

*Notes: Very effective=1, Effective=2, Neutral=3, Ineffective=4, Very Ineffective=5; **significant with e-government usage at the 0.05 level; ***significant with e-government usage at the 0.01 level.*

greater degree of information sharing among department (60.7%). E-government has fostered a greater level of teamwork in employees (40.1%); and this finding is statistically related to e-government usage. E-government has developed a new level of collaboration among department (38.4%); and this is statistically related to e-government usage as well. Finally, recruitment and retention of qualified e-government program management and support staff is one of the most critical issues according to 41.1% of IT directors.

Table 4. E-government usage and management, leadership, and goverance

E-government and Management	Strongly Agree %	Agree %	Neither Agree/Dis-agree %	Disagree %	Strongly Disagree %	Median Response
E-government has made me a more effective manager.	14.3	37.5	34.8	7.1	6.3	2.0
E-government has been adopted widely and quickly.	11.6	38.4	20.5	25.0	4.5	2.5
E-government has empowered employees to make more decisions on their own.	9.8	30.4	35.7	17.9	6.3	3.0
E-government has enabled us to achieve greater performance milestones and results.**	13.4	53.6	22.3	6.3	4.5	2.0
Leadership and E-government						
Having a champion of e-government is one of the most important critical success factors for e-government advancement.**	51.8	39.3	6.3	1.8	0.9	1.0
Top management has a vision and strategic direction for e-government.	17.9	28.6	30.4	18.8	4.5	3.0
Top management dictates what our e-government initiatives will be.	9.8	41.1	25.0	19.6	4.5	2.0
Top management is very supportive of my department's participation in the decision-making process for e-government.***	35.7	33.0	19.6	8.0	3.6	2.0
E-government and Governance						
E-government projects have created a more citizen focused government.	12.5	55.4	25.9	5.4	0.9	2.0
E-government projects require some input from stakeholders such as city council, citizens, and businesses but ultimate decisions tend to rest with city government.	12.5	63.4	16.1	6.3	1.8	2.0
E-government projects have increased citizen interaction with city government.	17.9	62.5	15.2	3.6	0.9	2.0
E-government projects are a top-priority of city government.	14.3	29.5	30.4	19.6	6.3	3.0

Notes: *Strongly agree =1, agree =2, neutral=3, disagree =4, strongly disagree=5; ** significant with e-government usage at the 0.05 level; ***significant with e-government usage at the 0.01 level.*

Table 5. E-governement usage and the workforce, resources, and administrative discretion

E-government and the Workforce	Strongly Agree %	Agree %	Neither Agree/ Disagree %	Disagree %	Strongly Disagree %	Median Response
Recruitment and retention of qualified e-government program management and support staff is one of the most critical issues.	12.5	28.6	24.1	27.7	7.1	3.0
E-government has allowed a greater degree of information sharing among departments.	20.5	40.2	25.0	11.6	2.7	2.0
E-government has fostered greater teamwork in employees.***	7.1	33.0	39.3	16.1	4.5	3.0
E-government has developed a new level of collaboration among departments.**	8.9	29.5	39.3	17.9	4.5	3.0
E-government and Resources						
Has the critical information technology infrastructure to promote e-government adoption.	24.1	56.3	11.6	6.3	1.8	2.0
Has adequate budgetary resources to fund e-government projects.	8.9	34.8	17.9	34.8	3.6	3.0
Has seen manual processes being reduced as a result of e-government.	17.9	54.5	19.6	6.3	1.8	2.0
Takes a holistic view of e-government when implementing e-government projects.**	10.7	32.1	38.4	15.2	3.6	3.0
E-government and Administrative Discretion						
When e-government is used, decisions are not often questioned.	2.7	13.4	55.4	25.0	3.6	3.0
When e-government is used, there is greater control over the implementation of policies.	3.6	29.5	49.1	16.1	1.8	3.0
When e-government is used, there is minimal contact by employees with citizens.	2.7	19.6	36.6	39.3	1.8	3.0
When e-government is used, there is greater accuracy of decisions made by employees.***	0.9	25.9	59.8	11.6	1.8	3.0

Notes: *Strongly agree =1, agree =2, neutral=3, disagree =4, strongly disagree=5; **significant with e-government usage at the 0.05 level; ***significant with e-government usage at the 0.01 level.*

Table 6. Correlations, descriptive, and reliability statistics for e-government usage and predictor variables

	Mean	Min	Max	SD	1	2	3	4	5	6	7	8	9
1. E-government Usage (Website and Email Contacts as a Percent)	33.30	2.0	90.0	19.08	1.00								
2. E-government has made me a more effective manager (1 Strongly Agree to 5 Strongly Disagree)	2.54	1	5	1.03	-0.33 ***	1.00	(1.78)						
3. Having a champion of e-government is one of the most important critical success factors for e-government advancement (1 Strongly Agree to 5 Strongly Disagree)	1.61	1	5	0.76	.202 **	0.05	1.00	(1.04)					
4. Effectiveness of citizen access to e-government information (summation of Website and Email effectiveness)	3.77	2	7	1.15	-.292 ***	.365 ***	0.14	1.00	(1.66)				
5. Effectiveness of e-government for citizens to solve a problem (summation of Website and Email effectiveness)	4.42	2	9	1.40	-.268 ***	.461 ***	0.07	.550 ***	1.00	(2.11)			
6. Effectiveness of e-government for citizens to access services (summation of Website and email effectiveness)	4.36	2	10	1.71	-.252 **	.432 ***	0.03	.607 ***	.689 ***	1.00	(2.32)		
7. E-government has enabled city to achieve greater performance milestones and results (1 Strongly Agree to 5 Strongly Disagree)	2.35	1	5	0.95	-.215 **	.611 ***	0.07	.407 ***	.447 ***	.462 ***	1.00	(1.83)	
8. Full-time equivalent employees (1=249 or less to 6=5,000 or more)	3.93	1	6	1.09	0.11	-0.09	-0.09	0.11	0.08	0.09	-0.14	1.00	(1.06)

Notes: *Total observations were 101; Variance Inflation Factors (VIF) are in parentheses; SD=Standard Deviations; **correlation significant at the 0.05 level; ***correlation significant at the 0.01 level.*

Table 5 provides information on e-government and resources in city governments. Some authors argue that the more citizens participate in government through e-government the more costly it is to govern (Chen, Huang, and Hsioa, 2006). Most of the IT directors agree that their city government has the critical information infrastructure to promote e-government adoption (80.4%). There is agreement that in their city government manual processes have been reduced as a result of e-government (72.4%). City governments take a holistic view of e-government when implementing projects according to only 42.8% of IT directors in this survey. E-government usage is statistically related to taking a holistic view of e-government projects. Many city governments have adequate resources to fund e-government projects (43.7%).

Some research argues that there is a change from the traditional street-level to system-level bureaucracies because of IT (Bovens and Zouridis, 2002). Table 5 provides information on the impact of e-government and administrative discretion in city governments. There is not much agreement that e-government had an impact on discretionary decision making in cities. For instance, only 33.1% of IT directors agree that when e-government is used there is greater control over the implementation of policies. There was only 22.3% of IT directors who believed that when e-government was used there was minimal contact by employees with citizens. A very small percent of IT directors believe that decisions are not often questioned when e-government is used (16.1%). There is a greater accuracy of decisions made by employees when e-government is used according to 26.8% directors; this was statistically related to e-government usage. Overall, the survey results showed little impact on employee discretion when e-government was incorporated in the city.

Perceptions of E-Government Effectiveness and Usage

In order to examine the relationship between perceived effectiveness and e-government usage, Table 6 provides some descriptive statistics of the dependent variable e-government usage and the seven predictor variables. The dependent variable e-government usage (Website and email contacts) was operationalized as a percent score of this type of contact with government. As previously shown in Table 2, citizen-initiated contacts by e-government was on average 33.3% of the possible contacts.

The independent variable in Table 6 of "E-government has made me a more effective manager" was a Likert scale variable ranging from strongly agree (1) to strongly disagree (5). The independent variable of "Having a champion of e-government is one of the most important critical success factors for e-government advancement" was similarly coded from strongly agree (1) to strongly disagree (5). The fourth through sixth variables ranged from very effective (1) to very ineffective (5) for the effectiveness of e-government for citizen access to information, to solve a problem, and access services. This variable was constructed by adding up the service channel of Website and email effectiveness questions; therefore, the scores are higher than the previous variable. Variable seven of "E-government has enabled city to achieve greater performance milestones and results" was coded from strongly agree (1) to strongly disagree (5). The final variable is the FTE of the city government being coded from (1) for 249 or less employees to (6) for 5,000 or more employees with the frequencies previously shown in Table 1 for this variable.

The Variance Inflation Factors (VIF) in parentheses are not above four, therefore, the risk of multicollinearity it not great for these variables (Table 6). The correlation coefficients were significant at the 0.05 level or greater for e-government usage having an impact on most of the predictor variables. However, FTE employees was not statistically significant with e-government usage.

Table 7. Regression model of e-government usage and effectiveness factors

	Beta Coeff.	*t-statistic*	*Prob. Sign.*
E-government has made me a more effective manager	0.25	2.06**	0.04
Having a champion of e-government is one of the most important critical success factors for e-government advancement	0.26	2.78***	0.01
Effectiveness of citizen access to e-government information	0.23	1.97**	0.05
Effectiveness of e-government for citizens to solve a problem	0.07	0.50	0.62
Effectiveness of e-government for citizens to access services	0.01	0.08	0.94
E-government has enabled city to achieve greater performance milestones and results	0.06	0.47	0.64
Full-time equivalent employees	0.14	1.44	0.15
Adjusted R^2		0.16	
F-Statistic		3.74***	
N		100	

Table 7 has examined the relationship between the perception of the effectiveness of e-governments and its usage. OLS regression was used with e-government usage being the dependent variable regressed against a series of independent variables identified in the literature as impacting usage. From the regression results there were three statistically significant coefficients found. First, usage was related to e-government making the IT director a more effective manager. Research shows that managerial innovation appears to be closely associated with the establishment of e-government adoption in local governments (Moon and Norris, 2005). Second, having a champion of e-government was related to e-government usage; this is also consistent with the literature (Garson, 2006). Finally, the effectiveness of citizen access to e-government information was related to e-government usage.

Overall, the results show that e-government usage had an impact on management for IT directors which is consistent with the existing literature. It also is incumbent for a city government to have a champion of e-government for its project success. Finally, e-government effectiveness is the greatest for accessing information, which is also consistent with the existing literature that indicates that e-government falls short for solving problems and accessing services (Norris and Moon, 2005).

Some of the independent variables that did not predict e-government usage were FTE employment of cities, which runs counter to the existing literature (Weare, Musso, and Hale, 1999; Moon, 2002). Another variable not statistically significant was e-government usage enabling the city to achieve greater performance milestones and results. This is also surprising with the movement towards results-based approaches through e-government.

Limitations and Future Research

Since this research has focused on the views of IT directors there was no independent verification of their claims about the effectiveness of e-government in their cities. One would expect that IT directors that are more optimistic about e-government would be more willing to participate in this survey. These officials have a self-interested view that what they are doing is effective, efficient, and responsive

(West, 2004). A study comparing bureaucrats and citizens enthusiasm for e-government found that bureaucrats were more enthusiastic about e-government (Moon and Welch, 2005). Another limitation is that this study examined larger-sized cities in the United States, and as a result smaller cities and e-government usage and effectiveness were not reported. However, the ICMA has conducted several surveys on e-government adoption focusing on some issues of effectiveness for small to medium sized cities. A final limitation of this study is that it has asked CIOs what citizens use when contacting their government. The argument for using CIOs was because they are very familiar with the communication channels within their city government; and should know the degree and effectiveness of contacts by citizens with these service channels.

Future research could possibly examine the effectiveness of e-government in other countries besides the United States. There also could be a study of e-government effectiveness of different levels of e-government, such as the views of CIOs in state governments and the federal government. It would be beneficial in future research to find more direct measures of the effectiveness of e-government, rather the self-reporting of a survey.

CONCLUSION

This study examined e-government usage and its impact on the perceived effectiveness of e-government in cities in the United States. This study has addressed a missing piece in the e-government literature, finding a relationship between citizen usage of e-government and managerial effectiveness. This work is a preliminary attempt to focus on evaluating e-government, while much of the existing research has focused on the adoption of e-government. E-government usage by citizens is composed of one third of citizen-initiated contacts. This was the most pronounced contact by citizens with government, just behind the telephone. Websites were the most effective service channel for getting information; the telephone was the most effective service channel for solving a problem; while in person at a government office was most effective service channel for citizens' to access city services. Through a regression model, managerial effectiveness, having a champion of e-government, and perceived effectiveness of citizen access to information were all positively related to e-government usage.

What do these results mean with respect to the evaluation e-government? First, cities should be cognizant that e-government is a major force in citizen-initiated contacts with their government. They should, as a result, make sure that they find better mechanisms to provide information, services, and ways of addressing problems online to an increasingly sophisticated cyber audience.

In addition, management capacity is a critical element in promoting e-government usage. E-government should be used as a way to increase the capacity of making the IT director a more effective manager, which has long been advocated in the public sector IT literature (Bozeman and Bretschneider, 1986). Having a champion of e-government has long been touted in the literature as critical, and this study confirms that finding (Garson, 2006). The views of IT directors on the effectiveness of e-government to gather information is also consistent with the literature which argues that e-government's greatest success factor is that it provides a good source of information for citizens (Norris and Moon, 2005). The greater issue is that providing information online for citizens in just one step towards promoting e-government adoption in city governments (Thomas and Streib, 2005). Reaching higher levels of e-government diffusion involves providing more transaction-based services and the ability for citizens to solve problems online.

REFERENCES

Bertot, J. C. (1997). The impact of Federal IRM on agency missions: Findings, issues, and recommendations. *Government Information Quarterly, 14*(3), 235-253.

Bertot, J. C., & McClure, C. R. (1997). Key issues affecting the development of federal IRM: A view from the trenches. *Government Information Quarterly, 14*(3), 271-290.

Bovens, M., & Zouridis, S. (2002). From street-level to system-level bureaucracies: How information and communication technology is transforming administrative discretion and constitutional control. *Public Administration Review, 62*(2), 174-184.

Bozeman, B., & Bretschneider, S. (1986). Public management information systems: Theory and prescription. *Public Administration Review, 46*, 475-487.

Bretschneider, S. (1990). Management information systems in public and private organizations: An empirical test. *Public Administration Review, 50*(5), 536-545.

Brown, M. M. (2007). Understanding E-Government benefits: An examination of leading-edge local governments. *American Review of Public Administration, 37*(2), 178-197.

Buehler, M. (2000). U.S. Federal government CIOs: Information technology's new managers – Preliminary findings. *Government Information Quarterly, 27*, 29-45.

Chen, D-Y., Huang, T-Y., & Hsiao, N. (2006). Reinventing government through on-line citizen involvement in the developing world: A case study of Taipei City mayor's E-mail box in Taiwan. *Public Administration and Development, 26*(5), 409-423.

Fletcher, P. D. (1997). Local governments and IRM: Policy emerging from practice. *Government Information Quarterly, 14*(3), 313-324.

Garson, G. D. (2006). *Public information technology and E-Governance: Managing the virtual state.* Sudbury, MA: Jones and Bartlett.

Green, K. R. (1982). Municipal administrators' receptivity to citizens' and elected officials' contacts. *Public Administration Review, 42*(4), 346-353.

Hirlinger, M.W. (1992). Citizen-initiated contacting of local government officials: A multivariate explanation. *Journal of Politics, 54*(2), 553-564.

Ho, A. T. K. (2002). Reinventing local governments and the e-government initiative. *Public Administration Review, 62*(4), 434-444.

Holden, S. H., Norris, D. F., & Fletcher, P. D. (2003). Electronic government at the local level: Progress to date and future issues. *Public Performance & Management Review, 26*(4), 325-344.

Jones, B. D., Greenberg, S. R., Kaufman, C., & Drew, J. (1977). Bureaucratic response to citizen-initiated contacts: Environmental enforcement in Detroit. *American Political Science Review, 71*(1), 148-165.

McClure, C. R., & Bertot, J. C. (2000). The chief information officer (CIO): Assessing its impact. *Government Information Quarterly, 17*(1), 7-12.

Milward, H. B., & Snyder, L. O. (1996). Electronic government: Linking citizens to public organizations through technology. *Journal of Public Administration Research and Theory, 6*(2), 261-275.

Moon, D., Serra, G., & West, J. P. (1993). Citizens contacts with bureaucratic and legislative officials. *Political Research Quarterly, 46*(4), 931-941.

Moon, M. J. (2002). The evolution of e-government among municipalities: Rhetoric or reality? *Public Administration Review, 62*(4), 424-433.

Moon, M. J., & Norris, D. F. (2005). Does managerial orientation matter? The adoption of reinventing government and e-government at the municipal level. *Information Systems Journal, 15*(1), 43-60.

Moon, M. J., & Welch, E. W. (2005). Same bed, different dreams? A comparative analysis of citizen and bureaucratic perspectives on E-Government. *Review of Public Personnel Administration, 25*(3), 243-264.

Norris, D. F., & Moon, M. J. (2005). Advancing e-government at the grassroots: Tortoise or Hare? *Public Administration Review*, 65(1), 64-75.

Pieterson, W., & Dijk, Jan van. (2007). Channel choice determinants: An exploration of the factors that determine the choice of a service channel in citizen initiated contacts. *The Proceedings of the 8th Annual Digital Government Research Conference*, 228, 173-182. http://www.dgsociety.org/documents/p173-Pieterson.pdf last accessed October 12, 2007.

Reddick, C. G. (2005a). Citizen-initiated contacts with Ontario local E-Government: Administrators responses to contacts. *International Journal of Electronic Government Research, 1*(4), 45-62.

Reddick, C. G. (2005b). Citizen-initiated contacts with government: Comparing phones and Web sites. *Journal of E-Government, 2*(1), 27-53.

Serra, G. (1995). Citizen-initiated contact and satisfaction with bureaucracy: A multivariate analysis. *Journal of Public Administration Research and Theory, 5*(2), 175-188.

Sharp, E. B. (1984). Citizen-demand making in the urban context. *American Journal of Political Science, 28*(4), 654-670.

Snellen, I. (1998). Street-level bureaucracy in an information age. In *Public Administration in an Information Age: A Handbook*, edited by Ig Snellen and Wim van de Donk, 497-505. Amsterdam: IOS Press.

Snellen, I. (2002). Electronic governance: Implications for citizens, politicians, and public servants. *International Review of Administrative Sciences, 68*(2), 183-198.

Streib, G., & Navarro, I. (2005). Citizen demand for interactive E-Government: The case of Georgia consumer services. *American Review of Public Administration, 36*(3), 288-300.

Thomas, J. C. (1982). Citizen-initiated contacts with government agencies: A test of three theories. *American Journal of Political Science, 26*(3), 504-522.

Thomas, J. C., & Streib, G. (2003). The new face of government: Citizen-initiated contacts in the era of e-government. *Journal of Public Administration Research and Theory, 13*(1), 83-102.

Thomas, J. C., & Melkers, J. (1999). Explaining citizen-initiated contacts with municipal bureaucrats: Lessons from the Atlanta experience. *Urban Affairs Review, 34*(5), 667-690.

Thomas, J. C., & Melkers, J. (2000). Citizen contacting of municipal officials: Choosing between appointed administrators and elected leaders. *Journal of Public Administration Research and Theory, 11*(1), 51-71.

Thomas, J. C., & Streib, G. (2005). E-Democracy, E-commerce, and E-Research: Examining the electronic ties between citizens and governments. *Administration & Society, 37*(3), 259-280.

Ugbah, S. D., & Umeh, O. J. (1993). Information resource management: An examination of individual and organizational attributes in state government agencies. *Information Resources Management Journal, 6*(1), 5-13.

Vedlitz, A., & Dyer, J.A. (1984). Bureaucratic Response to Citizen Contacts: Neighborhood Demands and Administrative Reaction in Dallas. *The Journal of Politics, 46*(4), 1207-1216.

Vedlitz, A., Dyer, J. A., & Durand, R. (1980). Citizen contacts with local governments: A comparative view. *American Journal of Political Science, 24*(1), 50-67.

Ward, M. A., & Mitchell, S. (2004). A comparison of the strategic priorities of public and private sector information resource management executives. *Government Information Quarterly, 21*, 284-304.

Weare, C., Musso, J. A., & Hale, M. L. (1999). Electronic democracy and the diffusion of municipal Web pages in California. *Administration & Society, 31*(1), 3-27.

Welch, E. W., Hinnant, C. C., & Moon, M. J. (2004). Linking citizen satisfaction with E-Government and trust in government. *Journal of Public Administration Research and Theory, 15*(3), 371-391.

West, D.M. (2004). E-Government and the transformation of service delivery and citizen attributes. *Public Administration Review, 61*(1), 15-27.

Westerback, L. K. (2000). Toward best practices for strategic information technology management. *Government Information Quarterly, 17*(1), 27-41.

This work was previously published in International Journal of Web Services Research, Vol. 5, Issue 4, edited by L.J. Zhang, pp. 89-104, copyright 2008 by IGI Publishing (an imprint of IGI Global).

Chapter 12
E-Government and Creating a Citizen-Centric Government: A Study of Federal Government CIOs

ABSTRACT

This chapter examines the relationship between e-government and the creation of a more citizen-centric government. This study provides a conceptual framework showing a possible relationship among management, resources, security, and privacy issues that would lead to creating a more citizen-centric government with e-government. It explores the opinions of chief information officers (CIOs) on e-government issues and effectiveness. A survey was administered to federal government CIOs in June and July 2005. The survey results revealed that CIOs who have higher management capacity and project-management skills were associated more with creating a more citizen-centric federal government. The contribution of this study to the literature on e-government is that it identifies two key attributes that CIOs can attain in order to reach higher stages of e-government advancement for their department or agency.

INTRODUCTION

Electronic government or e-government in this study is defined as the delivery of government information and services to citizens through the Internet 24 hours a day, 7 days a week. This definition has been used in other empirical studies of e-government adoption (Moon & Norris, 2005a). This research adds to this definition with Grant and Chau's (2005) interpretation of e-government as a broad-based transformative initiative, which is consistent with creating more citizen-centric government. Gronlund (2005) reviews the various definitions of e-government. That author has found they share a common theme of the need for organizational transformation through technological implementation. We realize that focusing on the Internet and e-government is a more limited way of examining e-government because of the rise of non-Internet technologies (Gronlund & Horan, 2004).

Citizen-centric government is the delivery of government services continuously to citizens, businesses, and other government agencies through the Internet (Seifert & Relyea, 2004). Citizen-centric government through e-government acts more as a transformation tool that provides a new government model based on being citizen focused (Schelin, 2003). Some scholars have argued that for e-government to fully realize its capabilities, it must transform government from agency centric to citizen centric (Seifert & Relyea).

The term e-government emerged in the late 1990s. It was born out of the Internet boom. The literature of IT use within government is different from e-government because it more often focuses on external use, such as services to citizens and organizational change (Gronlund & Horan, 2004). Definitions of e-government that focus exclusively on service-delivery components fail to capture the more complex aspects of government transformation because of IT (Grant & Chau, 2005). This study attempts to address this issue by focusing on citizen-centric e-government.

Existing Research on CIOs

The existing research on chief information officers (CIOs) or information resource managers (IRMs) has focused on the federal government (Bertot, 1997; Bertot & McClure, 1997; Buehler, 2000; McClure and Bertot, 2000; Westerback, 2000), state governments (Reddick, in press; Ugbah & Umeh, 1993), local governments (Fletcher, 1997), and comparisons between the public and private sectors (Ward & Mitchell, 2004). There have been no scholarly studies, of which we are aware, that examine public-sector CIOs and their opinions on e-government issues and its effectiveness. This is most likely attributed to the Internet being a relatively new research area in the public sector. In general, the management of IT in private-sector organizations has long been a focus of IS research, but the extent of diffusion has not been as extensively explored in public-sector organizations (Fletcher, 1997).

This study empirically focuses on the connection between e-government and creating a more citizen-centric federal government. The existing research has begun to explore the relationship between e-government and increasing citizen-initiated contacts with government; this study fits into that research area (Thomas & Streib, 2003; West, 2004). However, much needs to be done to identify the key attributes of CIOs, which enable them to create more citizen-centric organizations.

Existing Empirical Work on E-Government Adoption

In a survey of state and federal government CIOs and an analysis of their Web sites, West (2004) arrived at the conclusion that e-government has fallen short of its potential to transform government service delivery and trust in government, that is, creating a more citizen-centric government. E-government does have the possibility of enhancing the responsiveness of government and increasing beliefs that government is efficient and effective. There is also evidence that e-government increases citizen-initiated contact with public officials (Thomas & Streib, 2003). The potential of the Internet to improve citizens' access to government and involvement in policy making is well articulated in the literature. However, citizen-centric government is difficult to achieve in the public sector since governments need to provide universal access to their services (Mahler & Regan, 2002).

Citizen-centric e-government is consistent with the four-stage model of e-government adoption in that governments can reach higher levels of adoption if they become more citizen centric. Layne and Lee (2001) proposed a "stages of e-government growth model" that begins with first cataloging online information; second, moving to online transactions; and then third, moving to vertical integration in which local systems are linked to the national systems. The fourth stage of adoption is horizontal integration across different functions leading to one-stop shopping for citizens (e.g., a Web-site portal). Citizen-centric federal government would involve the final stage of the Layne and Lee model of horizontal integration whereby citizens use Web portals to attain services rather than get information from individual departments or agencies.

This study is different from the existing work on e-government adoption since it focuses on one of the highest stages of development, namely, citizen-centric government. Most of the existing empirical work that tests the impact of e-government adoption primarily examines the first two stages of providing online information and municipal e-service delivery (Ho & Ni, 2004; Moon & Norris, 2005b). Additionally, Andersen and Henriksen (2005) argue that the role of government in technological diffusion is studied the least and therefore is the focus of this chapter.

A study of local e-government over 2 years found that as local-government Web sites mature, they will become more sophisticated, transactional, and more integrated vertically and horizontally (Moon & Norris, 2005a). These authors and others found that e-government adoption is progressing rapidly if measured by the deployment of Web sites. However, a movement toward integrated and transactional e-government is progressing much more slowly in more of an incremental fashion (West, 2004). The key question that this study explores is, what can CIOs do to enable their departments or agencies to become more citizen centric to achieve higher levels of e-government adoption?

In order to examine the views of federal government CIOs on e-government and the creation of a government that is more citizen centric, this study is divided into several sections. In the following section, this study articulates the evolution of the roles and responsibilities of federal CIOs. There also is a description of how the public-sector CIO's environment is uniquely different from what can be found in the private sector. We identify what it means to create a more citizen-centric federal government through e-government. A conceptual framework is outlined explaining what factors one would expect to be associated with creating a more citizen-centric federal government. The final sections articulate how these findings can be used to move e-government to higher stages of development, and demonstrate two easily identifiable skills that CIOs can attain through graduate education.

CLINGER-COHEN ACT AND CIOs

The Information Technology Management Reform Act (ITMRA) of 1996 (P.L. 104-106), also known as the Clinger-Cohen Act, established the position of CIO in executive-branch agencies. This act requires agency heads to designate CIOs to lead reforms to help control system-development risks, better manage technology spending, and achieve measurable improvements in agency performance through the management of information resources (General Accounting Office [GAO], 2004b). However, almost a decade after the passage of this act and despite the government's expenditure of billions of dollars annually on IT, GAO's management of these resources has produced only mixed results.

The Clinger-Cohen Act is consistent with the Government Performance and Results Act (GPRA) of 1993 (P.L. 103-62) that requires agencies to establish clear and measurable objectives, to implement a process, to report on the degree to which those objectives are accomplished, and to report regularly to Congress on their progress in establishing and meeting performance objectives (McClure & Bertot, 2000). Together, the Clinger-Cohen Act and the Paperwork Reduction Act (P.L. 10413) of 1995 (which deals with the strategic acquisition and management of information resources by federal agencies) ushered in a new era of IT management practices in the federal government (Relyea, 2000; Westerback, 2000).

With the passage of the Clinger-Cohen Act, federal departments and agencies had the authority and responsibility to make measurable reforms in performance and service delivery to the public through the strategic use of IT (Bertot & McClure, 1997). Prior to this act, the majority of agencies and departments had an IRM official as their top information person who was viewed as an administrative overhead function. IRMs were far removed from the agencies' strategic decision making and program offices that they served with little or no access to senior agency officials. As a solution, the Clinger-Cohen Act states that federal CIOs will report to and work directly with agency directors. As a result, the CIOs were raised to the executive level and were expected to ask the tough questions about strategic planning, outsourcing, and attaining economy and efficiency (Buehler, 2000).

The importance that CIOs place on strategic planning for their department or agency can be found in existing survey research. A survey of senior IT officers and managers of federal departments and agencies revealed that their top priority was aligning IT with strategic goals (AFFIRM, 2004). Existing research on federal CIOs has examined whether proper management of information resources can lead to effective, efficient, and strategic organizations (Bertot, 1997). Evidence was found for a connection between federal agency strategic planning and agency mission attainment, which face different environmental constraints than private-sector organizations.

THE ENVIRONMENTAL CONTEXT OF PUBLIC-SECTOR CIOs

In the seminal work by Bozeman and Bretschneider (1986), these authors argued that management information systems (MISs) developed for business administration are not altogether appropriate for public administration. Essentially, the different environmental context of the public organization is an important constraint, which makes public MIS diverge from business. The environment of public MIS differs from that of its private-sector counterpart through greater interdependencies that create increased accountability, procedural delays, and red tape (Bretschneider, 1990). Budget and other constraints on purchasing make it impossible for comprehensive approaches to work well, such as strategic planning (Rocheleau & Wu, 2002).

In a survey of state agencies concerning the ability of public organizations to control and manage information resources, the following was found: (a) Public agencies find their programs and sources of information externally oriented, (b) recruiting and retaining a technically competent workforce in public agencies to manage information resources effectively was found to be a problem, and (c) public agencies are constrained by fiscal crisis and a political climate in which they must operate (Ugbah & Umeh, 1993). These unique differences make public-sector Internet use especially worthy to explore.

CITIZEN-CENTRIC FEDERAL GOVERNMENT AND E-GOVERNMENT

The E-Government Act of 2002 (H.R. 2458) defines electronic government as the use by the government of Web-based Internet applications and other information technologies. This act established the Office of Electronic Government within the Office of Management and Budget (OMB) to oversee implementation of its provisions. The E-Government Act was enacted with the general purpose of promoting better use of the Internet and other information technologies to improve government services for citizens and internal government operations, and provide opportunities for citizen participation in government (GAO, 2004a). According to the General Accounting Office, the OMB and federal agencies have taken many positive steps toward implementing the provisions of the E-Government Act.

Creating a more citizen-centric government can be found in President George W. Bush's management document, the *President's Management Agenda* (PMA) of 2002. This document argues that the "… administration's goal is to champion citizen-centered electronic government that will result in a major improvement in the federal government's value to the citizen" (EOP, 2002b, p. 23). In evaluating the PMA, the GAO showed that the results in terms of e-government implementation were mixed, with many goals only being partially achieved or there being no significant progress made (GAO, 2005b).

Citizen-centric e-government is further elaborated upon in the Bush administration's document *E-Government Strategy* (EOP, 2002a). President Bush has made expanding e-government part of a five-part management agenda for making government more focused on citizens and results. According to the Bush administration, the three main aspects of expanding e-government are to make it easier for citizens to obtain service and interact with the federal government, improve government efficiency and effectiveness, and improve government's responsiveness to citizens. E-government is "… critical to meeting today's citizen and business expectations for interaction with government" (p. 3).

Although the PMA does not specifically define citizen-centric government in its application to the federal government, we can discern from reading the document that it implies a focus on citizen expectations driving government responses rather than the other way around, with an emphasis on performance measures. Citizen-centric government essentially focuses on providing citizens with the services and information they require from their government.

CONCEPTUAL FRAMEWORK

The conceptual framework demonstrated in Figure 1 shows the relationship between six factors that are predicted to create more citizen-centric federal government. Each of these factors is discussed along with its respective hypothesis.

Management Capacity

The literature on public administration in e-government has often argued that effective management is a critical catalyst for its advancement (Brown & Brudney, 1998; Ho & Ni, 2004). The benefits in the public-administration literature of the impacts of IT are often associated with the efficiency and rationality of service provision (Danziger & Andersen, 2002). For instance, putting a strong CIO in place can be done to address the federal government's many information and technology management challenges

(GAO, 2005a). The literature on management capacity and its impact on federal e-government initiatives is not as well developed as the local e-government literature. For instance, has e-government made the federal CIO a more effective manager? Empowering employees to make more decisions on their own is a desirable trait according to the total quality management (TQM) literature. Has e-government facilitated the empowerment of employees in the federal government? Finally, the literature on public administration also mentions that performance measures are of critical importance in both public and private sectors. Have federal departments or agencies been able to achieve greater results because of e-government? These three management factors are expected to have an impact on creating a more citizen-centric federal government. Indeed, in a survey of all three levels of government, public-sector IS managers attach more importance to managerial issues than technical ones (Swain, White, & Hubbert, 1995). The following hypothesis can be used to show the impact of management capacity on creating a more citizen-centric federal government.

H_1: *As CIOs believe that e-government management capacity factors are important, this will create a more citizen-centric federal government.*

Security and Privacy

Besides the importance of management capacity outlined in the literature, there also is a growing trend to think about e-government in light of security and privacy concerns. Since the terrorist attacks of September 11, 2001, in the United States, there has been an emphasis on homeland security and emergency preparedness as it relates to information systems (Dawes, Cresswell, & Cahan, 2004). One of the crucial and growing issues for the near future of e-government is the security of information infrastructure and government information applications (Stowers, 2004). This trend is consistent with the security and privacy of digital information. For instance, threats or attacks on information systems could compromise national security. In addition, the privacy of citizens' personally identifiable information (PII) is of paramount importance with increased incidence of identity theft. The federal government must make sure that it has safe and secure information systems. IT security remains a top priority for federal CIOs in President Bush's second term in office (ITAA, 2005). Federal CIOs continue to focus on security and authentication as key building blocks for the advancement of e-government (ITAA, 2004). According to federal government CIOs, in the age of terrorism and identity theft, a clear authentication protocol is necessary for creating a more citizen-centric government (ITAA, 2004).

However, in past studies on differences in the priorities of public- and private-sector IRMs, evidence has shown that public-sector IRMs were much less concerned with protecting information. It was ranked almost last (out of 23 categories) compared to the private sector's relatively high ranking of sixth place (Ward & Mitchell, 2004). This finding is somewhat perplexing given the recent emphasis on privacy and security issues in the federal government. Therefore, we predict that security and privacy issues should have an impact on the ability of the federal government to initiate a more citizen-centric government.

H_2: *As CIOs believe that security and privacy are important issues that must be dealt with in e-government, this will create a more citizen-centric federal government.*

Figure 1. Conceptual framework of factors that predict creating a more citizen-centric federal government

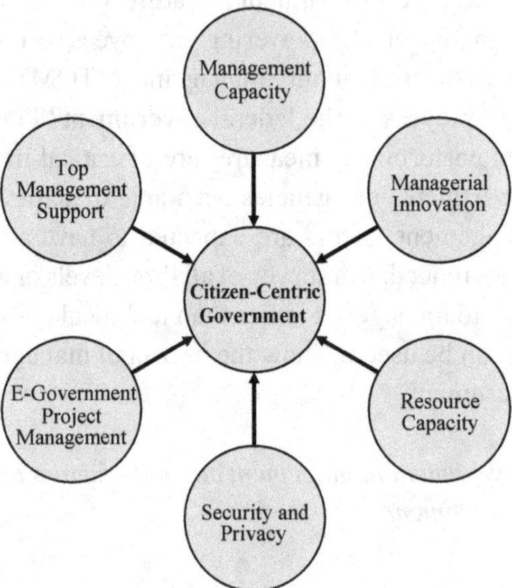

Top-Management Support

The literature also suggests that if top management is supportive of e-government, this provides for greater advancement. For instance, having a champion of e-government, someone who is essentially a cheerleader identifying the benefits of an e-government project and translating it into something of value, is of paramount importance (Ho & Ni, 2004). Additionally, with the increased emphasis on strategic planning in public organizations, leadership is said to be increasingly vital. If a manager is not enthusiastic about e-government and does not see its overall benefits to the organization, this is likely to wear against its advancement. Indeed, existing empirical research shows a connection between top-management support and IT planning at the local level (Ho & Ni; Ho & Smith, 2001). Therefore, support from top management is predicted to have an impact on creating a more citizen-centric federal government.

H_3: *As top management of a CIO's department and agency is more supportive of e-government efforts, this will create a more citizen-centric federal government.*

E-Government Project Management

Along with support from top management, there also is a need for finding and recruiting well-qualified project managers for e-government projects. Project managers are in short supply, especially for government agencies, which must compete for higher paying jobs in the private sector (ITAA, 2004). How widely and quickly have e-government projects been adopted in a department or agency is said to be the barometer of project-management success. Can e-government projects be seen through from start to finish on time and on budget? CIOs were unanimous in the belief that attracting and retaining qualified project-management personnel remains a significant challenge for moving e-government forward (ITAA, 2005).

How have e-government projects changed the interaction of a department or agency with the clients or customers that it serves? Ideally, one would assume that e-government has increased citizen and business interaction with government and has provided for more satisfaction with contacts (Thomas & Streib, 2003). Therefore, we predict that good project management should have an impact on creating a more citizen-centric federal government.

H_4: *As CIOs become more involved in e-government project management, they are more likely to agree that e-government has created a more citizen-centric federal government.*

Managerial Innovation

The transformation agenda of e-government has been promoted under the label of the *new public management*, which calls for reinvention of government as an institutional reform (Grant & Chau, 2005). This managerial innovation has been one of the major thrusts of the theoretical work on e-government. Scholars have argued that e-government is associated with a more decentralized, flexible, efficient, and effective public sector (Ho, 2002; Moon & Norris, 2005b). Research shows that public agencies do indeed face higher levels of formalization and red tape than the private sector (Rainey & Bozeman, 2000).

Existing studies maintain that e-government will break down the silos of information dissemination in government; it will decentralize government, allowing it to run more efficiently and effectively. Agencies will share information more readily and there will be a greater amount of teamwork toward reaching a common goal. Departments and agencies will collaborate more on projects and look at IT not as part of a functional unit, but in terms of serving customers.

An example of the managerial innovation having an influence on e-government is the http://www.firstgov.gov Web portal, where instead of listing departments, the federal government lists services that a citizen most often uses. A number of CIOs also believe that the process of working together across departments, agencies, and in some cases levels of government has resulted in a new model of collaboration through e-government (ITAA, 2005). However, CIOs have started to raise significant concern about the difficulty of changing ingrained cultural attitudes in order to manage change (ITAA, 2004). Existing research suggests a connection between managerial innovation and e-government at the local level (Ho, 2002; Moon & Norris, 2005b), but there is little empirical work in this area on the federal government and the creation of more citizen-centric government.

H_5: *As CIOs believe that they have managerial innovation in their agency, this is likely to have an impact on creating a more citizen-centric federal government.*

Lack of Resource Capacity

One area that should also have an impact on creating a more citizen-centric government is whether the federal government has adequate resources to fulfill e-government mandates. The lack of resource capacity is a perennial problem that federal CIOs face in IT implementation (ITAA, 2005). Is the budget Congress appropriates to an agency adequate to provide for e-government services? Has the government been able to save resources by eliminating manual processes through e-government? Does the department or agency have an adequate amount of IT infrastructure to fulfill its e-government mandates? What kind of outsourcing relationship does the agency have? Does the department or agency fit into the

Office of Management and Budget's vision of e-government project management—the OMB being the chief agency responsible for federal e-government? CIOs have expressed frustration with the difficulty of securing budget deliberations from Congress to fund e-government initiatives (ITAA, 2004).

Existing empirical research does not show that resource capacity is a major constraint on public-sector IT planning (Ho & Ni, 2004; Ho & Smith, 2001). However, this factor is included in our model because of its importance identified in focus-group discussions with CIOs (ITAA, 2005). Finally, this chapter predicts that resource capacity should have an impact on creating a more citizen-centric federal government.

H_6: *The more that CIOs believe that resource-capacity issues are a problem for his or her department or agency, the less likely he or she is to agree that e-government has created a more citizen-centric federal government.*

CHARACTERISTICS OF FEDERAL CIOs

This survey of federal government CIOs was administered during June and July of 2005. The contact information for the CIOs was taken from the CIO Council Web site at http://www.cio.gov. This Web site provides the most comprehensive listing of contact information for CIOs employed by the federal government. There were 115 federal departments and agencies that had a designated CIO official. All of them were sent a survey. In total, 38 CIOs responded to the survey, which indicates a response rate of 33%. This is a slightly lower response rate than West's (2004) study of CIOs and e-government service delivery.

The survey protocols were to initially send a cover letter to each of the CIOs indicating that in a few days they would receive a survey. The survey was seeking their opinions on e-government issues and effectiveness. Second, a formal survey and a cover letter with instructions were sent to the CIOs. This was an anonymous survey; therefore, we believe that the responses to the questions are candid. The majority of ideas for questions on the survey were taken from the series of ITAA focus-group discussions with federal CIOs and their views on IT planning and management (ITAA, 2004, 2005).

Table 1 provides the characteristics of CIOs who responded to the survey and their department's or agency's size. The majority of CIOs who responded were from large departments or agencies that employed 5,000 or more full-time equivalent (FTE) employees. Large-sized departments represented 56% of CIOs surveyed. Smaller agency CIOs employing 99 or less FTE composed only 14% of the sample. Therefore, this research is more representative of larger department CIOs than smaller agencies.

Table 1 also indicates that the typical age range of CIOs is between 45 and 54 years, representing approximately half of those surveyed. A third of the respondents were between 55 and 64 years of age. The smallest number of CIOs surveyed was between the ages of 35 and 44 years, representing around 17% of the sample.

According to Table 1, almost half of the CIOs have worked for the federal government for more than a quarter of a century. Therefore, their tenure in the federal government is substantial. However, those surveyed have not acted as CIOs for long. According to the survey results, 75% of the CIOs have been in that position for 10 years or less. This finding is most likely attributed to the Clinger-Cohen Act of 1996, which established the new position of CIO for most federal government departments and agencies.

The highest level of academic attainment for the CIOs was typically a master's degree, with just over

50% of them holding this advanced degree. Only 25% of CIOs hold a bachelor's degree as their highest level of academic achievement. This finding is what one would expect as the requirement (having an advanced degree) when working at an executive-level position in the federal government.

The characteristics of CIOs and their departments and agencies generally show that the CIOs are from large agencies. They tend to be baby boomers, are male, and have many years of experience in the federal government but fewer years of experience as a CIO. The majority of the CIOs are well educated. The survey results are more representative of large-sized federal departments and agencies than smaller ones. This should be kept in mind when interpreting the findings presented in the following section.

CIOs' OPINIONS ON E-GOVERNMENT

Structured Questions

In this section, the opinions of federal government CIOs on e-government are explored. It examines the views of CIOs on whether they agree that e-government has created a more citizen-centric federal government. We also outline the influences of management capacity, security and privacy, support from top management, project management, managerial innovation, and resource capacity on e-government.

Table 2 presents the impact of e-government on creating a more citizen-centric federal government. Over 60% of CIOs agree that e-government has indeed created a more citizen-centric federal government. However, 14% disagree that e-government has created a more citizen-centric government. A quarter of respondents indicated that they neither agree nor disagree with this statement. However, only 40% of CIOs either disagree or are uncertain of its impact on e-government.

Table 2 also shows the impact of management capacity on e-government. Has e-government made the CIO a more effective manager? First, approximately 40% of CIOs agree that e-government has made them more effective managers. Second, almost 50% of CIOs agree e-government has empowered employees to make more decisions on their own. Third, nearly 66% of CIOs believe that the performance of their agency has improved because of e-government. Overall, the management-capacity findings revealed that e-government has had a major impact on the federal government.

Security and privacy issues are of paramount importance for federal government IT systems. This issue is evident in the CIOs' opinions on security and privacy issues. Almost all CIOs believe that secure storage of citizen and business PII is the most important concern for the future advancement of e-government. Additionally, 92% of the CIOs believe that security and authentication are the key building blocks of e-government advancement. Finally, according to 95% of CIOs, information assurance and security is one of the most pressing concerns for e-government adoption. Not surprisingly, very few CIOs disagreed with these three above-mentioned security and privacy statements.

Another category investigated is the support from top management for e-government adoption, which is one of the critical success factors noted in the literature (Ho & Ni, 2004). Does having a champion of e-government, someone who will spearhead the implementation of e-government efforts, make a difference toward attaining greater levels of adoption? Nearly 90% of CIOs believe that having a champion of e-government is one of the most important, critical success factors. Top management, according to over 70% of CIOs surveyed, has a vision and strategic direction for e-government. Additionally, top management is supportive of CIOs in the e-government decision-making process, according to over 70% of CIOs. There is a general agreement that the OMB has a vision and strategic direction for e-government and has been inclusive in the decision-making process.

This survey outlines the level of adoption of e-government projects in the federal government. Project management has been identified as one of the most critical success factors for a department or agency to possess, according to the ITAA's (2005) survey. E-government projects have been adopted widely and quickly, according to over 50% of CIOs. Over 60% of CIOs believe that e-government projects have increased citizen and business interaction with the federal government. E-government projects are a top priority of departments or agencies, according to almost 60% of CIOs. Seventy percent of CIOs believe that recruitment and retention of qualified e-government project-management staff is of critical importance.

Has e-government been influenced by managerial innovation? The existing literature in this area shows that this has been the case (Ho, 2002; Moon & Norris, 2005b). E-government has allowed for a greater level of information sharing among departments, according to 70% of CIOs. Additionally, e-government has created more teamwork in federal departments and agencies, according to 42% of respondents. Two thirds of CIOs believe that e-government has created a new level of collaboration among departments and agencies. There seems to be support for these three aspects of managerial innovation that have a discernable impact on federal e-government.

A lack of resource capacity in a department or agency is also said to have an impact on e-government advancement. Does the CIO's department or agency lack the necessary IT infrastructure, which would inhibit e-government adoption? Only 20% agree with this statement of not having adequate IT infrastructure. However, approximately 50% of CIOs agree that they do not have an adequate budget to fund e-government in their department or agency. Only 28% of CIOs agree that they have not seen manual processes being eliminated because of e-government. Finally, there is a movement in the federal government to holistically and competitively outsource IT. Approximately 22% of CIOs agree that they do not take a holistic view when it comes to outsourcing e-government projects. The resource-capacity findings provide evidence that key e-government infrastructure is available, but the greater issue is not having adequate budgetary resources to fund e-government. This issue is also addressed in the open-ended question.

Open-Ended Question

An open-ended question was also asked of federal government CIOs on their opinions concerning e-government issues and effectiveness. The most common responses were that CIOs had issues with a lack of budgetary resources, the OMB dictating e-government projects, and no role for smaller agencies in federal e-government initiatives.

For example, in the budgetary-resources issue, one CIO believed that the most significant hindrance to implementing e-government is OMB's practice of mandating implementation schedules that are shorter than the budget cycle. This CIO argues that agency budgets are developed 2 years in advance. Consequently, the OMB needs to either provide planning guidance that announces e-government initiatives or mandates 2 years in advance of their issuance, or allow at least 2 years for the implementation of initiatives. Another CIO stated that e-government project managers spend far too much time begging for money from reluctant agency partners. Finally, a CIO said that a lack of funding is the biggest inhibitor to e-government advancement.

A second common theme was reaction from some CIOs about the role of top management being either the chief executive of the department or agency or the OMB. A CIO stated that he or she personally has not seen much value in the e-government policies promulgated by the OMB. According to another CIO, $60 billion in federal IT spending is simply too large to be managed on a top-down basis. According to another CIO, e-government is very important to my organization but has sometimes been stymied by the OMB. A CIO commented that executive leadership must really understand e-government opportunities. Thus, they must want and know how to leverage technology for successful e-government outcomes.

A third common response was the role of small agencies in federal e-government initiatives. The scalability of e-government initiatives presents problems for small and microagencies, according to one CIO: One size does not fit all agencies. E-government needs to address the needs of the very small agencies (10 employees or less) as well as the larger agencies, according to another CIO.

Less common responses indicated by CIOs were that too many silos of information and information technologies exist in the federal government. According to a CIO, departments and agencies are finding it difficult to keep up with new government regulations (privacy, security, etc.). A CIO commented that governments must close the digital divide for e-government to reach its full potential. One response that is consistent with creating a more citizen-centric federal government was the comment by a CIO that e-government initiatives are very worthwhile in giving citizens a participatory role in government and providing easy access to information.

The results in Table 2 support many facets of e-government advancement and effectiveness. There is ample evidence that management capacity is an important catalyst for e-government adoption. Not surprisingly, security and privacy were the priorities for e-government advancement according to the vast majority of CIOs. Top-management support and direction is also crucial for e-government development. Project-management skills and support were noted as being critical success factors. Finally, the lack of resources of the department and agency was also found to have a discernable impact on e-government.

The structured questions are also supported by some of the responses to the open-ended questions of a greater need for e-government budgetary resources, top-management support through the OMB of e-government initiatives, and the role of smaller agencies in e-government initiatives. There is some initial evidence that all of these categories are important factors that explain e-government advancement. The next section of this study investigates what impact they have as a group on creating a more citizen-centric federal government.

DESCRIPTIVE STATISTICS OF DEPENDENT AND PREDICTOR VARIABLES

In order to model these hypotheses on creating a more citizen-centric federal government, we composed indexes representing each of these categories. The indexes are presented in Table 3 along with their summary statistics. The dependent variable that is modeled creating a more citizen-centric federal government is shown in this table. All of the statement variables outlined in Table 2 were coded in the following manner. A 2 was recorded for a response of *strongly agree*, a 1 for *agree*, 0 for *neither agree nor disagree*, -1 for *disagree*, and -2 for *strongly disagree*. For the dependent variable, creating a more citizen-centric federal government, the mean score was 0.58, indicating that most of the CIOs agreed with the statement. However, they did not strongly agree with this statement since the mean was above 0 and less than 1.

Table 1. Descriptive characteristics of CIOs and their departments or agencies

	Frequency	Percent
How many FTE employees are employed in your department/agency?		
99 or less	5	13.9
100 to 499	3	8.3
500 to 999	2	5.6
1,000 to 4,999	6	16.7
5,000 or more	20	55.6
What is your age range?		
35-44	6	16.7
45-54	18	50.0
55-64	12	33.3
What is your gender?		
Female	9	25.0
Male	27	75.0
How many years have you worked for the federal government?		
Less than 5 years	5	13.9
5 to 10 years	4	11.1
11 to 15 years	4	11.1
16 to 20 years	2	5.6
21 to 25 years	5	13.9
26 years or more	16	44.4
How many years have you worked as a CIO?		
Less than 5 years	14	38.9
5 to 10 years	13	36.1
11 to 15 years	3	8.3
16 to 20 years	4	11.1
21 to 25 years	1	2.8
26 years or more	1	2.8
What is your highest level of academic attainment?		
High school diploma	2	5.6
2-year college degree	2	5.6
4-year college degree	9	25.0
Master's degree	19	52.8
Law degree	3	8.3
Doctorate degree	1	2.8

The responses for the six categories of independent variables are outlined in Table 2. We simply added the responses for each of the categories to get an index score for each respondent. For example, in order to compose the management-capacity index, we added up the responses to the three statements in this category of e-government making the CIO a better manager, empowering employees, and creating greater performance results (see Table 2). For management capacity, there was a minimum score of -5 and a maximum score of 6, which means that there was a substantial range of responses when adding the three categories together. However, the mean score was 1.29, which implies that there was more of a tendency for CIOs to agree that e-government affected management capacity.

The remaining five predictor variables are also reported in Table 3. All of the mean values are positive, with the exception of a lack of resource capacity, which was negative. In this variable, a majority of respondents disagreed that resources were not much of a factor. The strongest level of agreement was for the issues of privacy and security, with a mean score of almost 4. Top-management support for e-government registered the second highest mean score of just over 3.

RESULTS OF OLS REGRESSION MODEL

Using the six predictor variables alluded to in the previous section, which of these factors best explains creating a more citizen-centric federal government? Ordinary least squares (OLS) regression was used since we are modeling a dependent variable ranging from -2 to 2.

Table 4 presents two statistically significant impacts of the predictor variables management capacity and e-government project management on creating a more citizen-centric federal government. These variables are both statistically significant at the 0.05% level.

The management-capacity variable implies that as CIOs agree that management has been affected as a result of e-government, they are approximately 33% of a point more likely to increase their level of agreement that e-government has created a more citizen-centric federal government (beta coefficient=0.34). Additionally, CIOs who agree that project management has been affected are over 33% of a point (beta coefficient=0.38) more likely to increase their level of agreement with the statement that e-government has created a more citizen-centric federal government.

These results essentially imply that the statements that e-government has made the CIO a more effective manager, has empowered employees, and has enabled the CIO to achieve greater performance milestones are correlated with creating a more citizen-centric federal government. If e-government projects have been adopted widely and quickly within a department or agency, the CIO believes e-government projects have increased citizen and business interaction with his or her agency, e-government projects are a top priority of the agency, and recruitment and retention of project-management staff are important (the four project-management statements). These statements were correlated with creating a more citizen-centric government.

The six predictor variables in Table 4 explained just over 60% of the variance of the OLS regression model. The F-statistic of 10.65 indicates that the overall significance of the model is strong, being significant at the 0.01% level. However, since there were only 36 observations for the regression model, this limits the interpretation of the results.

DISCUSSION OF HYPOTHESES

The six hypotheses mentioned previously should be reviewed in order to find out whether the evidence found in this study refutes or confirms them. Hypothesis 1 inquired whether CIOs agreed that manage-

Table 2. Summary of CIO opinions on e-government

Category	CIOs' level of agreement and disagreement with the following statements about e-government	Strongly Agree (%)	Agree (%)	Neither Agree/ Disagree (%)	Disagree (%)	Strongly Disagree (%)
Citizen-Centric Government	Have created a more citizen-centric federal government	13.9	47.2	25.0	11.1	2.8
Management Capacity	Has made me a more effective manager	13.2	28.9	47.4	10.5	0.0
	Has empowered employees to make more decisions on their own	5.3	42.1	23.7	26.3	2.6
	Has enabled us to achieve greater performance milestones and results	10.5	55.3	23.7	7.9	2.6
Security and Privacy	Secure storage of citizen and business PII is one of the most pressing concerns for e-government advancement.	45.9	48.6	2.7	2.7	0.0
	Information assurance/security is one of the most important concerns for e-government adoption.	40.5	54.1	2.7	2.7	0.0
	Security and authentication are the key building blocks for the advancement of e-government.	35.1	56.8	5.4	2.7	0.0
Top-Management Support	Having a champion of e-government is one of the most important critical success factors for e-government advancement.	52.8	36.1	11.1	0.0	0.0
	Top management has a vision and strategic direction for e-government for my department/agency.	22.2	50.0	13.9	11.1	2.8
	Top management is very supportive of my department's/ agency's participation in the decision-making process for e-government.	27.8	44.4	16.7	8.3	2.8
E-Government Project Management	Has been adopted quickly and widely	13.2	42.1	28.9	13.2	2.6
	Has increased citizen and business interaction with my department/agency	22.2	38.9	22.2	13.9	2.8
	Is a top-priority of my department/agency	13.9	44.4	19.4	19.4	2.8
	Recruitment and retention of qualified e-government project-management and -support staff is one of the most critical issues.	41.7	27.8	25.0	2.8	2.8
Managerial Innovation	E-government has allowed a greater degree of information sharing among departments/agencies.	19.4	50.0	19.4	11.1	0.0
	E-government has fostered greater teamwork in employees.	5.6	36.1	38.9	19.4	0.0
	E-government has developed a new level of collaboration among departments/agencies.	13.9	52.8	16.7	16.7	0.0

Table 2. continued

Lack of Resource Capacity	Lacks IT infrastructure, which inhibits e-government adoption	2.8	16.7	16.7	44.4	19.4
	Does not have adequate budgetary resources to fund e-government projects	13.9	33.3	22.2	22.2	8.3
	Has not seen manual processes being eliminated as a result of e-government	5.6	22.2	19.4	47.2	5.6
	Does not take a holistic view of e-government when competitively outsourcing e-government projects	5.6	16.7	33.3	27.8	16.7

Table 3. Descriptive statistics of dependent and predictor variables

	Observations	Minimum	Maximum	Mean
Have created a more citizen-centric federal government	36	-2	2	0.58
Management Capacity	38	-5	6	1.29
Security and Privacy	37	-1	6	3.95
Top-Management Support	36	-3	6	3.06
E-Government Project Management	36	-8	8	2.67
Managerial Innovation	36	-3	6	1.69
Lack of Resource Capacity	36	-6	5	-0.97

Note: Dependent variable shaded

capacity factors related to creating a more citizen-centric federal government. The evidence found in this study indeed supported this hypothesis since management capacity was correlated with citizen-centric government. This confirms existing literature that argues managers are more effective if they set performance targets and empower employees to make more decisions on their own. This is consistent with the GPRA initiated in the federal government since 1993.

Hypothesis 4 was also supported in the survey of CIOs. There was evidence that CIOs who had favorable views of project management and its impact on their department or agency were more likely to be of the opinion that e-government has created a more citizen-centric federal government. The ITAA (2005) has also found through extensive interviews with federal CIOs that project management is one of the most important critical success factors for IT advancement. This study lends support that good project management is also applicable to e-government as well.

There is no evidence found in this study that top-management support is correlated with e-government. However, the open-ended question indicates that one of the issues that CIOs face is the OMB dictating e-government projects. Issues of security and privacy are critical to advancing e-government, yet they had no relationship to creating a more citizen-centric federal government. Security and privacy would override issues of citizen-centric government since it has dominated Washington agenda setting since September 11, 2001. There was no evidence found for the impact of managerial innovation popularized in the United States on creating a more citizen-centric federal government. This is surprising since the literature demonstrates such a connection. Finally, the hypothesis that a lack of resources in the federal department or agency decreases the creation of a more citizen-centric government was not supported. This finding coincides with some of the existing literature that resource capacity is not correlated with e-government advancement (Ho & Ni, 2004).

CONCLUSION

This study has examined some possible factors that might influence the creation of a more citizen-centric federal government. The existing literature on e-government has not provided a connection between e-government and the opinions of CIOs. This is an important area of IS research given that the federal government is the largest purchaser of IT in the United States. Creating a more citizen-centric government is one indication of the advancement of e-government into the highest stage of development (i.e., horizontal integration). This study has identified that having a greater management capacity, and project-management skills and development leads to the creation of a more citizen-centric federal government.

CIOs can use these identified skills in order to reach higher levels of e-government adoption for their departments or agencies. Working more on project management and the ability to manage more effectively are skills that can be easily acquired through education at, for example, the CIO University. This is a virtual consortium of universities for federal CIOs that offers graduate-level programs that directly address executive core competencies. Since just over 33% of federal CIOs do not have a master's degree, this would help in achieving these two important skills. Additionally, more emphasis should be placed on better recruitment and retention of federal project-management personnel. This issue was also mentioned in the ITAA (2005) CIO focus-group discussions.

One of the major limitations of this study is that it examines the opinions of CIOs. Such responses from CIOs are limited because they are based on perceptions, not assessments of actual figures or data. CIOs have a self-interested stake in promoting the view that what they are doing is effective and efficient. As a result, future work might involve independent verification of CIO achievements in their departments or agencies in terms of e-government projects actually being implemented. A comparison across time might provide further evidence as to whether CIOs are achieving results in terms of e-government advancement.

ACKNOWLEDGMENT

The authors would like to thank all of the CIOs who participated in this survey. Without their generous support, this project would not be possible.

REFERENCES

AFFIRM. (2004). *The federal CIO: Ninth annual CIO challenges survey.* Retrieved July 30, 2005, from http://www.affirm.org/

Andersen, K. V., & Henriksen, H. Z. (2005). The first leg of e-government research: Domains and application areas 1998-2003. *International Journal of Electronic Government Research, 1*(4), 26-44.

Bertot, J. C. (1997). The impact of federal IRM on agency missions: Findings, issues, and recommendations. *Government Information Quarterly, 14*(3), 235-253.

Bertot, J. C., & McClure, C. R. (1997). Key issues affecting the development of federal IRM: A view from the trenches. *Government Information Quarterly, 14*(3), 271-290.

Bozeman, B., & Bretschneider, S. (1986). Public management information systems: Theory and prescription. *Public Administration Review, 46*, 475-487.

Bretschneider, S. (1990). Management information systems in public and private organizations: An empirical test. *Public Administration Review, 50*(5), 536-545.

Brown, M. M., & Brudney, J. L. (1998). Public sector information technology initiatives: Implications for programs of public administration. *Administration & Society, 30*(4), 421-442.

Buehler, M. (2000). U.S. federal government CIOs: Information technology's new managers. Preliminary findings. *Government Information Quarterly, 27*, 29-45.

Danziger, J. N., & Andersen, K. V. (2002). The impacts of information technology on public administration: An analysis of empirical research from the "golden age" of transformation. *International Journal of Public Administration, 25*(5), 591-627.

Dawes, S. S., Cresswell, A. M., & Cahan, B. B. (2004). Learning from crisis: Lessons in human and information infrastructure from the World Trade Center response. *Social Science Computer Review, 22*(1), 52-66.

EOP. (2002a). *Implementing the President's management agenda for e-government: E-government strategy*. Retrieved July 30, 2005, from http://www.whitehouse.gov/omb

EOP. (2002b). *The President's management agenda*. Retrieved July 30, 2005, from http://www.whitehouse.gov/omb/

Fletcher, P. D. (1997). Local governments and IRM: Policy emerging from practice. *Government Information Quarterly, 14*(3), 313-324.

General Accounting Office. (2004a). *Electronic government: Federal agencies have made progress implementing the E-Government Act of 2002* (GAO Publication No. GAO-05-12). Washington, DC: U.S. Government Printing Office.

General Accounting Office. (2004b). *Federal chief information officers: Responsibilities, reporting, relationships, tenure, and challenges* (GAO Publication No. GAO-04-823). Washington, DC: U.S. Government Printing Office.

General Accounting Office. (2005a). *Chief information officers: Responsibilities and information and technology governance at leading private-sector companies* (GAO Publication No. GAO-05-986). Washington, DC: U.S. Government Printing Office.

General Accounting Office. (2005b). *Management reform: Assessing the President's management agenda* (GAO Publication No. GAO-05-574T). Washington, DC: U.S. Government Printing Office.

Grant, G., & Chau, D. (2005). Developing a generic framework for e-government. *Journal of Global Information Management, 13*(1), 1-30.

Gronlund, A. (2005). State of the art in e-gov research: Surveying conference publications. *International Journal of Electronic Government Research, 1*(4), 1-25.

Gronlund, A., & Horan, T. (2004). Introducing e-gov: History, definitions, and issues. *Communications of the Association for Information Systems, 15*, 713-729.

Ho, A. T.-K. (2002). Reinventing local government and the e-government initiative. *Public Administration Review, 62*(4), 434-444.

Ho, A. T.-K., & Ni, A. Y. (2004). Explaining the adoption of e-government features: A case study of Iowa county treasurers' offices. *American Review of Public Administration, 34*(2), 164-180.

Ho, A. T.-K., & Smith, J. F. (2001). Information technology planning and the Y2K problem in local governments. *American Review of Public Administration, 31*(2), 158-180.

ITAA. (2004). *CIO: Catalyst for business transformation. 2004 survey of federal chief information officers.* Retrieved July 30, 2005, from http://www.grantthornton.com

ITAA. (2005). *Issues in leadership: 2005 survey of federal chief information officers.* Retrieved July 30, 2005, from http://www.grantthornton.com

Layne, K., & Lee, J. (2001). Developing fully function e-government: A four stage model. *Government Information Quarterly, 18*(1), 122-136.

Mahler, J., & Regan, P. M. (2002). Learning to govern online: Federal agency Internet use. *American Review of Public Administration, 32*(3), 326-349.

McClure, C. R., & Bertot, J. C. (2000). The chief information officer (CIO): Assessing its impact. *Government Information Quarterly, 17*(1), 7-12.

Moon, M. J., & Norris, D. F. (2005a). Advancing e-government at the grassroots: Tortoise or hare? *Public Administration Review, 65*(1), 64-75.

Moon, M. J., & Norris, D. F. (2005b). Does managerial orientation matter? The adoption of reinventing government and e-government at the municipal level. *Information Systems Journal, 15*, 43-60.

Rainey, H. G., & Bozeman, B. (2000). Comparing public and private organizations: Empirical research and the power of the a priori. *Journal of Public Administration Research and Theory, 10*(2), 447-469.

Reddick, C. G. (in press). Information resource managers and e-government effectiveness: A survey of Texas state agencies. *Government Information Quarterly.*

Relyea, H. C. (2000). Paperwork Reduction Act reauthorization and government information management issues. *Government Information Quarterly, 17*(4), 367-393.

Rocheleau, B., & Wu, L. (2002). Public versus private information systems: Do they differ in important ways? A review and empirical test. *American Review of Public Administration, 32*(4), 379-397.

Schelin, S. H. (2003). E-government: An overview. In G. D. Garson (Ed.), *Public information technology: Policy and management issues.* Hershey, PA: Idea Group Publishing.

Seifert, J. W., & Relyea, H. C. (2004). Considering e-government from the U.S. federal perspective: An evolving concept, a developing practice. *Journal of E-Government, 1*(1), 7-15.

Stowers, G. (2004). Issues in e-commerce and e-government service delivery. In A. Pavlichev & G. D. Garson (Eds.), *Digital government: Principles and best practices.* Hershey, PA: Idea Group Publishing.

Swain, J. W., White, J., & Hubbert, E. D. (1995). Issues in public management information systems. *American Review of Public Administration, 25*(3), 279-296.

Thomas, J. C., & Streib, G. (2003). The new face of government: Citizen-initiated contacts in the era of e-government. *Journal of Public Administration Research and Theory, 13*(1), 83-102.

Ugbah, S. D., & Umeh, O. J. (1993). Information resource management: An examination of individual and organizational attributes in state government agencies. *Information Resources Management Journal, 6*(1), 5-13.

Ward, M. A., & Mitchell, S. (2004). A comparison of the strategic priorities of public and private sector information resource management executives. *Government Information Quarterly, 21*, 284-304.

West, D. M. (2004). E-government and the transformation of service delivery and citizen attitudes. *Public Administration Review, 64*(1), 15-27.

Westerback, L. K. (2000). Toward best practices for strategic information technology management. *Government Information Quarterly, 17*(1), 27-41.

This work was previously published in Modern Public Information Technology Systems: Issues and Challenges, edited by G. Garson, pp. 143-165, copyright 2007 by IGI Publishing (an imprint of IGI Global).

About the Author

Christopher G. Reddick is an Associate Professor and Chair of the Department of Public Administration at the University of Texas at San Antonio, USA. Dr. Reddick's research and teaching interests is in e-government. Some of his publications can be found in *Government Information Quarterly*, *Electronic Government*, and the *International Journal of Electronic Government Research.* Dr. Reddick recently edited the book entitled *Handbook of Research on Strategies for Local E-Government Adoption and Implementation: Comparative Studies.*

Index

K

L

M

N

O

P

R

S